44123

The Rise of Social Theory

Contradictions of Modernity

Edited by Craig Calhoun
University of North Carolina at Chapel Hill

The modern era has been uniquely productive of theory. Some theory claimed uniformity despite human differences or unilinear progress in the face of catastrophic changes. Other theory was informed more deeply by the complexities of history and recognition of cultural specificity. This series seeks to further the latter approach by publishing books that explore the problems of theorizing the modern in its manifold and sometimes contradictory forms and that examine the specific locations of theory within the modern.

The Rise of Social Theory

Johan Heilbron

Translated by Sheila Gogol

Contradictions of Modernity, Volume 1

University of Minnesota Press

Minneapolis

First published in The Netherlands as *Het ontstaanvan de sociologie*
by Prometheus Amsterdam © Johan Heilbron 1990

First published in 1995 by Polity Press
in association with Blackwell Publishers

Published simultaneously in the United States in 1995
by the University of Minnesota Press
111 Third Avenue South, Suite 290
Minneapolis, MN 55401-2520

Printed in Great Britain

Library of Congress Cataloging-in-Publication Data

Heilbron, Johan.
    The rise of social theory / Johan Heilbron.
        p.   cm. — (Contradictions of modernity ; v. 3)
    Includes bibliographical references (p.   ) and index.
    ISBN 0–8166–2712–6 (hc). — ISBN 0–8166–2713–4 (pbk.)
    1. Sociology—History.   2. Social sciences—History.   I. Title.
II. Series.
HM19.H357   1995
301'.09—dc20   94–40152
                                                                          CIP

Contents

Preface

The period from 1750 to 1850 is commonly associated with two revolutions, the Industrial Revolution and the French Revolution. It is less well known that the intellectual transformations of this period also marked the transition to the modern era, and that the emergence of sociology was an essential part of it. These transformations are the subject of this study, focusing as it does on how social theory emerged and how this process was linked to changes in the intellectual as well as the social context.

I wrote this book when I was at the Amsterdam School for Social Research and the Swedish Collegium for Advanced Study in the Social Sciences in Uppsala. I would like to express my gratitude to the faculty members at both of these institutes for their hospitality and the stimulating working conditions. I would like to thank Pierre Bourdieu and Roger Chartier for their suggestions, Maaike Dahler for her help and Nico Wilterdink for his comments. Most of all, I am indebted to Johan Goudsblom, my supervisor, whose critical sense served as my example. The English translation was funded by the Netherlands Organization for Scientific Research (NWO) and the Netherlands Universities Institute for Coordination of Research in Social Sciences (SISWO).

Introduction

The progress of knowledge, in the case of social science, supposes a progress in the knowledge of the conditions of knowledge.

Pierre Bourdieu

The social sciences are customarily viewed as being a recent phenomenon. They are thought to have emerged in the course of the nineteenth century, but not to have truly developed until the twentieth. This assumption is common among social scientists and laymen alike, even among historians in these fields.[1] What tends to remain obscure here is how the social sciences came into being. To gain insight into their genesis, it is widely admitted that one would have to go further back than the nineteenth century. However, that has only been done on rare occasions and in a highly unsystematic fashion. The reason for this is related to the function of written history.

Historical accounts of the social sciences are closely linked to the ubiquitous demand for information on the past. Educating new students about the disciplinary history is a regular component of professional socialization, and some basic knowledge is part of the intellectual equipment required for any discipline One of the most common ways to reconstruct the past is by drawing a border between 'history' proper and 'prehistory' or 'early history'. History then pertains to the past in as far as it bears a direct relation to the contemporary practice of a particular discipline. Examples from this past can be used to support or refute, to serve as a standard for evaluations, and to fulfil any number of symbolic and representative functions. In this sense, history acts as a storehouse open to everyone in the discipline. All and sundry can come to it for terms and concepts, examples and counterexamples, symbols and idols. Thus 'history' is a recognized part of the disciplinary identity.

'Prehistory' and 'early history', however, include the wide range of configurations and intricacies that no longer affect the identity of the

discipline. The precise location of this border may change and is subject to conflicts, but no matter how these are settled the early history is
no longer regarded as relevant. Early history is the history that might
legitimately be forgotten. It is no shame to be ignorant in this respect,
and whatever one might know about it is generally at second hand.

In sociology, the demarcation between history and early history is
drawn at the mid-nineteenth century. The great names of the second
half of the century are part and parcel of 'classical' sociology. Marx,
Weber, Durkheim and several others are still widely read, commented
upon and published. They have their followers and their critics, and in
the margin of the sociological craft there are always a few specialists
who stand guard over their texts and the various interpretations. But
this is not the case with earlier authors, who are no longer viewed as
being proper examples. They might sometimes be referred to as pioneers or predecessors, even as founding fathers, but their work is rarely
commented upon or included in anyone's curriculum. It is generally
read only as an enjoyable pastime, or to satisfy historical or literary
curiosity. It is typical of this lack of attention that there is no standard
model in sociology of the development of social theories before the
mid-nineteenth century. There are detailed interpretations pertaining
to the subsequent periods and most social scientists have no trouble
describing the developments since the 'classics'. Very few, however,
would be capable of sketching a comparable picture of the developments before 1850. Even in specialized literature there is little more to
be found than a rather vague awareness that the emergence of the
social sciences dates back to this period.[2] How and why this happened
remains unclear.

The disciplinary and the predisciplinary stage

Since the historiography of the social sciences is so closely linked to
present-day classifications and interests, what few studies are available are disciplinary histories.[3] This is already evident from the journals in the field. *The Journal of the History of the Behavioural
Sciences* (1965) contains mainly articles on the history of psychology.
Other journals reflect disciplinary ties in their titles: *History of Political Economy* (1969), *Journal of the History of Sociology* (1978) later
continued as *History of Sociology* (1985), *History of Political Thought*
(1980) and *History and Anthropology* (1984). This strictly disciplinary focus led to an extremely one-sided view of history. Particularly
in recent years, ample new information has become available on the

histories of specific disciplines. But many concepts and assumptions of modern social science date back to their 'early history'. This holds true for the modern meanings of such concepts as 'state', 'economy' and 'society', and for modern ideas on human action and notions such as 'interest'. For a proper understanding of the development of the social sciences, it is consequently necessary to subject their early history to more systematic examination. In many senses this 'early history' is not 'prehistory' at all, but constitutes instead an integral part of history.

From this perspective the very term 'early history' is confusing and might be replaced by 'predisciplinary history'. The history of the social sciences then consists of a *disciplinary* and a *predisciplinary stage*. The predisciplinary stage covers the period from about 1600 to the middle of the nineteenth century. It was during this period that modern notions on human societies emerged. These notions were formulated within far more general frameworks than disciplines. The institutional context consisted of academies and learned societies. Their members were not professors who wrote textbooks for registered students, but men of letters. More often than not, there was no specific professional practice. Ideas were informed by general conceptions in which such terms as 'reason', 'nature' and 'philosophy' were key concepts. Although there was no strict division of labour, this set of institutions and practices was not an undifferentiated constellation. One might speak indeed of a differentiation in *intellectual genres*. Despite the fact that they were viewed as branches of one and the same type of discourse, these various genres did have a certain autonomy, as is evident, for example, from their specific vocabularies. So in early modern times intellectual activities were organized in academies and learned societies, which competed with older church organizations; the discourses produced in this setting were divided into different intellectual genres, but these genres were part of more general frameworks in a cognitive and institutional as well as a social sense.

From a historical perspective it is typical of modern science that it is organized in disciplines. The formation of disciplines became dominant with the rise of modern universities, when separate curricula, journals and professional organizations were founded. Thus the transition took place from relatively flexible intellectual genres to far more strictly organized university disciplines. This transition meant not only more specialization, but also a more constraining type of organization. Disciplines can be defined as *units of teaching, research and professional organization*. This multifunctional type of organization reinforced ties *within* disciplines, while ties *between* disciplines

considerably weakened. General categories lost their central significance and made way for an orientation that was disciplinary and directly linked to new institutional arrangements (chairs, examinations,
journals) and a new audience (students). This phenomenon has long
characterized the structuring of the sciences in modern times.

Nowadays one might perhaps add a postdisciplinary stage to the
predisciplinary and disciplinary ones. With the unprecedented expansion of universities after World War II, disciplinary frameworks began
to lose much of their function. As of 1960 research increasingly called
for approaches that were interdisciplinary, multidisciplinary or
transdisciplinary.

The division into a predisciplinary and a disciplinary stage is more
in keeping with the factual development of modern science than the
customary division into history and early history. This does not only
hold true for the social sciences. In the development of the natural
sciences, a predisciplinary and a disciplinary stage can be distinguished
as well. The predisciplinary stage encompasses the rise of the classical
natural sciences in the seventeenth century and went on until approximately 1800. In this stage, celestial mechanics or astronomy was the
dominant paradigm of natural philosophy. In the decades around 1800
the founding of specific disciplines advanced, and 'physics', 'chemistry' and 'biology', in the contemporary sense of the words, emerged
more or less simultaneously.[4]

The predisciplinary history of social science

Although very little research has been conducted into the predisciplinary
history of the social sciences, a clear pattern can nonetheless be distinguished. At the most general level the rise of the social sciences was
part of the secularization of the conceptions and representations of
human societies. This secularization remained confined initially to a
rediscovery of the works of classical antiquity. Aristotelian 'practical
philosophy' played a key role in this respect. It was the point of departure for the elaboration of modern notions of human societies. The
emergence of these modern notions can be viewed as the beginning of
the predisciplinary history of social science. A number of stages can be
distinguished in this development.

The emergence of modern conceptions of 'state' and 'law' was the
earliest stage. Secular politico-legal theories were formulated in the
Italian city states and evolved in close conjunction with processes of
state formation. At the close of the sixteenth century, according to

Quentin Skinner, a modern concept of the state was formulated for the first time in France. In this conception, the state was viewed as a sovereign institution to which all the citizens were subordinate. This institution was impersonal, since the state was no longer perceived as the property of the monarch. It was an abstract concept that embraced more than just the government or certain legal and administrative agencies.[5]

The rise of modern economic theories represented the next stage. The *Traité d'économie politique* (1615) by Antoine de Montchrestien was one of the first publications to refer to 'political economy'.[6] The management of wealth was no longer the preserve of independent households; it was now defined as a public affair, and acquiring knowledge on it was the objective of a new intellectual genre: political economy. Up to the mid-eighteenth century, this type of knowledge was directly linked in France to state functions and state institutions. Compared with England, there were fewer publications and debates on these matters. It was not until around 1750 that this was to change. There was a sharp rise in the number of writings on economic topics, and new periodicals were founded, such as the *Journal économique* (1751–72).[7] At the same time, 'mercantilistic' perspectives began to be supplanted by conceptions in which economic processes were defined as an 'order' independent of the state. Political economy became less of a 'political' genre and more of an 'economic' one. The economic models of Cantillon and Quesnay were the first examples of this. According to the tenets of Quesnay and the physiocrats, knowledge of the 'laws' of the economic process was a prerequisite for state intervention. The 'economy' was a 'natural', self-regulating system that one could best leave unhampered: laissez faire. The primary task of the state was not to promulgate laws but to acknowledge the laws of this 'natural order'.[8]

At approximately the same time, in the mid-eighteenth century, a secular approach emerged as to the concept of 'society'.[9] Like the modern concept of the economy, the term 'society' meant a break with theology and church teachings as well as with political theories. In the church doctrines human communities were perceived in the light of divine dictates. In politico-legal thinking communities were subordinate to the state and individuals were seen solely as 'citizens' or 'subjects'. The new social theories provided an alternative to both of these traditions.

Social structures were no longer perceived in the light of the Fall of Man or Divine Providence, but as an affair of human beings. In the relations among them, even the most powerful institution, the state, and the most powerful individual, the monarch, were dependent on other institutions and individuals. In order to comprehend and improve human units it was essential to do justice to these forms of inter-relatedness and interdependence: 'states' had to be viewed as 'societies'.

These secular theories did not emerge in a random sequence. Political theories were the first to evolve into a more or less independent and modern intellectual genre. These early modern political theories were advanced in France by such legal scholars as Jean Bodin in pace with the political developments. The jurists constituted a powerful group in the state apparatus. *Vis-à-vis* the local power of the nobility and the church, jurists were a major ally of the monarch. As officials and advisors, men of the law had long been in the vanguard of the central authority. The conceptions they developed of the law, the state and the public sphere played a prominent role in this connection.[10] In the seventeenth century this development took a paradoxical turn. Richelieu utilized legal doctrines on 'sovereignty' to confine the power of the legal estate and transform the French monarchy into an absolute state.[11]

The establishment of absolutism, in other words the creation of a relatively permanent and far-reaching monopoly on violence and taxation, enabled numerous forms of peaceful competition to thrive and grow. Slowly but surely, this became the foundation for independent 'sectors'. Spokesmen of trade and industry began to make claims to greater independence from the state, and the emergence of economic theories was linked to this trend. A concomitant development could be observed in other fields. In the 'cultural sector' opinions were now also voiced emphasizing a greater degree of autonomy from church and state.

In the rise of social theories, this growing differentiation and relative separation of the various sectors played a crucial role. Various social groups had acquired greater autonomy from the state. The politico-legal idiom consequently began to forfeit its general validity. More and more activities took place outside the official politico-legal frameworks, without being 'private' or falling under the jurisdiction of the church. In an effort to designate and to promote this development, the term 'society' came into fashion. In social theories, 'social' relations had replaced what was formerly defined in politico-legal or ecclesiastical terms.

The rise of sociology

Against this background, three stages can be discerned in the predisciplinary history of French sociology:

(1) The first stage consisted of the rise of secular social theory. This took place in the period from 1730 to 1775, and its most prominent spokesmen were Montesquieu and Rousseau. In their work, social differentiation and interdependence were the central phenomena. In this sense, social theory differed from the existing intellectual genres (political theory, law, moral philosophy, political economy). Modern human communities were no longer viewed as fairly homogeneous religious or political units, but as differentiated and rather complicated bodies. This meant a kind of 'decentring'. The emphasis shifted from unitary concepts ('state', 'church', 'community') to terms and problems stressing differentiation and diversity. In a theoretical sense the dissimilarities to the existing genres were less sizeable. The models of social interdependence were still formulated largely in the language of a rationalist philosophy, frequently inspired by the pursuit of universal or 'natural' principles. Natural law served as the most important model for these constructions.

(2) In the second stage these modern concepts and constructs became part of an explicit scientific problematic. This took place from 1775 to 1814, with Condorcet and Cabanis as its two leading representatives. Social relations were now no longer viewed primarily as a subject for rational constructions, but as a topic for an empirical science. The term 'social science' was coined, and the new science was seen as an extension of the existing sciences. Efforts in this direction were made after Louis XVI ascended to the throne and became dominant in the revolutionary period.

(3) The third stage, from the fall of Napoleon in 1814 to the middle of the nineteenth century, was characterized by the further diffusion of social theory, the increasing diversity of approaches and the growing domination of disciplinary modes of organization. Auguste Comte was to be one of the most important figures of this period for French sociology. And not because Comte's sociological insights were of such great significance, but because he introduced a new theoretical orientation. Comte was the first to advocate an uncompromising scientific approach without taking refuge in any of the established sciences. He developed a theory of science in which the idea of relative autonomy played a central role. This attributed to social science a territory of its own and gave it the task of developing its own proper

theories and methods. By the end of the nineteenth century this contribution was to serve as the foundation for the French sociological tradition.

These three stages can be recognized as distinctive and successive phases in the history of sociological thought in France.[12] Since this development did not take place anywhere else in quite the same fashion, the explanation for this pattern must bear some relation to the French context. The periodization would seem to bear out the same conclusion. Secularization was a long-term process that peaked in the eighteenth century with the Enlightenment. The second stage, the period of 'scientization' following the example of the natural sciences, was of relatively short duration, at any rate in the first instance. It covered more than a quarter of a century and dominated social thought throughout the revolutionary period. The third stage ensued immediately afterwards. Comte and his peers wrote their works fully aware that the Revolution was over: a new era had commenced, industrialization went on and, despite successful opposition of sections of the nobility and the clergy, for most of them there was no way back.

In this study, each of these three stages will be discussed in turn. The main aim is to document and to explain this entire process. Part I focuses on the rise of social theory, Part II deals with its scientization, and in Part III the work of Comte is central.

Old and new approaches

In analysing this entire process, one can traditionally opt for either of two methods. The most common method is to read, compare and interpret texts. The ideas found are treated as an independent history as it were, which can be examined as something totally distinct from whatever might have occurred outside this particular set of texts. A method of this kind is routine in the history of ideas, *Begriffsgeschichte* and the history of science. This approach is based on the principle of rational reconstruction, which holds that texts can be comprehended by way of careful scrutiny and discovering the relation they bear to other texts. Thus one might arrive at the conclusion that a certain text is a variation, a response or an allusion to some other text. Relations between texts are then frequently interpreted as 'influences'. Although such links can clarify a great deal, it is impossible to find any explanations by using this method. Within the framework of rational reconstructions, it can be done only by assuming an immanent development whereby text B more or less logically follows from text A (or from a combination of A1 and A2 etc.). Since this type of 'natural development' of thinking à la Hegel or Comte is no longer plausible, historians of ideas usually refrain from the pursuit of explanation. This also holds true of the contemporary variant of this approach, discourse analysis. Although here more attention is devoted to the social functioning of discourses, efforts are rarely made to formulate explanations. Just as in the traditional history of ideas, in discourse analysis the focus is on the internal structure of discourses.

Diametrically opposed to these 'internal' approaches is the second method, where it is the context that is of central importance. In 'external' analyses, the point of departure is that texts can be comprehended only by exploring links with instances outside the text. Texts are asssumed to exhibit only a very limited extent of autonomy *vis-à-vis* the author, the author's social position and the social context. The assumed lack of autonomy is evident from the terminology used. Ideas are described as 'reflections' or 'expressions' of the interests or values of the group to which the author belongs. This perspective has been developed mainly by Marxist authors, for whom ideas could be 'explained' by the class position of the author or the structure of society as a whole (the 'basis'). In the first case the aim was to comprehend the work of a specific author or school, and in the second case to address far more general phenomena such as 'abstract art' or 'bourgeois literature'. Neither of these explanatory models has many adherents today, although the latter model is once again being propagated by spokesmen of system theory. The kind of sociology of knowledge they favour examines the correlations between the development of knowledge and that of society. Fundamental correlations are assumed to exist between cognitive and social systems, and this assumption is derived in turn from the functional requirements of social systems.[13] In this approach the individuals and groups who produce these ideas remain 'off-screen'. In *Gesellschaftsstruktur und Semantik* Niklas Luhmann was thus able to quote from any number of books and essays without ever referring to their authors. As to the highly general correlations he discussed, it remains unclear how they could be feasible. Why should relatively independent and respected authors care about the functional requirements of industrial society? In much the same way as in Marxist reflection theories, the fact is overlooked that intellectuals have formed specific institutions, acquiring a certain autonomy of their own, even in relation to far more powerful groups. In this fashion intellectuals have come to have specific interests and pursuits. This relative autonomy implies that every effort to trace the work of these intellectuals back to large-scale socio-economic or political structures is doomed to fail.

Both of these approaches, internal and external alike, are reductionist simplifications of a complicated problem. In the one case, the development of constructs is reduced to a non-social sphere of texts, ideas and discourses, and in the other to extra-intellectual factors and structures. Neither of the two constitutes a very fertile point of departure for research. The terms are misleading ('internal' is automatically understood as 'non-social') and they derive their authority more from academic conventions than from their heuristic force.

In contemporary research the dividing line between internal and external approaches has become increasingly vague. If present-day developments share any common factor at all, it is probably their tendency to contextualize. Nowadays the history of ideas is less of an isolated specialism than it was ten or fifteen years ago.[14] And in science studies the artificial border lines between theory of science, history of science and sociology of science have lost much of their pertinence.[15]

Pierre Bourdieu's work in the sociology of culture represents an early and systematic effort to transcend the dichotomy between internal and external approaches. The objective was to develop a sociological approach that would do justice to the specific nature of intellectual and cultural production.[16] He started from the observation that cultural products emerge and function in a specific context, in a relatively autonomous 'field' and with a structure and dynamics of their own. An intellectual field is a social constellation consisting of people who compete with one another for intellectual authority. Intellectual products derive their significance primarily from their position in this constellation. By accepting this 'intellectual field' as a specific and historically variable social constellation, one acknowledges not only that intellectual work is a specific activity but also that this activity is no less social than any other.

Given that intellectual products are created within a specific set of relations, this implies that a reconstruction of this set is a prerequisite for understanding what is created in and for a field of this kind. This reconstruction is also called for to understand which effects other fields bring about. Because of the relative autonomy of the intellectual field, political or economic developments have a specific kind of carry-over. They are translated, as it were, into the specific logic of intellectual exchange. Instead of reflection, there is a process of refraction.

The intellectual field is a configuration of people with various positions who, even if they have a comparable position, differ as to their capabilities and preferences. What these people accomplish is dependent on the structure of the field, on the 'capital' at their disposal, and on their 'dispositions' or 'habitus', in other words on their specific tendencies to utilize and invest this capital. This capital varies in amount as well as in composition. Some people have more of it, some have less, and always in a specific combination of economic, cultural and social capital. The very terms 'disposition' or 'habitus' draw attention to the fact that the way people manage this capital is rarely in keeping with the logic of 'rational choices'. Within a given field acts are guided by interests, but these interests have to be interpreted and evaluated in a certain way. In the course of this process rather intuitive sympathies and antipathies play a role, and derive their system in turn from the habitus of the individual or group in question. In short, 'ideas' and 'theories' are also the outcome of complex social dynamics. They are not simply the 'reflection' or the 'expression' of certain social structures or interests, but the result of the work of a specific group of 'producers'. As such, they are dependent on the relations under which these producers have to work, the resources at their disposal and their specific dispositions or habitus.

Social theories and intellectual regimes

For this study I elaborated upon Bourdieu's model to distinguish three types of question. The first type pertains to the development of social theory in relation to the intellectual field. What is involved here are such questions as: What kind of theories were they? How did they come into being and develop? What were the most important differences between rival points of view? What position did they occupy in the intellectual space? The fact that the intellectual context is central here does not mean it is mainly 'internal' questions that are posed. Doing justice to the specific character of intellectual work does not mean one has solely to pose text-internal questions or to devote attention to 'intertextual' relations ('sources', 'influences' and so forth). It is not only texts and theories that are important here, but also their producers, their colleagues and competitors and the groups and institutions they form.

The second type of question pertains to the social conditions under which the intellectual field functions. The autonomy of intellectuals is relative, and in their work they also depend on people who are not intellectuals, people who commission their projects, serve as their patrons, intervene on their behalf or read their work. In innumerable ways, what takes place among intellectuals is interconnected with other fields and other groups. For each author this fact implies a specific series of opportunities and restrictions. Different intellectuals react to this in different ways. Some are apt to shrink back from a wider audience and try to build up a career with the kind of support that comes mainly from their colleagues. Others prefer quick economic gains to intellectual authority in the long run. Others still try to find a *modus vivendi*; they want to take advantage of opportunities, but without running the risk of compromising themselves. Intellectual developments thus also depend on opportunities to gain support and recognition outside the intellectual world, if only because intellectuals do not refrain from taking advantage of these opportunities in their rivalry with one another. The structure of the intellectual field is the outcome of the acts and the strategies of a specific group, the intellectuals, but their opportunities are determined in part by their relations to other social groups and institutions. To do justice to them, it is important to devote attention to the social conditions of intellectual work and the social functions of intellectual products.

The third type of question pertains to the specificities of the French development in the international context. French contributions played a leading role in the rise of sociology. This raises the question of how the development in France compared with that in other countries. What role did foreign examples and challenges play? What role did specific French traditions and characteristics play? How did national aspirations affect the rise of social theory?

These questions, which allude to the intellectual, the social and the international context respectively, can be viewed as the three dimensions within which the rise of sociology took place.

In working on this book, it soon became clear that not enough material was available to study all three of these dimensions properly. Very little is known, for example, about the development of the intellectual field. For two centuries a myriad of volumes have appeared on the Enlightenment, but up until very recently no one had any idea how many writers there were at the time and how they managed to make a living. A great deal has been written about the famous few, but it is not always clear what their work meant to their contemporaries. Surprisingly enough, even less information is available on the revolutionary period. There are journals and research centres that focus all their attention on this period, but not one single comprehensive study has been conducted on the role of intellectuals during the Revolution or the effects of revolutionary change on intellectual developments.

One ramification of this dearth of information is that many researchers refrain from posing contextual questions — or, in the exceptional case, refrain from doing anything else. In the former case, they are firmly backed by tradition and need have no compunction about spending all their time interpreting one book, one person or one school of thought. And in the latter case, the promise of something new is enticing and attention is focused on institutional developments or changes in the book market, although it remains unclear what the relevance could be to a better understanding of the texts written in this context.

By uniting intellectual history and social history I tried to avoid both these snares. In doing so I had to narrow down the original problem. This was done mainly by examining social theories in relation to the intellectual field or the intellectual regime. For the period in question it might be more appropriate to speak of an intellectual regime,[17] since its autonomy was restricted and there was no open competition. A regime can then be defined as a specific, more regulated state of a field involving, for example, different forms of external censorship. Intellectual regimes or fields can be described as to their degree of autonomy, level of differentiation and type of hierarchy.

First and foremost, intellectual regimes are characterized by a certain degree of autonomy. In this sense, the intellectual regime that developed from 1750 to 1850 was one with an increasing degree of autonomy. The dependence on extra-intellectual institutions was considerably reduced. With the *philosophe* there came a figure on the scene who laid claim to expertise in all fields of knowledge without exception. During the Revolution the clergy lost once and for all the intellectual power it had monopolized for centuries on end. Now an intellectual regime was established that was not even dependent on the church in a purely polemical sense, and this increased autonomy also altered relations among secular intellectuals. At the beginning of the nineteenth century the groups of scholars that had previously assembled around the *Encyclopédie* each went their own way. There was no need to preserve the united front *vis-à-vis* church institutions, and the differences among secular groups became more important than their joint opposition to the church.

This last development heralds the second aspect, increasing differentiation. The intellectual regime of the early modern period was relatively undifferentiated, institutionally concentrated as it was around relatively unspecialized academies and learned societies and theoretically founded on the unity and immutability of reason. Modern intellectual regimes have a differential structure in which many unitary concepts (reason, nature, philosophy) have made way for a division into faculties and disciplines. Wolf Lepenies described this regime as a constellation of three cultures. The social sciences constitute the third culture,[18] in between 'literature' and 'sciences'.

Lastly, from 1750 to 1850 the intellectual regime witnessed changes in hierarchy. The intellectual scene in France was dominated initially by men of letters and literary means of expression. The status of the natural sciences did rise in the eighteenth century, but less than is generally assumed. It was not until after 1775 that the natural sciences came to occupy a central position in the intellectual field. Shifts of this kind in intellectual hierarchy are one of the most important aspects in the structure of intellectual regimes. New intellectual trends are frequently related to these changes in hierarchy: a group of intellectuals rises in status and threatens the leading position of dominant groups, and this challenge, regardless of whether it is successful, then leads to reorientation on the part of a third group. The social sciences are extremely sensitive to changes of this kind. This is why new developments in the 'third culture' are so often indicative of an altered relation between the 'first' and the 'second' cultures.

By exploring the development of social theory from the angle of changes in intellectual regimes, I have turned this into a kind of double study. I set out to examine the predisciplinary history of social theory, but, for each of the three stages that were distinguished in this connection, I also examined the structure of the intellectual regime. This was necessary not only because so little information was available, but also because the predisciplinary nature of intellectual production made it essential to engage the entire intellectual constellation in the study. The very fact that Voltaire was a writer, Montesquieu a jurist and Condorcet a mathematician indicates how futile it would be to even try and understand these social theorists without scrutinizing the structure of the intellectual regime and its transformations.

This is why, in each of the three parts of this book, such a wide scope of intellectual developments is included. Part I deals at length with the rise of a secular intellectual culture in seventeenth-century France. The relations and cultural traditions that emerged as a result shaped the opportunities and limitations the *philosophes* were to have. In comparison with the Scottish moral philosophers their work remained more contingent on a rationalistic problematic. This phenomenon can be understood only by comparing the intellectual regimes under which they worked.

In much the same manner, Part II focuses on the changes that took place in the intellectual regime in the period after the Enlightenment, the most important being that men of letters lost their supremacy and, for the first time, the natural sciences came to occupy a dominant position. This alteration in the intellectual hierarchy, which had to do with the Revolution, largely explains the scientization of social theories at the time.

Changes in the intellectual regime similarly play a central role in Part III. Auguste Comte can be viewed as one of the first to provide a theoretical account of the establishment of a modern intellectual regime. Cognitive differentiation and the formation of disciplines were central features in Comte's theory of science. In itself this constituted a major innovation, but, surprisingly enough, many decades later it was precisely this theory that was to serve as the foundation for the French sociological tradition. This, then, is the reason why his work occupies a central position in the last part of this book.

Part I

The Rise of Social Theory

Part I

The Rise of Social Theory

Introduction

There are few people who allow themselves a vigorous and auda-
cious usage of their reason and dare to apply it to all subjects in all
its force. Time has come to thus apply it to all subjects of morals,
politics and society; to kings, ministers, nobles, philosophers, to the
principles of the sciences, the arts, etc. Without which we would
remain in mediocrity.

Chamfort

The idea that human beings can be understood from the social arrangements they form is a modern one. Strictly speaking, it was not
until the eighteenth century that an approach emerged with this as its
central idea. Behind this line of thinking was the awareness that modern societies are not the same sort of units as 'states', nor should they
be. They encompass much more than the institutions recognized and
regulated by the state, and this greater diversity could no longer be
covered by the vocabularies available at the time. It was during this
period that the term 'society' acquired its modern meaning; the function of the word was to do justice to the increased diversity without
abandoning the idea of interconnectedness. In the simplest sense, a
society was a system of groups of people and institutions linked to
each other in a variety of ways. This linkage was many sided and
many faceted: it did not stem from a 'plan', was not stipulated in laws
or rules and was neither purely 'political' nor purely 'economic' —
and it was precisely this differentiation that made societies such
complicated units that were so difficult to manage. Though they did
constitute a more or less constraining whole, this constraint could not
be localized in any one person or group, nor could it be defined in
legal or political terms (rights, competence, obligations). In the development of societies, unanticipated causes and unintentional effects
played an important role, and in that sense as well the traditional
approaches failed to suffice. These themes, which came to occupy a

central position in social theory, were coherently formulated for the first time in France and Scotland. Much of it has since become part and parcel of the social sciences.[1]

The general question addressed in this first part is how and why these social theories emerged in France. In what fashion did this process occur? Who were the main authors? How can this development be explained? Two more specific questions are dealt with as well, each of which requires a short explication.

Social theory can best be defined as a new intellectual genre. Though it did not constitute a separate 'discipline', it did nonetheless differ from the existing genres (political theory, law, political economy and moral philosophy). An intellectual genre can be viewed as a distinct discursive practice or tradition, characterized at the very least by a specific vocabulary. In order to analyse a new intellectual genre, there are two matters to be clarified. One pertains to its relation to the terms and concepts of existing genres — in this case: what was the relative significance of political theory, moral philosophy and law in the genesis of social theory? In France, these genres and the persons specialized in them constituted a constellation that differed considerably from the English and German context. Without insight into the structure of this constellation it is impossible to comprehend the making of social theory. Like any other genre, however, social theory can be practised in very different manners. This is why it is also important to devote attention to the theoretical perspective from which this genre was pursued. Was it, as has so frequently been suggested, a predominantly scientific perspective in the sense of the natural sciences, or was it the procedures of modern natural law that served as examples for the French social theorists? Working from the distinction between *intellectual genres* and *theoretical perspectives*, between vocabularies and procedures, the two questions to be addressed in this part of the book can be specified as follows.

The first question is why social theories were formulated to such a great extent in relation to developments in moral philosophy and to such a limited extent in relation to political or legal traditions. Barely any attention has been devoted to this phenomenon in the literature. Recent studies focus their attention on the history of political theory.[2] There has been growing interest in political economy and law, but it is striking how little has been published on moral philosophy. The fact, for example, that the moralist tradition was also of great importance for Montesquieu is systematically overlooked throughout the enormous body of literature. The most important reason for this neglect is the contemporary academic division of labour. The only people still likely to write about French moralists are literary historians. Specialists in philosophy and the history of ideas confine themselves to writings of a more systematic ilk than the aphorisms and essays of the moralists. And since the 'moral sciences' no longer exist, the field no longer has custodians to keep the records of its past. As a result the history of the moral sciences has yet to be written. All that has been studied are literary, philosophical and social science aspects of the moral sciences, but this principle of classification has been in existence only since around 1800.

Moreover, special attention to the moralist tradition is not merely essential as regards the origins of social theory. It is not only that social theories emerged as a new branch of the 'moral sciences'; in France this relationship continued to exist for quite some time. At the end of the nineteenth century moral issues were still a central component of the social sciences. When sociology first became a required subsidiary subject on the university curriculum in 1920, what was entailed was *morale et sociologie*, which was taught to philosophy students. Forty years later, lectures for this 'certificate' still comprised the only official teaching course in sociology. It was not until 1958 that the institutional connection between morals and sociology was severed and sociology became a discipline in its own right. For a lengthy period of time, the connection between social theory and moral science was thus a major feature of French sociology.

The closeness of this connection between the social and the moral sciences is matched by their long-standing distance from political science, as is illustrated by their institutional history. Philosophy and such subjects as psychology and sociology were added to the *sciences humaines* in the eighteenth and nineteenth centuries, all of them being taught in the Faculty of Letters. This gradual extension did not, however, include forms of knowledge pertaining to the state. Political science developed along quite a different route. The science of politics was long to remain a state monopoly. No academies were founded in the seventeenth or eighteenth centuries for administration, law or politics. These matters were thus excluded from the intellectual world that had been instituted around academies devoted to literature, the arts and the sciences. Under the *Ancien Régime*, political concerns were the preserve of the servants of the Crown: politics and government were state matters rather than academic questions. In the nineteenth century this was to remain much the same. A separate institution was founded, the Ecole libre des sciences politiques (1871), but it was not affiliated with the universities and did not play a role of any significance in an intellectual sense. After World War II the Ecole libre was converted into the Fondation nationale des sciences politiques, but there was still a gap between this institution and the social sciences and the humanities.

This split between the 'moral' and the 'political' sciences was a fundamental division in France. It dates back to the seventeenth century, but has never really disappeared. In the human or moral sciences there was a clear preference for forms of behaviour outside the realm of official rules and laws: manners and morals and the emotional world, and the field of action where they prevail. These phenomena constitute the material for literary as well as moral writings. The moral sciences acquired their autonomy by relinquishing everything pertaining to the state. This held true very literally for treatises by the *moralistes*, but it is striking that in the works of Comte or Durkheim the state plays a similarly negligible role. The moral sciences remained, as it were, stateless.

In general, moral scientists had a great deal of difficulty incorporating political developments into their models. And political scientists found it equally troublesome to surmount the limitations of their policy studies. The Ecole libre des sciences politiques trained countless generations of highly placed officials, but not much ever came of the scientific ambitions of its founder, Emile Boutmy.[3] Moral scientists refused to incorporate political questions, just as political scientists were not particularly interested in the scientific dimensions of their work. Moral scientists did not hold official positions, political scientists seldom held intellectual ones. In 1969 Fernand Braudel, a leading representative of the human sciences, lamented the fact that the political sciences had not yet managed to become fully fledged sciences.[4]

This partitioning, with all its repercussions as to the questions posed and the concepts formulated in both of the fields, was reinforced by another division that plays an important role in France, that between 'intellectuals' and 'experts'. From the very start, the human or moral sciences were practised by a different group than the political sciences. The terms *moraliste, philosophe* and, later, *intellectuel* implied a fundamental distance from the 'specialist', who uses knowledge for purposes of government and management. In the eyes of 'intellectuals', political scientists were little more than civil servants or government officials. Their work was performed for different groups, fulfilled different functions and was done by another type of specialist.

The only social science that could sidestep this division has been economics. In the seventeenth century and at the beginning of the eighteenth, economics was still practised as a 'political science', just like statistics or demography. With the rise of classical political economy a division was born separating it from 'mercantilistic' doctrines, and in the course of the nineteenth century the distance from the state became greater. This was institutionally manifested in the fact that economics was awarded a place at the Law Faculty. Without getting any closer to the 'humanistic' subjects, it was separated once and for all from the 'political' sciences.

In France, the social sciences have thus arranged themselves in a triangle. The intellectually dominant pole in this constellation consists of the subjects positioned within the Faculty of Letters, which are traditionally dominated by philosophers. These disciplines, notably psychology, sociology and anthropology, continue in the tradition of the moral sciences and train students for intellectual functions in education or research. At the opposite pole, there are the political or policy sciences. The separate institutions for these disciplines did prepare students for higher positions in the civil services, but they failed to acquire an intellectual legitimacy of any significance. The economic sciences became increasingly important in the nineteenth century and constituted a third group. The main factor enabling their autonomy *vis-à-vis* the state was the link that was established with the expansion of trade and commerce and the concomitant demand for economic and financial know-how.[5]

The question as to how social theory is associated with moral science alludes, in short, to a major phenomenon in the history of the social sciences in France, and this is why I shall devote greater attention to it than is customarily the case.

The second question to be addressed at some length in this part of the book is why, in a strictly theoretical sense, these social theories remained so dependent on rationalistic procedures. Under the *Ancien Régime*, intellectual production was not only characterized by early and sometimes radical secularization and 'rationalization', but also by slow scientization. Here the term scientization refers to the tendency to take procedures from the natural sciences as a model for constructing social theory. The rise of secular and rational social theory was early in France, its expansion was rapid, but at the same time it was a process characterized by *slow scientization*, or perhaps more accurately by postponed scientization. This phenomenon has been widely misunderstood. Peter Gay wrote, for example, that the *philosophes* tried to 'identify their way of working with the methods of the natural sciences'.[6] Other authors have made similar comments and, in a somewhat vague manner, the Enlightenment is frequently associated with an unprecedented faith in 'science', particularly with respect to the veneration of Locke and Newton. One side effect of an interpretation of this kind is that the development of the social sciences from 1750 to 1850 is depicted as a continuous process, with no breaks or sudden changes. René Hubert thus concluded that all Saint-Simon and Comte had to do was continue advancing along the path laid down by the *Encyclopédie*.[7]

To illustrate why this view is questionable, it is important to draw a distinction between 'rational' and 'scientific' conceptualization. Empirical research and empirical testing are decisive for scientific theories, but not for purely rational ones. The social theory that set the tone in France remained strongly based upon rationalistic premises. Contrary to what is generally assumed, before about 1775 there is no evidence of a clear tendency towards scientization. Compared with the case of the Scottish moral philosophers, one could thus speak of slow or delayed scientization. To explain this phenomenon, it is necessary to deviate from the usual studies of the Enlightenment in two senses.

Firstly, it is imperative to devote more attention to details of the French context and to differences with other countries. In line with the cosmopolitan ideals of the period, French *philosophes*, Scottish moral philosophers and English scholars are usually quoted indiscriminately as examples of one and the same era. Surprisingly few comparative studies have been conducted. In addition to the more general studies on the Enlightenment, innumerable research projects have focused on the *philosophes* and the Scottish moral philosophers, but not one has ever systematically compared the two.[8]

Secondly, it is important to go back to the seventeenth century. Despite the classical studies by Hazard and Cassirer, the Enlightenment is far more often described from the perspective of the period following it than of the one preceding it. This holds true of its critics as well as its defenders. Both groups often see the Enlightenment as the beginning of modern times. But in France, more than anywhere else, the Enlightenment was linked to institutions (academies and salons) and traditions (classicism) dating back to the seventeenth century. This renowned period in French history goes by two names: *le grand siècle* and *l'âge classique*. In conjunction with the political supremacy France had gained in Europe, a new cultural system was created that was to serve as the foundation for national culture. With the support of the court and the nobility, a new cultural regime emerged around academies and learned societies which soon overshadowed the traditional intellectual centres, church and university alike. The new secular and more or less 'worldly' culture expanded in the course of the eighteenth century, and to a certain extent the work of the *philosophes* can be described as an elaboration and radicalization of this cultural style. In the transition from the classical period to the Enlightenment a wide range of changes occurred, but no fundamental break can be observed anywhere like the one between Enlightenment and Romanticism.

Since the resources and reputations of the *philosophes* depended so strongly on this heritage, in this part of the book I first focus on the establishment of this new cultural regime and the social conditions under which it was born. In the exchanges, particularly between writers and the court aristocracy, a cultural style developed that was incorporated into the education system via the Jesuits and continued to be dominant throughout the eighteenth century. Chapter 1 gives a general description of this style. Against this background, in Chapter 2 a number of general features of the work of the *philosophes* are discussed. Moral philosophy, which is the subject of Chapter 3, is of particular importance in this connection. Chapter 4 deals with the actual rise of social theory and Chapter 5 focuses on similarities and differences in comparison with the Scottish moral philosophers.

1

Intellectuals between Academy and Salon

For a long time, a wide diversity marked the conditions of intellectual production. During the *Ancien Régime*, writings on social phenomena were formally subordinated to political and church authorities. Specialists in these fields, especially jurists and theologians, were trained at the universities, but they were confined to official texts and had to adhere to more or less fixed rules pertaining to commentary and exegesis. In their professional practice they were subordinated to the authority of higher state and church institutions, and their work was subject to censorship. In all these senses, what they did differed from the activities that had acquired the right to be practised at an academy. The national academies were recognized as the highest authorities in their field and had been granted mandates and privileges guaranteeing a certain degree of autonomy, particularly *vis-à-vis* the church. The rise of a modern, secular culture in France centred mainly around academies. These academies emerged most often from private societies that had been subsequently recognized by the state. Together they formed a new cultural regime, distinct from the older church and university institutions.

When the first social science institution was founded after the French Revolution, it followed the example set by the academies. They were to remain the most prominent cultural and intellectual institutions far into the nineteenth century.

The shaping of the academies

The system of national academies arose in the seventeenth century during a decisive stage in the establishment of the absolute monarchy. Eight royal academies were founded between 1635 and 1671, six of them under Louis XIV. They submitted expert recommendations to the monarch, educated students for certain cultural professions and contributed to the prestige of the French monarchy. An academy was a state institution, situated in Paris and consisting of a limited number of representatives of the most prestigious arts and sciences. Most of them had their roots in societies of writers, artists and scholars that became increasingly prevalent in the seventeenth century. These societies were initially a private affair. More than seventy such gatherings are known to have followed the Italian example and referred to themselves as academies. Most of them (56 out of 71) were literary societies, nine were focused on the natural sciences, and the other six on music and art.[1] It was one of these circles of writers that was the breeding ground for the first official academy. The Académie française (1635) is the oldest and most prominent academy. Its forty members are qualified to view themselves as the literary authorities of the country and constitute a kind of supreme court for French literature and the French language. The foundation of the Académie française was instrumental in the rapid replacement of church and university Latin with French. Descartes was no longer ashamed of writing in French and the royal recognition of writers soon served as an example for painters, sculptors and scientists.

Within a few decades there were also academies for art, music, architecture and the natural sciences. It was usually a small group in a particular field who took the initiative. Sometimes it was done in conjunction with the authorities, and only in a few cases was it the state that took the initiative. For the groups involved this process of academization did not take place in the same way.[2] For painters and sculptors, academic recognition meant a break from the guilds and an effort to have their work recognized as a 'liberal' art rather than a craft or 'mechanical' art. In their case, upward social mobility was accompanied by partial 'deprofessionalization' and led to a wide range of conflicts with the rigidly organized corporation. The first generation of academic painters drew upon their knowledge of anatomy and geometry (for depicting perspective) and distinguished themselves in this way from the crafts they held in such contempt. Later generations, more apt to take academic recognition for granted, put more emphasis on the aesthetic qualities of their work. Skilful craftsmanship was no longer sufficient, nor were insight and learning; now it was a sense of beauty and taste that counted. In the eighteenth century this development resulted in the concept of the 'fine arts', and

'aesthetics' became a specialty in its own right.[3] After the division between craftsmanship and art, between *artisans* and *artistes*, a demarcation line came to be drawn between art and knowledge. In the
Romantic representation of the artist, craftsmanship and learning retreated even further into the background. For scientists – *savants*, as
practitioners of the natural sciences were called – developments followed a different course. For them academization meant a break
with university traditions. Their work had been categorized under the
'liberal arts', the *artes liberales*, though it was dominated by scholastic
customs and doctrines. In their case, the split from the university meant
a rapprochement with the 'mechanical' arts. Members of the university community devoted themselves to spiritual matters, manual
labour was foreign to them, and the use of Latin served only to accen-
tuate their aloofness from profane concerns. Performing experiments,
conducting measurements, detecting causal or mechanical relations,
all these ingredients of the classical natural sciences were alien to them.
University professors were learned men, schooled in logic and highly
skilled at drawing distinctions and constructing classifications – skills
that were essential to their disputes. The pioneers of empirical observation, experimentation and the tenets of causal thinking were not
employed at the universities. It was the skilled craftsmen, artists and
engineers such as Leonardo da Vinci and Simon Stevin who generated
these forms of knowledge in the cities. They often moved in circles of
merchants, instrument-makers and inventors, and when they put
their findings on paper they did so in the vernacular. Edgar Zilsel has
argued that empirical natural science could come into being only after
the gap between these two groups was bridged. From the university
tradition came the erudition, the systematic reasoning and the theoretical interest. From the world of skilled craftsmanship came the
practice of experimentation, the use of quantitative methods and the
habit of causal thinking, as well as contempt for school authorities
and the capacity for effective cooperation. It was around 1600 that
work was done in England (Bacon, Gilbert) and Italy (Galileo) that
bore witness to a coherent connection between these two traditions.
This connection was to serve as the basis for the scientific revolution
of the seventeenth century. Galileo's major work, the *Discorsi* (1638),
still bears traces of the old duality: he commented upon the mathematical deductions in Latin and discussed the experiments in Italian.[4]

In France the Académie des sciences (1666) became the centre for
the new natural sciences. Designed after the example of the existing
academies, the institution was primarily a response to the foundation
of the Royal Society (1662). Now mathematics and the natural

sciences could also be practised in France to the greater glory of the monarch. In addition, the new academy was assigned practical tasks; it evaluated inventions, for example, and inspected new machines. As a result new professional possibilities came into being that had been hitherto virtually non-existent. For scientists, academization thus went hand in hand with a rapprochement with the mechanical arts and a tendency towards professionalization. In the arts, however, academization coincided with an estrangement from the mechanical arts – first by way of intellectualization and then aestheticization – and partial deprofessionalization.

Since academies rapidly became the most highly esteemed and most dynamic cultural institutions, the authority of the church was soon reduced in these fields. Education at the *collèges* and universities did remain closely linked to the church, but for the actual practice of the arts, literature and the natural sciences the academies set the trend. Theology, law and medicine, the three higher faculties, remained purely university subjects. They were denied academic status, which was one of the reasons why their dependence upon the church and university orthodoxy was so much stronger. In the natural sciences, practised as they were at academies and universities alike, the universities lagged far behind. The universities either missed out on the latest scientific innovations or failed to introduce them until they were no longer called for. According to Biot, university professors were lecturing on Aristotle when scientists were admiring Descartes, and on Descartes when Newton was at the peak of his fame.[5] The cultural rivalry between the older institutions affiliated with the church and the newer state ones had already become clear somewhat earlier. Under Francis I, the Collège royal (1530), later known as the Collège de France, was founded to teach Greek and Hebrew, for which there was no place at the Sorbonne. A century later the Jardin du roi (1635) was founded, and the officialization of the academies provided a new opportunity to enhance the cultural prestige of the state and overshadow the church as well as other states. Secularization and academization of intellectual life were thus closely linked to the process of state formation.

The academic regime

Upon receiving official recognition, academies became specialized institutions bound to a fixed set of rules and regulations. As such, they differed from the far less rigidly organized societies of the sixteenth and early seventeenth centuries.[6] Theological disputes were prohibited, the rights and obligations of an academy pertained to a specific field, and, in order to become a member, in principle a certain competence was required. The assemblies had their own procedures, and certain symbolic attributes underscored the dignity of academic office. The first duty of the academician was to deliver an inaugural address. From that moment on his consecration was official and he was assured of a eulogy in praise of his merits upon his death. The *discours de réception* and the *éloge* were standard components of the ritual and in many senses typically academic genres. Since an academy was a state institution, its members also performed representative functions. The most prominent academies held their assemblies at the Louvre and, as a *corps*, the academicians participated in certain royal ceremonies.

An academy derived its position from the official recognition of its particular competence. Academicians had the right to select new members themselves, they exchanged knowledge, discussed new work and had publication rights without needing the permission of censors. In addition, they enjoyed the power to evaluate new developments, settle conflicts and stipulate general norms. In their field, the academies had a kind of *monopoly of judgement*. As Mannheim noted, they served as 'competitive monopolies' in relation to the church.[7] The Académie française, for example, published a dictionary defining the 'accepted' words in the 'right' way. The Académie de peinture et de sculpture concerned itself with aesthetic norms. And the Académie des sciences was authorized to pass judgement on technical inventions, sometimes pronouncing them 'approved by the academy'.[8] Periodicals such as the *Journal des savants* were run by academicians and served as inter-academic forums. All the academies regularly held contests, thus maintaining contact with 'young talent'.

Proper to the high status of an academic position, there was fierce competition for the vacancies. The title of academician was sought after and was also a great advantage in acquiring other positions. In a long-term perspective, membership increasingly became an honorary function, the ultimate reward for work that had long been completed. At the Académie des sciences, the average entrance age rose from 28 in 1730 to 39 just before the Revolution; by 1900 it had risen to 50 and in 1970 to 65.[9]

In the course of time, the academies lost various of the functions they had initially fulfilled. After 1800, scientific articles were increasingly published in journals that were not affiliated with academies. Discussions on scientific or literary work were conducted in specialized societies and associations, which was why the academies were less and less in a position to impose their standards. Multifarious conflicts throughout the nineteenth century between avant-garde artists and the academic authorities led in the end to the decline of 'academism' in all its facets. The academies lost their central and dominant position in every sector of culture. The situation altered to such an extent that for publications, performances and exhibitions there was no longer that sole dependence on the academy in question. A more differentiated and less centralized cultural regime evolved, and, since the social elite was also becoming somewhat more heterogeneous, there was a growing 'style diversity' in any number of fields, and a concomitant tendency towards 'taste uncertainty'.[10] In most cases all that the academies retained was their ordination function and a share in the granting of prizes and other tokens of esteem, with membership at the academy itself as the highest honour that could be bestowed.

The process of academization had promoted the autonomy and prestige of the arts and sciences, thereby reinforcing the tendency towards secularization. At the same time it had effectuated a considerable extent of centralization and officialization. Academicians had to reside in Paris and were promoted as the official authorities in their field. They could conduct their work in their own manner, but had to evaluate and supervise the work of others. An academy thus functioned as a distinguished club as well as a national tribunal. The condemnation of Corneille's *Le Cid* by the Académie française is a good example of the power of the academy. The same verdict, however, also illustrated the dependence on the central authorities. It was pronounced under pressure from Richelieu, the statesman to whom the Académie française owed its very existence.

The royal court and the salons

Although as of the seventeenth century the arts, literature and the natural sciences evolved mainly in and around academies, it would be misleading to speak of an academic culture. In the modern-day sense of the word, the academies were not all that academic. They developed in a field of tension between the closed world of the guilds and universities on the one hand and the flourishing culture of the royal court on the other. They attained a relatively high level of independence from the guilds and universities, but therefore had to rely on the support of the state and the court. In comparison with contemporary academic institutions, their dependence was greater and more direct. Each academy had a group of honorary members, the *honoraires*, consisting of noblemen and high state officials. Although they lacked the required competence, they did confer a special prestige on the academies. The very fact that they attended academic assemblies was the highest token of recognition for the work conducted at the academy. The court was also of crucial importance in other senses for cultural activities. Numerous features of cultural production were closely linked to the taste and distaste of the aristocratic elite. To a large extent artists were dependent on aristocratic circles in Versailles and Paris for commissions, support and recognition. The dancing masters illustrated how decisive the support of the court aristocracy could be, for they were able to found an official academy of dance that was on a par with the other academies. For the courtiers, dancing was as much an art as painting or poetry.

The dominant position of the court was also evident in the arts and literature. Not only were skills at dancing courtly virtues, but literary capacities and a certain artistic sense were as well. Members of the court nobility devoted much of their time to refining their manners and their taste. In the competition for prestige and favours a refined lifestyle had become their most important resource, and art and literature were automatically components of it. Via patrons, there were regular exchanges with artists, and various forms of courtly art could evolve. Since the bourgeoisie more or less followed the courtly examples, French culture came to exhibit a markedly aristocratic demeanour and was to become the dominant model for aristocratic groups in other countries.[11]

An important moment in the definitive establishment of the court was the failure of the Fronde, a series of civil revolts between 1648 and 1653. This was the last time the nobility was to oppose the sole rule of the monarch. Louis XIV was still a minor, Mazarin was ruling and various groups, *parlements*, urban corporations and members of the high nobility all tried to exploit the temporary weakness of the monarchy. 'Each of these people and groups', Norbert Elias wrote, 'wants to curtail royal power; but each wants to do it to his own advantage. Each fears that another's power might grow at the same time. Finally – not least thanks to the skill with which Mazarin takes advantage of this mechanism of tensions – the old equilibrium is re-established in favour of the existing royal house. Louis XIV never forgot the lesson of these days; far more consciously and carefully than all his predecessors, he nurtured this equilibrium and maintained the existing social differences and tensions.'[12]

By making use of the differences among these various groups, the monarchs managed gradually to improve their position and then to keep it for a long time. As far as the rising bourgeoisie were concerned, the king could rely on the nobility, who were rewarded for their support with positions at the court. And with regard to the court nobility, the king relied on bourgeois groups, particularly the civil officials. Much as the court had become a bulwark of the nobility, the civil administration had become a predominantly bourgeois affair.

Each position in this structure implied a certain ambivalence. Members of the high nobility shared with the bourgeoisie an interest in restricting the power of the king, but for their position as noblemen it was the king on whom they were dependent. Representatives of the bourgeoisie could contest certain of the nobility's privileges, but since their own existence was similarly based upon privileges they were rightfully wary of endangering the structure itself.

For the aristocracy, the failure of the Fronde implied that court domination had become inescapable. From then on there was no place but the court to turn for a diplomatic or military career – and indeed for a prospective marriage candidate as well. The hope for some measure of liberation from the severity of court etiquette and for restrictions to the power of the monarch had proved an illusion. Now there was no other option than to accept defeat. Whoever so wished could perhaps gain exemption now and then from the rituals of the court and make an effort to continue the opposition with peaceful means. After the Fronde, this was the need some of the salons were to meet. At the salons, entertainment and opposition could go hand in hand, as noblemen could combat their boredom there in properly dignified fashion – for example, by mocking courtiers.[13] As armed resistance had failed, they could only express their discontent symbolically by means of irony and satire, and later by being receptive to the *philosophes* or other manifestations of 'theoretical' opposition.

The advent of the salons dates back to the seventeenth century. After the Fronde, they witnessed an unprecedented boom up until about 1665, when court life became more attractive and salon activities once again declined.[14] Unlike events at the court, the salons were open to members of the bourgeoisie. They were places where people gathered together in keeping with aristocratic customs and habits, but without having to subject themselves to very strict rules of etiquette. The manners adhered to here were less ceremonious and rigid and some salons were known for a certain specialty. Thus in the eighteenth century, in the heyday of the salons, some were devoted to philosophy, others to music or gastronomy. In this fashion there were salons that earned for themselves a special role, regardless of what was in vogue at the court and in a sense in competition with the court. The social function the salons fulfilled was thus twofold: it was via the salons that courtly standards were disseminated and that members of the bourgeoisie could associate with aristocratic circles, but it was also via the salons that new developments could be introduced into the upper layers of the aristocracy.

Salons were dominated by women from the high nobility. In the seventeenth century approximately half the précieuses came from this group, and the other half from circles of aristocratic officialdom or high finance.[15] There were other admittance criteria besides noble blood, and assembling people from the highest levels of various groups was one of their functions. Resistance to this *mondain* elite was voiced mainly by members of the lower nobility. They had been outpaced by some members of the bourgeoisie and very few of them could afford a *mondaine* lifestyle of the kind required. It was mainly people from this group who spoke out in defence of the traditional virtues of rank. They held tenaciously to the old codes of the nobility and were fervently opposed, for example, to the new role of women.

Together the individuals who peopled the world of the court and the salons constituted a small, centralized and rather homogeneous elite. High government officials, merchants, clergymen and writers could all gain access to the *monde*, as it was modestly called, but only if they adjusted to courtly etiquette, only if they exhibited the proper manners. The division between this dominant elite and the lower orders was extremely sharp. It was possible to cross the boundary, but there could be no doubt as to its strictness. Compromises or intermingling 'distinguished' and 'vulgar' were out of the question. The lower classes were rarely depicted in either literature or the arts. It was in poor taste to describe a peasant or an employee of any sort, and having them actually open their mouth was unseemly. This is why English plays were long shunned in the theatres of France: so many things occurred on the stage that were viewed as indecorous in France and as flagrant violations of the *style noble*. Shakespeare was still virtually unknown in France at the beginning of the eighteenth century. This did change somewhat after 1730: commentaries by such authors as Voltaire were published, soon to be followed by the first translations and, after 1750, by the first debates on his significance. The first stage performances date back to shortly before the Revolution, but all things considered it was not until the age of Romanticism that Shakespeare was widely admired and imitated in France.[16] The rigidity of the propriety norms in comparison with other nations was illustrated by the custom of omitting 'coarse' passages from the translations. French versions were thus always polished adaptations.[17]

Artists, writers and scientists were not dependent to the same degree on the aristocratic and *mondain* circles in the capital. Some of them relied more on the court than the salons; others, however, turned mainly to their colleagues for help and to the academy for support. There were also differences in the structure of this dependence in the various genres. In genres in which the court was not apt to express interest, the artist could affort to take quite a bit of liberty as regards courtly preferences, but was then more dependent on the opinions of colleagues. On the grounds of these differences, various strategies evolved to gain recognition, and various types of careers. In general, it was artists who were presumably the most dependent on the court. Their product was a singleton, which made them directly dependent on someone to purchase or commission it. This did not hold true to the same degree for writers. Their work was for a more diffuse audience of readers and theatre-goers; their dependence was thus less direct and less personal, and on the whole they were probably more dependent on the salons than on the court. Lastly, scholars and scientists were the least dependent on either the court or the salons. There were forms of courtly art and courtly literature, but there was no courtly science. Science was associated with 'learning' or the 'mechanical arts', both of which merely aroused contempt at court.

In the cultural world of the *Ancien Régime*, writers occupied a dominant position. They were the first to acquire academic status; they were able to take advantage of the interest in literature at the court, but were not completely dependent on it. They could furthermore make direct use of their specific capacities in their interaction with members of the nobility. If they could manage to adjust to the aristocratic code of etiquette, they could even excel at the art of *mondain* conversation and gain the favour of many a *salonnière*. In that sense, artists and scientists were at a disadvantage. Their specific capacities could serve no immediate purpose, and in the case of scientists they were not at all appreciated.

Cultural effects of court domination

At an early stage, the salons came to have a special significance for writers. Conversation played a central role there, and this in turn gave literary skills a high status. A *bon mot*, a charming anecdote, an entertaining narrative, all these forms of verbal talent were widely appreciated at the salons. What is more, there were close ties between the Académie française and the literary salons. Literary reputations were subject to the judgement of the *honnêtes gens*, who were the reading audience for literature, and to the more specialized judgement of the academician. In the seventeenth century the relation between the two was such that the academy stipulated what had been received in *mondain* circles as proper and refined.[18] Not mistakenly, Taine described the Académie française as an official and central salon. The peculiar mixture of literary norms and aristocratic manners was characteristic of the Paris salons. As Abbé Voisenon observed, it was advantageous for noblemen and writers alike to come together there: 'The courtiers learned to reason, the men of letters learned to converse. The former were no longer bored, the latter no longer boring.'[19]

There was an atmosphere of refined and elegant entertainment at the salons. Writers took part in the conversations in a manner befitting the ambience and acquainted themselves with the rules of propriety and good taste. In this atmosphere of refined courtesy and subtle rivalry for status there was no place for serious treatises and long-winded discourses. A good play on words had more chance of success than a learned lecture, a surprising paradox was more apt to be appreciated than well-founded argumentation, an amusing story would lead to greater rewards than erudition or rigour. Certain stylistic procedures prevailed and an attitude evolved, a way of thinking still viewed as being typically French. Salon culture was the territory of generalists. The brilliant conversationalist was never at a loss for words, no matter what the topic was; the only thing that mattered was the ability to carry on an entertaining conversation. Even the most unmanageable subjects could be tamed with the instruments of rhetoric, so that, according to Mademoiselle de Scudéry, matters could be broached at the salons that no one else would even dare to think of.[20] Short turns of phrase that were singularly apt (aphorisms, maxims) were especially popular, particularly if they pertained to human conduct or passion.

Etiquette at the court and salons required skills that had not traditionally been given much attention in schools, and were mainly transmitted from one generation to the next in the privacy of the home. In the seventeenth century the Jesuits did a great deal to alter this situation. The education they provided was designed for the children of aristocrats. They succeeded in gaining the support of the court nobility and defeating the opposition of the Sorbonne and the *parlements*, earning for themselves a dominant position in the field of education. Logical and dialectical exercises were replaced by a predominantly literary curriculum. Writing skills and eloquence became central, and throughout more than two centuries, the education of the literate French was characterized by an omnipresent focus on *belles lettres*. Latin was taught mainly by the Jesuits in the form of style exercises, 'heathen' ideas were omitted altogether and no attention was devoted to the scientific advances of antiquity or in fact even the history of ancient civilizations. Knowledge and insight were overshadowed by the mastery of stylistic devices; eloquence was the very highest aim. This is why Renan spoke of 'pseudo-humanism'.[21] Durkheim commented much along the same lines when he referred to the dominant role of literary rhetoric as one of the main features of French intellectual history.[22]

It was not until the *écoles centrales*, founded after the Revolution, that new methods and subjects were to be introduced. Many elements of the Jesuit curriculum did, however, turn up again in the teaching programmes of the lycées. In the nineteenth century rhetoric retained its central position, although it was now French rather than Latin rhetoric that was entailed. By the end of the nineteenth century rhetoric had been officially eliminated from the curriculum altogether, but essays and *dissertations* were of undiminished importance. Writing skills and eloquence have continued to occupy a central position, for virtually the entire range of examinations. Paradoxically enough, it was thus through the school system that a tradition was reproduced that was initially as far from schoolish as could be. Ever since the rhetoric of the salon was granted a place in the school system French pupils have been evaluated for their *brille*, their ability to shine and sparkle. It is not necessarily the 'right answer' that counts, but the manner in which it is presented (the tone, the style, the demeanour). The fact that this mode of behaviour, with the emphasis on polish and lustre, also became the highest norm in the school system is an indication of the predominance of the courtly models. *Brille* was a kind of *grandeur* for classroom and salon. *Grandeur* was reserved for the monarch, but for his subjects at any rate there was *brille*. This tendency towards aestheticization and ostentatious demonstration, combined with a very specific attitude, is still evident in any number of fields. The tone, the gestures, the expression, the stance, all are in keeping with a certain style that is still around. Montesquieu observed that, in a monarchy, behaviour was not commended as 'good' but as 'distinguished', not as 'right' but as 'grand', not as 'reasonable' but as 'exceptional'.[23] The fact that these models remained of such importance has to do with the perpetuation of a central elite concentrated in Paris. For the dominant groups, courtly forms of style and prestige retained their function.[24]

Traces of this continuity can still be discerned in contemporary intellectual commerce. The essay, for example, still occupies a prominent place in France, although in such countries as Germany, with a predominantly university intelligentsia, it has either lost much of its significance or was never accepted in the first place because of its 'frivolous' or 'superficial' nature. In France, where aristocratic traditions are strong and scholarly traditions comparatively weak, the essay continues to be one of the most widely practised genres. As a literary medium, the essay is a form stripped of technical jargon and professional terminology, devoid of footnotes, references and indexes, in which an original and clever discourse is far more important than systematic reasoning and empirical evidence. In the essay, Adorno wrote, rhetorical intentions are sublimated to the idea of a happy freedom *vis-à-vis* the object.[25] The writer can freely resort to puns and *double entendres* and organizes his thought according to a musical logic, yielding pleasures the sciences have been forced to abandon. As the art of unattached reflection, of the unbound discourse, the virtuosity of the French essay still recalls many of the peculiarities of the salon culture.

A stylistic tradition

Cultural production in France from the early seventeenth to the late eighteenth century exhibits considerable continuity and coherence. This period, from the Renaissance to the Revolution, was dominated by what the French call Classicism. A style evolved that set the tone in numerous fields and was frequently viewed in fact as the cornerstone of French culture. Its institutional framework consisted of the court, the salons and the academies. Around these institutions a new system of cultural production unfolded, a schism widened with the old cultural powers (church and university), and secularization became one of the main features.

One striking aspect of this new constellation is that none of the well-known philosophers of this period pursued a university career. Many of them were in the service of aristocratic families or under the patronage of the monarch; others were independently wealthy to the extent that they could freely devote time and energy to activities of their choice. Throughout the entire period, from Montaigne to d'Alembert and Diderot, intellectual innovations were initiated outside the universities.[26]

The process of secularization was more intensive and comprehensive in France than in many other countries. The departure from university traditions was marked and nowhere else did national academies gain as prominent and as dominant a position. With the backing of aristocratic groups, writers achieved unprecedented esteem. The foundation of the Académie française (1635) became the symbol of a whole series of new developments which were concluded in a certain sense with the publication of the *Encyclopédie* (1751-72). In this century and a half a sizeable secular intelligentsia emerged and, in addition to new rights and institutions, they also introduced a new division of labour. The medieval categorization of the arts still embedded in the university structure was now replaced by a more modern division into the fine arts, literature and science. This new system was characterized moreover by growing autonomy. The Académie française was still an official institution with limited competence. The *Encyclopédie* was the work of an independent 'society of men of letters' who laid claim to expertise in all areas of human knowledge, and the result of their efforts was not commissioned by any one person or body but was designed for the free market. The commercial success of this enterprise illustrates that, in the course of time, an audience had also evolved for the writings of this new class of secular intellectuals.[27]

The writers who stood at the threshold of this development constituted the dominant group and made a crucial contribution towards the formation of Classicism. Classicism has been defined as a 'doctrine' said to consist of a number of compulsory 'rules'.[28] In reality, it was more a stylistic tradition born of the merging of artistic intentions and aristocratic manners. The only 'rule' that was generally accepted pertained to the function of art. Art was supposed to please the *monde*, and *plaire* was the most important criterion, with all the other 'rules' either ensuing from it or subordinate to it. The functioning of cultural skills in an aristocratic setting led to a style that can be discerned in any number of fields. In music, garden design, architecture, painting and literature, everywhere there is the same intention of restrained and elegant harmonies. All these arrangements, whether of notes, words or steps in a dance, fulfil the same compositional principle: they all exhibit a transparent and graceful arrangement. Since the work of artists was attuned to the lifestyle of a courtly aristocratic audience, a certain unity of style developed, a certain 'way of doing things' that was not linked to any single sector. Even today the turns of phrase in French, the *tournures*, are still reminiscent of the restrained grace with which one was supposed to walk, talk and gesture at court.

The peculiarities of this style can be most clearly illustrated by what was not done, by what was viewed as indecent behaviour. Norbert Elias demonstrated that behavioural standards evolved at the court that were characterized by an increased constraint to exercise self-control. Whatever the situation, a great extent of self-control was called

for. Even the slightest sign of sensitivity could be interpreted as a form
of 'moral inebriation', as Stendhal once described it. Courtiers had
little choice but to exercise the utmost restraint in everything they said
and did, and the features of Classicism were closely linked to this courtly
habitus.

Classicism was first and foremost a style of moderation and restraint.
Italian music, for instance, was viewed in France as being overly exuberant and too emotional. The same phenomenon could be discerned
in literature. Boileau had described and classified the various literary
genres, but without awarding any place at all to lyricism. French poetry was prosaic, lyrical outbursts were taboo, and here again the work
of Rousseau was certain to be categorized as outrageous. Classicism
was not expressive, it was far more a representative or decorative style.
The artist was not expected to express feelings or arouse emotions,
but simply to enhance entertaining gatherings.

The second feature of Classicism was its widely acclaimed clarity.
The striving to be comprehended and immediately understood meant
a rejection of odd and bizarre or mysterious arrangements and of overly
complex design. The rejection of the 'obscure' was born of a kind of
aristocratic scepticism: anything beyond the understanding of a courtier
could not be of any significance. This self-assurance was accompanied
by a strong emphasis on what was viewed as 'reasonable' and 'natural'. The 'reason' at issue here was the intellectual counterpart of good
taste. It had less to do with philosophical categories than with the
skirmishes for prestige at the court. Due to the never-ending rivalry
for status, the most reasonable thing a courtier could do was to behave rationally: keep passions in check, observe with the utmost scrutiny, take into consideration all the possible ramifications of any act
and exercise foresight. This courtly rationality, as Elias called it, with
the emphasis on *le bon sens*, was the reason why faith in religious
explanations and interpretations declined. In ideas on art, reason was
lauded as the highest virtue. The mind ought to curb the imagination
and guard against excessive stimulation of the senses. This is why,
during the age of Romanticism, Classicism was referred to as a style
that was reserved and intellectual.

The emphasis on clarity also meant a rejection of complexity and
abstruseness. For well-bred laymen, art had to be comprehensible and
recognizable. Looking at a painting was not a separate activity in a
special room, presented and commented upon by experts, it was an
everyday component of a lifestyle. The enjoyment of art was not
supposed to require any special knowledge or expertise. As at receptions, the main thing was good taste rather than specialized and out of

the ordinary expert knowledge; these were bourgeois virtues, useful in the world of professional activities, but beneath the dignity of the *honnête homme*. Much along the same lines, the French language was simplified and a conversational style evolved that avoided specialist expressions of any kind. Technical terms were not listed in the first dictionary of the Académie française published in 1694, the only exception being terms pertaining to hunting or warfare, traditional skills of the nobility.[29] The aristocratic mistrust of specialization and professional values was perpetuated in the salons, and Madame de Staël felt that the 'division of labour discovered by Adam Smith' was only valid for the mechanical arts. In matters of the mind, a division of labour would only lead to deterioration.[30]

The third feature of Classicism, the striving for elegance and refinement, is related to what is generally called 'baroque'. The incorporation of baroque elements and motifs has been referred to as characteristic of French Classicism.[31] The combination of these three features, restraint, clarity and elegance, constituted the basis of the style that came into vogue in the seventeenth century and continued to set the tone far into the eighteenth. On the grounds of this general description it is possible to say a bit more about the concomitant intellectual developments.

In the years after the Fronde, with accelerated centralization taking place, Classicism evolved into the dominant cultural model. Aristocratic families that had played a role in the patronage system before 1650 had either left, lost their fortune or joined the court scene. The position of the literate bourgeoisie around the *parlements* had similarly weakened. For writers and artists, opportunities for support were scarce all over, except at the court. This helped bring the courtly tradition to the foreground, and, together with the increasing role of the state in the patronage system, there was a growing tendency towards officialization.[32] Writers, artists and scholars were all eligible for official pensions, but at the same time censorship intensified and a wide range of efforts were made to codify the genres, as if a cultural code of etiquette had to be drawn up as well. To a large extent intellectuals and artists came to rely for support on aristocratic circles in the capital, and, according to Henri Peyre, French literature had never been such an exclusively Parisian affair as in the heyday of Classicism.[33] This was a period rich in famous writers, and they are the ones who went down in history as the classical French authors whose works are still read and taught. It was no less characteristic of this heyday that everything that was *not* appreciated in aristocratic circles was condemned to the periphery.

Pedantry, the stigma of scholarship

What a delicate country we have. One cannot be learned in any
subject without being taken for a prig.

Saint-Evremond

In *mondain* circles, there was an intense aversion to everything
'schoolish'. The noblemen's contempt for the school system was of
lengthy duration. For many aristocrats it was incomprehensible and
probably unbearable that people laid a claim to esteem simply because
they had 'stuck their nose into some books'. They could not muster
the slightest respect for someone who could master some extinct language but was at a loss when it came to conducting a 'decent conversation'. They had two words to express this distaste: *cuistre* and *pédant*.
A *cuistre*, or 'egghead', was a person with too much book learning of
the type acquired at school. *Pédant* was a term with a much more
general meaning and referred to all the knowledge the courtiers held
in contempt. *Pédant* initially just meant a schoolteacher.[34] The term
acquired its pejorative connotation in Italian comedies of the sixteenth
and seventeenth centuries. The figure of the *pédante* was associated
with an ostentatious show of learning, a cumbersome style of speech
replete with Latinisms and little sense of the realities of the world.
Montaigne began his essay 'Du pédantisme' with a reference to the
comedia pedantesca. Montaigne, 'flabbergasted' by these plays in his
youth, held that the most gallant of men were the ones who had the
greatest contempt for pendantry. In the work of Montaigne, the term
pédant still had a rather precise meaning. It stood for all those forms
of knowledge that did not contribute anything to a better life and
stood in the way of wisdom.[35]

In *mondain* circles, the terms pedant and pedantry expanded in the
course of the seventeenth century to include scholarliness and all the
scholarly knowledge it led to. Learnedness and erudition were viewed
as a transgression of good breeding and almost as a sign of poor taste.
Scholars were the target of mockery, difficult words a source of amusement. In plays by Molière and others, the *pédant* would appear on the
stage as an ill-mannered fool, regardless of whether he was a theolo-
gian, a scientist or a doctor. The differences between scholasticism,
humanism and science were irrelevant in these circles. 'Un galant',
Boileau wrote, 'condamne la science, et, blamant tout écrit/Croit qu'en
lui l'ignorance est un titre d'esprit.'[36] Aristocrats basked in their superior ignorance, and 'learned' became synonymous with 'pedantic'. What
few noblemen had any interest in learned matters in the seventeenth

century were well advised to camouflage it and feign ignorance. Knowing the rules of etiquette was the only knowledge that mattered: whatever else one knew was best concealed. Just as it was inappropriate to demonstrate one's true feelings, it was similarly improper to make a show of the book learning one had accumulated. Ferdinand Brunot gave a good example of this norm. In the coterie around the Queen Mother, one day a lady happened to use the word 'vowels'. The others looked at her and exclaimed, 'Oh madame, vowels?' They looked at each other and enquired, 'Do you know what they are, vowels?' All of the women belied their knowledge, and in the end only Madame de Montauzier had the courage to admit she knew what they were.[37] The same attitude pervaded seventeenth-century guides to conversation. It was indecorous to mention 'learned' subjects; only *belles lettres* were a legitimate topic for conversation.

The fact that it was permitted to talk about poetry or drama but not about vowels was indicative of the division that evolved in the seventeenth century between *belles lettres* and *lettres savantes*. At the beginning of the seventeenth century *belles lettres* were still barely a separate category. In the humanistic tradition the study of literature covered linguistic and historical as well as 'aesthetic' considerations. With the increased significance of *mondain* assemblies, the *belles lettres* came to occupy a far more central position at the expense of all the other facets of the study of language. Linguistic questions that were not related to *style* but to *knowledge*, such as etymology or grammar, were now of subordinate importance and anyone concerned with them ran the risk of banishment to the realm of *pédantaille*. This division in the study of literature heralded a development that was to lead to the modern concept of literature.[38] A more specific explanation for the decline of the *lettres savantes* was the repeal of the Edict of Nantes (1685), driving sizeable numbers of Huguenots out of France. Among their ranks were numerous *érudits* who settled in Switzerland, Germany and the Netherlands. Pierre Bayle, for instance, was to complete and publish his famous dictionary in Rotterdam.

Such distinctions as the one between *doctes* and *mondains*, which were still drawn at the start of the seventeenth century, had made way for the reign of the *mondain* tradition by the end of the century. Very few traces remained of the innumerable conversation circles and private academies.[39] Even the jurists around the *Parlement* of Paris, the powerful executive elite known for its learned traditions, increasingly looked to the court for orientation. People began to wonder whether Latin quotations were not pedantic, and after 1630 young barristers preferred to write plays rather than legal or historical dissertations, and *parlementaire* rhetoric was soon obsolete as well.[40] The various forms of intellectual activity that had flourished in the early seventeenth century had been overshadowed by the elegant style of the court. Whoever wished to be admitted to the *monde* had to adjust accordingly and refrain from demonstrating any trace of contemplation or scholarliness; otherwise one was doomed to a life of relative obscurity. The centralization of cultural life around the court had led to a strict and permanent intellectual hierarchy. In their concord with the *monde*, French writers not only acquired social prestige, they also gained supremacy over the *érudits* and the *savants*. Literary activities merited the highest esteem and provided opportunities for brilliant careers. The *érudits* and scientists were excluded from these opportunities; only if they were able to couch their knowledge in a literary form did they have any chance of gaining access to the *monde*.

'Esprit' as intellectual model

This entire development was to have vast ramifications. The decisive factor in this respect was that, among French aristocrats, a strong literary and cultural interest was accompanied by a simultaneous stigmatization of science, erudition and scholarship. This combination led to the very specific phenomenon the French are wont to refer to as *esprit*. If there is any single intellectual style that can be referred to as typically French, then *esprit* is a good name for it. *Esprit*, one might say, was in France what *Bildung* became in Germany. *Avoir de l'esprit* referred to much the same quality as *gebildet sein*. These codes constituted the intellectual dimension, as it were, of the far wider contrast between *civilisation* and *Kultur* that was analysed by Norbert Elias.[41]

At the French court, and in the salons, everyone was fond of verbal and intellectual games. Even if they were of bourgeois descent, the people most skilled at them could be admitted to the highest circles. The French court differed in this sense from the Viennese. It was immediately obvious to French men of letters that, in Vienna, aristocrats and men of letters lived in separate worlds; noblemen were not 'spiritual' and writers had no manners.[42] This was certainly not the case in France. Eloquence in spiritual matters was highly esteemed, although the French court and salon style did differ from the more bourgeois cultural styles, which were more university oriented (such as the German) or more practical and application oriented (such as the Dutch).

At the salons, verbal virtuosity and a capacity for refined and witty observations were clearly at a premium. But at the same time, studying was viewed as a waste of time, detailed knowledge as dead weight, and technical expressions and lines of reasoning demonstrating any complexity as pedantic. This peculiar combination, aptly expressed in the term *esprit*, led to the cultivation of a strongly verbal and rhetorical type of intelligence. It cannot be denied that this does have a certain charm, particularly in situations where tact and graciousness are consequential. However, in circumstances where there is an opportunity for 'study', a chance to read and re-read, where it is possible to think and rethink, to take various factors into consideration, to make corrections, in short, when the written word is more important than conversation, then much of this *esprit* soon appears to be based upon superficial, short-term effects. In a more scholarly culture, where a certain distance is maintained from *mondain* gatherings and one is interested mainly in making an impression on colleagues specialized in the same field, *esprit* is apt to be perceived as little more than eloquent ignorance. This is why Kant, a spokesman of a more scholarly orientation, was of the opinion that one 'could not be cautious enough' with the writings of the French. They ordinarily contained a great deal of 'schönes Blendwerk' that did not hold up under the cold eye of scientific scrutiny.[43]

In France this *esprit*, this mixture of elegance and eloquence, grew into the paradigm of intellectual excellence. A style was established in which insight and comprehension could easily be confused with wit. A line of reasoning did not have to be sound, it had to be elegant; the precision of phrases was less important than their polish and refinement. The attitude befitting this style was that of the ultimate conversationalist who – in a manner of speaking – knew nothing but could talk about everything. The main aim was to please; well-founded argumentation and proof were matters of secondary importance. In a context of this kind, cultural and intellectual achievements were automatically perceived as the light-hearted improvisations of gifted individuals. In this perspective, lengthy efforts and indeed the entire learning process vanished to make way for the flash of wit, the inspiration and the gift.[44] Patient and careful enquiry was discouraged in favour of overwhelming flashes of intuition. Due to the inordinate sensitivity in matters of style and elegance, 'sound' and 'thorough' were soon associated with 'ponderous' and 'laborious'. There has been a permanent enticement in France to write facile and surprising essays, and time and time again more scientific-minded intellectuals have opposed the glorification of *esprit* without knowledge and *brille* without understanding. As witnessed by the work of Auguste Comte and Emile Durkheim, French sociology developed as a critique of this dominant model. For a large part, the 'positivistic' tradition evolved as opposition to a culture where sparkling turns of phrase were more highly acclaimed than serious research. Contrary to what is frequently assumed, however, positivism was never a dominant movement in France. The most celebrated accomplishments of other cultures are quickly assumed to be 'typical' of whatever culture produced them. Since positivism was initiated in France, it is widely assumed to be in one way or another 'typically French'. In so far as positivism played any role in France, however, it was more as a *counter-tradition* than anything else. In a predominantly literary and essayistic culture it served as a counterpoint, a defence of research and rigour, and as a refusal to attribute any cognitive value to aesthetic qualities.

2

Conflict over Reason

In our century, philosophy, or rather reason, extending its empire
over all the sciences, has achieved what the Roman conquests
achieved in earlier times; it has united all the parts of the literary
world.

Turgot

In exchange for their services and as acknowledgement for their achievements, writers in the seventeenth century had been granted their own
rights and considerable social status. This gradually also altered the
relations they maintained with their benefactors. At the salons they
consorted as equals with members of the nobility, with whom they
shared a growing extent of mutual recognition rather than a one-sided
service relation. Alain Viala described this development as a shift from
'clientelism' to 'recognition'.[1] This development continued after the
death of Louis XIV. The court lost something of its attraction, the
salons flourished and numerous provincial academies were founded
throughout the country. Especially as the last years under Louis XIV
had witnessed so little to boast of, this gave writers greater leeway.
The altered mood was manifest in the success of the satirical letters
Montesquieu published in 1721. The *Lettres Persanes* gave this provincial magistrate access to prominent circles in the capital, and within
a matter of years he even had himself a seat at the Académie française.
The main characters in the book, two Persians, observed Parisian life
in the latter years of Louis XIV. Their astonished reactions were amusing and, particularly in their misconceptions – mistaking as they did
highly placed persons for footmen – criticism of absolutism was unmistakable.

   Among the landed nobility and representatives of the magistracy,
this critical stance was not new. But via his Persian heroes Montesquieu
managed to find a legitimate form for this criticism: the Orient was in
fashion, letters were a popular genre and there was always a demand
for amusing satire. Montesquieu spent lengthy periods of time in the
capital and enjoyed his success. Shortly after he joined the Académie

française, he was to leave Paris. He travelled and spent two years in England, where he admired the parliamentary system. Here he discovered new ways to counterbalance the omnipotence of the monarch.

Voltaire's alliance

For Montesquieu and many of his peers, England became the symbol of the reforms that were needed in France. There was every indication that the English had surpassed the French. Not only had they succeeded in restricting the power of the monarch and establishing a parliamentary regime, with their deism they had also developed a 'reasonable' form of religion, in the natural sciences they had ascended to a prominent position, and in literature and philosophy new forms were in full bloom. The discontent with the latter reign of Louis XIV appeared to be a fertile breeding ground for the accelerated reception of English writings. Locke was one of the first to have his work translated. In the years before 1730, translations ensued of the work of Shaftesbury, Mandeville, Addison, Pope, Swift and Milton. In 1733 the first volumes were published of a comprehensive *bibliothèque brittanique*, which was soon followed by widespread 'anglomania'.[2]

The English example played a crucial role in Voltaire's development. He was of the same generation as Montesquieu, but more than anything else he was a poet and a writer. His first literary and *mondain* successes came when he was still quite young; throughout his lifetime he was to retain his weakness for salon life, and he was known and indeed feared for his witty mockery and sarcasm. Voltaire felt so at home in the *monde* that he could not accept the allusions a high nobleman once made to his bourgeois descent. He responded by commenting that he might not bear an illustrious name, but that at least he knew how to be a credit to it. The distinguished aristocrat, a less articulate man, saw to it that the writer got a beating while he watched from his coach. Voltaire then challenged him to a duel and took fencing lessons, but soon discovered he had to pay the price for his impertinent conduct: imprisonment at the Bastille. He was released on the condition that he would leave the country, and spent the next three years in England. In 1734 he published a series of letters about his experiences in England. The *Lettres philosophiques*, the uncommon title of the work, was published anonymously, upon which the *Parlement* of Paris immediately voiced its disapproval. Voltaire described England as the most enlightened nation of Europe. Freedom ruled, people were unprejudiced and men of letters enjoyed such high esteem that were they even occupied government positions: Addison was Minister of State, Newton had served as Warden of the Mint and Swift was an important official in Ireland. In France, they would have been members of an academy and would have received a pension from some aristocratic lady or other.[3] The respect the English had for intellectual achievement also led to Voltaire's acquaintanceship with the natural sciences. It was not Newton's books or theories that made an overwhelming impression on Voltaire, but his royal funeral.[4] Not even a writer had ever been honoured that way in France.

The *Lettres philosophiques* was one of the first books to combine several of the main themes of the French Enlightenment. During his stay in England Voltaire probably realized for the first time that there were other options open to writers besides entertaining aristocrats. He discovered philosophy and the natural sciences there, wrote about Bacon, Locke and Newton, and probably also perceived that an alliance between writers and scientists would provide a chance for greater independence from the nobility. It was inconceivable for the author of a panegyric such as *Le Mondain* to dissociate himself from the *monde*, but Voltaire certainly wished to propagate a greater respect for writers, and one way to achieve it was by entering a coalition with other cultural producers. After his English period, two new subjects came up in Voltaire's work. Firstly, he analysed the developments in France starting at the beginning of the seventeenth century. In his interpretation of the heyday of court society, 'culture' played a central role. This touches upon the second topic, that is, the role of cultural producers, of writers and their place in and outside the republic of letters.

In *Le siècle de Louis XIV*, which was finally published in 1751, Voltaire praised this era for having been a glorious time for the 'human spirit'. His book was neither a biography of the Sun King nor an account of political history, it was a description of the 'spirit' of the people. The best example of this new spirit was to be seen in literary life. Writers were protected and supported, and it was this 'enlightened spirit' that eventually brought about the revolution for which the French were so widely admired. It was the 'culture of the spirit', as Voltaire called it, that was central in his account, and no longer the monarch or the state. What was soon to become known simply as 'culture' was more important than politics, diplomacy or military escapades, and the attitude of the people in power towards their 'culture' was the touchstone for blossoming or decay. Voltaire's version thus had the *grand siècle* start with the foundation of the Académie française.

On the grounds of the decisive significance he attributed to this 'spirit', he also drew a distinction within the group of cultural producers. Voltaire acknowledged that the French did not in any way set the trend in the sciences and that the French reputation in the arts left much to be desired. The explanation he gave was that these activities were not solely dependent on the 'spirit'.[5] Manual skills were as indispensable for conducting experiments as for making paintings. The old division into mechanical and liberal arts, into working with the hands and working with the mind, was once again referred to in explaining the supremacy of literature.

Voltaire praised Louis XIV for providing what he wanted even more of: the protection and promotion of 'letters'. At the same time, however, he was no longer focused solely on literature, but rather on the connections between the various cultural activities. He no longer viewed art and literature as activities with the sole purpose of pleasing the *monde*, but as products of the human mind. In contrast to the courtly or *mondain* definition of culture, Voltaire formulated a definition that was more in keeping with the interests of the producers, in particular with those of writers. But since what was involved was the 'culture of the mind' in a more general sense, the traditional conception of writing and of being a writer was inadequate. Voltaire formulated a new conception. In short, from then on it pertained to the writer as *philosophe*, to the *philosophe* as spokesman of culture, and to culture as the main or one of the main sectors in society. Voltaire's aspiration to achieve greater respect for writers led him to make an overture to other cultural producers, particularly those for whom there had been no place at *mondain* gatherings. This overture gave rise to a wide range of questions regarding the unity of the various cultural manifestations, and in that light philosophy was called upon.

The discovery of philosophy

The introduction of philosophy into the world of letters was relatively new. Up to about 1730 the term *philosophe* stood for a person who wanted no part of worldly matters.[6] Philosophy was viewed as an esoteric endeavour engaged in either by scholastics or by wise stoics. In a review of Fontenelle's *Entretiens sur la pluralité des mondes* (1686), the *Mercure galant* had written, for example, that this book presented an elegant spectacle, 'even though it was about philosophy'.[7] In the decades before 1750 a new definition emerged. In the works of Voltaire and others, the *philosophe* was attributed with a place in the world of letters and consequently with an explicit task in society. Philosophy became the common foundation for the practice of the arts, letters and sciences, and the *philosophe* was presented as the spokeman of this enlightened alliance. In this light, the *Encyclopédie* can best be described as the realization and the justification of this new alliance. From 1750 to 1770 this new concept of philosophy took hold, as it were, and heated disputes broke out between its advocates and opponents. Via salons and local and national academies, the *philosohes* managed to settle the dispute in their favour. After 1760 they eclipsed the 'pious' in the Académie française and in 1772 d'Alembert even became secretary of this illustrious society.[8]

Around philosophy in this sense of the word, a wide scope of new opportunities dawned. For the first time there was a coherent alternative to the antithesis between *mondain* and learned culture. In opposition to the court and the salons, the reference to philosophy symbolized the importance of studying and acquiring knowledge. For this purpose, *philosophes* sought the support of writers and scientists. In opposition to the traditional specialists at the universities, philosophy functioned as a substitute for theology and scholasticism, and in this struggle the *philosophes* benefited in turn from the support of enlightened segments of the nobility. *Vis-à-vis* both of them, nobility and university alike, the *philosophes* called upon the English example and insisted on the importance of the natural sciences. The specific details of these relations varied from one individual to the next. In an institutional sense, the position of the *philosophes* had barely been stipulated. With the exception of such wealthy individuals as Holbach and Helvétius, no one but Voltaire was economically independent. The others relied for their livelihood on allowances donated by noblemen, their incomes as academy members and the fees paid by publishers. Voltaire had the most ties with the nobility, d'Alembert with members of the academies, and Diderot was dependent largely on the work he did for publishers. These social differences regularly led to disagreements as to what tactic to follow. Voltaire did not want to offend the high nobility and the monarch, since he deemed their support and protection to be of great importance; d'Alembert had little faith in them, however, and advocated a more autonomous stance focused on gaining positions that were based primarily upon support in literary and scientific circles. These differences came to light, for example, in connection with the play *Les philosophes modernes* (1760), which was a satirical attack on the *philosophes*; d'Alembert wanted an unambiguous countermove from the least vulnerable and most authoritative *philosophe*, in other words from Voltaire. But, as the author could boast of the protection of a number of prominent noblemen, Voltaire hesitated. Diderot's position was initially close to d'Alembert's, but there were increasing overtures on his part to the group around Holbach. By the time his *Système de la nature* (1770) was published, Diderot had joined his side and found himself opposed to Voltaire and d'Alembert, who had both by then adopted a moderate and more 'academic' stance.[9]

For a large part, the campaign of the *philosophes* was directed against the church's claims to knowledge and the jurisdiction of theology. The arts and sciences, they reasoned, were a vital component of enlightened nations and could be practised independently of religious convictions and doctrines. The finely meshed totality of human knowledge, summarized and illustrated in the twenty-eight volumes of the *Encyclopédie*, was based on nothing other than the 'natural capacities' of the human being. Each part of this whole could be linked to one of these capacities: knowledge, for example, stemmed from the capacity to observe and reason. Essentially, the philosophy of the *philosophes* was not much more than the pursuit of a number of these common principles. All the aspects of what human beings can do and know were classified in this manner, and these 'natural' classifications made every allusion to 'supernatural' principles superfluous. Theology had been deposed, philosophy could take its place.[10] Philosophy in this sense was neither a separate realm of knowledge nor a detailed system derived from Newton, Locke or Descartes. It did not coincide with a specific doctrine and d'Alembert described it simply as 'the dominant taste of the century'.[11]

In a theoretical sense, this form of thinking was an unbridled continuation of various seventeenth-century currents. In particular, the pursuit of 'natural' principles had already been elevated to the highest norm in the heyday of classicism.[12] What was new about the contributions made by the *philosophes* was that they used this way of thinking in new fields, conceived of human knowledge as a coherent and concrete unity (where nothing was any longer reserved for higher authorities), and linked societal ramifications to their analyses (*écrasez l'infâme*). These three phenomena, personified by a new figure, the *philosophe*, constituted the nucleus of the 'Enlightenment' in France. If this global description is accurate, the question remains as to how fundamental was this change from the seventeenth century and what was its significance as regards thought on societal questions.

A new figure, the philosophe

Ever since the seventeenth century the term *gens de lettres* has been used as the collective term for secular intellectuals. The *Journal des savants* (1665) did not address scientists, but 'all men of letters'; and the *Encyclopédie* was also presented as the work of a 'society of men of letters'. Other terms were of secondary importance. In legal documents, for example, scientists would never describe themselves as *savant*, but preferred to use their professional title (doctor, professor and so forth) or the term *homme de lettres*.[13] Men of letters constituted a recognized group, and in medical handbooks they were even attributed with ailments of their own.[14] Judging from these terms, the literary tradition continued to be dominant. What did change, however, was the description of what a man of letters was and should be. The campaign of the *philosophes* implied a broader conception of the literary craft. The *philosophes* represented a unique combination of intellectual and social involvement: most of them were not solely moralists, philosophers or scientists, but a combination of the three. They were not philosophers but *philosophes*; the term has rightly remained untranslated and, if one were called upon to give a synonym for it, 'intellectual' would be as close as one could get. They were not bound to any one institution or professional field and their work was generally simultaneously meant for colleagues, literate citizens and sophisticated salon-goers.

The item on *gens de lettres* in the *Encyclopédie* was written by Voltaire, and in it continuity and innovation are both clearly visible.[15] In order to call oneself a man of letters, according to this article, first there was a certain minimum requirement: one had to practise more than one genre. People who happened only to have written sermons were not men of letters in the true sense of the word. When Voltaire went on to give a positive definition, he used two ingredients which, in good harmony, characterized the true man of letters. Men of letters, Voltaire held, were individuals who were just as well suited for the 'salon' as the 'study'. It is from this trait that they derived their superiority as compared to earlier times. It had only been since the beginning of the seventeenth century that they had access to the *monde*. Ever since then their competence was no longer based on mastery of Greek and Latin, on the *esprit grammaire*, but on a 'healthy philosophy'. This philosophy, which made prejudice and superstition disappear, had become a property of men of letters. For this reason a gap had also grown between the men of letters and the *bel esprit*, who had no need for philosophy or study; a rich imagination and pleasant conversation were enough.

The consummate man of letters, in Voltaire's view, was able to combine a philosophical mind with good taste. In the item on the *philosophe* published in the *Encyclopédie* a few years later, it was also stressed that the *philosophe* was an *honnête homme*.[16] In this definition as well, every effort was made to avoid associating the philosopher with scholars who never left their studies or teachers who were overly pedantic.

Analytical rationalism

This redefinition of the writer, as time has told, turned out to be extremely successful. In the eighteenth century literature was no longer the only intellectual activity accepted in the *monde*, and acceptance in the *monde* no longer automatically earned one literary recognition. The true writer distinguished himself from the *bel esprit* as well as the reclusive scholar. And yet this change was not as drastic as is often assumed. Indeed the individuals who played a key role in this change were virtually all writers. It was not until they came forth as intermediaries between scientists and aristocrats at the end of the seventeenth century that the contempt for science was somewhat reduced. Fontenelle was the first to fulfil this role. As an admirer of Descartes, he had exhibited interest in the natural sciences. On the grounds of this interest, in 1699 he was appointed secretary of the Académie des sciences, a position he was to hold for more than forty years. Never before had scientists had such a prominent spokesman. Fontenelle translated their activities into clear and elegant French, promoted their interests, praised their insight and devotion, and wrote a widely read account of the history of the academy. It was largely thanks to his efforts that 'learned' was no longer held to be synonymous with 'pedantic'. Voltaire and others followed him and helped give the sciences a place in the enlightened world view.

Like Fontenelle, most of the *philosophes* were writers, and the few exceptions who had had a career in the natural sciences, such as d'Alembert, went to whatever effort was required to comply with the ideal of the *homme de lettres*. For the *philosophes*, scientific work was important primarily as example of the powers of reason. What mattered to them was not so much science but reason. The scientific work of a man such as Newton was one way of using rational procedures. Newton's work, however, was often more important as an illustration of the existence of 'natural' and universal principles than as an example of a scientific method. Most of the *philosophes* were not engaged in the actual practice of an empirical science. Reason was the central, all-embracing point of view. Cassirer wrote that in all their work, the unity and immutability of reason was presumed: reason was essentially identical for all thinking human beings, all eras and all branches of intellectual activity. The difference from seventeenth-century rationalistic movements was that reason was no longer conceived as a fixed system of principles and truths, a metaphysical system, but far more as an intellectual power – a form of 'energy', as Cassirer put it.[17] Nothing was as characteristic of the Enlightenment as this spirit, this yearning to subject everything to rational enquiry. In so far as this was a form of rationalism, it was a more concrete rationalism. Cassirer gave a description of it without introducing a term, but *analytical rationalism* would be a good expression for the approach. It was no longer metaphysical or speculative rationalism though it did remain a form of rationalism because its starting point was reason and the existence of universal or 'natural' principles. It no longer involved abstract systems, nor did it focus on empirical research and scientific explanations. The major theoretical problem of this form of rationalism was how to reconcile the diversity of the phenomena with the belief in universal principles. How could the idea of universal standards for law, morality and so forth be reconciled with the overwhelming diversity evident in the accounts of travellers and the chronicles of historians? For the *philosophes* and their contemporaries, the awareness of this diversity was a shared experience. More and more information was available on a widening range of societies and eras. In the sixteenth century a total of approximately 450 books had been published giving accounts of travels abroad; in the seventeenth century this figure rose to 1,560, and in the eighteenth century to 3,500.[18] The trend was unmistakable. The depiction of human societies became more detailed and more comprehensive in the eighteenth century than it had ever been before, and more significance was attributed to this knowledge. The question arose as to what was the meaning of all this new information with respect to the existing conceptions and the current manners of thinking. This question was all the more oppressive for the *philosophes* because they were not specialists who could withdraw to a restricted area. The answer they developed was that rational principles and procedures would have to be used for constructing new forms of ordering and classification. This would make it possible to do justice to the diversity without giving up the existence of rational standards. If any publication was typical of this form of rational ordering and classification, it was the *Encyclopédie*, which is rightly viewed as the symbol of the French Enlightenment.

Analysis was one of the catchwords of the French Enlightenment. In a more technical meaning, it was a concept from mathematics and logic, but in the first half of the eighteenth century it became more or less synonymous with rational enquiry.[19] For Condillac, 'analysis' was the universal method for all forms of knowledge. Analyses began with the dissection of an object into smaller units ('decomposition') , which was followed by the rearrangement or restructuring of these elements ('composition'). According to Condillac, both of these procedures were characterized by 'simplicity', 'precision' and 'obviousness'. In this description there are no 'first' or 'final causes', nor has use been made of any other traditional concept from metaphysics. But it is equally unfeasible to call the criteria Condillac used scientific ones. 'Obviousness' and 'simplicity' were not criteria for validity in the natural sciences, and Condillac did not view the procedures he described as scientific principles, but merely as the way the human mind worked. He was not concerned with the methods of doing research, but with determining what was rational and reasonable. Despite his admiration for Locke, Condillac remained completely in the rationalistic tradition.[20] His work was the most systematic formulation of the analytical rationalism to which the *philosophes* were all dedicated in one way or another.

Thus the *philosophes* cannot be categorically described as followers of Newton. It is difficult to call the way they worked and reasoned a 'scientific' one, and indeed it was not their intention to follow scientific procedures. Even in the case of d'Alembert, who is generally classified as a Newtonian, it has been demonstrated that the rationalistic tradition affected his writings far more than his statements sometimes led one to believe.[21] Upon closer examination, a mathematical ideal, the *esprit géometrique*, appears to have served as guideline, and in fact d'Alembert never engaged in any empirical or experimental research. At the Académie des sciences, this mathematical style was the dominant form of scientific practice. Physics was still called 'mixed mathematics' and, for Marquis de l'Hôpital and Malebranche, Newton's work was primarily a new step towards mathematical refinement. In the course of the eighteenth century, d'Alembert, Lagrange and Laplace were to make important contributions towards transforming classical mechanics into a solidly founded, mathematically formulated system. While Newton served as the great example for experimental research in the Netherlands, in France he was viewed as the epitome of a mathematical orientation.[22]

Natural sciences in the French Enlightenment

Whenever references are made to science in the writings of the *philosophes*, the meaning of the term remains strongly dependent on a rationalistic problematic. In the rivalry with theology and the church, they probably could not do without an encompassing concept, an alternative unit of analysis. In countries where relations between secular intellectuals and the church were different there was less of a necessity for a concept of this kind. To a certain extent, this explains why the *philosophes*, even with all their admiration for the English empirical tradition, retained a rationalistic orientation. There were also other reasons; in general they had not been extensively educated in the sciences, and in France scientists had a lower status than writers. For writers, and consequently for most *philosophes* as well, it was certainly not obvious to emulate the example of natural scientists. To varying degrees, the *philosophes* had furthermore remained dependent on the support of the nobility and the interest of the salon audience, and in these circles scientists were not held in particularly high esteem. For all these reasons it was improbable that a French writer would have taken the trouble to study the natural sciences as an example for his own work.

It is true that in the course of the eighteenth century science did become a topic of conversation at many a salon. These conversations, however, focused on very specific forms of what was later to be called popularization. The matters that were written about in the publications of the Académie des sciences remained largely outside the field of vision of laymen, and there was barely any interest in 'academic' science. For the *philosophes* science was there to serve reason, for salon-goers it was there to entertain and amuse. Ever since Fontenelle's *Entretiens sur la pluralité des mondes* (1686) the conversation value of scientific work gradually rose, and by the mid-eighteenth century, according to Buffon, the sciences had indeed become 'more pleasant' and 'more enjoyable'.[23] However, this type of science was not focused on discoveries, proof or refutations; the aim was merely entertainment and amusement. Experiments with electricity and magnetism were extremely popular. For a while the Leyden jar was a great attraction, and on special occasions 'gala experiments' were conducted. These gatherings, which were more theatrical than scientific, became more and more exotic as the years passed. There seemed to be no end to the manipulations with 'invisible powers', and the first balloon flight in 1783 heralded a new craze. There were balloon hats, balloon sweets and balloon pantaloons, and any number of other bloated products were put on the market.

The most popular 'science' was natural history. *Le spectacle de la nature* (1732–50) by Abbé Pluche consisted of eight volumes of illustrated descriptions of nature, and by 1770 more than twenty editions of it had been printed. *Histoire naturelle* (1749–89) by Buffon, with no fewer than thirty-eight deluxe volumes published by the *Imprimerie royale*, was richly illustrated and teeming with exotic plants and animals described in Buffon's inimitable style. In the overwhelming enthusiasm for natural history the fascination with the picturesque and the exotic was accompanied by an aestheticization of the descriptions of nature.

It was only a tiny step from these forms of more or less *mondain* science to outright pseudo-science. At the end of the eighteenth century the conduct of Lavater (the founder of physiognomics) and Mesmer (the inventor of animal magnetism) was sharply condemned in the circles around the Académie des sciences, although this did little to detract from the popularity of their theories.[24] All kinds of notions came into fashion, but they were rarely grounded on the writings of scientists or the experiments of researchers. At best they were based on popularized versions or amateur sciences such as natural history.

Simplifying a bit, one might say the natural sciences in France tended in two directions. In the small circle of professional scientists around the Académie des sciences, a strongly mathematical style of work was adhered to. Outside this group science was associated with *mondain* gatherings and its entertainment value remained a decisive factor. This type of science, the *physique amusante* or natural history, remained largely dependent on literary forms of expression. It would be erroneous to interpret its popularity as a sign of a flourishing scientific culture. Even in the eighteenth century, more would be required for this kind of culture than spectacular demonstrations, collections of butterflies or picturesque elaborations upon nature.[25]

D'Alembert, the only *philosophe* with a natural science background, wrote an uncommonly acrimonious commentary on this situation. His entire *Essai sur la société des gens de lettres et des grands* (1753) was about the difficulties that ensued from the dependence on *mondain* circles. As a renowned mathematician, he was undoubtedly more sensitive to the disadvantages of salon culture than the other *philosophes*. In England, he wrote, people were quite satisfied to accept Newton as the greatest scientist of his day, but in France they would have wanted him to be 'delightful' as well. If one had nothing to contribute to the pleasures of salon life, one was not respected. For this reason no attention was devoted to the work of the *érudits*, nor for that matter to the work of the scientists, until quite recently. The fact that there was some interest here and there in the sciences, d'Alembert felt sure, was to be of short duration. The only reason he could discern for this sudden attention was that, to their surprise, the nobility had discovered that mathematicians were not 'wild animals'. This led to their being treated like Turkish or Persian ambassadors: with amused amazement, people noted that these creatures were not lacking in common sense. D'Alembert's conclusion was that, for the sake of veracity, one should sever all ties with the nobility. A life of poverty was the price to be paid for the right to pursue truth in freedom. Abbé de Canaye, an *érudit* to whom d'Alembert dedicated his essay, had demonstrated that one could live very happily without the *grands*.[26]

D'Alembert's essay was poorly received. The men of letters were not about to jeopardize their privileges and the nobility was offended by his diagnosis.[27] D'Alembert himself was never again as sharp in his criticism, and his further career was not in keeping with his supplication to sever relations with the *monde*. His analysis does, however, indicate that the period of the Enlightenment did not differ as sharply from preceeding the period prior as is frequently assumed. The dependence on the aristocratic elites remained crucial, as did the predominance of literary activities, and the position of *érudits* and *savants* continued to be subordinate to that of writers.

The social composition of the academies in the eighteenth century confirms this ranking. The majority of the members of the Académie française were from the aristocracy, whereas most of the scientists at the Académie des sciences were from the Third Estate. The historical and literary erudition engaged in at the Académie des inscriptions held an intermediate position. With respect to the role of the clergy, the relations were the same; the proportion of clergymen was greater among writers than among scientists, and of all the academies the Académie des sciences had the fewest ties with the church.[28] Thus, in the eighteenth century as well, representatives of the most powerful social groups had little or nothing to do with the natural sciences.

Data on book production and book ownership indicate the same thing. In the eighteenth century there was a sharp decline in the production of theological and religious literature. In 1724, 34 per cent of all the officially published books were in this category; just before the Revolution this was true of only 8.5 per cent. This decline was accompanied by a slight increase in works on 'law', 'history' and 'literature', but the most marked increase was in the books about 'the sciences and arts'. Although this category was extremely heterogeneous, the increase also held true for 'the sciences' in the stricter sense of the word.[29] On this general level there would thus seem to have been a clear correlation between a declining interest in religion and a growing interest in the sciences. If one examines the book ownership of each estate, the nobility and the clergy appear to have played a very small role indeed in the rise of scientific writings. The contents of the libraries of the nobility confirmed the sharp decline of religious and ecclesiastical literature. However, this decline was not accompanied by a clear increase in interest among the noblemen in 'the sciences and arts'. What did rise among these readers was an interest in 'history' and 'literature'.[30]

The fact that scientific practice was held in relatively low esteem under the *Ancien Régime* and remained a markedly bourgeois affair does not mean no changes took place in this respect. In the course of the eighteenth century there was an unmistakable rise, be it a very slow one, in the number of aristocrats in the Académie des sciences. Around 1700 their role was still negligible, but by the end of the eighteenth century they constituted a very small though not insignificant minority. This increase was related in part to the somewhat higher esteem of the sciences in *mondain* circles; it was even more important, however, that science had become indispensable for warfare purposes. Courses in the natural sciences became part of the military training curriculum, so that for men in military positions, which had traditionally been held by the aristocracy, the sciences were no longer taboo. It is striking that the increase in the number of aristocrats in the Académie des sciences is explained in large part by the increase in the number of military men there. In 1700 only 1 per cent of the academy members held a military position; by the end of the century this figure had risen to 10 per cent.[31]

Secularization without scientization

In the period from the start of the seventeenth to the end of the eighteenth century, a sizeable group of secular intellectuals emerged in France. As they were supported by the monarch and the court nobility, they were able relatively rapidly to liberate themselves from the power of the church, and an all-encompassing secularization of French culture ensued. At the beginning of the seventeenth century the majority of all the 'authors', that is, all the people who had written at least one book, had been members of the clergy. By the end of the seventeenth century this was true of only approximately half of them, and just before the Revolution the figure had dropped to 20 per cent.[32] Though secularization was thus well advanced among cultural producers, the educational curriculum at the *collèges* and universities was as closely linked to ecclesiastical dogmas as ever. This contrast was the principal opposition of the French Enlightenment.

It was not only the proportions of the various groups that changed; the absolute figures exhibited sizeable alterations as well. The book market grew and, particularly in the eighteenth century, there was a rapid rise in the number of authors. After the death of Louis XIV, publication opportunities expanded. With the introduction of the *permissions tacites* it became possible to publish books that would have otherwise been censored. This led to a sharp rise in the total annual number of publications, from 1,000 in 1720 to 3,500 in 1770. There was a comparable rise in the number of daily, weekly and monthly periodicals.[33] After 1750 there was also a spectacular increase in the number of authors. The success of the *Encyclopédie*, which was made possible by this increase, stimulated and reinforced in turn the increase in the number of authors. In 1757 there were 1,200 individuals in France who had published at least one book. Ten years later there were almost 2,400, and just before the Revolution the figure had risen to at least 3,000.[34] In three decades the number of authors had thus almost tripled. The social composition of the group had changed as well: a slight but not surprising increase was exhibited by the Third Estate, the clergy fell from 32 to 20 per cent and the nobility rose from 9 to 14 per cent.

These figures illustrate once again that the loss in power suffered by the church authorities was owing mainly to the role of the nobility. Not only as theatre-goers, readers and patrons, but to an increasing degree as authors as well, the nobility played an increasingly large role in the realm of letters. This was also illustrated by the people who worked for the *Encyclopédie*. In comparison with the population of authors as a whole, the *Encyclopédie* was a thoroughly secular project: only 5 per cent of the writers were clergymen. The percentage of noblemen (20 per cent) was higher than among all the authors, as was the percentage of members of the Third Estate (75 per cent).

Thus the French Enlightenment was certainly not solely the manifestation of the rising bourgeoisie, as is so often claimed. It was first and foremost the triumph of a secular culture over church and university institutions, and the nobility played an extremely important role in this process. It was the nobility that had given certain categories of bourgeois intellectuals the opportunity to take part in *mondain* life. This participation was frequently a precondition for their very subsistence. Since virtually no one could live off the revenues of writing alone, it was necessary either to own property or to be able to rely on support and protection. Especially for that rather small group of pro-fessional writers, the increased autonomy in relation to church and university authorities had only been possible thanks to the support of the monarch and the nobility. This led to new forms of dependence: the world of letters was strongly centralized, with national academies as its most important institutions, and was quite closely linked with the court and *mondaine* elites. Against this background a marked and rather stable hierarchy had developed as to literature, erudition and the natural sciences. Writers had the best chance of improving their position. They were the first to be awarded academic rights and played an important role at *mondaine* gatherings. In the seventeenth century literature thus became the most prestigious, least specialized and most comprehensive sector of the republic of letters. Scientists were the least likely to gain support and recognition. They were confronted with the opposition of the traditional cultural powers, the church and the uni-versity, and with the contempt or indifference of the court nobility. Their achievements were acknowledged for their usefulness, but failed to be awarded much cultural status. In the French situation, historical and literary erudition also remained an inferior genre, which was even viewed by the *philosophes* as being tiresome drudgery barely worthy of any respect.

The social and intellectual conditions in France were thus favour-able for literature and essays and for the development of secular ideas, but relatively unfavourable for work based upon erudition or natural science procedures. In the quasi-literary modes of contemplation and reflection that were dominant in this constellation, scholarly norms, scientific requirements and utilitarian considerations were all secondary to the standards for *brille* and *esprit*. In the course of the eighteenth century a less exclusively literary orientation emerged. The success of the *Encyclopédie* and the attitude and demeanour of the *philosophes* were clear indications of growing autonomy. In the work of the *philosophes*, however, there was still a considerable distance from the empirical natural sciences. Their contributions marked an important step in the rise of secular and rational forms of historical study and social theory. At the same time, it is also evident in their contributions that French intellectual development was long charac-terized by a secularization without scientization.

French intellectual culture in a comparative perspective

A variety of terms is used to describe modern intellectual culture:

disenchantment, secularization, scientization. They are often used interchangeably. In view of the 'secularization without scientization' discussed above, a further examination of a number of Protestant countries might be useful. Quite the opposite process took place there, a kind of 'scientization without secularization'. These phrases are somewhat schematic, but from a comparative perspective what is involved here is an interesting and important contrast that calls for a comparative study of the 'disenchantment of the world'.

A completely different relation developed between the church and intellectuals in the Protestant countries. After the Reformation, Protestant theologians did not hesitate to deploy rational and scientific arms against Catholic orthodoxy. Especially in England, extremely close ties were tethered between religion and the new sciences. From the Royal Society (1662) to the British Association for the Advancement of Science (1831), relations continued to be extremely close between the Anglican Church and representatives of the scientific community.[35]

There were three reasons for this phenomenon. Firstly, there was the rivalry between Catholicism and Protestantism. The Protestant teaching was an oppositional doctrine and pounced upon every Catholic *faux pas*. The condemnation of Galileo thus immediately led the Protestants to sympathize with him; his work was translated and he was honoured in many ways. The anti-Catholic politics made it possible for an alliance to be forged between the natural sciences and religion.

The second reason for the ties between Protestantism and the natural sciences was the organization of the Protestant churches. Since there was no centrally formulated dogma, there was room for various interpretations. In the hope of gaining the support of the church, scientists could present new discoveries as confirmations of biblical truths. In England, this is how such doctrines developed as physico-theology, which professed harmony between science and religion. As long as their research represented a worthy homage to the Creator, scientists were supported by church authorities. Jan Swammerdam coined a fitting metaphor when he said he wanted to descry the greatness of God in the anatomy of a louse. This attitude, in which Christian orthodoxy went hand in hand with scientific research, was inconceivable in the French situation and presumably in other Catholic countries as well.

The third reason was that Protestant clergymen could raise a family. The children of parsons and vicars played an important role in intellectual life, and there are indications that English scientists frequently came from the families of ministers.[36] Priests were at a disadvantage in this respect, and French scientists usually came from secular families whose resources were mainly cultural (physicians, engineers, barristers). Via descent and family relations, direct links between the clergy and scientists continued to exist for a much longer period of time in England. In this way, the intellectual culture in the Protestant countries remained linked to the religious traditions and institutions much longer. Until far into the nineteenth century every scientific innovation in England was accompanied by debates on religious questions. In countries such as the Netherlands and Sweden, the situation was very much the same.

In short, the secularization of French culture took place mainly through support from the court and the state. The court nobility and state authorities played a key role in the making of an intellectual regime in which literary genres were dominant and science was accepted merely as a useful but barely prestigious activity. The rapid and far-reaching processes of secularization long remained devoid of any marked scientization. In a number of Protestant countries, science and research were deployed at an early stage in the rivalry with the Catholic Church. Thus an alliance could be forged between the Protestant churches and the practitioners of the new sciences. They took advantage of the support of church authorities and the interest of the faithful. The result here was a limited process of secularization or, better yet, scientization without secularization.

3

French Moralists and the Social Order

> It is the desire to please that gives coherence to society, and such is
> the good fortune of the human species that this self-love, potentially
> capable of dissolving society, on the contrary reinforces it and
> makes it firm and stable.
>
> Montesquieu

For a proper understanding of the originality of social theory, it is
necessary to examine more precisely its relation to the existing intellectual genres. As regards social and intellectual history, moral
philosophy and moral theory were of special significance in this
connection, especially in France.

Classical and modern divisions

Modern conceptions of the social world presumed a departure not
only from theological doctrine but also from the classical heritage. In
classical views, which were indeed the starting point for modern theories, social theory was divided into political theory and moral theory.
Questions were defined either as 'political' or 'moral', supplemented
now and then with a special category for matters of household management. In this categorization, which goes back to Aristotelian
models, these subjects were classified under 'practical philosophy'. They
constituted a certain unity and were taught at the universities, but
they had a lower status than 'theoretical' disciplines.

In Germany, where intellectual development was closely bound to
the universities, 'practical philosophy' was to remain the only formal
framework for ideas on the social order until far into the eighteenth
century. Early modern political theory (Machiavelli, Bodin, Hobbes)
was introduced quite late there,[1] and Pufendorf, the prominent spokesman of modern natural law, still formulated his ideas entirely within
the framework of practical philosophy.[2] In general, German authors
were more traditional, more academic and less politically and socially

involved than kindred spirits in England or France. Modern theories of the state, the economy and society emerged later there than in England and France. In the German literature, the modern concept of society, for example, was not introduced until Hegel published his philosophy of law.[3]

In contrast to the situation in Germany, French university courses in 'practical philosophy' remained virtually unaltered throughout the seventeenth and eighteenth centuries.[4] In France, intellectual innovations were introduced by people working outside the faculties and collèges. For this extra-university intelligentsia, early modern political theory and moral philosophy were of far greater consequence than the Aristotelian tradition.

Around 1760 these subjects came to be known collectively as sciences morales et politiques.[5] The term was soon incorporated into the official jargon and remained in use until the second half of the nineteenth century. It was on conventional grounds that people in France had become accustomed to speaking of 'moral and political sciences'. The combination of moral and political in one expression was not linked to any one specific orientation; in fact it was the new ideas that surmounted this kind of division. Reasoning in terms of 'economic' and 'social' relations came to play a major role, and these relations were granted a greater significance than political structures. The new theories thus had to vie with church doctrines as well as political theories, and this two-sided criticism was something they shared with developments in moral philosophy and moral theory.

In general it was a humanistic or anthropocentric point of view that served as the foundation for these new ideas. Ever since the Renaissance the point of departure for secular approaches had been sought in human nature. Such human inclinations as the urge for self-preservation or such human capacities as the cogito served as the foundation for secular and rational constructions. Since these constructions were based upon reasoning on 'the nature' or 'essence' of phenomena, the central concepts had the status of suprahistorical entities. The formulation of 'natural' and universally valid principles was the highest aim of intellectual activity. Dilthey referred to the 'natural system' of law, morals and politics. This system was based on the conviction that human institutions were also grounded upon 'natural' principles and that, if one was to know these principles, all one needed was reason. In this line of thinking, 'reasonable' and 'natural' were virtually synonymous.[6] It was not until this 'rationalization' had been adopted in various fields and theologians came to be on the defensive that the tendency towards historicization emerged. The historical works of Voltaire and Turgot were among the first efforts to analyse comprehensive historical processes and thus find alternatives for the fall of man and providence. Without the rationalist orientation forfeiting its significance in France, models in terms of phases and stages became more important.[7]

The decline of political theory

Secular and rational points of view had been part and parcel of political theory and moral theory long before the Enlightenment. However, there was a marked divergence in the way the two genres developed in France. In the eighteenth century political theory was no longer a prestigious and attractive topic. Up to the seventeenth century it had been mainly jurists who had focused on it. The first formulations can be found in their work, of a modern conception of the state; they belonged to the country's intellectual elite, and in addition to the fields of law and the state they made important contributions in other areas.[8] In the course of the seventeenth century, however, their leading role in intellectual life came to an end.[9] Under Richelieu and Louis XIV the jurists lost their political positions. The *parlements* were stripped of their political powers and there were fewer opportunities to formulate independent theories on political questions. In the eighteenth century jurists confined their attention to the elaboration of existing legal arrangements. At the universities, the curriculum continued to be concentrated upon traditional legal systems and, up to the very end of the *Ancien Régime*, there was no place in the educational system for such approaches as natural and international law, which had already been taught at Dutch and German universities for more than a century.

The development of the state apparatus had given legally trained citizens opportunities for upward social mobility, and for the French bourgeoisie careers in civil service had a considerably higher status than careers in trade or industry.[10] As a result of the growing importance of the state, the differences between the military nobility and the nobility of officials, the *noblesse de robe*, were gradually reduced. But the prominent social position magistrates had earned for themselves had been accompanied by a loss in intellectual importance. Not only Jean Bodin, but also Montaigne, La Boétie and others had been magistrates. In the seventeenth century there were no longer any jurists of comparable intellectual status, and the same was the case throughout the eighteenth century.

The comments made by the *philosophes* often bore witness to their contempt for jurists and aversion to the conservatism of the *parlements*. In a letter to Voltaire, Condorcet remarked that ever since the seventeenth century, the *robe* had only produced one man whose work was worth reading: Montesquieu. The magistracy consisted solely of men of the most mediocre sort: 'One only remains in a *parlement* if one is incapable of anything better. Montesquieu immediately left the *Parlement* as soon as he discovered his talents.'[11] With the intellectual decline of the legal estate, political theory disappeared from the stage as well. Whatever touched upon affairs of the state was reserved for official agencies, and even the results of studies on the size and composition of the population usually remained confidential.

The *philosophes* were also hesitant to write about political matters in a direct sense. As men of letters, they played no role in politics or administration and were not permitted to voice unorthodox opinions in these fields. The regulations of the Académie française stipulated, for example, that 'moral and political questions' could only be dealt with in accordance with the authority of the king, the government and the laws of the monarchy. Provincial academies adopted this same stipulation and followed in this sense as well the example set in Paris.[12] Outside the official institutions, in clubs, salons and freemason lodges, these controversial issues were discussed among intellectuals. Efforts made to found official political societies, the first of which dates back to 1692, were all in vain. There was a short period when a society gathered around Abbé Choisy held weekly discussions on moral, political and theological questions.[13] Afterwards several new plans and efforts were made, and it was the Club de l'Entresol that was to function for some time as a kind of political academy, although this too was forbidden in 1731. Half a century later there was still no academy of this kind in existence, as an anonymous author noted: 'All over I see academies for all branches of knowledge, but nowhere do I see one for the political and moral sciences. What could the source of this exclusion possibly be?'[14] To counter the growing criticism of the authorities, in 1774 a proposal was advanced to found an Académie du droit public. This academy was to be focused on refuting arguments that cropped up with increasing frequency in subversive writings. But even this attempt was futile.[15] Statements on the organization of the state remained the preserve of the authorized agencies, and unauthorized persons were expected simply to do their duties as loyal subjects.

The rise of moral philosophy

One might conjecture from the official regulations that politics and morality were subjects to be avoided with equal avidity. However, that was not the case. Moral considerations had witnessed a development in France that was in many senses contrary to that of political theory. The decline of political theory in the seventeenth century coincided with a surge of moralistic literature. This phenomenon, although generally overlooked,[16] was to be of crucial importance for the formation of the French social sciences.

Morals was a subject much closer to literary culture than to political theory or law. Ever since the Renaissance moral philosophy had been included in the humanities. Together with poetry, grammar, rhetoric and history, it was on the curriculum of the *studia humanitatis*; other philosophical specialisms such as logic and metaphysics were not.[17] Following the ancient philosophers' example, moral theory covered a wide range of questions pertaining to human existence and human conduct. The central issue was the role of the passions. In Christian ethics the passions were subject to prohibitions and served to encourage penance and willingness to sacrifice. In secular conceptions they were viewed not so much in a positive but more in a neutral way. They gradually came to be perceived less as sinful shortcomings and more as the motives or driving forces behind human action. However unworthy greed, envy and vanity might be, it was sensible to take them into consideration and try to gain more insight into them.

Since the passions were viewed as the true motives for human conduct, they also constituted the point of departure for questions of lifestyle. In aristocratic circles, there was thus a special interest in this problematic. Hidden motives and passions were among the favourite topics of conversation at the salons, and literary as well as more philosophical discourses in this field witnessed a veritable heyday. The *Maximes* (1664) by La Rochefoucauld, the *Pensées* (1670) by Pascal, the numerous volumes of *Essais de morale* (starting in 1671) by Nicole and the *Caractères* (1688) by La Bruyère were all widely read and imitated. The sharp increase in moralistic writings throughout the seventeenth century was not paralleled by any other genre.[18] In stories and novels, moralistic themes gained a prominent position as well.[19]

This wide interest was related to the functioning of the *monde* and the leading role it played *vis-à-vis* other groups. Not only did a whole etiquette and conduct system develop around the court, there was also growing indifference towards Christian moral codes and an increasing demand for a new perception of human conduct. In order to maintain oneself at the court, it was now necessary to have insight into human behaviour and to scrutinize the changes affecting it carefully.[20] Owing to the high level of self-constraint among courtiers and the rich variety of polite manners at their disposal, it had become extremely difficult to detect their 'true' feelings. Careful attentiveness and a certain 'psychological' insight were required to comprehend what the motive could be for a certain act, and the same attentiveness and insight were called for if one was to react properly. Finesse and tact were also needed in dealing with one's opponents and rivals. There, too, the more 'striking' and 'apt' remarks and allusions were, the more effective they were likely to be. A compliment is most effective if it actually 'touches' the person to whom it is addressed; the same holds true of insults. *Plaire* and *toucher* were mentioned in one breath as requirements with which courtly conduct had to comply. Both required insight, which in turn called for diligent hours of study.

Knowing how to behave was therefore not enough. One also had to know why it was the proper way to behave, and why some courses of behaviour were more effective than others. This was why so much time was spent talking and thinking about the passions that were so carefully concealed in social intercourse. Madeleine de Scudéry's comment that, at the salons, one could talk about things other people would not even venture to think about presumably referred to the difference in this respect between the aristocracy and the bourgeoisie. Among aristocrats passions were popular topics of contemplation and conversation. Among the bourgeoisie, where conduct was subject to stricter rules, they were more frequently repressed and silenced.

Not all forms of knowledge were thus frowned upon in aristocratic circles. Insight into human nature and human action was highly esteemed and to a certain extent even indispensable. Observation and careful scrutiny of the people with whom one associated was part of the aristocratic lifestyle. 'In Germany', Madame de Staël wrote, 'one studies books, in France one studies people.'[21] Without this special attention to human behaviour, court life and salon culture would have been virtually inconceivable. And the same preoccupation was clearly in evidence in classical French literature. Character sketches and portraits became prestigious literary genres, the depiction of manners and morals became an accepted facet of literary works, and in the writings of the *moralistes* the dissection of human behaviour was elevated to a special art. In acutely observed details, La Rochefoucauld demonstrated that it is not courage that makes people act bravely and seldom virtuousness that makes them act righteously. Human behaviour is neither noble nor disinterested. Self-love and self-interest are the most common and most powerful drives, even in cases where it looks as if disinterestedness prevails. From Montaigne to Chamfort, these moralists never failed to demonstrate that even the most sublime acts were inspired by human – and often all too human – strivings. Nietzsche called this moralistic tradition the most important reason for the supremacy of French culture. Nowhere else, he wrote, not on the part of the 'mediocre' English and certainly not on the part of the Germans with their bloodless *Begriffsgespensterei*, could any equivalent be found for the psychological sensitivity and curiosity that one came across in France, even in the daily newspapers and the 'boulevard theatres'.[22]

One of the features of this moralist literature was that the authors refrained from moral lessons.[23] What the *moralistes* meant by *morale* had less to do with moral principles than with mores and manners, less with ethics than with *ethos*. Morality pertained to the intertwining of temperament and custom. Moralists observed without being concerned with commandments or ethical doctrines. They described and dissected human reality. Montaigne depicted this activity as 'contemplating the nature and circumstances of various people and the customs of various nations'.[24] Montaigne's work was one of the major examples of what was to expand in the seventeenth century into classical French moral philosophy. That was also when this current of moral philosophy acquired its classical form. Montaigne had written *essais* which, with the exception of the quotations, were entirely in French. In the works of later authors Latin disappeared completely, as did the quotations, and the aphorism soon replaced the *essai*.[25] Everything that could be interpreted as pedantry was avoided: quotations, long-winded reasoning, theoretical reflections, abstract concepts and a more or less systematic line of argumentation. The result was a genre featuring acute observations and short sketches and portrayals alternating with witty comments. Moral philosophy would not be the right word for it, which is why the term 'moralistics' is used.

Since they had become the medium for philosophical and ideological conflicts, moralistics and moral theory came to occupy a significant position in the course of the seventeenth century. Morals and manners constituted a perpetual bone of contention for Jesuits and Jansenists, believers and sceptics, courtiers and commoners. Not a single group was indifferent when it came to questions of conduct, virtue and morality. In England these differences of opinion were more frequently settled in a political and administrative setting, but that was inconceivable in France. The process of parliamentarization that imposed such considerable restraints on the English monarchy did not occur in France.[26] 'The English', Madame de Staël wrote, 'live with-drawn in their families or come together at political meetings for na-tional discussions. They are barely familiar with the intermediary area we call *société*; it is here in this frivolous sphere of life, however, that sensitivity and taste are formed.'[27] The discourses generated in this *société* were less academic than the German tradition and less political than many of the English contributions; moralistics was one of its most typical products.

A new anthropology

In the moralist tradition, the question 'why do people behave as they do?' was linked to the question 'what is a wise way to react?' Human conduct was no longer perceived in relation to obligations and duties, but in terms of motives and effects. The practical theories of action that thus emerged were instrumental to the rise of social theory. In this framework, ideas were formulated on self-interest and self-love, *amour-propre*, which were to serve as the foundation for much of the social theory of the eighteenth century. The notion gradually crystal-lized that, of all the passions that ruled man, interest was the most stable and predictable.[28] In this new anthropology man was no longer viewed as the unpredictable prey of passion, but as a creature who consistently promoted his own interests. According to this view, then, human behaviour was more stable and more orderly than Christian teachings assumed.

This new anthropology can be seen as one of the most important intellectual preconditions for the rise of modern social theory. Human acts were not simply random and accidental; they were focused upon gaining advantages and this was precisely why so much depended on their context. The anarchy of passions, which had to be tamed from 'outside' and from 'above', that is, by the strict imposition of religious and political obligations, was replaced by a totally new concept. The core of it, one might say, was the idea that people could be left to themselves. That was a new thought. Compliance with religious and political obligations was not a precondition for social order. In de-fiance of church doctrines and the tradition of political theory (Machiavelli, Hobbes), a *société* had come into existence where peo-ple who solely followed their own interests and preferences nonethe-less managed to live together in an orderly fashion.

This very observation was initially formulated as criticism. Pascal, Nicole, La Rochefoucauld and other visitors to Madame de Sablé's salon were the most renowned authors to write about the predominance of *amour-propre*. For Jansenists such as Pascal and Nicole, the analyses were the continuation of a long theological tradition. Nicole demonstrated that it was impossible for people to determine whether any given act was good or not. Judgements of this kind were the realm of God and God alone, since, even in what appeared to be altruistic, selfish motives prevailed. This point of view was defended on the grounds of detailed observations and analyses, which such secular authors as La Rochefoucauld would in turn make use of. The predominant role of *amour-propre* was something La Rochefoucauld borrowed from the Jansenists. He was a well-known *frondeur*, and after the defeat of the Fronde he devoted his time and energy to the psychological exposure of courtly life. If he showed that virtue was most often a mask for vice, he was following the Jansenist line of reasoning, but without their theological premises or conclusions.

The originality of Nicole and La Rochefoucauld was not that they discovered the predominant role of self-interest. The fact that they gradually arrived at a positive evaluation of *amour-propre* was something newer and far more striking.[29] They detected signs of self-interest in even the noblest of deeds, and this was perhaps what made them so receptive to the conclusion that there was reason for a re-evaluation of this drive. In the first instance this led to a distinction between ordinary and enlightened self-interest (*amour-propre raisonnable et éclairé*), this enlightened self-interest being the legitimate form of self-interest. According to Hans-Jürgen Fuchs, the decisive step had thus been taken towards a positive appreciation.[30]

In the late seventeenth century, in the 1670s according to Fuchs, a notion emerged that for the very first time took interest or self-interest to be a positive trait. *Amour-propre* was not solely a powerful motivation (diametrically opposed to love of God or respect for the state), it was in fact the urge that served as the very foundation for all human activity and social intercourse. The model for this notion was the functioning of the *monde*.

The virtues of sociability

By 1700 the idea that *amour-propre* was the basis for all human passions and acts was relatively widespread. The fact that this indestructible urge was also the true cornerstone for social relations was increasingly accepted. None of the authors drew a fundamental distinction between individual acts and their social context. For noblemen it was evident that behaviour was a social phenomenon. They were all too aware that everything they did was attuned to the things other people did. At the court and in the salons they barely had a chance to doubt this. At regular intervals, sometimes several times a day, there would be receptions and gatherings, and one could not fail to act in accordance with the rules without immediately endangering one's reputation. Life in the *monde* consisted of coming together and being together, and it was not without reason that one spoke of *société*.

In this aristocratic upper layer, what Pierre Bourdieu called social capital was one of the most important resources.[31] The totality of the relations one had, their 'value' and one's skills to sustain and develop these relations were of decisive importance for social success. For specialists in good manners and the art of social intercourse the behaviour of people with less social capital was a constant source of amusement. The clumsy provincial and the over-eager bourgeois became stereotypes at the theatre, and for noblemen misanthropy was an ailment as comical as it was fatal. The widely renowned sociabilité was often depicted as a typically French virtue. The English were characterized as enlightened and tolerant but also taciturn, dull and a bit melancholy, the Germans as serious and solemn, and the French as frivolous but charming and pleasant. 'L'esprit de société', Voltaire wrote, 'comes naturally to the French; it is a virtue and a pleasure for which other peoples have also felt the need.'[32] 'Sociability', according to d'Alembert, 'is the most important feature of the French nation.'[33]

The upper classes in French society were characterized by a strong ethic of sociability. There was vast appreciation for the virtues that were so essential at gatherings (manners, tact, charm); virtues that were linked less to social intercourse and more to the individual personality (righteousness, authenticity) or to private life were held in far less esteem. In writings on moral theory this hierarchy of values was also backed by theoretical arguments. The *Traité de la société civile* (1726) by Claude Buffier is a good example of an aristocratically toned ethical treatise. Buffier discussed the courtly etiquette in the standard concepts of moral philosophy (virtue, happiness, supreme goodness and so forth). The result was an ethical treatise in which social relations had become decisive. Ordinarily, as Buffier put it, moral philosophy was the study focused on regulating the customs and behaviour of people in a sensible manner. That meant that moral philosophy could be conceived as the science of how people live together with one another. The point of departure was courtesy, in other words, familiarity with what pleases or displeases other people. That is why the following rule could be taken as the general principle of moral philosophy:

'I want to be happy but I live together with other people who also want to be happy, so let us pursue the method that will make me happy and provide them with happiness as well.'[34] Viewed in this light, virtuous behaviour was nothing but the effort to achieve one's own happiness by making other people happy – or at any rate without doing any damage to their happiness. This precept was to be the 'general principle' of moral philosophy and the foundation of the 'entire civil society'.

It is clear that Buffier's principle coincided with the prevailing prestige economy. For courtiers, after all, prestige was something they acquired by pleasing others. Other instruments were excluded or of secondary importance: people competed for other people's favour, particularly for the favour of persons higher on the social ladder, and did so by providing pleasure for one another. Someone who knew how to please other people would be held in higher esteem, and indeed the only way to rise in other people's esteem was by pleasing them. Buffier reformulated this type of social relation, this reciprocity or interdependence, in the language of moral philosophy: individual happiness could be achieved only by contributing towards the happiness of others.

In accordance with a long tradition in moral philosophy, Buffier viewed happiness or well-being as the general designation for human desires. What was relatively new in his line of thinking was the strong emphasis on 'living together'. In the living together Buffier had in mind, the contradiction between individual desires and moral obligations was eliminated. Sociability was the most important source of happiness, and happiness was not feasible outside this sociability. Buffier's dissertation thus illustrated the tendency Robert Mauzi felt was characteristic of so many authors in the eighteenth century.[35] The striving for happiness increasingly replaced the Christian doctrine of salvation. The social dimension of this striving – sociability – came to occupy a central position and sociability was viewed as the true foundation for moral philosophy, law and politics. It was completely in keeping with this line of thinking that Abbé Pluquet, a professor in moral philosophy at the *Collège de France*, wrote *De la sociabilité* (1767). Since the striving for happiness was not feasible in isolation, people entered into relationships with other people. The societies that came into existence as a result were thus based upon human needs, and their aim was 'common happiness'.[36] This was a recurrent notion in many of the descriptions of the moral sciences. Condorcet, for example, described the moral sciences as the sciences that had the human being as their subject and happiness as their goal.[37]

However, the introduction of 'sociabilité' in moral philosophy was soon to lead to an unforeseen problem. If one formulates Buffier's reasoning in a slightly different manner, it becomes clear. If happiness could be achieved only by providing other people with it, one might also say that virtue did not result from having a dutiful attitude or loving thy neighbour, but from enlightened self-interest. This was also the *moralistes'* lesson. It led, however, to a paradox: virtue issued from vice! In the eighteenth century, particularly in Mandeville's succinct formulation, this paradox played an important role in the development of moral theory. Mandeville did not hold that it was virtue in the general sense that issued from vice, it was private vices that led to public benefits. This specification was essential. In *The Fable of the Bees* Mandeville outlined how the vices of the individual led to the comfort and prosperity of society as a whole. The fame and wealth of a country were not based upon virtuousness and diligence but on the vanity and greed of its citizens. If they were to behave in a truly virtuous manner their prosperity would soon be a thing of the past.[38]

Mandeville's parable addressed the discrepancy between 'is' and 'ought'. In this sense, one might view his narrative as symbolizing the fate of moral theory. At the end of the eighteenth century it was split in two: the normative questions accrued to new forms of moral philosophy and the more factual questions became the domain of the emerging human sciences. The new moral philosophy was most clearly manifested in the work of Kant. In his *Grundlegung zur Metaphysik der Sitten* (1785) he ousted once and for all the notion that morality could be founded upon such 'empirical principles' as the striving for happiness or the feeling of sympathy. Moral rules were obligations and their rational foundation was one of his best-known contributions. The transition from moral philosophy to social science emerged most clearly in the work of the *philosophes* and the Scottish moral philosophers, where multifarious notions rooted in moral philosophy were incorporated into a new problematic.

Moral philosophy and social science

The moralist tradition played a significant role in the rise of the social sciences in two senses. Firstly, a new image of human conduct emerged from this tradition. Human acts were less arbitrary than had been assumed. They exhibited a certain stability, and, since selfish motives were so preponderant, people could often be left to their passions. It was not necessary to prescribe love of one's fellow man or to stipulate a system of obligations and rules. The baker baked bread because it was to his own advantage. This argument, which Smith used in his *Wealth of Nations*, served as the anthropological basis for numerous economic and social theories. Religious and political precepts were partially superfluous: interest was a 'natural' and sufficient precondition for the functioning of many sectors in society. This idea emerged at the end of the seventeenth century in the work of such moralists as La Rochefoucauld and Nicole. It was elaborated upon and honed by various authors, especially Mandeville, and was to be an important presupposition in the work of Montesquieu and Smith.

In a second sense, as well, this new anthropology played an important role in the formation of the social sciences. The fact that people were less unstable than had been hitherto assumed did not necessarily mean human nature was simple. In the realm of *amour-propre*, as La Rochefoucauld observed, there were still numerous discoveries to be made. As a means to this end, conduct had to be carefully studied in its social context. Thus the moralistic tradition was not as 'individualistic' as it has been called.[39] Social customs and individual conduct were closely intertwined in writings by the *moralistes*; the awareness of this interlacing was another contribution to the rise of the social sciences.

4

The Construction of Social Theory

*The multitude which is not reduced to unity is confusion,
the unity which does not depend on the multitude is tyranny.*

Pascal

For the *philosophes*, moral theory and moral philosophy represented the most important point of departure. They constituted a vast and recognized theoretical field with a reasonable extent of autonomy from the intellectual orthodoxy. In the language of moral philosophy, the *philosophes* were able to express their views on all manner of human affairs, including controversial matters regarding church or state. It enabled them to appropriate certain subjects, achieve intellectual authority and dispute the position of official experts. In a rather unacademic way, moral philosophy was thus to become the point of departure for discourses focused not only on human behaviour, but equally on law and the state, culture and history, politics and society. In order to comprehend human relations individuals were no longer to be viewed as 'subjects' who owed obedience to the monarch or as sinners whose salvation depended on their penance, but as human beings capable of rational understanding and reasonable conduct. The approach from this perspective was the focal point for an enlightened science of man, and moral science was consequently the most comprehensive and, as Voltaire noted, the first of the sciences.[1]

For the *philosophes*, moral science was thus no more and no less than the science of human conduct and the human sciences were moral sciences. In his introduction to the *Encyclopédie*, d'Alembert cited three areas of knowledge: knowledge of God, knowledge of nature and knowledge of man. In the human sciences he drew a distinction between logic and morals. Logic pertained to a number of formal skills, and morals could be divided into a general and a specific part. *Morale générale* concerned concepts that were universal and generally valid, such as virtue or happiness, and *morale particulière* the duties of man as an individual (law), in the family (economics) and in society (politics). In this line of thinking, the word 'moral' served as a general term for human reality, at any rate in so far as it differed from nature – in other words, in so far as there was 'civilization'.[2] Theology and man's duties to God were not viewed by d'Alembert as part of human science, and in his opinion political and legal phenomena were part and parcel of morals.

The views expounded in his introduction were not very original. What was more interesting was the way certain moral categories and questions were used. Descriptive and normative statements overlapped. In itself, this too was nothing new. In classical rationalism the 'nature' of phenomena similarly served as object and norm alike. In the work of the *philosophes*, however, this type of reasoning took a far more concrete turn. Treatises on human nature led to arguments about what was or was not 'natural' and criticism of existing institutions was then formulated in this idiom: moral categories were brought to bear against existing political prescriptions.[3] In their criticism of theology and the church, the *philosophes* set to work in much the same way. Here again notions on the nature and rights of man served as critical substitutes for orthodox doctrines. Thus the whole notion of morals gradually acquired a critical undertone. Holbach and Helvétius, for example, advocated the 'moralization' of politics. They branded Christian morals a fraud and, according to Holbach, only the rule of morals, the ethocracy, could put an end to all despotism. Holbach opened his *Systéme de la nature* by stating that 'man is only unhappy because he denies his nature'.[4] Virtue and happiness, Holbach felt, would be man's fate if he would acknowledge his true nature. Helvétius displayed the same radicalization of moral philosophical points of view.[5]

Despite their subversive position, Holbach and Helvétius remained more or less within the tradition of moral philosophy. Holbach founded his 'natural morals' on the principle of sociability, and Helvétius' utilitarianism was a kind of codification of the thoughts on self-interest developed by seventeenth-century moralists. What distinguished them from their predecessors was that, with the help of these notions, they formulated ideas on the function and design of the state. This was inconceivable in the seventeenth century. French authors of those days were careful to abstain from commenting on political issues. Descartes wrote his *Traité des passions* (1649) but, unlike Hobbes or Spinoza, failed to draw even the slightest conclusion as to the design of the state.

A theoretical synthesis

The most important contributions to social theory, however, did not issue solely from a generalization or expansion of moral philosophy. For Montesquieu and Rousseau, widely viewed as the most significant writers at the time, moral philosophy was an important source but not the only one. As a jurist, Montesquieu was familiar with politico-legal thinking, and Rousseau also had thorough knowledge of modern legal theory. Their own theories were mainly syntheses of insights from moral philosophy and the politico-legal tradition. The concept of sociability that played such a key role in both traditions was their common ground – their interface, as it were. In moral literature sociability was intertwined with etiquette and manners and with treatises on human conduct in smaller groups. In modern natural law sociability was perceived as the drive upon which political communities were all founded. This view was clearly not in keeping with the *droit divin*, which held that the power of the state had a divine origin and the monarch had supernatural gifts (such as the ability to heal by laying on hands). Just as the natural law of Grotius and Pufendorf presented a rational and secular theory about such institutions as 'law' and 'the state', moral literature provided insights into human conduct and the meaning of practices and customs that were outside the reach of the state. Montesquieu and Rousseau used these traditions in very different ways, but for both of them these currents of thought were their major frame of reference.

Social theory, in other words, emerged from efforts to integrate politico-legal theories with the insights of moral theories. What was involved here, one might say, was an integration of micro-analyses with macrotheories. Macrophenomena played a central role in the politico-legal tradition, whereas in moral theories it was small-scale human interaction that was in the limelight. If this is an accurate description, it is easy to see why this integration became feasible only after intellectuals had gained a considerable extent of autonomy in regard to the state as well as *société*. And that did not occur until the decades following the death of Louis XIV. Criticism of absolutism was voiced, censorship became more flexible and there was a revival of critical interest in political issues. At the same time writers began to become less dependent on the courtly and *mondaine* elites. New intellectual societies were founded, philosophical salons developed, and in the *philosophe* a personality emerged that laid claim to far greater independence than the seventeenth-century man of letters. This increased autonomy made it possible to elaborate more systematically on the thoughts of the *moralistes* and combine them with political theories. The first steps in this direction were taken by Montesquieu.

Montesquieu

Montesquieu is known as one of the leading social theorists of the eighteenth century. With Voltaire, he belonged to the first generation of *philosophes*. In his grand study on 'the spirit of the laws' he drew attention to a whole range of phenomena and principles that eluded the power of the state. Habits, customs and conventions did not conform to the will of the monarch or in fact to the laws of the land. What 'ruled' people, Montesquieu stated, was a complex of 'physical' and 'moral' factors: climate, conventions and legislation. Differences in forms of government were related to differences in the physical and moral constitution of nations.[6] Each climate precipitated certain customs, and these customs were the building blocks for the form of government and the legislation that a nation adopted. Montesquieu examined the links between various seemingly unrelated factors. In modern terms, one might say he focused on the interdependence of relatively autonomous phenomena.

Montesquieu's quest for the 'spirit of the laws' went well beyond the traditional divisions. He wrote about manners and morals, but unlike the moralists he associated them with specific kinds of political regimes. He produced a typology of state forms, but linked them to moral and climatological conditions. The result of his research was such a differentiated description of the social world that neither the politico-legal nor the moral philosophical vocabulary was any longer adequate. The very term 'the spirit of the laws' indicates that he presented his work as a study on the prerequisites for political and legal structures. In his work, however, he made mention of a far more general phenomenon, which he called 'the spirit of the nation'. This 'general spirit', more powerful than any official institution, was the combined result of various physical and moral factors. Nations were ruled far more by this spirit than by their ruler. Legislation and politics, or so Montesquieu held, should be attuned to this spirit; without insight into this complex phenomenon, no reasonable system of governance was feasible.

Montesquieu's major work consisted of a compilation of elements from various intellectual traditions. It is true, as has frequently been noted, that it was inspired by his desire to restrict the power of the state and improve the position of the aristocracy. Montesquieu was a true defender of the *thèse nobilitaire*: he advocated the restoration of the power the nobility had lost to the monarch. The landed aristocracy to which he himself belonged served vital functions as the intermediary group between the monarch and the people. And yet there was no direct link between *De l'esprit des lois* and Montesquieu's position as either a magistrate or a nobleman. For a link of this kind, the genesis of *De l'esprit des lois* is far too complex and the specific logic of intellectual production too important. In actual fact his major work was the unanticipated result of a rather long and intricate course of development. Montesquieu's early writings, for example, eradicated any doubt as to his ambitions as a moralist, and his first work, *Lettres persanes*, was anything but a youthful impetuosity. The question to which his work gives rise is thus: how did he arrive at the synthesis aspired to by and achieved in *De l'esprit des lois*?

When Montesquieu began writing *Lettres persanes* in 1717, not yet two years after the death of Louis XIV, he was twenty-eight years old. It was more or less clear what his prospects were: he had studied law, was married in 1715, and a year later inherited the estate of *La Bréde* and the chairmanship of the *Parlement* of Bordeaux. In that same year he was admitted to the Bordeaux Academy, a local society for men of letters, the arts and sciences, which had been founded in 1712. Montesquieu was an established man, but he was not content with his provincial life. Nor did his function in the *parlement* grant him the satisfaction he sought. According to his biographer he was not a great magistrate, and as soon as he got the chance, in 1726, he sold his office. This gave him the time and the money to devote all his energy to writing and managing his estate. What he missed, however, was the contact with Paris, the opportunity to exchange ideas with other writers, the latest news, the rumours about imminent intrigues. It was not unusual for Montesquieu to express his appreciation of the tranquillity and isolation of the countryside and disparage the social scene in the capital. With some degree of pride he spoke with the accent of the region, but time and again he returned to the Capital; he could not live without it, if only to gather the energy for his mission as provincial nobleman. These ambivalent feelings towards the court and the capital were at the very basis of his later work.

Within three years the *Lettres persanes* had been completed. Montesquieu showed the manuscript to a friend in Paris, who reacted as he had hoped: 'President, this is going to sell like hot cakes'.[7] And the letters, which were published anonymously, did indeed meet with enormous success. The author proceeded to Paris, where he was invited to various salons and was even introduced at the court. *Lettres persanes* addressed the widespread discontentment with the last years of the reign of Louis XIV. It was a comedy of manners in which Montesquieu also satirically voiced his own preferences. The absolute power of the monarch was depicted, for example, as a form of magic, as a bizarre superstition that did not fail to amaze the Persians. The descriptions of certain specific customs were entertaining, but the book lacked the psychological sensitivity exhibited by so much of the moralistic literature. There were no finely sketched portraits, no characters skilfully explored, and according to Lanson it was a superficial satire devoid of any psychological depth.[8]

It is quite feasible that Montesquieu did not begin intensively to examine the body of problems Lanson felt was so sadly lacking in his work until he became part of Parisian salon life. It was at any rate precisely these themes that were the favourite topics of conversation at the salon of Madame Lambert, which Montesquieu was soon to frequent. Madame Lambert was herself the author of a short treatise on friendship, and in the circle she gathered around her the preferred topics of conversation were such moralistic issues as happiness, love, taste, duty and virtue. In this period of his life Montesquieu was writing a new literary work. It was published in 1725, but was not a success. At the same time he was working on a number of moralistic treatises. He wrote an article on taste, which was later to appear in the *Encyclopédie*, a piece on happiness, and a short discourse on esteem and reputation. At a session of the Academy of Bordeaux in 1725 he recited parts of his *Traité des devoirs*, which had been directly inspired by conversations at Madame Lambert's salon. A French translation of *De officio hominis* by Pufendorf had served as an example.[9] Several years later the support of the people with whom he had conversed at Madame Lambert's salon proved to be instrumental in another sense as well. It was thanks to the influential *faction lambertine* that Montesquieu was elected to the Académie française.

The years after the publication of *Lettres persanes* and before his journeys to Italy (1728–9) and England (1729–31) represented an important stage in Montesquieu's development. He recorded numerous plans, particularly literary ones, and the notes in his journals pertained to a myriad of subjects. No clear direction was evident, although according to Shackleton after 1725 he exhibited growing interest in political theory.[10] The fiasco of *Le temple de Gnide* (1725) undoubtedly played a role in the process, and Montesquieu's interest was sure to have been aroused by meetings at the *Club de l'Entresol* (1724–31), a political society with which he was associated. At any rate his stay in England reinforced his interest in politics, and in 1734 he decided to set to work on a comprehensive study of law and the state. His *Considérations sur les causes de la grandeur des Romains et de leur décadence* had just been published and Voltaire's *Lettres philosophiques* was very much in the limelight. Intense interest in the enlightened English nation was widespread, by then the Club de l'Entresol had been prohibited, and the time seemed ripe for an effort to shed new light on the great political issues.

In 1748, fourteen years after his decision, *De l'esprit des lois* was published. Many of the components were borrowed at least in part from earlier works; others are known to have been common notions at the time. But before Montesquieu it is not likely that anyone had ever written such a comprehensive and differentiated description of nations. Interestingly enough, the central concept in this connection, the 'general spirit of the nation', was already evident at an early stage. It seems to be linked to his experiences at Madame Lambert's salon and to his moralistic writings. Montesquieun arrived in Paris as the author of an entertaining satire. For seven years he was very much a part of the social scene in Paris and remained faithful to his literary ambitions. He sold his office and did indeed manage to penetrate the Académie française, but his literary career failed to really materialize. After his stay in England he returned to the themes of law and the state with which he had long been familiar. His writings on these themes were inspired by his opposition to absolutism, but were equally based upon a very specific integration of moralistic points of view. The originality of *De l'esprit des lois* lay mainly in the fact that it was a synthesis of political, legal and moralistic points of view. In this synthesis the incorporation of the moralistic tradition played a crucial role, and one that literature on the topic has systematically ignored.[11]

An early text written for his 1725 *Traité des devoirs* contained a paraphrase that seems to have been taken directly from the moralistic tradition. What Montesquieu was describing, however, was not a person but a nation. 'Societies', he wrote, are only a 'union of the spirit' and are distinguished by a 'common character'. This 'character' was the 'effect' of an endless sequence of causes, but as soon as it was formed it was in fact the ruling power.[12] Here Montesquieu used the way people were observed and described at the salons to characterize a society. One might assume from his early work that what he had in mind was to draw a character portrait, but of a nation as a whole. This seemed to have been the key motive behind the writing of *De l'esprit des lois*. The most significant part of what he later called the 'esprit général' was already in evidence in this early fragment. The power of the monarch and the legislative authorities was limited because they had to rely on the 'character' of the nation; this character was the result of an endless succession of causes that could not be controlled by any one person or group. This anonymous power, or 'conscience collective' as Durkheim would say, was more important than any law or political rule. Montesquieu's originality was based upon an elaboration of this idea. It is impossible, however, to view this idea as an 'expression' or 'reflection' of the interests of the landed aristocracy or magistracy. They were the groups from which Montesquieu came, but his early work was inspired more by literary and intellectual ambitions than by the desire to be recognized as spokesman of the magistracy or landed aristocracy. It was indeed characteristic of the French constellation that the two were so difficult to combine. The magistracy no longer had any intellectual esteem to speak of and writers had no political or executive power. As a writer, this was why Montesquieu had little choice but to reconcile himself to the standards of the literary intelligentsia. In the first instance, what he was writing was a satire; in conjunction with his role in salon life he then turned to the realm of morals. It was not until that turned out to yield such negligible rewards that he returned to questions of law and government, but with the intention of making moralistic notions productive for a better understanding of political systems. It was not until after this lengthy detour that he finally had an opportunity to approach questions of politics and government in a new manner and award them a new legitimacy.

In *Considérations sur la grandeur des Romains* (1734) the existence of a 'national spirit' played an important role in the analysis; the system was completed somewhat later in *Essai sur les causes qui peuvent affecter les esprits et les caractéres*. According to Shackleton, this short text was written in the period from 1736 to 1743.[13] The title alone was an allusion to moralistic literature. In the first part Montesquieu wrote about the influence of the climate, and in the second part he turned to moral causes. Personal upbringing and education were central, and, just as they shaped the individual's character, the 'general character' of a nation was inculcated into every individual via a 'general upbringing and education'. This character was informed by a combination of the well-known 'physical' and 'moral' causes.[14]

This pattern recurred in *De l'esprit des lois*. Montesquieu began with a typology of forms of government (republic, monarchy, despotism). This part fitted into the political theory tradition. He then dealt with the influence of the climate and the composition of the soil. This was followed by the famous book XIX, where the 'esprit général' was treated, after which a wide range of 'moral' causes were described.

This sequence illustrates the fact that Montesquieu was still adhering in part to a traditional politico-legal approach. In many senses the terminology and structure of his study represented compromises. Although he surmounted many of the limitations of conventional theoretical models, he did not succeed in developing a conceptual system of his own. In his formulation he remained dependent on the existing vocabularies, as is well illustrated by the title and subtitle of his study, *De l'esprit des lois, ou du rapport que les lois doivent avoir avec la constitution de chaque gouvernement, les moeurs, le climat, la religion, le commerce, etc.* The fragmentary form of his study similarly indicated that he had not really succeeded in creating a systematic alternative for the existing approaches. Perhaps this failure was precisely the reason that his work was so successful. Although old questions and concepts could still be discerned, it was an effort to undertake something new. Montesquieu differed in this sense from such authors as Rousseau or Hume, both of whom worked more systematically but were long doomed to remain unappreciated.

The concept of society

If Montesquieu's work is viewed today as one of the earliest examples of modern social theory, it goes by a term he himself never used. Montesquieu did not refer to 'social' relations or 'social' institutions; he either confined himself to 'the spirit of the laws' or 'the character of a nation' or avoided any strict system altogether and was content to position various phenomena side by side, as in the subtitle of *De l'esprit des lois*. In all probability he never even heard the term 'social theory'. For the new intellectual genre he helped create, the noun 'society' and the adjective 'social' were crucial terms, but these were to occur largely after the publication of his work. The emergence and expansion of this terminology is interesting evidence of the rise of social theory.

Up to the start of the eighteenth century the term 'society' had two meanings.[15] *Société* was used to refer to the leading social circles of Paris and Versailles. In this sense it was synonymous to *monde* and was associated with a courtly or sophisticated lifestyle. But *société* was also the term for an association or society in the sense of an organized group of people who gathered in connection with some common interest. This connotation, of particular relevance to city dwellers, was closely linked to the laws. A *société*, a legally recognized organizational form, whether a commercial association or a *société savante*, was comparable with the *societas* specified in Roman private law.[16] In both of these senses the term referred to small social units that belonged neither to the realm of 'the state' nor to that of the family or household.

In the writings of the *philosophes*, both these senses were still in evidence. The new meaning of the word did not manifest itself until the mid-eighteenth century. One indication of this new meaning was that combinations were created of the older meanings. As the traditional meanings came to overlap, a new concept emerged. Montesquieu, for example, described his predecessor at the Académie française as a man pre-eminently fit for the 'society' because he was 'amiable' and 'useful' and 'gentle in his manners and strict in his morals'.[17] Amiable and gentle were typical terms of aristocratic etiquette, whereas usefulness and strict morals were bourgeois virtues. This combination led to a new concept that soon gained far more general validity. This is comparable with the development Roger Chartier described regarding the concept of *civilité*.[18] Chartier observed that the diffusion of aristocratic models in the eighteenth century was accompanied by growing criticism of them as 'unauthentic' and 'external'. Writers and intellectuals used the words and the values of the *monde*, but tried at the same time to invest them with new contents. The same thing occurred in connection with the term *société*.

Another aspect was that the term *société* expanded to include all social units. As such, it was soon to replace theological notions, for example, the *corpus mysticum*, and notions in politics or public law (state, status, corporation). This expansion was descriptive, polemic and normative at the same time. It was descriptive because every institution, every human arrangement implied social interaction and could thus be defined as a 'society'. It was polemic because these social arrangements were viewed as a purely secular matter and because 'social' relations were thought to be more fundamental than the politico-legally defined relations. Lastly, it was normative because the term society had a positive connotation that was linked to the original meaning of a form of free association, in which the rights of individuals were respected. In this sense the concept was indicative of a pacified social sphere, one might say of a moral space that could serve as an example for the social world as a whole.

In the works of Montesquieu or Voltaire the term *société* was equivalent to 'nation' or 'country'. In *Lettres persanes*, Montesquieu referred to society in a very general sense and wrote the word with a capital letter, apparently to make it clear he was using it in a more abstract way, just as *Etat* is written with a capital letter in French. The term *la grande société*, which was used by a number of authors, served a comparable function. Buffon, for example, called human units 'large societies' and communities of animals 'small societies'. Small societies were solely natural units, and could thus easily be differentiated from *sociétés policées*.[19] But the term was not employed that frequently in the work of Montesquieu or Voltaire, nor was its use very systematic. It probably did not become a key concept until the work of Rousseau. Lexicographic studies show that, in the French language, Rousseau was the first to use the word *social* as the adjective of *société*.[20] Via *Du contrat social*, a study that Rousseau initially wanted to call *De la société civile*, it entered the French language by way of Latin. Rousseau was probably one of the first to use *société* as a key concept and explicitly to reason in terms of 'social' relations.

Rousseau

It is only by becoming sociable that man becomes a moral being, a reasonable animal, the king of all other animals, and the image of God on earth.

Rousseau

Although Rousseau occasionally referred to his 'clandestine preference' for France,[21] as a foreigner with a petty bourgeois background he never felt at home there. In all his writings his was the position of the opponent, and it was always clearer what he disapproved of or detested than what attracted him. Rousseau found it unbearable that the flourishing of art and literature, the refinement of manners and everything that was considered civilized was also viewed as moral progress. Time and again he repeated that virtue had nothing to do with good taste or literary qualities. In contrast to the *philosophes*, he was not eager to act as a spokesman of an enlightened era. In him, the triumph of reason and the expansion of civilization inspired doubt and distrust. His work centred round the opposition between civilization and righteousness. His criticism did not confine itself to the absolute state and the church but extended to cover society as a whole, including the salons and the academies. For Rousseau, the term *société* did not have a positive connotation. In fact it was 'society' that was the problem. If one was to gain even a semblance of understanding of society's shortcomings, one could not make do with only moral or political analyses: 'anyone who wishes to deal separately with political and moral issues will never have any understanding of either of them'.[22]

In his thinking, Rousseau's point of departure was the problem of 'evil', and more specifically of inequality. For theologians and many philosophers this was the question of theodicy: how could the existence of a good and almighty God be reconciled with the existence of evil in the world? In the moralistic tradition it was a problem of human nature. But, according to Rousseau, responsibility for evil could be attributed neither to a hidden wish on the part of God (the Fall of Man) nor to the evil nature of man himself. Cassirer demonstrated that what was so original about Rousseau was that he excused God and man alike and localized the responsibility for evil in 'society'.[23]

In an effort to comprehend something of evil, it was pointless simply to assume man was by nature wicked. Rousseau did not doubt the commanding role played by *amour-propre* and did not question any of the moralists' analyses. But, to him, what was involved was a historical phenomenon rather than a fact of nature. There was every indication, he felt, that what the moralists described was a product of the development of society. Society had become such a powerful entity that individuals had very little leeway to deviate from what was stipulated and prescribed. Society, Rousseau wrote, differed from the individuals of whom it consisted in much the same way as a chemical compound differed from its separate elements.[24] Rousseau thus arrived at the conclusion that it was the 'social system' that should be studied and that people should be viewed as 'social beings'.

Rousseau's extraordinary sensitivity to social constraint and to a 'social system' that had come to operate independently of individual desires and intentions was closely linked to the feelings of powerlessness that tormented him. His writings were the work of a man who felt himself to be a misunderstood and powerless outsider. By transforming these feelings into his own thoughts and publications, he turned his work into an effort to do something about it. 'Society' was the name Rousseau gave to the lack of transparency and the inauthenticity that bothered him in human interaction.[25] He could not believe these relations were 'natural' or that they would become any 'more natural' if the bishops had any less power. Nor could he agree that the enlightened lovers of culture were any more genuine than the artisans of Geneva. Rousseau could not concur with any of the existing diagnoses, and his own analysis was more general and more radical.

Just as his diagnosis differed from what was generally accepted, so did the remedy he proposed. In the political theories of his day the relation between the monarch and the people occupied a central position. In natural law this relation was conceived as a contract assuming that the people delegated certain powers to the monarch in exchange for protection. Rousseau, who was quite familiar with the political and legal literature in this field,[26] chose to challenge the very terms of this agreement. The 'social contract' that served as the foundation for the nation's politics was an agreement among all the members of the community on behalf of the entire community. It was an alliance of equals and, as such, was incompatible with any form of sub-ordination. Rousseau departed from the idea that the state was based upon a contract between the ruler and the people. He rejected this kind of 'political contract' and felt that politics could be rightly founded only upon a social contract.[27] Since the cause was 'social', the solution had to be 'social' as well. So Rousseau's recurrent use of the word society and his introduction of the adjective social were no mere coincidence. As he himself emphasized, they were the outcome of his study.[28]

Rousseau initially began working on a study of political institutions. What he published in 1762, however, was *Du contrat social* and *Emile*. He replaced the strained dualism between morals and politics with an analysis of society and social relations. Rousseau thus brought under one common denominator issues that for many of the *philosophes* had exhibited essential differences. He did not draw any basic distinction between enlightened and less enlightened sectors. Instead he viewed all institutions collectively as being a component of that alien and alienating reality he called society. Consequently, Rousseau's writings could no longer be classified as either moral philosophy or political theory. Side by side with Montesquieu, he was one of the earliest and most important proponents of social theory. Rousseau formulated the foundation of this new intellectual genre more clearly than Montesquieu ever had: '. . . il faut étudier les hommes par la société, et la société par les hommes'.[29]

Social theory after Rousseau

Despite the admiration of a few individuals, the systematic nature and the theoretical significance of Rousseau's work long failed to be appreciated by either enlightened critics or romantic admirers. Yet the fact remains that it was partly due to Rousseau's efforts that think-ing in terms of social relations became more widespread in the last few decades of the eighteenth century. After the publication of *Du contrat social* there was a definite increase in the use of the adjective 'social'. Though it was certainly not in common usage, it was no longer so unusual to define and comprehend human relations as 'social' relations.[30] The *Encyclopédie* contained several illustrations of how thinking in terms of social relations represented a significant new trend. In the article on *société* Diderot referred to the family as a society; villages and towns similarly constituted a society, and all the people of the same country or even of the entire world joined to form a 'general' or 'universal' society. The justification he gave for this use of the word was interesting because he alluded to a moral philosophical line of argumentation that seemed to have been taken from Buffier's *Traité de la société civile*. Every form of human communal living, Diderot felt, was based upon the principle that people wanted to be happy. But since each individual lived together with other individuals who wanted to be happy as well, it was necessary to pursue means that would provide common happiness, or at any rate would not be detrimental to the happiness of others. This made it feasible to derive several other principles, which were then viewed as the formal or tacit agreement among all people. Although the argumentation for it was still amply based upon concepts from moral philosophy (the striving for happiness) and the politico-legal tradition (contract), here the term *société* acquired an extremely general meaning.

In the *Encyclopédie* it also appeared that defining human arrangements as societies did not serve solely an analytical function. The article on the *philosophe* stated that *société civile* was the only 'deity' recognized by a *philosophe*. In a certain sense the *philosophes* took civil society as a model. Whenever ecclesiastical or political institutions were defined as societies it implied that they were evaluated according to the norms of civil society. Here again it was clear that the term society was open to various interpretations and served various functions at the same time. Society was simultaneously a part and the whole. As a 'part', it was a sector that was very much on the rise and within which activities were arranged that did not fall under the strict jurisdiction of either the church or the state. This included not only economic and cultural activities, but also more or less informal gatherings in clubs or salons. As they grew in importance, in the last few decades of the eighteenth century 'society' and 'the state' were increasingly opposed to each other, and criticism of the state was expressed in the name of society.[31]

The work of Abbé Raynal contained a highly articulate example of this. In his once famous *Histoire philosophique et politique des deux Indes* (1770), a multi-volume work published in more than thirty editions before the Revolution, accounts of specific societies were alternated with more 'philosophical' passages such as the following:

Society is a product of the needs of people, and government a product of their shortcomings. Society always tends towards goodness, government should always be predisposed to suppress evil. Society comes first, it is in origin independent and free; government is set up on its behalf and is solely its instrument. It is the task of the one to command and of the other to serve. Society propagated public power; government, receiving this power, should totally devote itself to the task thus granted. Lastly, society is in essence good; government can be evil, as we well know, and all too often is so.[32]

This long forgotten fragment is, I believe, one of the earliest examples of 'society' and 'the state' explicitly addressed as opposites. As the diffuse sector Raynal called 'society' became more and more important, the term 'the state' became less applicable to the whole. A wide range of activities more and more obviously eluded the authority of the state. The people who acted as the spokesmen of these activities, such as the physiocrats and the *philosophes*, formulated ideas on their specificity, laid claim to greater autonomy and developed a different representation of the whole. To them, a nation was no longer a legally defined unit of orders and corporations with an absolute monarch at the top; it consisted instead of various sectors that joined to form a rather complex whole. Relations among these sectors were characterized by ambiguity, cooperation and competition, dependence and hierarchy, but in any case no longer by simple political subordination. This kind of differentiated unit was not so much a 'state' as a 'society'.

Thus social theory was not, as conservative critics since Burke have claimed, the work of uprooted intellectuals who engaged in politics under the guise of principles unrelated to reality.[33] Nor were these theories simply the result of patient observations on the part of disinterested scholars. Social theory came into being as part of the struggle for a more autonomous intellectual culture. In a political sense there were important differences between Montesquieu and a proponent of the *thèse royale* such as Voltaire. And Rousseau occupied another position entirely. But all of them had enough in common to work side by side on the *Encyclopédie* and to stand up to censorship and the domination of the Sorbonne. This striving for a greater extent of intellectual autonomy implied that treatises on social questions were no longer left to official theorists in their capacity as church or state spokesmen. As distinct from the theologians and jurists, the *philosophes* chose to act as the spokesmen of *société civile*. The ideas presented by the *philosophes* were developed as an alternative to the theo-centrism of the one group and the state-centrism of the other. This resulted in a decentring of thinking about human communities. Political and moral phenomena were redefined as 'social' phenomena, which led to a more general and more abstract mode of thinking. At the same time new groups laid claim to their own competence. They were no longer theologians and jurists, but writers and *philosophes* who professed an accurate interpretation of human communities.

5

Theoretical Models Compared: France and Scotland

While social theory expanded in the latter decades of the eighteenth century, Montesquieu and Rousseau remained, alongside the physiocrats, the most original authors. Both classified as *philosophes*, they occupied singular positions within this relatively loose-knit network. Montesquieu differed from most *philosophes* in that he was trained as a jurist, had experience as a magistrate and belonged to the landed aristocracy. He was also one of the oldest among their ranks, and died in 1755, when the first volumes of the *Encyclopédie* had just been published. Rousseau was of the same generation as Diderot and d'Alembert, but he was a foreigner who – after a period of closeness – had broken his ties with the *philosophes*. Neither of the two was very typical of the mentality of the *philosophes*.

If Montesquieu and Rousseau had one thing in common, it was their ambivalent attitude to Parisian intellectual life. In a certain period in their lives, at any rate, neither of them could do without it. They picked up skills and information there they could not have acquired anywhere else, but neither could reconcile himself to the fate of a Parisian man of letters. Montesquieu was too much of a scholarly landed aristocrat to be able to accept Parisian nobility or Parisian writers as his example. And Rousseau was too much of an outsider. For very different reasons, neither Montesquieu nor Rousseau could truly identify with Parisian men of letters nor was apt to continue working within the existing traditions. They began more or less as moralists, but none of the existing genres could offer what they were looking for, and both men refuted the division between moral and political analyses. Their distance from the established perspectives enabled them to conceive links that were unfamiliar, even to the *philosophes*.

Montesquieu was a provincial nobleman and jurist who had gained access to Parisian salon life by publishing an entertaining satire. After vain efforts in literary and moralistic genres he returned to his study of law and the state, but not without using notions borrowed from the moralists to develop a new approach to political and legal questions. What Montesquieu presented in his major work was not so much the expression of a position or the elaboration of a point of view, it was the outcome of a particular development. The synthesis of the various perpectives that he advanced was also a synthesis of various stages in his life. *De l'esprit des lois* was rightly called a magnum opus, a mosaic of thirty-one books and hundreds of chapters that served as a backdrop for notes taken throughout his life. The leitmotif was the detection of linkages and the analysis of relations or *rapports*. The formulation of laws, or so one of his conclusions went, ought to be based upon insight into the relation between the laws of a country and its physical and moral constitution. Montesquieu began with the problem of law and legislation; via the moralists, he arrived in the end at the study of social interdependence. Though he failed to draw any theoretical consequences, he was well aware of the political ones. If the pronouncement of good laws depended on so many uncontrollable factors, it was necessary to divide the tasks and devote special attention to mediation mechanisms and intermediary groups. Since the administration of modern nations was far too complicated for an absolute ruler, there was the permanent threat of despotism. In order to ward it off, he advocated a division of powers and a renewed role for the landed aristocracy. *De l'esprit des lois* was thus simultaneously a modern version of the *thèse nobilitaire*.

Rooted in a very different background, Rousseau also developed a representation of human societies in which social linkages and interdependence played key roles. In the work of Rousseau, however, interdependence was viewed as a negative phenomenon. The emergence of a vast and differentiated 'social system' was, in his view, the cause of inequality and alienation. For Rousseau, this analysis also gave rise to new questions about his own life. Rousseau examined society because it was alien to him. In much the same way he then launched a study of himself. Just as he could not feel at home in the world of others, others made it impossible for him to be content with himself. In this sense he differed from many *moralistes* who preceded him. Rousseau did not share the tranquillity of Montaigne or Montesquieu, nor did he have the esteem of a distinguished nobleman such as La Rochefoucauld. At unexpected moments his tact would abandon him, causing him to forfeit whatever he had already attained.

Calm acceptance of life is a privilege of the established; patient efforts and trying again is the hope of newcomers. But neither of the two were in store for Rousseau: fitful and restless as he was, both 'society' and his own self were to present him with problems. And with the same amazement and impatience with which he had written his first discourse, Rousseau began to dissect his own observations and feelings. Instead of being satisfied with one character, he created a whole cast of them. It was a game played from a continually fluctuating perspective: Emile was viewed through the eyes of Julie, just as Rousseau was assessed by Jean-Jacques. These contributions, manifesting themselves mainly in a literary form, constituted the complement of his social theory.[1]

The significance of natural law in France

If social interdependence is indeed central to the writing of Montesquieu and Rousseau, and if they are consequently to be ranked among the very first modern social theorists, this still does not say much about the theoretical status of their work. Both of them may well have made decisive contributions to the rise of social theory; the question remains as to what kind of theories they formulated.

It was not Newtonian natural science that played a decisive role in their theoretical orientation but natural law. Modern natural law was the most comprehensive and most systematic theoretical framework available for social theory in the early eighteenth century. Montesquieu seems to have been familiar with Newton's work, but rejected his ideas on gravity and, just like many other members of the Bordeaux Academy, preferred Descartes and Malebranche.[2] He did, however, make use of natural law, which he combined with analyses that had long been in common use among French jurists. Rousseau might have exhibited somewhat less scientific interest than Montesquieu, but he did go to a great deal of trouble to construct a strictly rational theory. His main examples were the theorists of natural law.[3] Ample use was also made of natural law in the Encyclopédie. It was not unusual for articles on social issues to be compilations of what the great natural law theorists had written.[4]

The point of departure for natural law was the assumption that, in addition to the existing, 'positive' legal forms, there was a legal system independent of local customs and the specific ordinances of the magistracy and the monarch.[5] This 'natural' law, which could be addressed by reason, was based upon suppositions regarding human nature. It consisted of a system of obligations, rights and laws that was universal and immutable and that could be more or less deductively inferred from assumptions regarding the nature of man.

The existing legal forms could exhibit a wide range of discrepancies, but could not deviate in principle from what had been stipulated by this natural law. Thus natural law served as the final legal norm. Grotius played a central role in the revival of this school of thought in the seventeenth century. His work represented a veritable assault on the doctrine of *droit divin* that put the monarch above the law. This modern natural law also played an instrumental role in founding the unity of law. By granting the study of law a foundation of this kind, jurists could lay claim to fundamental independence from the church and moral theology. Whereas natural law centred round the obligations of the individual to himself and to his fellow human beings, theology was concerned with man's obligations to God. Thus natural law not only functioned as a final legal norm, but could also serve as the basis for secular moral philosophy.

In the first instance, natural law spread in Protestant countries, where it also acquired great significance in the field of political theory (Locke, Spinoza). Particularly via the writings of Pufendorf, it was to continue to expand in the eighteenth century, and ultimately led to the American Declaration of Independence (1776), which held that 'all men are created equal . . . endowed by their Creator with certain unalienable Rights', and the *déclaration des droits de l'homme et du citoyen* (1789).

In France, modern natural law did not acquire any degree of prominence until the first half of the eighteenth century. In the seventeenth century jurists and clergymen alike had rejected this newly emerging school of thought, the jurists because it was too 'philosophical' and the clergy because it was too 'Protestant'. Grotius and Pufendorf were not widely known until the publication of translations by Jean Barbeyrac. Barbeyrac, a Protestant scholar who had been driven from France after the repeal of the Edict of Nantes, worked in Germany, Switzerland and the Netherlands. His translations of Pufendorf, which he provided with his own extensive comments, were published in 1706 and 1707 and were followed in 1724 by a new translation of the major work of Grotius. There was no place for this school of thought at the French universities, but interest was all the more widespread outside them. In particular, Pufendorf's shorter work *Les devoirs de l'homme et du citoyen* was reprinted time after time and repeatedly paraphrased in the *Encyclopédie*.

Rousseau deliberately derived his mode of enquiry from the tradition of natural law. He repudiated the custom of referring to phenomena that were really 'social' as being 'natural'; he adhered to a different definition of what was natural, and went on to wonder which societal forms might be the least unnatural. The state of nature and the social contract he postulated were both characteristic of the rational constructions of natural law. In a theoretical sense, Montesquieu's work was less unequivocal than Rousseau's. In *De l'esprit des lois* he went to a great deal of trouble to scrutinize factual patterns, and many readers consequently hailed his study as one of the first examples of social scientific investigation. This view has been refuted in more recent interpretations. Mark Waddicor demonstrated that Montesquieu had not in any way broken with the tradition of natural law.[6] Montesquieu analysed law in the light of immutable natural laws as well as of specific circumstances. He acknowledged the existence of 'natural laws' and used them in numerous passages to evaluate existing legal forms. In that sense, he subscribed to the notion that positive law ought not to deviate from natural law. Unlike a university legal scholar such as Pufendorf, however, Montesquieu did not concentrate on the system of natural law but on the relation between natural and positive law. To penetrate the multiformity of positive law, it was not enough simply to compare it with natural law. One had to be familiar with the background and 'spirit' of positive law if one was to comprehend the 'letter' of the law. This was important mainly in the event of contradictions between, for example, common law and civil law. The French legal tradition had long been familiar with analyses of the 'spirit' of laws.[7] From a theoretical point of view, the work of Montesquieu was still within the tradition of natural law, be it that he focused on one component of this tradition, the relation between natural law and positive law, which had hitherto been largely overlooked.

Montesquieu's analyses of certain legal forms might perhaps be called 'empirical', but the theoretical framework within which he was working did not have much to do with science in the modern sense of the word. Strictly speaking, natural law and natural science were exact opposites. Representatives of each of these orientations did speak of 'natural laws', but in the one case they were referring to empirically testable regularities and in the other to normative rules based upon a priori reasoning as to the nature of man or society.[8] Utilizing the first type of law reality could be described and explained, and with the second reality could be evaluated. In natural science laws were tested against reality, in natural law reality was either tested against laws or served to illustrate them.

In the seventeenth and eighteenth centuries secular thinking was dominated by the search for 'natural principles' and 'natural laws'. The fact that a 'natural law' could mean very different things and could even refer to diametrically opposed theoretical procedures was not to become clear until later. It was characteristic of the thinking of the *philosophes* that they never systematically discussed this opposition. It was perhaps d'Alembert who approached it most closely when he drew a comparison between the natural sciences and literature. 'In the natural sciences and in literature', he wrote, 'the philosophical spirit has had opposite effects. In the natural sciences, it fixed strict borders to the mania of wanting to explain everything, which the drive toward systematism had introduced; in literature it began to analyse our pleasures and to examine everything that our taste addresses.'[9] In respect of the 'wise reticence' of the modern scholar, there was the 'outspoken candour' of the author, who even wished to subject personal pleasures to analysis. This passage was not followed by further elaboration upon these comments, but merely by a defence of the 'philosophical spirit'. The line of reasoning d'Alembert then proceeded to follow was typical of the analytical rationalism of the *philosophes*. Like other natural capacities, taste was based upon certain principles; one could come to know these principles, and the knowledge of them, he assured his reading audience, was a sturdy underpinning for *le bon goût*.

After the publication of Montesquieu and Rousseau there was a certain expansion and radicalization in how people thought about social relations, though there was not yet any clear tendency towards scientization. This radicalization and 'politicization' of social theory coincided with the formation of what Darnton called a 'literary underworld'.[10] From the early 1760s there was a far sharper rise in the number of writers than in the amount of available positions. More and more authors were excluded from the established circuits and regular professional careers. They constituted a sizeable intellectual proletariat, a 'literary underworld' that often looked up to the successful *philosophes* with a mixture of admiration and abhorrence. For many of them Rousseau, the *philosophe* who had severed his ties with the cultural establishment, became a key figure. It was mainly his work that was used in the lampoons and pamphlets that became increasingly conspicuous in the years just before the Revolution. A journalist by the name of Linguet was an early example of this tendency. His *Théorie des loix civiles, ou principes fondamentaux de la société* (1767) was published several years after Rousseau's *Du contrat social*. It contained an odd mixture of revolutionary and reactionary notions, culminating in a petition for a 'social monarchy'. Linguet and many of his companions in adversity developed into opponents of the intellectual as well as the social elite. They did not hesitate to make use of new ideas, but in their writings pessimistic and bitter comments were predominant.[11]

In more established circles, a rationalistic problematic continued to prevail; reasoning on the 'nature' of man and society retained a central function. The idea of 'natural' classifications that could be discerned by reason were at the core of the secularization of thinking. In the course of the eighteenth century this way of thinking was instituted in virtually every field. In a distinctly critical manner, the *philosophes* supported this mode of thinking as opposed to all the forms of intellectual activity that appealed to non-rational principles (religion, tradition, authority). They even went so far as to criticize certain social institutions that were not based upon 'reasonable' principles. Reason was their *idée-force*; however, to paraphrase Jean Ehrard, it was also an *idée-frein*.[12]

Despite their criticism of the *esprit de systéme* and despite their admiration for Locke and Newton, the *philosophes* continued to adhere to the primacy of rational constructions. In battling ecclesiastical and political authorities and in fostering an alliance between writers and scholars, reason was the most important weapon they had at their disposal. Reason was the foundation of the intellectual coalition around the *Encyclopédie*; in the form of natural law, it was also the buttress for their criticism of society. In an intellectual and social sense, the *philosophes* operated by the grace of what they called rational and reasonable; this held true to an equal extent of a moderate individual such as Voltaire and a more radical man such as Holbach. What there was no room for in this constellation was a critique or an examination of the limitations of reason. Efforts in this direction would have meant a weakening of the position of the *philosophes*. Abandoning the preference for rational constructions for more empirical procedures would have meant a loss of possibilities. The *philosophes* were not about to let go of their most important weapon and refused to give up the advantages reason allowed them to have. This resulted in a kind of delayed scientization. In addition to the more structural aspects referred to above, they thus had a strategic interest in holding on to a preponderantly rationalistic orientation.

Hume and Scottish moral philosophy

Viewed in this light, it is interesting to draw a brief comparison with the social theory being formulated at the time in Scotland. There the empirical procedures of the natural sciences had come to serve as a model at quite an early stage, especially since the criticism of Hume had undermined purely rational constructions.

Scotland had become a part of Great Britain in 1707.[13] Its parliament was disbanded and much of the high nobility left Edinburgh to settle in London. The low nobility, local merchants and professionals remained behind, but without any central institution comparable to a parliament. In the first few decades after the union there was a great deal of political insecurity and continuing economic hardship. It was under these circumstances that a new intellectual elite emerged with a considerable degree of independence from traditional institutions and customs. The members of this new cultural elite were quick to organize their own clubs and societies and soon lost interest in political and theological controversies. They were far more engrossed in the work of Locke, Newton and Berkeley and the moral philosophy of Shaftesbury, Mandeville and Hutcheson.

The young David Hume, born in 1711, was similarly fascinated by these authors. He shared many preferences with his teachers and peers, but none of them dared go quite as far as Hume. Based in part on the practice of the natural sciences, he developed a critique of all forms of knowledge that were not empirically but solely rationally founded. As the subtitle revealed, his *Treatise of Human Nature* (1739–40) was 'an attempt to introduce the experimental method of reasoning into moral subjects'. Such human institutions as law and the state did not come into being as the result of conscious agreements, as was assumed in natural law. Social and political contracts were 'fictions', imaginary constructions about the origin of the state and society that had little to do with reality. According to Hume, the social arrangements people formed were historically variable conventions. Legal rules and regulations were 'conventional' rather than 'natural', coming about as they had in processes of custom formation on the grounds of common interests.[14] Hume's more empirical approach also implied a stronger historical orientation. Human history, Hume wrote, was to moral philosophy what the experiment was to natural philosophy.[15] This is why his six-volume *History of England* (1754–62) was written as 'theoretical history'.

David Hume was not the first to view the experimental method as the only appropriate way to acquire knowledge. Some of Newton's followers had expressed opinions in much the same vein. What was so original about Hume, according to Duncan Forbes, was that he reasoned that searching for 'first or final causes' was incompatible with the experimental method. Far more strictly than his predecessors, Hume drew a distinction between statements about nature and statements about the 'origin' or 'purpose' of nature. He was criticizing not only the doctrine of natural religion, but also that of 'natural morality'. Hume wished to abandon the 'religious hypothesis' on the origin of the world and the moral imperatives derived from the 'natural systems' of law and morality. As he said himself, he just wanted to engage in 'moral anatomy'. He wanted to dissect human nature to gain a better understanding of human history, not to uncover obligations or commandments. In this sense, Hume's thinking was totally secular and empirical.[16]

Hume's *Treatise of Human Nature* was published eight years before *De l'esprit des lois* and more than twenty years before *Du contrat social*. 'Never did any literary work meet a sadder fate', Hume noted in an autobiographical fragment.[17] It was not until he presented his thoughts in the form of essays that his name came to gain fame. In France, Hume was known mainly as the author of a weighty history of England. *Le bon* David was a popular guest at various salons and in more literate circles he was acclaimed as the Tacitus of England, but no French translation of his *Treatise* was published until 1878. In Scotland the great David was a celebrity, but here again it was mainly as a historian. Hume did not hold a university position and lived largely from the revenues accrued via his writings. In more informal networks he did, however, play a prominent role and it was thus that he was to serve as an example for such authors as Adam Ferguson, John Millar and Adam Smith.

Together with a coterie of young men, Hume founded the Select Society in 1754.[18] Within the ranks of this successful society the initiative was taken to found the *Edinburgh Review*, to institute prizes and to set up the Edinburgh Society for the Encouragement of Arts, Sciences, Manufactures and Agriculture. All these efforts played an integral role in the heyday of the Scottish Enlightenment from 1750 to 1780. One of the young men whose help was so instrumental to Hume during this period was Adam Smith. This young professor in moral philosophy exhibited attitudes comparable with those of his friend and mentor Hume. Smith also praised 'Newton's method' as the most effective one for the moral sciences, and in the lectures he gave before the publication of *The Wealth of Nations* (1776) he tried to apply this orientation to various fields.[19]

Recent studies have shown that, to a large extent, the experimental approach was formulated in the language of more traditional conceptions. Hume's work did not signify a total rejection of natural law. According to Duncan Forbes, what Hume sought was a new foundation for natural law. This also appears to have held true of Adam Smith.[20] From a comparative perspective, it is nonetheless undeniable that the method of the Scots was more empirical than that of the *philosophes*. The natural sciences were taken as a model earlier in Scotland than in France and generally in a more systematic manner.

Smith on the intellectual situation in Europe

An article in the newly founded *Edinburgh Review* gave a good impression of the Scottish orientation: in 1756 Adam Smith surveyed the intellectual situation in Europe and his analysis emphasized the predominant position of the French and the Scots. He noted a number of important differences and, based in part on these differences, there was the clear implication that an extremely important role was awaiting the Scottish intellectuals of his generation. Smith's article read like a market research survey. He stepped back for an overall view, evaluated the chances and specified the choices he felt ought to be made. In this sense, Scottish moral philosophy developed in explicit competition with the French.

First and foremost, Smith emphasized how important it was for the Scots to familiarize themselves with what was happening on the Continent.[21] Articles in the new journal ought not confine themselves to English and Scottish literature, and it was of particular importance to follow the developments in France. Italy and Spain had lost their once so prominent position in art and science. German scholars were accustomed to writing in a different language, and consequently rarely succeeded in expressing themselves in a manner that was 'precise' and 'fortuitous'. It was only in sciences where 'taste' and 'wit' were not required and where common sense, diligence and perseverance sufficed that Germans were able to make important contributions. Essentially it was only the English and the French, according to Smith, who could attract the attention of literate audiences beyond the borders of their own countries. These two nations, rivals in trade, science, politics and warfare, both exhibited a wide range of merits. Imagination, wit and ingenuity were the talents of the English. Taste, judgement, propriety and order were the virtues of the French. French literature lacked perhaps the awesome imagination of Milton or Shakespeare, but it excelled in elegant and finely balanced compositions. Nowhere was there any aversion to French literature, as it rarely failed to be pleasant and entertaining.

In the natural sciences, virtually all the discoveries that did not come from Italy or Germany were made in England. The French contributions were negligible. Cartesian philosophy had been ingenious and 'deceptive' alike, and had disappeared altogether with the triumph of Newton. The superiority of English philosophy was acknowledged in the 'new French encyclopedia'. With barely concealed pride, Smith noted 'as a Briton' that the ideas of Bacon, Boyle and Newton were lucidly explained and praised in the *Encyclopédie*. He found it flattering, but at the same time he was somewhat upset by the possibility that people in other countries or in the future would come into contact with the ideas of the English via the writings of the French. Smith commented in this vein not only on the first volumes of the *Encyclopédie* but also on Buffon's *Histoire naturelle*. No science was practised in France with greater verve than natural history, which Smith felt was linked to the French yearning for 'perspicuous description' and 'just arrangement'. It was true that Buffon's philosophy was 'completely hypothetical' and confused here and there, but his pleasant eloquence amply counterbalanced these shortcomings.

Except for the Cartesian tradition, French moral philosophy could not boast of much original work. In Britain Hobbes, Locke, Mandeville, Shaftesbury, Butler and Hutcheson had nurtured the ascent of this field, but the English seemed to have since lost all interest in it. It was precisely this line of thinking in which the French were now increasingly interested. As an example Smith concluded with a lengthy account of Rousseau's *Discours sur l'origine et les fondements de l'inégalité*, which had been published a year earlier. In the first part of his discourse Rousseau described man in his natural state, and in the second part he turned to the emergence and development of societies.

Oddly enough, Smith did not even allude to the whys and wherefores of Rousseau's methodology. Rousseau wanted to demonstrate, as he himself observed, that inequality was not a 'natural' but a 'social' phenomenon, and in a certain sense consequently an 'unnatural' one. In order to make this clear he depicted the natural state and then went on to describe how private property and the division of labour alienated people and estranged them from themselves, made them more and more dependent on others and drove them to be increasingly influenced by other people's opinions. In their desire to achieve esteem and a good reputation, all they were interested in was the judgement of others, and life itself became a vain and frivolous game. The situation that emerged in the end was one where 'honour' existed without 'virtue', 'reason without wisdom' and 'pleasure without happiness'.[22]

Rousseau concluded that this situation, which was legitimated by the existing legal system, was contrary to natural law. Inequality was contrary to what was by nature characteristic of man. Whether this natural state had ever actually existed was irrelevant. The 'facts' could be disregarded, for what mattered was not 'historical truths' but 'hypothetical lines of reasoning'. The purpose of these lines of reasoning was to enable man to comprehend the 'nature of things' and not to shed light on their 'true origins'.[23]

It is significant that Adam Smith failed to mention this theoretical framework. He confined himself to observing that Rousseau's discourse was 'rhetorical' and 'descriptive', and thus felt no further analysis was called for. Smith did not conceal his admiration for Rousseau's style, but was apparently far less impressed by his theoretical intentions. Smith and other Scottish authors had formulated theories of their own on the development of human society.[24] Adam Ferguson wrote *An Essay on the History of Civil Society* (1767) and John Millar published *The Origin of the Distinction of Ranks* (1779). But these writings were more historical than Montesquieu's major work and more empirical than Rousseau's studies. Smith's item on the continental developments read in fact like a recommendation to work in that particular direction. Smith pointed out that by then the superiority of the empirical direction had been acknowledged in the French *Encyclopédie*. There was also growing interest in French moral philosophy, a branch barely engaged in at all by the English. Since the French were still plagued by their literary and rationalistic traditions, or so Smith suggested, there seemed to be great opportunities for the Scots in the moral sciences. Smith's text was published in 1756, in other words at the start of a period of flourishing intellectual development unparalleled in Scottish history.

Similarities and differences

The rise of modern social theory occurred mainly in Scotland and France. In these two countries the old cultural powers, the church and the university, had lost a considerable part of their intellectual authority, which meant there was now room for theories linked neither to the church nor to university traditions. Flexible and relatively autonomous clubs and societies played a prominent role in the exchange of information and ideas. In both cases moral philosophy remained the point of departure. In France political questions continued to be more or less taboo, and in Scotland, since it was no longer a state but a province, they had lost much of their direct relevance. For very different reasons there was a great deal of interest in each of the two countries in non-political phenomena, and there was a marked shift from politico-legal to economic and social theory. The central theme in this social theory was social differentiation. With the increased division of labour, relatively autonomous 'sectors' had come into existence. The all-embracing state and the small traditional communities had both made way for a differentiated body of interdependent units and groups; from then on, 'states' were to be viewed as 'societies'.

In all these senses there were similarities and parallels between the *philosophes* and the Scottish moral philosophers. The most significant difference pertained to their theoretical orientation. For the French, modern natural law was a more important model than the natural sciences. Natural law concurred with the rationalistic traditions and fulfilled vital cognitive and social functions for the *philosophes*. In that sense, developments in Scotland followed quite a different course. The Scottish moral philosophers joined to form a network that was less dependent on the court aristocracy, the universities already played a more important role, and after 1700 the natural sciences were granted a position of relative importance there. Via Hume the 'experimental method' became the guideline for much of the research in moral science. It also became a basis for the criticism of certain constructions that were common to natural law. In France there were few traces of any comparable development. The sciences were commended and praised, some authors described societies as 'machines' or reasoned like Newton in terms of 'powers', but these efforts were embedded in a predominantly rationalistic problematic and remained largely dependent on literary conventions.

Part II
From Social Theory to Social Science

Introduction

Legislators, philosophers, jurists, this is the moment of
social science.

Cambacérès

After Louis XVI ascended the throne in 1774, a change occurred in
the relation between social theory and the natural sciences. A number
of scientists became involved in policy-making and administration,
and they were the first to use natural science methods to analyse social
phenomena. The group consisted of younger members of the Académie
des sciences. Turgot had been appointed Minister and, to an unprecedented extent, scientists and technicians were now employed in the
modernization of state administration. Turgot was not to remain
Minister for long, but several of his plans were implemented and his
policies had inspired scientists to embark upon any number of new
projects. Existing scientific institutions were expanded and reorganized, new chairs were introduced, scientific associations were founded
and refounded, and this institutional expansion was accompanied by
new intellectual projects. The work of Laplace in mathematics and
astronomy and of Lavoisier in chemistry was closely linked to these
new opportunities. The same held true of Condorcet's programme for
the mathematization of the human sciences. As secretary of the
Académie des sciences, Condorcet was actively involved in the politics
of Turgot. It was in this context that he was confronted with the question of how natural science methods could be employed in the analysis
of societal questions. In the framework of scientific expansion and
political reform, Condorcet began his work on a mathematical social
theory. He was to present the first results in the years before the Revolution. This work was one of the earliest efforts to arrive at a systematic scientization of social theory.

In the years just after 1789, Condorcet continued working in this
direction and generalized his findings. After the Revolution scientization

had become a dominant trend, as was clearly illustrated by changes in vocabulary. In the circles around the Société de 1789, where Condorcet played a leading role, the term 'social science' was coined in the initial stage of the Revolution. It was presumably analogous to *art social*, a sort of social policy approach already propagated by the physiocrats. *Science sociale* was to be the proper theoretical basis for this *art social*, and it was the goal of the Société de 1789 to see to it that it was further developed. Although *science sociale* was initially still translated as 'moral science', the term 'social science' was introduced to the English language via the writings of Condorcet.[1]

For Condorcet, social science was a field where mathematics could be applied, and in 1793 he introduced the term 'social mathematics'. In an explanatory note he observed that he was referring to 'mathematics' because it was not only probability theory but also algebra and geometry that could be put to good use in the new science. For a similar reason he preferred the adjective 'social'. 'Moral' and 'political' were too 'restricted'.[2] What Condorcet had in mind was a comprehensive and 'separate' science that would be able to hold its own with mechanics.

After the Terror the new forms of social theory were usually referred to as *science sociale* or *science de l'homme*. Natural science models played an important role in these new sciences, but mathematics was not the sole component. As of 1795 physiology was to serve as its most prominent model. Cabanis examined the physiological foundations of the human sciences, Say redefined political economy as the 'physiology of society' and Saint-Simon alluded to the need to create a 'social physiology'. These various efforts at scientization constituted the main feature of French social theory after 1789.

Side by side with scientization, two other important changes in social thinking occurred in the period between the Revolution and the Restoration.

Firstly, social theory began to play a far more important role in a social as well as an intellectual sense. This increased significance was related to the Revolution, whose spokesmen used terms and modes of reasoning less than half a century old. Historians of ideas have linked them mainly to the work of Rousseau. The words *société* and *social*, both of which were widely used, were central to the new vocabulary. In numerous pamphlets and speeches a new state order was demanded in the name of 'society'. The authority of the monarch was disputed, and his function would not have any legitimacy unless he represented 'society' and actually subordinated himself to that role.[3] Attempts to define the notion of 'society' officially in this sense were not long in coming. In August 1789, just after the Declaration of the Rights of Man, there was a proposal to draw up a *déclaration des droits des sociétés*. Every society should have 'the common good' as its goal and should be set up in the way that would best serve the 'interests of all'.[4]

The new role of these terms and theories was institutionally established in 1795. In the Institut de France, which replaced the academies, a separate 'class' was set up for the social sciences. Alongside 'classes' for the natural sciences, literature and the arts, this was the first institutional recognition of the social sciences. Nothing can illustrate the increased significance of social theory better than the fact that, even for conservative thinkers, 'society' became a central category. In the work of de Bonald and de Maistre, 'society' began to serve as a new foundation for old doctrines. They could only defend the old institutions by making use of new arguments. In that sense, they owed more to their opponents than they cared to admit.

A second change that took place after 1789 was that social theory acquired more of a national emphasis. This was similarly related to the Revolution. The cosmopolitan ideals of the Enlightenment had been superseded by more 'national' sentiments. In the first stage of the Revolution the appeal to the 'nation' was still inspired mainly by criticism of absolutism. The 'nation' (or 'society', as the two terms were used interchangeably) constituted the true foundation of the state to which the monarch ought to be subjected. This notion did not remain confined to purely doctrinal disputes. In many fields initiative was taken with the aim of achieving national unity. Local diversity and the impenetrable system of privileges were replaced by national codifications. Under the auspices of the Académie des sciences, weights and measures were standardized, laws were codified by jurists, and plans were developed by politicians and intellectuals to reduce the role of dialects in favour of one 'national' language. These efforts to create and enforce national standards soon acquired a more traditional meaning. Now it was no longer just the 'nation' as opposed to the monarch and absolutism, but as opposed to other 'nations', as well. The noblemen who had fled France had betrayed the 'nation', and after the outbreak of the first coalition war in 1792, the Revolution became a 'national affair' in the new as well as the old meaning. *Patrie* was increasingly in evidence instead of 'nation' or 'society'.[5] For quite some time there was rivalry between France and virtually all the other powers of Europe, and in the new France, as well as the countries hostile to it, the unceasing warfare gave rise to a strong upsurge of 'nationalism'. The dedication of a French soldier by the name of Nicolas Chauvin still lives on in the term 'chauvinism'.

National borders also came to have more significance for intellectuals. Voltaire had pronounced England the great example of an enlightened nation. In intellectual circles this 'wise' and 'generous' statement made such an impression that only Voltaire's fame could 'console' Julie de Lespinasse for not having been born an Englishwoman.[6] The rampant Anglomania was born of the awareness that France had lost its predominant position in Europe, and only by learning from the English would the French be able to reconquer their former position. At the outbreak of the Revolution, once again a vanguard role seemed to be reserved for the French, and this new mood did not fail to affect the sciences. French chemists proclaimed Lavoisier the 'founder of modern chemistry'. According to this line of thinking Lavoisier's contribution was not restricted to his efforts in the new chemistry of oxygen or his work on a new nomenclature; he was indeed the founder of all of modern chemistry. Priestly, Scheele, Cavendish and others may have made significant contributions, but none of them could compare with the Frenchman. For much the same reason that Lavoisier was acclaimed in France, he was eyed with suspicion in Germany and England. 'French chemistry', as it was called by friend and foe alike, remained controversial for many years to come. Much later, after the defeat by the Prussians in 1870, the controversy flared up again, as it did once more in 1916, during the next war, when Pierre Duhem resumed the leitmotif with his *La chimie est-elle une science francaise?*[7]

The tendency towards nationalization was similarly evident in the social sciences. Here too parallels were drawn between political and scientific achievements. According to Saint-Simon, political revolutions were followed by scientific ones. He 'sensed' beforehand that there would be a 'great scientific revolution' and that this time the leading role would be played by France.[8] Destutt de Tracy expressed a similar expectation. In his *Elements d'idéologie* he wrote that, as soon as people were able to unite a sizeable quantity of scientific knowledge with 'complete freedom', a new era would commence. 'This era is truly the age of the French.'[9] Comparable sentiments could be found in the work of other authors, and later in Auguste Comte's writings. In all these comments the notion was discernible that the new social theory corresponded to new social relations and that the authors regarded their work as a step in this direction.

All three of these changes – the scientization of social theory, the heightened esteem of these theories and the trend towards nationalization – were linked to the upheaval of the Revolution. In order to examine this development more closely, I shall first touch briefly upon the years from 1775 to 1814 and the course of the Revolution. I shall then proceed to the repercussions of the Revolution for various groups of intellectuals. In the new intellectual regime the natural sciences gained a dominant position. Changes in the intellectual hierarchy were the key to many of the cultural transformations in this period. The intellectual supremacy of the natural sciences had three effects, and I have devoted a section to each of these.

Firstly, there was a more marked differentiation within the natural sciences themselves. In many branches of science there were new institutions, societies and journals, many of which were more or less independent of the Academy. This expansion and rise in status promoted not only the development of classical mechanics, but also that of other types of science in addition to the mathematical-mechanical disciplines. It was no coincidence that important breakthroughs in modern chemistry, medicine and biology all occurred during this period, and that the French made such crucial contributions. Since this process of scientific differentiation was later also of decisive importance for Comte, a separate chapter has been devoted to it.

Secondly, this development led to efforts to introduce natural science methods in other intellectual provinces. The social sciences were the clearest example. Condorcet was the first representative of this trend, which was to become dominant during the Revolution. The revolutionary circumstances stimulated scientists to view social sciences as a relevant field, and their growing power enabled them to redefine this new area as part of their empire. This is the most important explanation of the scientization processes that came to the fore so markedly in this period.

Thirdly, the expansion and prestige of the natural sciences gave rise to a striking reaction on the part of the literary intelligentsia. There was a widespread feeling among writers of being *déclassé*: the Revolution had deprived them of royal pensions and aristocratic patrons and helped bring the scientists to power. In their aversion to the new situation many of them were convinced it could all be blamed on what the *encyclopédistes* had started. Thus an anti-rationalistic and anti-scientific reaction emerged, even among writers whose sympathies had been with the *philosophes* before the Revolution. This reaction had a conservative and religious undertone, though it did also lead to the exploration of new stylistic devices. Utilizing earlier examples as well as foreign ones, these writers severed their ties with classicist traditions, and this was to be the start of French Romanticism. The rejection of the classicist tradition also meant the final rift between 'science' and 'literature'. In the eighteenth century writers and scientists had still been on the same side. They were members of societies and academies, and were both competing with the clergy for intellectual authority. Once the intellectual power of the church had crumbled, secular circles soon divided into competing groups and there was a definitive split between writers and scientists. Since then, antagonism between science and literature has remained a recurrent theme. De Bonald and de Maistre were closely linked to the literary opposition. They were the most important spokesmen of anti-scientific social theory, another product of this period.

6

Reform, Revolution and the Napoleonic Era

After Louis XVI succeeded to the throne in 1774, efforts were made to implement reforms. The major efforts, however, were to no avail. What the conflict came down to in the end was the question of who was to foot the bill for the financial crisis. The state debt was higher than ever, and in 1788 half the total national income went to redeem debts.[1] The nation needed a complete financial reconstruction, but the proposed tax reforms kept meeting with opposition, first from the *Assemblée des notables*, then from the *Parlement* of Paris. The *Parlement* would not approve tax measures without first convening the States-General, which had not met since 1614. None of the ruling groups was in a position to settle the crisis in their favour, a compromise was unfeasible, and in August 1788 the decision was finally made to convene the States-General.

The political crisis coincided with an economic recession. The harvest had been extremely poor in 1788, the winter of 1789 was harsh and the 1789 crops were mediocre. Sharp price rises were the result. These were the circumstances under which the elections for the States-General were held. Large numbers of political clubs and associations openly came to the fore for the first time. In May 1789 the States-General was opened in Versailles with all the pomp and circumstance of a state ceremony. Representatives of the Third Estate immediately took the offensive and demanded a different voting procedure. A month later, when it turned out that not the slightest advance had been made, they proclaimed themselves the National Assembly and swore not to adjourn before a constitution had been drawn up. The statement they issued noted that the Third Estate represented almost the 'entire nation'; its members were thus entitled to view themselves as the legitimate representatives of the 'general will' of the 'nation'. As opposed to an absolute monarchy based on the *droit divin*, there was now a National Assembly demanding to be recognized as the sole representative body of the 'nation'. The king tried in vain to break the spirit, but representatives of the clergy and nobility joined forces with the National Assembly. The king now had little choice but to recognize it and agree to have a constitution drawn up.

At approximately the same time revolts broke out all over France, and in Paris the Bastille was stormed. The notorious prison was almost empty, but it was clear the National Assembly was no longer the only place from which reforms would be coming. Pressured by the revolts, the National Assembly abolished the privileges of the Estates. A few weeks later, in anticipation of the constitution, the Declaration of the Rights of Man, the 'credo of a new era' (Michelet) was proclaimed.

In the succeeding years reforms were carried out which changed the entire face of the nation. Church property was confiscated, the separation of powers was furthered and an administrative reorganization divided the country into eighty-three more or less equal units (*départements*). In 1791 the king swore the oath that put the constitution into effect. France had become a constitutional monarchy headed by an elected body of representatives of the people. The fact that more than half the people in this legislative assembly were lawyers was characteristic of the new political dynamics. From then on, political battles were to be fought among 'parties' and political clubs, and no longer among representatives of Estates and occupational corporations. The ability to serve as a spokesmen for others was now of vital importance, and political eloquence had become a formidable weapon.

All the parties involved were soon confronted with the problem of growing opposition. There were counter-revolutionary rebellions throughout the country, and across the borders a coalition army had been formed, on which France was to declare war in 1792. The outbreak of warfare led to a further polarization of internal relations; people were suspicious of opposition, and anyone who expressed criticism of certain measures was viewed as betraying the Revolution. The king, who had tried to flee the country, was now imprisoned; the National Assembly was disbanded and elections were announced. In the newly elected National Convention, republicans were in the majority; they pronounced the end of the monarchy and proclaimed the republic. The Revolution had entered a new stage. The introduction of the republican era, with 1789 as year 1, was indicative of the enormous changes.

The National Convention (1792–4) was dominated by growing conflicts between the more moderate Girondins and the radical Montagnards. It was upon the proposal of Robespierre that Louis XVI was sentenced to death for high treason and beheaded. Great Britain, the Netherlands and Spain now became involved in the war, and under the pressure of international encirclement, royalist rebels and a number of military setbacks emergency measures were enforced. The *Comité du salut publique* was given an absolute mandate and began to set up revolutionary committees. Political commissioners supervised local governments. They purged regular governmental bodies of 'suspicious' individuals, closed churches, collected revolutionary taxes and issued certificates of 'civisme'. With the introduction of the draft, national troops were transformed into a people's army. In the course of these developments the Girondins were also deposed, as it were, and the Terror broke out. Violence was directed not only against individuals, 'enemies' and 'traitors', but also against institutions and certain customs. For a while it looked as if the whole world could be reshaped. Forms of address were changed, and everyone had to say *tu* and *toi*. Streets and cities were given new names, people solemnly shed the names with which they had been baptized, churches were turned into assembly halls or stables, and in addition to the republican era there was now also a new calendar with ten days to the week and new names for the months. Everything reminiscent of the Catholic and feudal past was eradicated. With new names for time and place, the world looked very different indeed.[2]

Two years later, in the summer of 1794, the Terror came to an end. Robespierre met his downfall and moderate republicans took power. Revolutionary tribunals were dismantled and the score was settled with what Grégoire called 'vandalism': 'j'ai créé le mot pour tuer la chose', he said. For several years to come efforts were made to safeguard the achievements of the Revolution. The new electoral system favoured the wealthier bourgeoisie and the former nobility in so far as they had no immediate relatives who had fled the country. Some areas were now stable to a certain extent. A national education system was set up, for example, which was to replace the *collèges* and universities that had been closed down in 1793.

Since internal opposition continued from the right as well as the left and the war was not over, the very survival of the republic depended largely on the military leadership. This was one of the factors that enabled Napoleon to rise to power. Napoleon was a young, successful general who had joined the Revolution at an early stage.[3] He had contact with leading politicians and intellectuals in the capital, and on the eighteenth of Brumaire in the year VIII (9 of November 1799) he ventured a *coup d'état*. Under the guise of thwarting a Jacobin plot, the Directory (1796–9) was abolished.

The Consulate (1799–1804) was presented as a moderate system of government led by three Consuls that would provide stability and put an end to the unrest. Power shifted to the executive bodies, extensive centralization was implemented and, in an effort to make the policies 'legitimate', plebiscites were held. Each department was now under the leadership of a prefect directly appointed by Napoleon and accountable solely to the Minister of Foreign Affairs. The revolutionary laws were codified in the *Code Civil* (1804). Equality before the law, private property and personal freedom were formally guaranteed, but the freedom of opinion was curtailed and a separate ministry was set up for police affairs. In much the same spirit of order and discipline, steps were taken towards a reconciliation with the church, as was later officially confirmed by the Concordat of 1801. In 1804 Napoleon felt the moment had come to depose his two fellow Consuls. In the course of the Napoleonic era, the process of militarization advanced further and further. Censorship became stricter and a social elite came to the fore that increasingly reverted to the old signs of distinction. In 1807 the aristocratic ranks and titles were reintroduced. The core of the new aristocracy consisted of high state functionaries, mainly military men (59 per cent) and officials (22 per cent). The world of trade and industry was barely represented in the new aristocracy (0.5 per cent). Since more than 20 per cent of these new noblemen were from the old aristocracy, old aristocratic families were far better represented than the 'modern' economic elite.[4] In the rural regions the continuity of the *Ancien Régime* was probably stronger. In a *département* such as the Var, which was far from tranquil, more than 85 per cent of the richest residents had also belonged to this category before the Revolution.[5] Many of the aristocratic families had retreated to the provinces during the Revolution. With new names or at the homes of friends or relatives, they waited for times to change, and this was how many of them managed to survive.

In the end, the sixth coalition war led to the defeat of the *Grande armée* and thus to the fall of Napoleon. The Empire crumbled and Napoleon's fate was sealed at Waterloo in 1815.

7

Intellectual Transformations around 1800

For the country's cultural and intellectual life, the Revolution meant a succession of radical changes. Some were to be more or less permanent; others were of a temporary nature. The most general effect was that the monopolistic organizational structure of the guilds and occupational corporations was shattered. The academies retained a dominant role but lost their monopolistic position once and for all. From then on other institutions existed as well – at any rate, there was the right to found other institutions. There were greater possibilities for a more differentiated cultural production, the significance of the market increased vis-à-vis the patronage system[1] and numerous new organizations emerged. Royal collections were put on display at national institutes, and, together with items confiscated from the church and émigrés, they provided ample material for the Bibliothèque nationale founded in 1793 and the first French museums, the Louvre and the Muséum d'histoire naturelle. In the succeeding years these 'national' collections were enhanced by numerous valuable objects seized as loot during the wars.

Cultural goods, changes in supply and demand

The abolition of censorship and the demise of the system of occupational privileges and monopolies led initially to an enormous growth in the cultural supply. Detailed regulations and precepts were replaced by unprecedented freedom. Developments in the field of art are a good example of the new opportunities and the problems they entailed.

Before the Revolution the art world was dominated by the Academy. State commissions were reserved for its members, as was participation at the only officially permitted exhibition, the *salon*, and it provided the only recognized art training. Internal relations were strictly hierarchic and the artist's rank was carefully stated at exhibitions. In 1789 young Academy members such as David and Restout ventured to criticize the rigidity of the institution. Their critical words appealed to artists outside the Academy, and in 1791 a petition was submitted to the National Assembly for a revision of the regulations. The Assembly agreed to a number of reforms, and starting in 1791 no artists were to be barred from the *salon*, regardless of whether or not they were members of the Academy. The number of participants rose from 53 in 1789 to 172 in 1791, including 128 who were not Academy members. By 1793 the number of exhibiting artists had risen to 258. This spectacular growth was followed by a decrease in 1795 and 1796 to 182 and 189 respectively.[2] The same pattern was evident in the theatre world, where the number of theatres in Paris rose from ten in 1789 to thirty-five in 1793. This too was followed by a decrease in subsequent years and there were only twenty theatres left in 1797. Actors, musicians and theatre directors joined forces to contest the position of such official institutions as the Théâtre française and the Opéra, which had sole rights to the classical repertoire and the most distinguished genres.[3]

The biggest problem of the new situation was that the growing supply was not accompanied by a similar rise in demand. In art there was even a decrease in demand. Commissions from the royal family, the court nobility and the church were no longer forthcoming, but without their role having been taken over by new groups. The result was a sharp fall in prices, and by 1791 complaints about financial distress were ubiquitous. Exhibitions were held by such organizations as the Société des arts, founded by artists and art lovers in 1790, in an effort to reach a new audience. In 1800 David charged an entrance fee when he put one of his paintings on exhibit, after which he bestowed it upon the nation as a gift. But since private initiative of this kind could not really do all that much to solve the problem, at an early stage an appeal was made to the state. Theatres submitted requests for subsidies, and painters and sculptors demanded commissions. The revolutionary governments were quick to respond which led in turn to revolutionary and patriotic themes figuring quite prominently in the new art. The newly acquired freedom was paid for in the arts by a greater dependence on current event themes and on the new regime. This was to remain the case throughout the Napoleonic era. Napoleon liked to see 'national subjects' depicted. The painters who were awarded prizes and other distinctions in the days of the Empire were largely those who looked to contemporary history for their inspiration. The fact that this genre occupied such a prominent position was relatively new. David was the most renowned representative of the new direction.[4] The dependence on current events and politics was also evident in the vicissitudes of the Cercle social, founded in 1790 and one of the most active organizations for writers in the early years of the Revolution. The output of this circle consisted mainly of hastily written pamphlets to be read and discussed without further delay. Very few of them were reprinted or remembered.[5]

The battle over the academies

In the revolutionary debates about culture, two related themes were emphasized. The first involved the position and organization of cultural producers, and the second the social function of their work. The first theme was related to the criticism of privileges and inequality, and the second to the criticism of the lavishness and ostentation of aristocratic culture. As opposed to the privileged position of the cultural establishment, demands were made for equality and accessibility, and, in contrast to aristocratic culture, the importance of social usefulness was emphasized.

These themes came together in criticism of the academies, which were the symbol of the old cultural order. In itself, this criticism was nothing new. Even before 1789 the academies had been a target, mainly from exponents of the 'literary underworld'.[6] At the end of the eighteenth century there was a far sharper rise in the number of intellectuals than in the jobs available to them. In the decades before the Revolution an increasing number of publicists came to the fore who were excluded from the established circuits and traditional careers. If they had no paid employment or property, it was virtually impossible for them to make a living unless they were willing to do 'dirty work', such as writing pornographic stories and articles for the scandal sheets or spying for the police, as did Brissot, later leader of the Girondins. The mandarins viewed these writers as 'the scum of literature' (Voltaire), and it is no wonder that precisely this group of 'mercenary scribblers' should have expressed such radical criticism of the cultural establishment. Marat was a striking example. Like that of Brissot, his career as a writer and scientist had been a fiasco. Despite tenacious efforts, his work had never been given the recognition he sought. Voltaire wrote a scathing review of one of his early publications, and the Académie des sciences refused to attribute any significance to his 'discoveries'. This eliminated any chance he might have had of an academy membership, a pension or any other form of official support. But in 1789 his chance came to get revenge. He began a journal entitled *L'Ami du peuple*, and two years later he published *Les charlatans modernes, ou lettres sur le charlatanisme académique*.[7]

The criticism of the academies was not voiced solely by cultural outcasts, and the Revolution was not solely an act of revenge on the part of what Max Weber called a 'proletaroid intelligentsia'.[8] There was also criticism within the academies themselves. There had long been discontentment about the internal organization at the Académie des sciences as well as the art academy. Objections were repeatedly raised about court and state intervention in the appointment of new academy members.

The Revolution gave various groups an opportunity once again to express their wishes. A dividing line soon separated the conservative academy members from the more reform-minded ones. At the Académie des sciences, for example, the astronomer Cassini wanted to preserve the ties with the royal family, whereas Laplace was in favour of having the academy fall under the auspices of the National Assembly. Cassini, also referred to as Cassini IV, was the hereditary director of the Observatory in Paris. His great grandfather had been personally appointed to the post by Louis XIV and he had every reason to fear that, for him, innovations would not necessarily be improvements. And he was right. His pupils turned against him in 1793 and he was imprisoned during the Terror. In the late 1790s he refused to have any more to do with the new academic institutions. He had lost his position, his pupils and his home, and Laplace's celestial mechanics rendered his work obsolete. He admitted to a former colleague that he could hardly remember ever having been an astronomer. He devoted the rest of his life, in the countryside, to writing a family chronicle.[9]

Internal confrontations such as the one between Cassini and Laplace could easily be reinforced by the pamphlets of Marat and others expressing far more radical criticism. In 1790 the question of the academies was discussed for the first time at the National Assembly. Reorganization plans were discussed for three years, up until the decision was made in 1793 to abolish 'all the academies and official literary societies'. Despite this radical solution, a distinction was drawn by many revolutionaries between the Académie des sciences and the other academies. The Académie française had been not only the most distinguished but also the most obsequious of the academies. For example, there had been a place there for neither Rousseau nor Diderot. The Académie des sciences however, had a long tradition of doing useful advisory work and devoting attention to applications of scientific knowledge. Louis-Sébastien Mercier thus distinguished between 'frivolous' and 'useful' institutions. Frivolous institutions such as the Académie française and the Académie des inscriptions would die out of their own accord, as it were, and only a useful institution such as the Académie des sciences was deserving of respect.[10] This was why, in 1793, Assemblyman Grégoire proposed abolishing all the academies except the Académie des sciences. At the time, however, the aversion to privileges and the privileged was so great that this last part of his proposal was not approved.

The status of the natural sciences rose even higher during the revolutionary wars. Scientists played an important role in the war efforts, which were led by Lazare Carnot. Carnot was a mathematician and a military engineer. Owing to his bourgeois background he had not been able to rise any higher in the army and had concentrated on activities of a more scientific nature. Another scientist, the mathematician Monge, was Naval Minister (1792–3), and the production of arms and munitions was led by a group of younger chemists and physicists. Scientists developed production techniques, wrote manuals and gave instructions and lessons at the numerous new workshops and factories that were opened.[11] Chaptal, similarly an extremely active scientist, had been a chemist and a small entrepreneur before the Revolution. In 1794 he was responsible for the production of gunpowder. In 1795 he was elected to the Institut de France and under Napoleon he was to ascend to the position of Minister (1800–04). The employment of scientists in warfare to this extent was unprecedented. And, in a technical sense, it was a great success. Immediately after the Terror the chemist Fourcroy, one of the most active scientists, wrote a number of reports attributing a decisive role in the successful defence of the republic to scientists. Perhaps not everyone was convinced of this, but according to Biot the scientists' contribution to the war effort had been of overriding importance for the 'unparallelled fame' of the natural sciences. There was no longer any doubt as to the usefulness of scientific work, and scientists now gloried in 'infinite esteem'.[12] Their fame also enabled them to embark upon political careers. For the first time scientists were to rise to high political office.

Discrediting 'belles lettres'

As far as literature was concerned, matters were quite different. The literary culture of the *Ancien régime* was disparaged and belittled to a far greater extent than the natural sciences. Chamfort, himself a member of the Académie française, painted a scathing portrait of the literary academies in *Des académies* (1791). The great authors who had belonged to them, or so Chamfort held, were already great when they were elected, and in many cases their literary merits had diminished rather than flourished after their election. The dictionary compiled by the academy was viewed extremely critically by writers themselves, and for the rest the illustrious membership was characterized solely by expressions of mutual admiration and an obsequious attitude to the authorities.

The fate of the salons that had served as informal literary societies was not much brighter. Many of them ceased to exist or moved with noblemen who fled the country. For writers, the disappearance of old institutions and privileges was barely counterbalanced by new opportunities, at least not in the usual literary genres. There were numerous possibilities for journalism, pamphleteering and the art of rhetoric, and a veritable heyday for patriotic verses and related forms of revolutionary devotion, but, measured by traditional standards, it was all little more than literary propaganda. Traditional literature was now suspected of representing a frivolous and aristocratic pastime. Not only had it been produced by a privileged group, it was incapable of serving the social functions that had endowed the natural sciences with such high esteem. The problem with literature, Madame de Staël observed, was that it had not been 'useful'.[13] In her defence of literature she was consequently one of the first to emphasize that it was a social phenomenon. Just as Montesquieu had demonstrated that political regimes were dependent on a physical and moral substructure, Madame de Staël reasoned that the same held true for literature. De Bonald also noted that revolutionary criticism of *belles lettres* completely overlooked the fact that literature was the 'expression of the society' in which it was written.[14] Madame de Staël and de Bonald tried to compensate for literature's loss of function by means of 'sociological' argument. In either case, their reasoning was intended as a social rehabilitation of literature and as a form of resistance to the notion that only the natural sciences were useful to society.

It was not only literature but also men and women of letters that were discredited, and even the most prestigious among them, the *philosophes*, were depreciated. The celebrities of the Enlightenment were increasingly mocked and criticized. This criticism was initially formulated by counter-revolutionaries such as Burke or Barruel. But as soon as some of the writers who had been affiliated with the *philosophes* publicly dissociated themselves from the Revolution, criticism was unleashed in revolutionary circles as well. In a widely publicized letter to the National Assembly in 1791, Raynal voiced his opposition to revolutionary changes, and others were quick to follow suit. The more conservative successors to the *philosophes* (Marmontel, Morellet, Suard) would have been satisfied with a few small-scale reforms, and were aghast at the actual course of the Revolution. Others, however, such as Condorcet and Chamfort, reacted enthusiastically and took part in various revolutionary activities, though both of them were surprised by the Terror, which neither was to survive. The radical stage of the Revolution was not supported by any of the successors to the *philosophes*, and in 1794 Robespierre described them as a 'sect of ambitious charlatans'. The people had seen through their 'egotistical doctrines' and cowardly salon morals, and the Revolution had gone through without them. In Robespierre's view this criticism held true of 'men of letters in general', all of whom had remained passive, fled the country or turned against the Revolution.[15] Rousseau was the only exception. For the Montagnards, he served as idol and alibi alike.

In the Napoleonic era aversion to the Enlightenment came to be far more systematic. Among dignitaries there was a re-evaluation of religious faith and the church, among writers there was an anti-scientific revolt, and for both these groups the Enlightenment increasingly represented a reprehensible past.[16]

The altered reputation of the *philosophes* was the result of much more than a changing intellectual mood. The Revolution had brought about a structural change in intellectual relations. Whereas the natural sciences were viewed as the most useful disciplines, literature was associated with aristocratic salons and frivolous gatherings with no applicability of any importance. The status rise of the natural sciences coincided with a virtually proportionate loss in the prestige of 'belles lettres'. The result was a rather sudden transformation of the intellectual hierarchy. In the institutional reforms, the new order of ranking was clearly discernible.

A new education and research system

In the years from 1791 to 1794 various proposals were submitted to the National Assembly and the Convention for the revision of the education system. After the fall of Robespierre various elements of these plans were combined and the first steps were taken towards a new education system. The most influential plan was the one submitted by Condorcet. In a report of 1792 he propagated an education system based upon a predominantly scientific and technical syllabus. Latin was to lose its privileged position ('there is no truly important work that has not been translated'), and he viewed the traditional literary curriculum as being too restricted and of use only to a small group of people. Without a certain extent of talent, the emphasis on literature led merely to 'envy' and 'ridiculous pride'. The sciences provided a much better training. They were within the reach of far more people, they were more useful and the results were more certain.[17]

On the highest level, the important thing was to find an alternative for the academies, which was why the Institut de France was founded in 1795. In a ranking order antithetical to the pre-revolutionary one, it was divided into three classes. In keeping with Condorcet's proposal the first class was reserved for the 'mathematical and physical sciences' and the third and last class was for 'literature and the fine arts'. The second class covered the new field of 'moral and political sciences'. The literary department had not only suffered the greatest loss in esteem, in comparision with the days of the *Ancien Régime* it also exhibited the largest extent of discontinuity. A majority of the sixty scientists of the first class had already been members of the Académie des sciences, whereas only two members of the literary department had belonged to the Académie française.[18]

Much the same picture was presented by the educational reforms. A new public education system replaced the universities and *collèges*, which had been directly or indirectly affiliated with the church. The new institutions for higher education were vocationally oriented state schools modelled after such institutions as the Ecole des ponts et chaussées (1755) and the Ecole des mines (1783). With the foundation of the Ecole polytechnique (1794) and the Ecole normale supérieure (1794), this type of school came to dominate French higher education. The Ecole polytechnique had a curriculum especially designed for civil and military engineers, but it was soon to become renowned as the place to go for the most modern scientific education in the world. The Ecole normale was a teacher's training college, and had a literary as well as a scientific department.

The syllabus at the *écoles centrales*, which replaced the *collèges*, was even more noteworthy. The plan for the curriculum had been drawn up by a group of republican politicians and intellectuals who were to rise to fame as the *idéologues*. In this new curriculum the natural sciences and their applications occupied a central position, the moral sciences were similarly instrumental (law, history) and, in addition to French, a number of practical subjects such as drawing were also taught.[19] Here again, usefulness and science were the key concepts.

Natural science in the Napoleonic era

Initially, relations between the natural sciences and literature underwent very few changes under Napoleon. In a certain sense Napoleon's rise to power even presented scientists with new opportunities. While training to be an officer, Napoleon himself had had a relatively extensive scientific education. He was interested in mathematics, history and geography, though not at all in languages, and had very little respect for either art or literature.[20] His military career in the artillery was based in part on his technical and mathematical know-how. During the Italian campaign (1797) Napoleon came into contact with Monge and Berthollet, who were assigned as 'scientific commissioners' to the army. Napoleon befriended Berthollet, which was one of the reasons why Napoleon was selected in 1797 for the first class of the Institut. The successful and popular general was known for his favourable opinion of the sciences.

After his election Napoleon made every effort to present himself as a patron of the sciences. He was accompanied on the Egyptian campaign (1798) by an impressive scientific committee. It consisted of 142 persons, most of whom were scientists and engineers, and included a few of the most renowned, such as Monge, Berthollet, Fourier and Geoffroy Saint-Hilaire. The group was assisted by pupils from the Ecole polytechnique. There were also several artists, though not in any way comparable in number with the scientists. There was a total of three painters, four draughtsmen, one sculptor, one engraver and four writers.[21] The Institut d'Egypte (1798) emerged in fact from this group of scientists. The institute was commissioned to study the history and the flora and fauna of the country and, if necessary, to submit recommendations to the French government. The work resulting from this expedition was to be the start of the field of Egyptology.

When Napoleon rose to power in 1799, he appointed many of the scientists who had accompanied him to Egypt to positions of importance. He expressed a great deal of sympathetic interest in other scientists as well, and the Institut de France was referred to as his favourite mistress of all. Scientists were appointed a Prefect (Fourier) and Minister (Laplace, Chaptal) and numerous members of the Senate were employed in the natural sciences. At the first count, six of the thirty-one Senators worked in the natural sciences, as did nine out of sixty at the second count.[22] For one of the highest political offices in the country, this was an unprecedentedly high proportion. Prizes and honours were also granted to scientists from abroad. In the course of time, however, the significance of the natural sciences did wane. Growing numbers of old and new dignitaries and fewer and fewer revolutionary politicians and scientists were elected to the highly lucrative and not very time-consuming position of Senator.[23] Another change in comparision with the revolutionary period was the foundation of the *lycées*, which were to replace the *écoles centrales* as of 1802. The curriculum was based largely upon what had been taught at the *collèges* before the Revolution. Latin was 'reinstated', the natural and moral sciences disappeared and only mathematics retained a position of importance.[24] In a number of cases the declining esteem of the natural sciences benefited the literary intelligentsia, but, for the Senate or other such state functions, scientists were not superseded by writers or other intellectuals but by military men, high officials and noblemen.

The reorganization of the Institut de France in 1803 was an indication of the changes taking place in the Napoleonic era. The most thorough change was the elimination of the separate class for social sciences. Its leading members were known for their anti-clerical and liberal views, which Napoleon felt were not in the interest of the state. The third class for literature and the fine arts was divided into three new classes. French literature, the subject matter of the old Académie française, was moved up to the second class at the Institut. The third class now corresponded to the old Académies des inscriptions and was devoted to historical and literary erudition, and the fourth and last class was reserved for the fine arts. At the time of the Empire there was a clear upgrading of literature at the expense of the social sciences, but the natural sciences retained their position as first class.

The intellectual supremacy of the natural sciences in the period from 1789 to 1815 was confirmed by the reports of foreign visitors. Foreign scientists were surprised at the prominent position occupied by the natural sciences, and many of them observed feverish activities and numerous new journals, societies and schools.[25] For laymen, the change was similarly unmistakable. Englishmen who visited France before the Revolution did so to improve their manners and widen their knowledge of art and literature. The Grand Tour was part of the upbringing of a true gentleman. Critics of the Grand Tour, such as Adam Smith, noted that, upon their return, young men were often even more unfit for serious studies or business than before their departure. In the eighteenth century English visitors frequently expressed their admiration of the theatre, literature, fashion, salons and good manners of the French. The intellectual level of their hosts made less of an impression, especially as regards the mastery of the classical languages. After the Revolution it became customary to come back with tales of outstanding scientific activities, often commenting that scientists seemed to have taken the place of writers.[26]

Restructuring the intellectual regime

Although no comparative research has been conducted into the development of various groups of intellectuals in this period, two conclusions are inevitable.

Firstly, there was every indication of a restructuring of the intellectual regime in favour of the natural sciences. The first signs of this process were evident in 1775, and the breakthrough came with the Revolution. Book production figures show that this was not confined to the small group of producers, but corresponded to changes in the taste of the reading audience. In 1785, purely scientific books accounted for approximately 12 per cent of production. This percentage rose to 15 per cent in 1798, 19 per cent in 1803 and around 20 per cent in the last years of the Empire. There was then a reduction at the time of the Restoration, and by 1816 the figure had dropped to 15 per cent.[27] The men of letters lost most after 1789 and benefited least from the new situation. For literature the break with the *Ancien Régime* was far more dramatic than for the natural sciences. This might go someway towards explaining why it was in the ranks of writers that such spectacular counter-revolutionary conversions took place (Raynal, La Harpe). In part it can also explain why intellectual opposition to the new regime seems to have come mainly from within the literary world (Chateaubriand, Madame de Staël). The representatives of the natural sciences benefited the most. Particularly after the Terror, their esteem was unprecedented. A small group of politically active scientists took advantage of this situation to found such institutions as the Ecole polytechnique, to attain a dominant position at the Institut de France and to rise for the first time to high positions in the state bureaucracy.

Secondly, the Revolution heralded the definitive secularization of intellectual life. One of the lasting effects of the revolutionary changes was that, from then on, education and research were primarily state matters. Neither the Concordat nor the *lycées* nor the establishment of the universities in 1808 could do much to change that. The predominant role of the church in education was a thing of the past. This meant that the struggle between secular and ecclesiastical doctrines lost much of its significance. The Revolution liberated secular culture, as it were, from the need to legitimate itself *vis-à-vis* theology and the church. Relations among various secular groups thus changed as well. Since the antagonism between ecclesiastical and secular groups diminished, competition intensified among secular intellectuals. Writers and scientists were no longer linked by their joint opposition to the church. The enlightened alliance crumbled: *philosophie* lost its function, the reputation of the *philosophes* dwindled, and the old contrasts (natural versus supernatural principles, reason versus faith) were overshadowed by new ones.

Thus the restructuring of intellectual relations led not only to an intellectual culture more or less dominated by the natural sciences, but in fact to a new kind of cultural schism.[28] After 1800 science and literature were no longer viewed as belonging to the same family. They ceased to be depicted as branches on the same trunk, as had been the case in the *Encyclopédie*, and for the first time they were seen as opposed and even antagonistic enterprises. There had been a certain degree of rivalry since the seventeenth century, when separate academies were founded for literature and the sciences. Pascal had drawn his distinction between the *esprit de finesse* and the *esprit de géométrie*, and in the eighteenth century the contrast between the two was a regular topic of discussion. But shared interests and reciprocal dependencies served to keep this rivalry in check. When this mutuality faded and men of letters felt *déclassé*, the rivalry burst into open hostility. With the decline of the intellectual power of the church, writers and scientists became entangled in a process Mannheim referred to as 'polarizing competition'.[29] Men of letters had the tendency to dissociate themselves from the new order and pursue totally new pathways. The result was the kind of division that manifested itself in 1808, when separate faculties were set up for letters and the natural sciences.

8

Natural Science and Revolution

Natural science flourishes

The flourishing of French natural science around 1800 was based on changes that had taken place in the last fifteen years of the *Ancien Régime*. The accession of Louis XVI to the throne in 1774 had heralded a new period. One reform followed another, the most important ones occurring when Turgot was Minister. In his short term in office this former *Encyclopédie* collaborator effectuated a whole series of measures to make more systematic use of scientific knowledge, and these measures led to numerous plans and projects in scientific circles. They initially involved mainly applications of scientific knowledge, a subject that now also featured in academy-organized contests.[1] But initiatives of this kind did not remain confined to the applied sciences.[2] In 1774 professorial chairs were established at the Collège de France for physics and chemistry, and the courses were soon reputed to be the best in the country. Courses at engineering schools were also quick to improve. As of 1775 the Ecole des ponts et chaussées was entitled to call itself Ecole royale, and the Ecole des mines was founded in 1783. The Société de médecine (1776) became the centre for a wide spectrum of new initiatives in the field of medicine. It was a learned society that conducted studies for the government on epidemics and such public health matters as the effectiveness of certain remedies and the quality of mineral water. Following the example of the Académie des sciences, the society admitted only a limited number of members. It functioned in fact as an academy of medicine, and competed with the conservative medical faculty. Under Lavoisier's supervision reforms were also introduced at the Académie des sciences. This led to the founding of a separate section for experimental physics, which had quite characteristically been hitherto non-existent. The work of Lavoisier himself was one of the most striking successes of French science in this period. And the fact that Lagrange moved from Berlin to Paris in 1787 illustrated the altered mood.

The two decades following these years of innovation were perhaps the most unique in the history of French science. In no other period did such far-reaching changes take place so rapidly, and in no other period did French scientists play a role of such international prominence. Existing scientific institutions were either abolished or thoroughly reformed and numerous new ones were founded. These innovations, facilitated by the new esteem of the natural sciences, improved the research and career opportunities markedly, thus making the natural sciences even more attractive. Specialists in the history of science have frequently noted that, around the year 1800, Paris was the centre of the scientific world. This held true for mathematics and physics, most probably for chemistry and the *sciences naturelles*, and certainly for the medical sciences. Comparative research has demonstrated that there were more 'top researchers' in France at the time than anywhere else and that they were more productive than their competitors in other countries.[3]

Three generations, three fields of enquiry

These scientific developments can best be described by generation and by field of enquiry. Generally speaking, there were three generations and three fields of enquiry. The first generation consisted of the 'older' scientists whose careers began before 1789.[4] They had had a classical education and, for lack of regular scientific training, their careers had often begun in a wide variety of ways. By 1789 they had an established position and were members of the Academy. For all of them, gaining the support of a prominent Academy member had been a decisive moment in their career, and in general their own Academy membership represented the most important position they held. The second generation consisted of scientists who did not yet have an established position in 1789. The large majority had a positive attitude towards the Revolution, from which they tried to benefit. The founding of various new institutions stimulated their careers, which were more rapid, more differentiated and less exclusively dependent on the Academy than those of their teachers. The scientists of the third generation, too young to take part in the Revolution, were educated at the new institutions and started their careers in the Napoleonic era.

These three generations were divided over three fields of enquiry. The mathematical sciences were dominant: mathematics, astronomy, mechanics and the rapidly developing field of physics. This vast research field differed from the others in that mathematical formalization played a decisive role and a certain level of quantification was required. The work of Lavoisier was in keeping with the ideal of an 'exact' science, which was a criterion in these disciplines for true knowledge. Lavoisier went to a great deal of trouble to conduct more exact measurements and worked together with Laplace for this purpose. His work was initially distrusted by chemists, although at the Academy he immediately gained the support of mathematicians.[5] The work of Berthollet, the leading French chemist after the death of Lavoisier, similarly exhibited this orientation. Thus, in a sense, the dominant forms of chemistry can be categorized as part of the mathematical and physical sciences. In the two other fields of enquiry mathematics did not play a role of any significance, which might explain why they were barely accepted as 'sciences' at all. Natural history consisted mainly of botany and zoology, as practised at the Jardin des plantes, which had gradually been expanded under its director Buffon. The third field of enquiry was the medical sciences. Taught at the university, they were not practised at a separate academy, nor were there extra-university research opportunities – at any rate not until 1776 – comparable with those at the Jardin des plantes.

Mathematization and the ideal of an exact science

At the end of the eighteenth century the notion was widespread among mathematicians that their field was at an impasse. Lagrange had repeatedly expressed the fear that mathematics was doomed to the same fate as Arabic: a professorial chair here and there, respected enough but without any real significance.[6] The mathematization of mechanics had been virtually completed, and opportunities for mathematical research thus seemed to have been exhausted. Against this background, three tendencies could be discerned among mathematicians: a current that was to lead to pure mathematics,[7] a school that focused on mathematizing new scientific fields, and forms of mathematics that were linked to new applications.[8] The two latter tendencies were by far the most important. The leading exponent of the mathematization of new scientific fields was Pierre Simon Laplace and the main spokesman of more application-oriented mathematics was Gaspard Monge. Both of them were about forty when the Revolution broke out, were ranked among the greatest mathematicians of their day, and fulfilled important positions and official functions after 1789, including that of Minister.

Monge's systematization of descriptive geometry was closely linked to the growing demand for more adequate descriptions of machines. He himself had taught at military academies, and the military and industrial potentialities of their geometry were to be an important reason for the success of his work. Monge played a decisive role in the founding of the Ecole polytechnique. The Ecole centrale des travaux publics, as it was initially called, was established in 1794 to provide a joint basic curriculum for all engineers. After a thorough 'polytechnical' syllabus, students would go on to specialize at an *école d'application* (military engineering, artillery, mining engineering, bridge and highway engineering). A *concours* was organized to decide which students would be admitted to the polytechnical school. Their social backgrounds were no longer taken into consideration, although good morals and republican sympathies were required. The teachers were among the leading scientists of the day; in addition to Monge, Fourcroy and Berthollet, the founders also included Lagrange and Laplace.

In the first years of the Ecole polytechnique Monge and Carnot's technological applications more or less dominated the syllabus. Slowly but surely, especially after Napoleon's coup in 1799, Laplace's influence grew and the practical and experimental components of the curriculum receded into the background. There was now more emphasis on courses in mathematics, and the mathematizing of physics as propagated by Laplace. In his *Exposition du système du monde* (1796) he explained that physical phenomena could be comprehended as the result of 'forces' that elementary particles exerted upon each other. Much as the discovery of gravity had made it possible to predict the movements of celestial bodies with one single law, it would now be possible, Laplace stated, to analyse such physical phenomena as electricity, heat, light, magnetism and chemical 'affinities' in the same way. This meant they would have to be quantified on the basis of precise measurements. The results would then have to be reduced to forces that attracted or repelled and could be represented by way of algebraic equations. This meant an enormous expansion of Newtonian mechanics, and Laplace's reputation as the Newton of his day soon spread beyond the borders of France. French work in physics and chemistry was soon dominated by Laplace's Newtonian conceptions and his mathematical style of working.[9] Via positions at the Institut de France, the Ecole polytechnique and the Bureau des longitudes (1795), and good relations with Napoleon, Laplace and the chemist Berthollet came to dominate the French natural sciences.

The special position of the circle around Laplace and Berthollet was clear at the *Société d'Arcueil*, a private society that functioned for a number of years as a kind of semi-official centre for research in physics.[10] It consisted of a small group of followers and students of Laplace and Berthollet: the chemist Chaptal who, like Laplace, had been a Minister under Napoleon, and various younger men who were soon to gain fame in physics and chemistry (Biot, Thenard, Gay-Lussac, Malus, Arago, Dulong, Poisson). Almost all of them were former students of the Ecole polytechnique. For a number of years the group would gather at Berthollet's country home in Arcueil, where Laplace also had a summer residence. They published three volumes of *Mémoires* (1807, 1809, 1817) and were highly successful in winning prizes and securing seats at the Academy. The society received personal financial support from Napoleon, who gave Berthollet 150,000 francs to pay his debts.

Berthollet was already one of the wealthiest scientists in France. None of the members of the *Société d'Arcueil* were from the aristocracy and all of them relied on their scientific activities for a living. The income they might earn as a professor or Academy member was not especially high, so accumulating functions was the best way to accrue higher earnings. In addition to positions in the scientific world, after 1789 it became possible to hold political posts as well. Berthollet thus increased his annual income from 2,000 francs in 1785 to 67,000 in 1812.[11] By 1812 his income was approximately a hundred times higher than that of the average Parisian worker, consisting as it did of his earnings as professor at the Ecole polytechnique, Academy member, senator, officer in the Legion of Honour, and Imperial Count, a title he held as of 1808. Laplace, Lagrange, Monge, Chaptal, Lacépède, Cuvier, Carnot, Fourcy and Fourier had all attained comparable positions. All of them combined functions in the scientific world with important political offices, and all of them were awarded Napoleon's highest distinctions. Posts in the scientific world were considerably less lucrative, and scientists who built up positions solely in education and research earned considerably less. Although the institutional differentiation of scientific work increased rapidly after the Revolution, this system of *cumul* led to the perpetuation of a regime dominated by a small number of extremely powerful *patrons*. The refounded academies did indeed lose some of their functions to other institutions but, due to the combination of positions, actual power frequently remained in the hands of a small group of scientists. Laplace was one of the most successful examples of this phenomenon.

Laplace's school played a decisive role in the making of modern physics. In the eighteenth century mechanics was virtually the only discipline in physics recognized as a 'mathematical' one. All the other fields of research were classified as 'experimental physics' or as *sciences physiques*.[12] Thus a clear distinction was drawn in the organization of the Academy between the mathematical sciences (mathematics, astronomy and mechanics) and the 'physical' ones, which included all the natural sciences. The difference was also expressed as 'general physics' versus 'special physics', and in much the same way a distinction was drawn between mathematicians or *géomètres* and physicists or *physiciens*. The former practised an 'exact', coherent and quantitative science, and the latter engaged primarily in qualitative or experimental work and focused on the 'special' properties of matter. This classification did not change until the last decade before the Revolution. Before then, mathematicians looked down upon the *sciences physiques* and referred to their practitioners as the *physicaille*. One of the factors contributing towards this attitude was their contempt for the 'gala' experiments of the *physique amusante* and the 'phraseology' of Buffon and other proponents of natural history. *Vis-à-vis* these forms of knowledge, professional mathematicians such as d'Alembert held high the ideal of a 'pure' mathematical science.

The *Memoire sur la chaleur* (1783) by Laplace and Lavoisier was one of the very first results of collaboration between a 'mathematician' and a 'physicist'. Two years later the new section for 'experimental physics', which had been added to the Academy upon Lavoisier's instigation, was already considered part of the department for 'mathematical sciences'. According to Lavoisier, the 'physical' sciences were 'almost entirely neglected'. However, Laplace, the leading younger mathematician, was already convinced there was a special task for him.[13] What he set out to do was draw up a research programme for the field. The aim of his programme, based upon classical mechanics, was to mathematize such phenomena as electricity, heat conduction, magnetism and light. This was the cornerstone of the Société d'Arcueil. Even when there emerged after 1810 a generation of physicists (Fourier, Fresnel, Ampère) who opposed Laplace's reductionist programme, their orientation remained strictly mathematical.

Physics in the modern sense of the word thus came into being via the mathematization of the experimental *sciences physiques*, which in France had been totally distinct from the mathematical sciences. This process began after 1780, accelerated enormously as of 1795 once Laplace and Berthollet were enabled to recruit students from the Ecole polytechnique, and reached a peak at the time of the Empire with the

Société d'Arcueil. According to some historians, almost all the important contributions to the new physics were made by French researchers.[14]

There was a clear decline during the Restoration, with the repeated reorganizations of the Ecole polytechnique as a major contributory factor. After 1804 the Ecole polytechnique was militarized. In parallel with the war efforts, the school was increasingly transformed into a military institution housed in barracks and administered with uncompromising discipline. Growing numbers of students opted for a military career and, since the 1804 reorganization replaced the scholarships with relatively high tuition fees, the school became less and less accessible to students without economic capital.[15] In view of the social background of many of the scientists, this was undoubtedly an important reason for the decline of French physics. Another reason was that, partly owing to the efforts of the group around Laplace, the applied and experimental subjects were overshadowed by more mathematical courses. This was the case not only at the Ecole polytechnique, but at secondary schools as well. Mathematics retained its importance at the Napoleonic *lycées*, but the empirical sciences were replaced by Latin. These measures had a similarly detrimental effect on the development of French physics and chemistry.

Natural history

The second field of enquiry, natural history, represented a type of knowledge very different from the mathematical disciplines. Initially the domain of physicians interested in the medicinal properties of plants, natural history gained unprecedented popularity in the course of the eighteenth century, and 'amateurs' began to engage in it as well. Neither Buffon nor the former army officer Lamarck had had any medical training. Work in the field of natural history was generally conducted by the custodians of collections and consisted mainly of describing and classifying the items. The most important natural history collection was the one that belonged to the king. In 1739 Buffon was put in charge of the Royal Botanical Gardens. He enlarged the collection and appointed several co-workers and assistants, who helped him produce his *magnum opus*, gave courses and in some cases rose to positions at the Académie des sciences. They were assigned mainly to writing detailed descriptions of plants, and to a lesser extent of animals, minerals and crystals. The descriptions were confined to visible features (shape, number, size, arrangement). Anatomy played an extremely minor role; Buffon refused to use a microscope and questions pertaining to the function of certain organs or patterns affecting the entire organism remained largely unasked.[16] The naturalists' goal was to provide as complete and accurate descriptions as possible of the plant and animal kingdom. Since more and more information was available on the various species, classification was a pressing problem with which naturalists were increasingly confronted. In the course of the eighteenth century several classification systems were developed, and classification was in fact the highest aim of natural history activities.

In 1793 the Jardin des plantes was converted into the Muséum de l'histoire naturelle. The new institution was a combination of the Royal Zoological Gardens and the Botanical Gardens. A library was opened and the number of professors was increased from three to twelve. They were all entitled to a residence in the grounds, over which they were to exercise collective custody. Buffon's function ceased to exist, and each of them was now responsible for a certain part of the collection and gave courses in that particular field. There were still no examinations or diplomas in any of these fields, and anyone who was interested could attend the courses. There were professorial chairs for mineralogy, geology, anatomy, botany, zoology and chemistry. Mathematics and physics were not taught here, and chemistry was the only subject that was also given at the Ecole polytechnique. With the Société linnéenne (1788), later converted into the Société d'histoire naturelle (1790), naturalists had a society of their own, and when the *Annales du Muséum d'histoire naturelle* was founded in 1802 they had their own journal as well.

The Muséum was one of the largest natural history institutions in the world and for decades probably the most authoritative as well.[17] Its fame was based upon the extensive collections and work of such professors as Georges Cuvier and Jean-Baptiste Lamarck. Cuvier was twenty-six years old when he was invited to join the Institut de France in 1795. Within a few years, he was also appointed to professorial chairs at the Collège de France and the Muséum d'histoire naturelle, and in 1803 he became permanent secretary of the natural science department at the Institut. He also held numerous other official positions.[18] Cuvier was to natural history what Laplace was to the mathematical sciences. Lamarck was considerably less successful, at any rate in a social sense. One of the older generation, he had begun his career under Buffon, and by the time he became professor he was fifty years old. He had indeed been a member of the Académie des sciences, but up until Buffon's death in 1788 he had occupied a position of minor importance there. Of the various professors at the Muséum,

Cuvier and Lamarck were to gain the greatest fame. In the years around 1800 they both departed from the traditional forms of natural history. Cuvier, responsible for the rapidly growing anatomical collection, developed the field of comparative anatomy. He worked from the traditional postulate of the immutability of the species but, because of the emphasis on anatomy, his classifications were no longer based upon external properties. Cuvier held that species were characterized by their internal organization rather than the surface features that naturalists had traditionally described. By systematically comparing the species' internal organization, Cuvier drew up new classifications. It was on the grounds of these classifications that Foucault ascribed a central role to him in the making of modern biology.[19] Cuvier's originality was not that he was the first to use the concept of internal organization. The notion that living creatures were 'organized bodies' – unlike the *corps bruts* of mechanics – was not a new one. In the final decades of the eighteenth century it was of vital importance in the work of Jussieu, Vicq d'Azyr and Lamarck, and during the Revolution the concept of organization acquired markedly political connotations.[20] Even before Cuvier, 'organization' had already become more or less synonymous with 'life'. Using this organization concept, Cuvier developed a programme for the systematic comparison of species. These comparisons led to new classifications and to a more functional view of living creatures.

Just as Cuvier took a significant step towards a comparative and more functional approach to species, Lamarck introduced the concept of development. In *Recherches sur l'organisation des corps vivants* (1802), and at greater length in *Philosophie zoologique* (1809), he developed the idea that species were not fixed units, but changed in the course of time. These changes were indicative, he felt, of a tendency towards increasing complexity in the organization of living creatures.[21] Lamarck's 'transformism', as it was later called, is an important example of the temporalization of representations of nature. At the end of the eighteenth century the image of immutable nature that was adhered to in mechanics as well as in natural history began to make way for more dynamic representations. Chronologies were introduced as a new way to classify phenomena in various disciplines, and these new views of nature stimulated in turn the further historicization of the social sciences.[22]

Medicine as clinical practice

The development of the third field of enquiry, the medical sciences, differed not only from that of the mathematical and mechanical disciplines but in a number of senses from that of natural history as well. For the mathematical disciplines the Academie des sciences was the centre, and for natural history it was the Royal Botanical Gardens. The medical sciences, however, were neither an academic nor a predominantly non-academic field, but a university discipline dominated by the medical faculty in Paris. Like other faculties in the eighteenth century it was a conservative institution. Efforts at innovation were viewed as violations of its century-old privileges and were fervently opposed. Thus the medical faculty had succeeded in preventing a medical academy from ever even being founded. Group spirit, *esprit de corps*, was apparently so strong that individual interests were repeatedly sacrificed to the privileges of the group as a whole. But despite the privileges on which the faculty prided itself, French physicians were not held in high esteem. Their training was old-fashioned and their curing capacities often mocked. Medicine had remained a theoretical study. Prospective physicians were required to be acquainted with medical literature, but their actual training and many of the medical theories bore no connection whatsoever to clinical practice. Illnesses and treatment options were learned from books, and medical disputes remained theoretical. Students had barely any experience performing autopsies or prescribing medication, and it was common practice to diagnose patients based on their own descriptions of their symptoms. The physician was wont to interpret the complaints – in a manner befitting the particular theoretical or therapeutic school to which he adhered – in conjunction with the patient, who usually came from a higher social class. This social distance made it impermissible for patients to be examined or even touched.[23] It was not until the rise of the modern clinic that physical examinations became acceptable. In the eighteenth century, however, hospitals were predominantly charity institutions where the poor were cared for but rarely actually treated.

Although medical practice did not undergo that many changes in the eighteenth century, three developments were to play a key role in the medical reforms implemented during the Revolution. Firstly, physicians were increasingly confronted with competition from surgeons.[24] Surgery was traditionally a form of manual work categorized under the mechanical arts, and surgeons were in the same guild as barbers. In 1731, however, Louis XV granted surgeons the right to found their own academy. The guild was divided by royal decree in 1743, and from then on a preliminary university diploma was required for admission to the training course for surgeons. Backed by the king, surgeons had managed to surmount the opposition of the medical faculty. Like painters and sculptors in the seventeenth century, by founding an academy they had earned for themselves the status of a 'liberal art'. In the course of the eighteenth century French surgery rose to quite a prominent position in Europe. For reform-minded physicians at the end of the eighteenth century, the more practically oriented surgery curriculum served as an example to the medical faculties. In fact the anatomical knowledge of the surgeons, their empirical approach and their practical skills were of central importance at the new Ecoles de santé (1794).

In addition to the surgeons there was also the Montpellier medical faculty, which increasingly competed with its Parisian counterpart. The professors in Montpellier were far more open to new medical doctrines than their colleagues in Paris. One aspect the new theories all had in common was a form of vitalism. The mechanical models presenting the body as a machine had been replaced – partially if not totally – by a concept emphasizing the specific properties of organized bodies. The German physician and chemist Georg Ernst Stahl held that, to live, organisms needed a force he called *anima*, the full meaning of which is not well caught in the usual translations as 'soul' or 'spirit'. His 'animism' was one of the first doctrines explicitly refuting the mechanical models of Descartes and Newton, which Boerhaave had developed for the field of medicine. One of the major challenges for the mechanical explanations came from a pupil of Boerhaave's around 1750. The Swiss physiologist Albrecht von Haller demonstrated by way of experiments that animals had a certain extent of 'sensibility' and could be 'irritated' by stimuli, phenomena for which there were no purely mechanical explanations. He localized animals' sensibility in their nerves and their irritability in their muscles. Colleagues all across Europe were interested in Haller's work and for almost half a century it served as the standard for physiological research. In the theoretical sense, it played an essential role in the shift from mechanical to vitalistic models that occurred after 1760 in various countries.[25] In France vitalism was elaborated upon mainly at the medical faculty of Montpellier. Paul-Joseph Barthez was a prominent representative of the school, and his *Nouveaux élements de la science de l'homme* (1778) was one of the major publications in the rise of French vitalism.

A third change that threatened the position of the Parisian medical faculty was the founding of the Société de médecine (1776). This society conducted research for the government on what later came to be called 'public health'. The systematic attention devoted to epidemics led to a whole new field for medical expertise. Up to then health and hygiene had been problems for individuals. Now that epidemics had become a subject for research, attention shifted from individual hygiene to *hygiène public*, and from health to 'public health'. This tendency continued throughout the Revolution and led in the early nineteenth century to the institutionalization of *hygiène public* as a separate field of research, education and administration.[26]

By the start of the Revolution, the distinctions between these three developments could barely be discerned. Many of the younger physicians felt an urgent necessity for reform and combined a clear awareness of the significance of surgery with a vitalistic orientation and avid interest in 'public health'. Barthez, for example, not only propagated vitalistic medicine, he was also a member of the Société de médecine. Vicq d'Azyr, who was secretary of the Société de médecine, had also been trained as a surgeon and was in favour of an autonomous science of medicine inspired by vitalism. Among young, reform-minded physicians in 1789, this combination was the rule rather than the exception.

These various elements were to come together in the radical reorganization that was the result of the Revolution. Together with the guilds, the National Assembly also did away with the professional privileges of physicians. In 1792 the medical faculties were closed down. Unlike the technical subjects and natural history, the medical sciences were in disrepute. This was why so many of the reform proposals were simultaneously attempts to reinstate the profession to its position of esteem.[27] Members of the Société de médecine played an important role in this connection. They drew up plans for a new syllabus, emphasized the social functions of medicine, particularly with respect to *hygiène public*, and stressed the need for a more scientific approach.

However, it was not until 1795 that the Ecoles de santé actually started serving the purpose for which they were designed. Up until then health care meant ministering to the war effort, and these experiences were incorporated into the new framework of the Ecoles de santé. Hospitals were transformed from charity institutions often affiliated with churches into state clinics for wounded soldiers. These clinics suddenly found themselves at the core of medical practice. After the Terror the clinics officially became centres for treatment, research and training. Medicine and surgery each had a place within the same curriculum, and the medical sciences were integrated into one institution. This reorganization meant a complete transformation as regards medical practice and the medical sciences.[28] Medicine became a clinical field of study based upon observation and research. This clinical approach was more similar to the methods and attitudes of surgeons than to the courses in medicine taught at the universities before the Revolution. Pathological anatomy became an important part of the training and research, and anatomical knowledge became the basis for diagnostics.[29] Various studies were devoted to the theoretical foundations of the new medicine. Using vitalistic arguments, many of them stressed the autonomy of the medical sciences *vis-à-vis* mechanics. At the same time this vitalism was no longer confined to theoretical disputes. It was linked to clinical practice and to experimental physiological research, which had largely been overlooked or even rejected by the vitalists.[30] The more scientific practice of medicine also meant a rapprochement with natural history. And among the attentive followers of Cuvier's comparative anatomy there were numerous physicians.[31]

In the years from 1776 to 1814 the medical sciences that had undergone such essential changes also came to account for more and more of the scientific publications of the day. It would seem as if, by the start of the nineteenth century, medicine had replaced natural history as the most popular field of science. In 1799 a third of all scientific books (33 per cent) were about medical subjects. Next came natural history (24 per cent), followed by mathematics and astronomy (17 per cent). During the Restoration there was an even greater increase in the role of medicine in scientific literature. By 1818 half consisted of medical subjects.[32] This expansion, directly related to the growing number of physicians, had been made possible by the emergence of new fields for medical expertise such as 'public health', the hospital revolution and the medical profession's more 'scientific' image.[33]

Expansion, professionalization and the formation of disciplines

The development of the natural sciences after 1789 was characterized by accelerated expansion and differentiation. In a number of cases this process had gone into effect after 1774, when multifarious steps were taken to develop research that would help modernize the administration of the monarchy. In the ten or fifteen years before the Revolution there were several significant breakthroughs, for instance in the field of chemistry, although in other cases changes took place at a much slower pace. For all the fields of science, however, the Revolution heralded a new period. Old institutions were discontinued or reformed, and within a short period of time a whole new system of education and research was set up. Career opportunities improved considerably and science became a 'profession' once and for all.[34] Training courses led to recognized degrees, fixed careers and hierarchies: from secondary-school teacher to lecturer at the Ecole polytechnique, or *aide-naturaliste* at the Muséum d'histoire naturelle to professor and member of the Institut de France. The new educational system played a crucial role within this process of accelerated expansion. Natural sciences were taught not only at secondary schools, but also on a more advanced level at the Ecole polytechnique, the Ecole normale supérieure and the Ecoles de santé, and as of 1808 at the Napoleonic universities as well. From then on teaching was a fixed part of a scientific career. Before the Revolution a scientist was first and foremost dependent on admission to the Academy; he conducted research, discussed it at the Academy and had the results printed in Academy publications. Although some scientists were employed as private tutors or instructors at military academies, teaching was usually not one of their tasks. In general teaching was done by clergymen. The Revolution put an end to this situation, and important findings were now even published as teaching material. Monge systematized his descriptive geometry for a series of lectures at the Ecole polytechnique, Laplace's *Système du monde* originated in much the same way, Lamarck first presented his transformism in lectures at the Muséum d'histoire naturelle, and Cuvier developed his comparative anatomy in the course of lectures at the Collège de France. In addition to introductory surveys, numerous systematic *traités* were published which presented a comprehensive view of an entire field of science.[35]

This expansion and professionalization was accompanied by an accelerated process of differentiation. The Institut de France, which replaced the academies, remained the highest authority but was no longer the undisputed centre for research and evaluation. Separate societies were founded for various fields of science, some of which were private, like the Société d'Arcueil. These societies were more specialized and took over certain functions traditionally fulfilled by the Academy. The same type of differentiation also affected scientific publications. Up until 1770 specialized and independent scientific journals were non-existent. The only media for scientific findings were such official organs as the Academy proceedings or the *Journal des savants*. The first periodical of a different nature was the monthly *Observations sur la physique* (1771), also known as *Journal de phys-*

ique.[36] Confined to the experimental *sciences physiques*, it was independent of the Academy but was nonetheless a professional periodical in which prominent researchers published their results. A few comparable journals were published up to the Revolution, but it was not until after 1789 that the exception was to become the rule. The Academy *Mémoires* were increasingly supplanted by independent and more specialized journals such as *Annales de chimie* (1789), *Annales du Muséum d'histoire naturelle* (1802), *Journal de l'Ecole polytechnique* (1794) and *Annales de mathématiques* (1810).

These new periodicals had two advantages over the official organs. Firstly, they published articles much more rapidly. This was why Lavoisier published many of his findings first in the *Journal de physique*; many years later they were published again in the Academy *Mémoires*. Secondly, 'supradisciplinary control' was no longer feasible.[37] The Académie des sciences was dominated by the mathematical disciplines, and the procedures of these 'exact' sciences were long viewed as the standard for 'scientificity'. Thus it was no coincidence that the first specialized scientific journal was focused on the experimental and non-mathematical *sciences physiques*. The *Journal de physique* was the organ of the more descriptive and experimental sciences. It was founded in a period when mechanical models in the life sciences began to make way for more vitalistic approaches. For the further development of these sciences, independence from the Academy was of vital importance.

The most fundamental aspect of this process of scientific differentiation was undoubtedly the rise of 'biology'. In 1802, independently of each other, Gottfried Reinhold Treviranus coined the term in Germany and Lamarck introduced it in France. Two years earlier the word had been used in a medical publication, but with a less specific definition.[38] In the same period other terms were proposed (zoonomy, general zoology) to refer to a general science of life, indicating that it was certainly not an isolated phenomenon. The word and the idea behind it illustrate the breakthrough of a new type of science. Biology was neither a *physique particulière* nor a purely descriptive discipline like natural history, but an empirical and general science with its own subject matter and its own research methods. Just as 'physics' became the general term for the study of inorganic nature, 'biology' was gradually accepted as the term for the study of living organisms. In both cases, institutional and professional growth coincided with cognitive expansion. Just as Laplace generalized Newtonian mechanics into the paradigm for the study of physical phenomena, knowledge of plants, animals and human beings was gradually accepted as all part of one and the same science of life. It was a different science from mechanics, but barely any less general and certainly no less important. This cognitive differentiation meant a clear departure from the ideas of the Enlightenment. In the eighteenth century nature was viewed predominantly as one harmonic unity. The tiniest and the most complex creatures were part of the same long, unbroken chain.[39] In nature differences were only gradual, and just as nature itself constituted a whole, so did the study of it. In keeping with this monistic ontology there was a monistic epistemology. It was no coincidence that the words 'nature' and 'reason' were used only in the singular. By the late eighteenth century, however, and particularly after the Revolution, both of them had lost much of their polemical function. The secularization of education and research made it less imperative – and less feasible – to define all forms of knowledge as branches of one and the same 'reason'. In the life sciences a dualistic conception of nature gained acceptance, and with the recognition of an essential distinction between animate and inanimate bodies, between matter and life, it had become considerably more difficult to speak solely of nature in the singular. The same held true of 'reason'. Instead of 'reason', it became more common to refer to 'the sciences'. This shift is a good illustration of the two most fundamental changes in comparision with the Enlightenment: scientization and cognitive differentiation. This tendency was evident in the successor to Diderot and d'Alembert's *Encyclopédie*. The *Encyclopédie méthodique* (1781–1832), which ultimately consisted of 166 volumes, had separate volumes on various branches of knowledge: eight on medicine, two on surgery, three on mathematics, three on chemistry, eight on law and so forth. The fact that there were three volumes on theology and three on philosophy makes it clear that they had lost their supradisciplinary status and, like the other branches of knowledge, were in the process of becoming 'disciplines' in the modern sense of the word. The volumes were clearly separate and no effort was made to impose coherence or congruity from any specific point of view. The *Encyclopédie méthodique* was written by a staff including fewer noblemen and considerably more professional scientists than Diderot and d'Alembert's precursor. Virtually all of them were experts in their fields and their articles were confined to their areas of competence. There was no longer any room for *philosophes*. The *Encyclopédie méthodique* was an encyclopedia in the neutral sense. It no longer aspired to reclassify knowledge, nor was knowledge presented as an alternative to religious faith. The aim was no more and no less than to present the progress that had been made in all fields of knowledge.[40]

The cognitive differentiation that took place around 1800 was not only a process of segmentation and specialization, it was character-ized first and foremost by the formation of disciplines. This was an essential change. Not only did physics and biology emerge in their modern versions; the whole intellectual framework changed as well. With their own journals, societies and curriculums, these branches of knowledge had attained a degree of autonomy that made them discip-lines for which supradisciplinary frameworks lost their significance. This was true on the institutional level, of the Académie des sciences and periodicals such as the *Mémoires*, and on the cognitive level of conceptions pertaining to the role of 'philosophy' and notions such as the 'great chain of being'. The new intellectual field was divided into relatively autonomous 'disciplines'. This change manifested itself in a positive way in the formation of disciplinary networks and in a negat-ive way in the rapid decline of supradisciplinary institutions and concepts. The altered status of philosophy is a good example. To Auguste Comte, the philosopher was now only a 'specialist in gener-alities'. Even philosophy had been driven back within the borders of a discipline.

9

The Literary Opposition

Mais, ô déclin! quel souffle aride De notre âge a séché les fleurs?
Eh quoi! le lourd compas d'Euclide Etouffe nos arts enchanteurs!
Elans de l'âme et du génie!
Des calculs la froide manie
Chez nos pères vous remplaça:
Ils posèrent sur la nature
Le doigt glacé qui la mesure,
Et la nature se glaça.

Lamartine

In literary criticism, the years of the Revolution and the Empire are at best considered a period of transition. For most critics, that was just about their only virtue. Classicism disappeared and republican art made an entrance, be it followed just as rapidly by an exit, and only a few early Romantics were to find favour in their eyes. During the Revolution, or so Sainte-Beuve held, there was no art at all in the true sense of the word. As an 'independent persona', art had been 'ravaged' and 'exterminated'. Nonetheless, he wrote, poetry was soon to be pervaded by the Revolution as well. While the French celebrated their victory on the battlefields of Europe, unrelated to all this and far from the new intellectual centres, the seeds of an artistic revolution began to sprout. Madame de Staël and Chateaubriand inconspicuously set out on pathways that were soon to coincide. The Empire had allowed no latitude for this 'pure art'. It was not until the Restoration that a generation of poets came forth who took the lessons of Chateaubriand to heart. In the opinion of Sainte-Beuve, art owed the revival of its dignity to these Romantic poets. Despite their glorification of the Middle Ages, the monarchy and Catholicism, they were the ones to breathe new life into literature, and when the militant years were over, they abandoned their political illusions and concentrated on their real work.[1]

The opinions of literary historians did not differ from those of Sainte-Beuve. Lanson wrote in his textbook that literary production had never been 'more trivial', 'inconsequential' and 'unauthentic' than at the time of the Revolution and the Empire. Since the salons were closed and, for a decade if not more, there was no *mondaine* life to speak of, the new literature was no longer linked to the group that had served as literary audience for two centuries. Its style and ways of thinking had long been the standard for poets and writers. At the time of the Revolution, quite different groups and new media came to the fore, and, by the time the salons finally opened again and social life began anew, Classicism had become a thing of the past. Even during the Restoration the salons never regained the significance they had once had. According to Lanson, this meant women had lost their power over literature, and from then on literary work was conducted by and for men. In the revolutionary period the role of salons and *mondaine* conversation was taken over by journalism and public speaking. Newspapers and magazines came to play as important a function in literary appraisal as the salons before them, and political rhetoric and republican poetry were now the genres that filled the pages of these periodicals. Lanson did discuss a few examples of this, but then proceeded to devote all his attention to the two authors Saint-Beuve had focused on as well: Madame de Staël and Chateaubriand.[2]

Innovation born of conservatism

Since literary production was not as directly linked to institutional arrangements as the natural sciences, it is somewhat more difficult to survey its developments concisely. There were no schools and diplomas for writers, and the Academy had lost much of its prestige. The most important division in literature was between the writers who remained in France and those who emigrated. For both groups the Revolution was the all-important event, although each perceived it from a totally different position. Very little of the literature produced to glorify the Republic could later meet with approval. As in the field of art, much of this work was linked to the moment of the Revolution and often served merely to reinforce efforts to create a republican mythology. The neo-classical literature of the Napoleonic era fared hardly any better. Work from this period was described as a 'vapid and colourless pastiche of classical literature'.[3]

The opposition was a fertile breeding ground for literary innovations, particularly among emigrants and ex-emigrants. For a while some

of them, such as Chateaubriand, pinned all their hope on Napoleon
in what was virtually always an alliance of convenience. Napoleon
exiled Madame de Staël, and in the end the Emperor himself had to
admit that all he had was the support of second-rate writers. Although
world-famous scientists dedicated their books to him, he had to con-
cede that only the 'petite litérature' was on his side, and all he could
expect from 'grande litérature' was animosity.[4] This was one of the
most striking aspects of the literature of the period. Several writers of
greater renown combined counter-revolutionary attitudes with the
pursuit of new literary forms and means of expression. For some time,
social conservatism and literary innovations were closely linked. And
an unmistakable nostalgia for the past went hand in hand with an
aversion to literary tradition. This unusual combination characteristic
of early French Romanticism came to the fore in the course of the
emigration period.

For emigrants, the Revolution meant spending time in some other
country under totally different circumstances. Some of them stayed
away for a few years, many returned when Napoleon came to power,
and others waited until the Restoration. The cultural changes that typi-
fied the Empire and the Restoration were often rooted in these experiences abroad. Having to remain in a foreign country for years on end,
coming into contact with total strangers who shared one's background
and one's plight, unanticipated trials and tribulations, all these aspects
of life in exile contributed towards a reorientation that exerted enormous influence on literature and art alike. For many of the emigrants,
the most drastic loss was having to leave their *mondaine* life. The fact
that *mondaine* centres were no longer easily accessible also meant a
sudden and perhaps drastic change in the lifestyle of non-aristocrats.[5]
In the French colonies that gathered at various spots, desperate efforts
were made to keep traditions alive, but there were profound changes
in the attitudes towards them. First and foremost there was a growing
predilection for lyricism and emotional literature rather than the
more objective psychology of Classicism. The old ideals of a sense of
'measure' and 'grace' no longer sufficed. In the unusual circumstances
of the time, Rousseau's emotional dramas met better with readers'
needs than Classicist literature. Moreover, religious feelings came to
play an important role in this new sensibility. Before the Revolution
scepticism and indifference to religion had been widespread in aristocratic circles. In the emigration period religion was re-evaluated and
Catholicism was rediscovered not only as a source of comfort and a
doctrine of salvation, but also as a social institution, a guarantee for
law and order. This return to the faith, or revived devotion to it,

coincided with a more general glorification of the past. The present had become unbearable and few could resist the temptation either to cling to the past or to escape into the fantasy of the imagination. The yearning for carefree times or deeds of proud heroism overshadowed whatever interest there might have been in the present and nourished feelings of hatred towards the people held responsible for the losses.

Enchantment regained

After Napoleon's *coup d'état*, some of the *émigrés* returned. By the end of 1799 churches were open on Sunday again, and only a few weeks later sixty of the seventy-three political periodicals were banned, after which half the registered emigrants were given permission to return to France if they so chose. Negotiations were opened for an official reconciliation with the church, and around 1800 numerous emigrants returned to their native soil filled with hope and confidence. Some of them were cast in leading roles in the counter-revolutionary reaction emerging at the turn of the century around such periodicals as *Mercure de France* and *Journal des débats*. Counter-revolutionary writings and periodicals had hitherto solely been published abroad. The first confrontation between republican intellectuals and repatriated emigrants was sparked off by the publication of *De la littérature considérée dans ses rapports avec les institutions sociales* (1800). In this study Madame de Staël presented a comprehensive survey of the development of literature as a social phenomenon. Her guidelines were Montesquieu's idea of social interdependence and the notion of social progress elaborated upon by Condorcet. Her analysis expanded upon the legacy of the Enlightenment, there was enthusiastic appreciation of the Revolution, but criticism of the new relations was expressed as well, be it only because her entire book constituted a defence of the significance of literature and eloquence. And there was also the fact that her criticism of certain evils or wrongs had been motivated by her religious convictions. In Madame de Staël's opinion, altruism and virtue were products of religious consciousness, and in this sense her Protestant preferences differed from those of the republican intellectuals. *De la littérature* immediately came to play a key role in public discussions on literature, religious faith and the Enlightenment.[6] The first issue of *Mercure de France* after it was refounded featured a lengthy article by Fontanes touching upon all the themes that would soon constitute the standard repertoire of the literary opposition.

Fontanes' criticism pertained mainly to the notion of progress. He

viewed the very idea that human history was characterized by progress and that modern times were thus superior to previous eras as a
fanciful illusion. Progress was confined to science and technology. And
since this progress was based upon little more than perseverance and
coincidence, it was for good reason that scientists had such erratic
reputations. 'There is no getting round it, the most splendid and most
lasting creations are those of eloquence and poetry.'[7] The reason was
that their power was based upon 'human passions and emotions' which
were 'immutable'. There was no moral, artistic or political progress,
nor any new discoveries to be made in these fields. It was a misconception to think human life could be approached by calculations or
reasoning. 'If everything is subjected to philosophical analysis, it all
loses its charm.' The 'charm' of things, according to Fontanes, lay in
their enigmatic aspects; it was only 'mysterious and infinite feelings'
that gave pleasure to the 'soul'. People with a weakness for 'fame,
virtue and beauty' would be wise to devote no further attention to
'doctrines that wither the heart and the imagination'. It would be a
foolish mistake to 'glorify the sciences at the expense of the fine arts'.

In his ode to poetry and the imagination, Fontanes was bolstered
by Chateaubriand, with whom he had been friends since their emigration. Chateaubriand discussed the same themes, but put more emphasis on religious faith. Since 'only Christianity has understood man . . .
everything Madame de Staël ascribes to philosophy I ascribe to
religion.'[8] Only Christianity had granted a certain extent of insight
into the world of human feelings, all the great writers had been
Christians, and, according to Chateaubriand, any writer who refused
to believe banished 'the infinite' from his work. Instead of progress
and *perfectibilité*, it was this 'infinity' that was important, the eternal
mystery. 'Genius' was nothing but the awareness of it.

The discussion on literature and religion became even more heated
when the Concordat was signed in 1801. Shortly afterwards, simultaneously with its official inauguration, Chateaubriand's *Génie du
christianisme* (1802) was published. Its aim was to demonstrate that
Christianity was 'the most poetic and most humane' of all religions
and the one most conducive to 'art and literature'. Chateaubriand's
book was an immediate success and became the manifesto for a new
literary sensibility. This orientation was presented as part of the alliance between literature and Catholicism. Like Fontanes, Chateaubriand
constructed an all-embracing opposition between literature and science, with literature representing emotion and passion and science
representing unfeeling reason. This duality coincided with a whole list
of others, with religion on the side of literature, emotions, morality

and humanity, and science on the side of reason, skepticism, callousness and ultimately even crime. 'Various people', he wrote, 'have noted that science wilts the heart, strips nature of its enchantment, steers weak spirits to atheism and from atheism to crime; the fine arts, on the other hand, add a glow to our lives, stir our souls, fill us with faith in the Divinity and lead via religion to virtue.'[9] According to Chateaubriand, science and philosophy constituted a threat to poets and writers, and, to no less an extent, to emotional life, the church, and society as a whole. He later added one more argument to the reasons he viewed the sciences as inferior: Laplace, Lagrange, Cuvier, Monge, Chaptal, Berthollet, all 'those child prodigies' who had once been such proud democrats, had become Napoleon's most 'obsequious servants'.

> To the greater glory of literature it can not be denied that the new literature was free and science sycophantic. . . . the very people whose thinking soared to the highest heavens could not elevate their soul above Napoleon's feet. They claimed to have no need for God, which is precisely why they needed a tyrant.[10]

In the years following Napoleon's rise to power, a circle of intellectuals emerged around Fontanes' *Mercure de France* who began to propagate emotion and the power of the imagination as the major sources of literary inspiration. These forms of literature were presented as an alternative to the intellectual models prevailing at the time, and had an explicitly anti-scientific and anti-rationalistic slant to them. Faced with the arrogance of reason and the oppressive world of science, Chateaubriand and his like-minded circle defended everything that eluded calculation and comprehension. Thus a new conception of literature was also formulated. In Chateaubriand's exuberant prose, the Classicist ideals soon faded into oblivion. 'Taste' was replaced by 'genius'. Literature and poetry were one; it was no longer a matter of clear and elegant depictions of reality, but of the poetic re-creation of everything that existed. The writer was no longer a man of letters, which had become a pale and somewhat suspicious term, but was now a troubadour and a seer. To Chateaubriand, the deep dark mysteriousness of reality was overwhelming. This was a way of saying it was unfathomable. The desire to understand creation was mere vanity, and the conviction that one could indeed understand it was pure arrogance. Lamartine invoked this same archaic distrust of knowledge. In *L'homme*, a poem dedicated to Byron in 1819, he wrote: 'Notre crime est d'être homme et de vouloir connaître: Ignorer et servir, c'est la loi de notre être.'[11] In one way or another, all the early Romantics in France emphasized that the important thing was not to dissect and examine nature, but to praise and glorify it and acclaim its beauty and lustrous secrets. In contrast to the earthly and the finite, they sought the enchantment of the 'mysterious', the 'inexhaustible' and the 'infinite' and assigned to the writer the task of bearing witness to it.

The Romantic revolt and the two cultures

Virtually all the themes of this Romantic reaction were formulated in the years following Napoleon's rise to power. With the experiences accrued in the Revolution and emigration period, and in the battle against the new intellectual rulers, a literary counter-movement assembled that exchanged philosophy for religious faith, reason for feeling, and scientific knowledge for the enchantment of miracles and mysteries. The yearning for faraway countries, distant times and unfathomable phenomena was no longer nourished by the need for entertainment, as it had been in the eighteenth century, but was far more a product of the mood of crisis among the victims of the Revolution. Writers such as Chateaubriand reforged these experiences into a literary doctrine centred around criticism of reason and science. To Chateaubriand the imagination was a challenge to reason, and, as if it were his fondest desire to silence the scientists, he mobilized everything that defied reason. Religious faith was deployed in this battle as an ally and metaphysical mainstay in the pursuit of everything exceeding human capacities.

Chateaubriand and the circle around him were quick to gain ground. The *Journal des débats*, founded in 1799, had a circulation of more than 30,000. A confidential report to Napoleon in 1803 stated that the journal's main aim was to wage 'open warfare' on the sciences. The development of the sciences, it was felt, had led only to moral corruption and atheism.[12] When Madame de Staël completed *De l'Allemagne* in 1810, it was evident that religion and criticism of the sciences had become more important to her as well. She lauded Chateaubriand's 'beautiful work' and stressed that poetry, art, idealistic philosophy and religion all drew on the same source and served the same purpose.[13] Although the differences between 'liberals' and 'conservatives' had not disappeared, both groups had witnessed a revival of a form of spiritualism. In both, criticism was focused on the 'materialism' of science. And in both it was stressed that the denial of a higher being and spiritual intangibles such as the soul had had disastrous repercussions, and that a revival of religious and moral values was imperative. Writers and poets alluded to this development in their efforts to upgrade literature. Lamartine, born in 1790, a great admirer of Chateaubriand and one of the leading Romantic poets, described this development as follows:

> I remember that, when I came into the world, only one voice spoke of the irreparable decay and of what had in fact been the cold-blooded murder of this mysterious capacity [poetry] of the human spirit. It was the era of the Empire, the period when the materialistic philosophy of the eighteenth century ruled the government and morals alike. All those mathematical men who would not let anyone else get a word in edgewise and who crushed us, the other youngsters, under the unprecedented tyranny of their victory did indeed believe they had succeeded in shattering in us the very thing they had tarnished and destroyed in themselves: the moral, divine and melodious side of human thinking. For people who did not experience this first hand, nothing can evoke the arrogant sterility of this era. It was the satanic smile of an infernal wizard once he has managed to degrade an entire generation, to uproot the enthusiasm of an entire nation, to ravage virtue; these gentlemen had the same feeling of triumphant powerlessness in their heart and on their lips when they said to us: 'love, philosophy, religion, enthusiasm, freedom, poetry, all of it is nothing! Calculation and force, the number and the sword, that is everything! We only believe what is provable, we only feel what is tangible; poetry perished with the same spiritualism with which it was born.' And they spoke the truth, for in their souls it has perished, in their minds it had expired, and in them and around them it was dead . . . Everything was organized to counter a rekindling of moral and poetic feeling; it was a universal alliance of mathematical studies against thought and poetry. Only number was permitted, honoured, protected and rewarded. . . . Ever since that time I have abhorred number, that denial of all human thinking, and I have retained the same abhorrence of the exclusive and jealous power of mathematics. Mathematics was the chain imprisoning human thought. I can heave a sigh of relief, for it has been shattered!'[14]

Lamartine wrote this in 1834 as a preface to a new edition of his collected works. The Romantic elements in his writing were no longer new, but it could not have been easy for younger writers to empathize with the resentment he obviously harboured towards mathematicians. Flaubert described similar feelings in a letter written in the same period, but expressed them in a much more stylized fashion:

... it is sad for criticism and studies to penetrate deeply into science and discover nothing there but vanity, to analyse the human heart and find only egotism, to comprehend the world and discern solely misery. Oh, what I adore far more is pure poetry, supplications from the heart, sudden effusions and, furthermore, deep sighs, voices of the soul, musings of the heart. There are days when I would gladly exchange all the science of past, present and future twaddlers, all the foolish erudition of nitpickers, fusspots, philosophers, novelists, druggists, grocers and academics for two lines of verse by Lamartine or Victor Hugo. You see I have now become fervently anti-prose, anti-reason and anti-truth, for what is beauty but the impossible, and what is poetry but barbarism . . .[15]

If they reacted at all, scientists were apt to belittle the literary-cum-religious *Mercure de France* campaigns. Republican intellectuals defended their position in the *Décade philosophique*. Cuvier, a Protestant, held that Chateaubriand and the circle around him did not serve the interests of their faith by refuting, in the name of religion, what little was known.[16] Other scientists who joined in the discussion took it a step further. The physicist Biot, one of Laplace's most productive students, contested the kind of literature Chateaubriand was defending. 'Common sense' and 'good taste', he wrote, had not yet ceased to exert influence. 'They who strive to introduce a new kind of poetry based upon unreasonableness and extravagance will not only have to deal, as they have surmised, with enlightened and learned people; their true enemies, their arch-enemies, are the great writers of the era of Louis XIV, and in particular Fénelon, Boileau and Racine, who taught us by their example and their work not to accept any sources of literary beauty other than nature and truth.'[17] Above his piece, Biot quoted the famous words of Boileau *rien n'est beau que le vrai* (nothing is beautiful but truth). Just as Chateaubriand's reactionary preferences were accompanied by a marked innovative drive, many progressive scientists adhered to ideas on literature that were quite conservative. Biot clung to the most traditional Classicist formulations. The *Décade philosophique* defended the political revolution as a step forward, but 'viewed the literary revolution as a step backward'.[18] The editorial staff of the *Décade* refused to abandon the traditional division into genres. Each genre had its own themes and its own tone, and even a 'genius' had no right to deviate from them. Part of this aesthetic conservatism, as Marc Regaldo called it, was that these republican intellectuals rejected any notion of a dichotomy between literature and science, between imagination and reason.[19] At the time, however, the separation between the two was well under way.

In France the theme of an irreconcilable difference between two cultures, a scientific and a literary one, was increasingly in vogue in the first years of the nineteenth century. It was the first time this had ever occurred.[20] The notion was formulated and elaborated upon by representatives of the literary opposition as part of their resistance to the intellectual supremacy of the natural sciences. The poets and writers in question wanted to withdraw their work once and for all from the critical judgement of scholars and philosophers, and thus severed whatever ties remained with the Classicist tradition. It was not only forms of literature with an anti-rationalistic and anti-scientific slant that emerged from this process, but also doctrines that provided the theoretical foundation for this split. The expression *l'art pour l'art*, or art for art's sake, was coined in this period, probably by Benjamin Constant in 1804. The idea that aesthetic activities ought to be completely separate from cognitive ones became more prevalent and was incorporated into the cultural ideology of Romanticism.[21]

De Bonald and de Maistre

The Romantic reaction in France pertained to literary prose and poetry. There was no sign of Romanticism in the natural sciences, and philosophy and the human sciences occupied an intermediate position. The situation was somewhat different in other countries. Partly due to anti-French sentiments, the natural sciences in Germany and England were, to some extent, open to Romantic motifs.[22]

In France there were clear links between political conservatism, criticism of the natural sciences and literary commitment. This also held true of social theorists such as de Bonald and de Maistre. In 1807 de Bonald noted that a 'rift' had grown between the natural sciences and literature.[23] For centuries no distinction had been drawn between the two, and it was only recently that it had become clear how essential the differences were. In de Bonald's opinion, the most important cause of this rift lay in the emergence of a group of independent men of letters at the beginning of the eighteenth century. Writers had then acquired a 'title' without having a 'function', and like other 'redundant' individuals they were a source of strife and turmoil. In their 'hatred of religion' and 'ignorance' as to matters of faith, morality and politics, they identified the sciences with the natural sciences. Their satirical writings had been well appreciated by bored noblemen, there were plenty of conspirators from the Third Estate, and thus the moral sciences, which were based upon Christian teachings, had lost more and more ground. Viewed in this light, the *Encyclopédie* had been the first part of a work of which the Revolution was part two: 'the two parts have the same composition and, one might add, the same format.'[24]

De Bonald then addressed the matter of why every 'sensible person' ought to prefer moral sciences and literature. The Revolution had demonstrated that negligence as regards moral and social truths unavoidably led to chaos. For the individual as well as society as a whole, the moral sciences were superior to the natural sciences. They were more useful and more exalted; what is more, they were 'more perfect' because the existing theories did not have to be revised every couple of years. A study in physics could well serve the reputation of an individual scholar, but not of his nation. The fame of France was based upon the work of its poets, rhetoricians and politicians and not on the merits of its physicists.

Shortly afterwards, de Bonald wrote some notes for an essay on the same subject entitled 'Sur la guerre des sciences et des lettres'. Here he no longer presented any descriptions or arguments, he merely calculated. 'If war were to break out between the sciences and literature', he wondered, who would be on which side? Literature would go to battle with the pride of an illustrious past, and the sciences with confidence roused by recent successes. But, militarily speaking, literature's prospects would be poor. The classical genres (comedy, tragedy, epic poetry) had suffered losses in their most sensitive spots, so that literature could only count on the 'irregulars' (novels, serials, translations) and would thus be forced to summon the assistance of melodrama. The sciences, on the other hand, could count on the support of the 'learned nations to the north' and 'pedagogology [*sic*], statistics, cameralistics [*sic*], technology, archaeology etc.'. The arts would be divided. The mechanical arts would take the side of the sciences, and the liberal arts that of literature. But the liberal arts would be a 'dubious and perfidious ally'. Music was already 'ardently learned', dancing had its own science, choreography, and poetry, generous but always imprudent, would open negotiations even before the first shot was fired. 'So there would be every indication of the imminent fall of the republic of letters and consequently the universal rule of the exact sciences.'[25]

De Bonald's imaginary warfare calls to mind a picture of extreme intellectual polarization. In the contest between science and literature, nothing and no one could avoid taking sides. Perhaps it was the scales tipping towards the sciences that kept de Bonald from completing and publishing his essay. It would only have served to undermine the morale of the troops further. It was not until after a decisive battle was won and Napoleon left the arena that de Bonald elaborated upon his notes in a collection of essays. The essay is not dated, but, judging from its place in the collection, it must have been written some time between 1806 and 1810. By the time the collection was published in 1819, the Restoration was in full swing and the supremacy of the natural sciences had been relegated to the past.

What linked de Bonald and de Maistre to the literary opposition was their resistance to the new power of the scientists and their conviction that personal preferences should be rooted in religious faith. They were both in their forties when the Revolution broke out, they were both aristocratic *émigrés*, and they both tried to find new phrasing for the foundations of the Catholic monarchy. They were not inspired Romantics like Chateaubriand, but they did share his aversion to modern science, which they held directly or indirectly responsible for the Revolution. However, it was not so much the 'disenchantment' of the world to which de Bonald and de Maistre were opposed, as were Chateaubriand and Lamartine; rather it was the repercussions it had on the relations of authority. *Philosophes* and scientists were viewed as the main culprits when it came to undermining authority, thus leading to the Revolution. This theme was prevalent in the works of all the counter-revolutionaries, and for all of them this diagnosis was linked to a reassessment of Catholicism and absolutism. The aristocratic criticism of absolutism, still so widely formulated in the first stage of the Revolution, disappeared from counter-revolutionary writings. After the fall of the monarchy in 1792, pleas in favour of a division of power or a constitutional monarchy and criticism of arbitrary rule and despotism were replaced by new formulations of absolutist doctrines. These political theories were frequently accompanied by a renewed focus on organicist and corporatist ideas in which individuals were subordinate to the social tasks they were presumed to fulfil. The writings by de Bonald and de Maistre were the most systematic efforts in this direction.[26]

Independently of each other, the two men published their first larger works in 1796: de Maistre's *Considérations sur la France* and de Bonald's *Théorie du pouvoir politique et religieux dans la société civile*, both of which criticized the modern sciences. Throughout his lifetime, Joseph de Maistre was obsessed by the power of science. According to him, the natural sciences and the people who engaged in them could only be tolerated in subordinate positions. The educational system had to remain in the hands of priests and executive functions in those of noblemen, officers and high clergymen. As soon as other groups

attained positions of authority the Catholic monarchy would be a thing
of the past. In de Maistre's view, it was the scientists who – 'impertinent as they were' – had begun to ask God to account for his decrees.

> We could not manage to keep them in their place. There used to be very
> few scientists and not many of them had no religious belief. Nowadays
> all you seem to see are scientists: it is an occupation, a mass, a people,
> and among them the exception has become the rule. . . . If one thing is
> certain in this world, it is that science is not entitled to lead humanity.[27]

In *Examen de la philosophie de Bacon* (1836), de Maistre traced the
pernicious influence of modern science back to Bacon. *Vis-à-vis* the
empiricism of the English, he defended religious faith and metaphysics
as the indispensable foundations for the moral sciences. These sciences
were incommensurate with the natural sciences in that they were based
upon fundamental articles of faith (from the Fall of Man and Providence to the infallibility of the Pope, which de Maistre defended in a
separate book).

The defence of traditional Christian 'moral sciences' was also the
central theme of de Bonald's work. The groundwork for his doctrine
was outlined in his first book, and his later publications were elaborations upon it. His essays were frequently illuminating, as they were
of greater contemporary relevance and more lively than his longer
treatises. De Bonald's social theory was directed primarily against the
expansion of individualism and pluralism. His conception of science
was directed against the introduction of natural science methods in
the moral sciences. As in de Maistre's work, these two aspects were
closely connected. De Bonald's social theory was based on the assumption of an original order created by God. Existing societies were nothing but 'manifestations' of this original society and any encroachment
upon it would lead to crisis phenomena. Relations in this society were
permanently fixed, in fact they were 'laws', and de Bonald referred to
a 'législation primitive'. Just as the relations between a father, a mother
and a child constituted a natural hierarchy, so did the relations between the monarch, the nobility and the people or, in more abstract
terms, between power, ministership and subservience. To de Bonald,
subjects were beholden to their subservience, just as noblemen were
beholden to public service. Notions of individual rights or independence and liberty would disrupt the original order. There was but one
society, and that was the unity of religious society (the Catholic Church)
and political society (the monarchy). The church guarded over man's
moral well-being, and political society over his physical well-being.

There was no space in this arrangement for independent 'sectors' or 'markets' or for any real division of powers. This also applied to intellectuals. It had been their claims to independence that had led to the making of modern philosophy, in other words to attempts to understand and systematize everything without calling upon the Divinity and the society created by Him.

De Bonald's social theory was a kind of socio-political theology. The original society and the obligations it entailed preceded the rights and preferences of individuals. There was a certain amount of leeway for individuals' actions, but if they deviated too much from the original design it would endanger physical or moral health. De Bonald's theory, elaborated upon in greater detail and more strictly than de Maistre's, reads like a scholastic exercise. Everything depended on preconceived definitions, from which a number of conclusions were then deduced. 'Metaphysics', so de Bonald held, 'is to the moral sciences what algebra is to the natural sciences.'[28] He felt nothing was as detrimental to the moral sciences as the imitation of the modern natural sciences.

De Maistre and de Bonald's ideas originated as criticism of the revolutionary developments. They reverted back to old theological and political convictions, but the selection and explication of these conceptions were inspired in part by ideas held by their opponents. The ideas for which de Maistre and de Bonald sought alternatives were mainly modern conceptions regarding society and science. Concerning the modern conception of society, which assumed a dynamic and decentred whole, they proposed a static theory holding that an unchanging centre was indispensable to a society. Social differentiation was feasible solely within the previously determined division of labour between the family, the church and the state. All other forms of social activity ought to be subordinate to these institutions and functions. It was not the interdependence of relatively autonomous sectors that was central, but the metaphysical need for unity in subordination. From a theoretical point of view, this reactionary dream could be supported only by defending the type of theory that disputed the rationalistic and natural science traditions. The criticism of modern philosophy and science was indeed a major component of their work, and, when either of them now and then emphasized their scientific diligence, they were alluding to science in the scholastic sense of the word. De Bonald and de Maistre shared their critical attitude to the modern sciences with the literary opposition. Louis de Bonald wrote articles for the *Mercure de France* and, together with Chateaubriand, founded the *Conservateur* (1818).

The work of de Bonald and de Maistre illustrated the diffusion of social theory as well as the resistance to it. Their writing was traditionalistic, but, since it originated as criticism of the revolutionary developments, it acquired a whole new dimension: it became 'reactionary' or 'conservative' in Mannheim's sense of the terms; it became a traditionalism that 'had become conscious of itself'. Neither de Bonald nor de Maistre could be content to repeat old doctrines. De Maistre's work, with its mystical slant, stressed the historical role of Providence. He interpreted the Revolution as punishment, as a kind of penance that would lead in the end to the resurrection of the church and the original relations of authority. In de Bonald's work, the return to an 'orderly society' occupied a central position. He viewed the Revolution more as a repercussion of the gradual erosion of the social relations in the course of the eighteenth century. Both men turned against modern social theory, which they viewed as part of the evil that was, but, while they scorned it, in part they had to reason in the same terms, and de Bonald in particular had a preference for rational derivations. The decisive difference between them and modern authors was not so much their vocabulary as their theological premises.

Cultural and cognitive diversity

The intellectual transformation that occurred around 1800 in France was characterized by the expansion, flourishing and differentiation of the natural sciences. At the same time, and mainly as a reaction, a counter-movement gained momentum in literary circles and broke with the conventions of Classicism. These writers of poetry and prose defined literature as an activity completely independent of rational and scientific criteria. On the one hand an essential differentiation developed within the natural sciences, and on the other a split occurred between the sciences and the various literary activities. Intellectual and cultural diversity now became a dominant motif, and by the start of the nineteenth century it was no longer possible to formulate any one general point of view that would apply to all intellectual activities. Auguste Comte, although he was never considered a particularly modern thinker, was one of the first French intellectuals to address this problem. To Comte the dichotomy between science and literature was an established fact, and any attempt to save Classicism was a mere illusion. Procedures had become stricter in the sciences, chemistry and biology had developed into positive sciences, and literary coquetry à la Buffon was now a thing of the past. If anything was typical of the sciences, it was this accelerated progress. The notion that there were criteria for knowledge unrelated to time or scientific subject was a fiction. This awareness constituted the point of departure for Comte's theory of science. In 1817, not yet twenty years old, Comte wrote that it was an illusion to believe that 'absolute principles' could be found – totally erroneous illusion. And as regards human societies, 'everything is relative, that is the only thing that is absolute.'[29] Neither reason nor any other principle could now make a claim to suprahistorical and general validity.

   The split between science and literature was one of the prerequisites for this insight. But the fact that this rift could be interpreted as progress illustrates how ambivalent de Bonald and de Maistre's attitude was to the literary opposition. Chateaubriand and the early Romantics fought for a literature about which philosophers and scientists would no longer have any say. Catholicism initially played a role in this battle. None of the Romantics were willing, however, to conform to the wishes of the ecclesiastical authorities, and the more prestige the writers gained, the less of a role Catholic and royalist aspects of their work were apt to play. Lamartine and Victor Hugo began their careers as fervent admirers of Chateaubriand and as Catholic royalists. But they soon found themselves in a situation of growing dissension with the spokesmen of Christian literature, who were opposed to the idea of art for art's sake. For the church spokesmen, the Romantic movement was an enormous disappointment. The Romantics aspired to free literary forms, they elevated art to the highest manifestation of spirituality, but their spirituality was of a totally different kind to that of the church. In a way, the religious bent of the Romantics was possible only because of the dissolution of the church after the Revolution.[30] In this sense, de Bonald and de Maistre adhered to quite different convictions. To them the autonomy of literature was no less reprehensible than the autonomy of philosophy or science. Intellectual activities could be useful and could serve to make life more pleasant, but ought to remain subordinate to political and moral authority. Thus their support of the Romantic rebels was not unconditional. And, as time went on, de Bonald and de Maistre would appear to be as tenacious regarding this point as they were isolated.

10

Models for a Social Science

In the development of social theory, the first systematic efforts at scientization were made after 1775. The initial steps were taken during Turgot's term in office as Minister, with scientists involved in governmental reforms on an unprecedented scale. Members of the Académie des sciences turned their attention to social questions, and it was Condorcet who first converted these experiences into a programme for a 'social science'. Condorcet's work was continued by Laplace and several of his pupils, but, since mathematical competence was a prerequisite, this attempt at scientization was confined to a small group of professional mathematicians.

A very different form of scientization coincided with the expansion of the medical sciences. Its start was similarly linked to Turgot's period as Minister. The founding of the Société de médecine (1776) represented the first stage. The new society focused on 'public health' and was active in reforming hospitals. During the Revolution a totally new medical system emerged: the position of the church weakened and medicine became a clinical and more scientific profession. Efforts to use medical science as a foundation for the human sciences were part of this process. The work of Cabanis, a physician, exemplified many of these changes.

Before the Revolution a new and more scientific orientation evolved in the mode of thinking about societies. It became dominant in the course of the revolutionary period, and one of the ways it was perpetuated after the Terror was in the framework of the Institut de France. Interest waned somewhat during the Empire, and further endeavours in this direction were hindered by authoritarian Napoleonic policies and the literary and 'spiritualistic' reaction.

In the first instance, the leading spokesmen of the new social theory were scientists themselves. Condorcet, who was the first to represent this development, was a mathematician. His work is now viewed as one of the earliest examples of a mathematical social science. The work of Cabanis, on the other hand, set a major example for the *idéologues* and related thinkers.

Condorcet and social mathematics

The only basis of belief in the natural sciences is the idea that the general laws, known or unknown, which control the phenomena of the universe are necessary and constant; and why should this principle be any less true for the development of the intellectual and moral faculties of man than it is for the other workings of nature?

Condorcet

Condorcet was the last *philosophe* and the first representative of a social theory founded on the natural sciences. His work embodied the transition to a social theory that was oriented primarily towards natural science and, following scientific examples, focused mainly on applications.

Condorcet was born in 1743, half a century after Montesquieu and Voltaire and about twenty-five years after the generation of Diderot, d'Alembert and Rousseau. He did not work on the *Encyclopédie* itself, although he did write a few articles for the 1776–7 supplement. With his first publications Condorcet gained the support of leading mathematicians in the Académie des sciences. His first book in this field was published in 1765, when he was twenty-two. He initially devoted all his time and attention to calculus, in other words to the mathematics that was in the limelight at the time and had taken the place of the older, more geometrical approaches. On the basis of these early publications, in 1769 Condorcet became an auxiliary member of the Académie des sciences. In keeping with its tradition, his family would have preferred a military career for him and opposed the appointment. 'Many noblemen', d'Alembert reported to Lagrange, 'view the title and profession of scientist as beneath the dignity of the aristocracy.'[1] Condorcet, however, proceeded along the path he had chosen and was elected assistant secretary of the Académie four years later. Via his mentor d'Alembert, he had by then also entered the salon of Julie de Lespinasse, one of the most prestigious meeting places for writers and *philosophes*. In addition to d'Alembert, it was frequented by Turgot, Morellet, La Harpe and Suard and visited on occasion by Condillac, Raynal and Chamfort as well as Diderot and Holbach, who had set out in a somewhat more radical direction. Julie de Lespinasse helped Condorcet make his way in the *monde*. She urged the young mathematician to improve his posture and hair-style, not to bite his nails in company, and not to spend the entire day in his study. The aging Voltaire, who had withdrawn to Ferney, encouraged d'Alembert's student as well, and in 1782 Condorcet was elected to the Académie française.

Condorcet's career illustrates the academic successes of the *philosophes*. By 1770 their battle had been won. The *Encyclopédie* had been completed, and at the academies, as well as elsewhere, they were among the most widely admired authors. Between 1767 and 1770 all four of the vacant seats at the Académie française went either to *philosophes* themselves or to their supporters. This was followed by a reaction of the 'pious', who had the required backing at the court, but in 1772 d'Alembert was elected secretary of the Académie française. This simplified new appointments, and from 1774 to 1776, with Turgot as Minister, no fewer than five members were appointed who could be classified as *philosophes*. Although Holbach and his circle continued their 'fatal work' (Voltaire) outside the Académie française, d'Alembert stated that he had no other wish but to have Condorcet accepted among their ranks. This wish was to be fulfilled in 1782, a year before his death.[2]

Condorcet owed his admission to the Académie des sciences in part to d'Alembert's support. This held true to an even greater extent of his appointment as secretary of the Academy, his acceptance into the salon of Julie Lespinasse and his membership at the Académie française. At the salon of Julie de Lespinasse, Condorcet met his second mentor, Anne-Robert-Jacques Turgot. His contact with Turgot was ultimately to alter the very direction of Condorcet's work. Starting in 1770, the reform-minded quartermaster from the province corresponded regularly with the young mathematician. Condorcet kept Turgot informed as to the latest developments in the capital and advised him on technical and scientific questions. When Condorcet became assistant secretary at the Academy in 1773 and Turgot Minister a year later, they began to communicate even more intensively. In the twenty months that Turgot was Minister he did everything he could to employ scientists and technicians in the administration of the state. Condorcet acted as his most important advisor in this respect, and was greatly disappointed by Turgot's fall in 1776. Condorcet returned to his study of calculus, although he was never to complete it. Step by step, he found a way to combine his mathematical capacities with his desire for reform, and abandoned his older mathematical studies. In about 1780 Condorcet realized that the probability calculus, on which Laplace had published several important essays, could serve as a new basis for the moral sciences. Renewed in this manner, the moral sciences were in turn to provide the certainty and precision which Turgot's reforms had lacked.

Condorcet first expressed this conviction in his inaugural lecture at the Académie française in 1782. To Condorcet, the development and expansion of the modern natural sciences meant there were no further obstacles to virtually unlimited progress. The continual proliferation of knowledge had evaporated prejudices and made numerous useful inventions feasible, and the fine arts benefited from it as well. Poets had new inspiration for their imagination, and, all things considered, the entire development had been solely at the expense of a few vain pleasures. However, one important task had yet to be completed: natural science methods had not been extended to the moral sciences. If one contemplated the nature of the moral sciences, Condorcet wrote, one could not fail to conclude that they 'had to follow the same method, ought to acquire a language as exact and precise, and should reach the same level of certitude'.[3] Once that had been achieved, in principle there would no longer be any difference between moral science and natural science, the only dissimilarity being that in moral science the observer is part of the object he studies, thus making scientific development 'slower'. For the same reason, perhaps a certain degree of coercion would be needed before the results of these sciences were accepted.

Condorcet's inaugural lecture was not well received in literary circles.[4] A few years later he was nonetheless able to publish the lengthy study that was the first outgrowth of his line of thought. For quite some time this *Essai sur l'application de l'analyse à la probabilité des décisions rendues à la pluralité des voix* (1785) was considered an extremely cryptic work. It was not rediscovered until after World War II, and has since been viewed as one of the earliest efforts to formulate a mathematical theory of social processes.[5] The subject was a direct product of Turgot's plans for reform. One of the main plans Turgot had in mind was to found representative organs at various levels of administration. At the local level, these councils would be responsible for collecting taxes and executing public works. The composition was independent of status and profession. What mattered was the possession of land: the more land one owned, the more taxes one would pay and the more of a say one would have over how revenues were spent. This system of councils or *municipalités* gave rise to questions as to elections and electoral conduct, and Condorcet's study was a mathematical treatment of these questions.

According to Granger and Gillispie, Condorcet's study did not contain anything new in a mathematical sense. He followed Laplace, whose work continued to play a key role in shaping the mathematical foundations for probability calculus far into the nineteenth century. Nor did Condorcet's book contain much that was directly useful in a practical sense, although he did demonstrate that a simple majority decision did not necessarily reflect the wishes of the majority.[6] The most original aspect of Condorcet's work was that he explained how mathematical techniques could be used to analyse social phenomena. Laplace, whose interest was focused on natural science problems, had not devoted any attention to this possibility. To Laplace, probability calculus was the mathematics of incomplete knowledge. Probability was not a matter of causality, but of knowledge; it was not indicative of an absence of mechanical causality, but only of faulty knowledge of it. Probability calculus could be used if and when causes or events were not all known. This form of mathematics could be used especially in the field of astronomy to analyse irregularities in the orbits of planets. To Laplace, probability calculus was an underutilized opportunity for mathematization, and he later adopted Condorcet's deployment of it to analyse social phenomena. In his classic *Traité analytique des probabilités* (1812) Laplace wrote about electoral procedures and judicial decisions, two topics taken from Condorcet's work.[7]

Condorcet's project to mathematize the moral sciences originated in response to the demand for scientific expertise to accompany Turgot's reform policies. Laplace's new techniques made it possible to meet this demand, and, as a mathematician, *philosophe* and secretary of the Académie des sciences, Condorcet was in the strategic position to do so. For Turgot, Condorcet served as a link with the Académie des sciences, and the fact that Turgot was Minister gave Condorcet his first opportunity actually to put into practice what had hitherto been only wishes and ideas. Condorcet's 'social mathematics' thus materialized in conjunction with the mathematization of new research fields (with Laplace as their leading exponent) and the reform policies initiated by Turgot. At the intersection of these efforts at mathematization and political reform, the idea was born of a mathematical and 'exact' social science. Scientists and political reformers crossed paths, and the centre of social theorizing began to shift. It was no longer solely men of letters or jurists, who were interested, but scientists as well. Questions of application began to play a more important role, and demographic and statistical data that had previously been kept secret now became available. For the first time scientists could work with quantitative data, and during Turgot's term in office as Minister the Académie des sciences began to publish demographic data. In 1786 Laplace used these data to estimate the population of France.[8] Access to quantitative data was a prerequisite for mathematization, and Condorcet firmly advocated setting up special departments for statistics. After 1789 what had begun on a small scale around 1780 unexpectedly came to serve as an important example.

Thanks to former links with the *philosophes* and his academic functions, Condorcet found himself in an auspicious position when the Revolution broke out. He was one of the first and most active to try and formulate answers to the problems with which intellectuals were confronted. In pursuit of new applications for scientific knowledge, he focused on the foundations of the social sciences and the place they were to occupy and on reforming the school system and the academies. He summarized his confidence in the course of history in *Esquisse d'un tableau historique des progrès de l'esprit humain*, which was published posthumously in 1795.

The Société de 1789 was one of the first projects in which Condorcet was involved. The group consisted of reform-minded politicians and intellectuals eager to play a role in drawing up a constitution. Condorcet was a leading figure in the group, which also included Lavoisier, the physiocrat Dupont de Nemours and such future *idéologues* as Cabanis, Destutt de Tracy and Garat. The objective of their activities was to develop the kind of applied social science they described as an *art social*. Just as moral philosophy had focused on individual happiness, social science would be concerned with the 'happiness' of society as a whole. Various sciences had already made separate contributions towards this end, and now these efforts could be combined and coordinated.[9] This description, dating back to early 1790, recalls the vocabulary of moral philosophy.

The objective of the Société de 1789 was to make scientifically sound and well-considered contributions towards a new constitution and other questions on the agenda of the National Assembly. The group came together in early 1790 from within the ranks of a small circle around Condorcet, Lafayette, Dupont de Nemours and Sieyès. In the following months it was transformed into an official society with members, correspondents and a journal of its own. As Baker suggests, it was a kind of academy for the social sciences. Most of the intellectual members of the Société de 1789 were from the Académie des sciences and the Société d'agriculture, a farming reform organization officially recognized in 1788. Like the Société de médecine, this society combined scientific research with plans for reform. Prominent politicians were among the members of the Société de 1789, as were a sizeable group of financiers and bankers involved in various ways in state affairs. Some had sole rights to such financial transactions as insurance policies, others were interested in attaining privileges of this kind, and many had speculated in state loans. Judging from the members of the society, there had been a shift from a predominantly literary salon culture to a culture where scientists who helped run the state occupied prominent positions.

Within a year, however, the Société de 1789 had been dismantled. Condorcet made a new effort in 1793, but no more than six issues of the *Journal d'instruction* were ever issued. It was in this journal that Condorcet published his last contribution to what he now called 'social mathematics'. According to Condorcet, the enormous potential usefulness of probability calculus was in itself a good reason to create a 'separate science'.[10] Further progress would be feasible only if existing insights were systematized and generalized. Condorcet's discourse was intended as an initial survey of the new science. His essay was published in two instalments in June and July 1793, and had apparently been hastily written shortly beforehand. Amid the confusion and chaos, Condorcet felt there was more of a need than ever for lines of reasoning that were 'precise' and 'strict'. Probability calculus was a means towards this end, and could be used to combat 'active ignorance' and the 'pernicious perfection' of eloquence.

The metaphor upon which his generalizations were based was that of a game. Players who are able to calculate their chances have an advantage over those who play purely by instinct or routine. In cases where there was no complete certainty, which was virtually always, probability calculus could be used. Condorcet believed that absolute truths, in other words principles independent of measurements and calculations, were only very rarely applicable and often remained vague. Without measuring and calculating, there was a greater risk of making mistakes or being misguided by prejudices. In principle, Condorcet did not believe there was a single individual or collective interest to which this mathematical treatment could not be applied. Although mathematicians were the only people who could practise social mathematics, the results were within everyone's reach.

'People' and 'things' or a combination of 'people and things' constituted the object of social mathematics. The basic outline for Condorcet's programme consisted of these three categories. Where electoral or demographic data were concerned, people were the object, where lottery chances were involved, things were the object, and where life insurance was entailed, a combination of people and things was the object. Condorcet proceeded from these three categories and went off on any number of tangents without being overly concerned about his original model. He barely made any further reference, for example, to the third category of 'people and things'.[11]

If people were the object, attention was focused on 'individuals' or on the workings of the 'human mind'. For individuals, there was the question of how probable it was that they would reach a certain age or catch a certain disease. This part pertained to probabilities that could be derived from statistical series. The second part pertained to what Condorcet called *motifs de crédibilité*, in other words how credible certain evaluations (decisions, testimonies, verdicts) actually were. In Condorcet's view, the chance of a miscarriage of justice could thus be calculated, and a rational verdict could then be based upon this calculation. Laplace and his students later elaborated upon this branch of social mathematics, which was severely criticized in the nineteenth century by such thinkers as Comte and Mill, and then sunk into oblivion.[12]

In the part of social mathematics that was focused on 'things', criteria were developed to measure, assess and compare them. Without units of this kind it would have been impossible to use mathematical techniques. The examples Condorcet used all had to do with what he called 'social economics'. His criteria were 'money' and, in later stages of societal development, such indicators as national income. Concorcet was probably following the analogy of the standardization of weights and measures, in which he played an active role. The implication was that the task of social mathematics was to contribute towards the development of what have come to be called economic and social indicators.

Various parts of Condorcet's social mathematics were further pursued via the work of Laplace. Statistics, a field that mushroomed after the Revolution, came to play an increasingly important role. A public Bureau de statistique was opened in 1801, although its activities were reorganized in the last years of the Empire. First the comprehensive regional surveys and descriptions made way for more limited statistical information on specific subjects, and then the bureau was closed altogether and the accumulated data became confidential again. In 1817 the city of Paris founded its own statistics department, and some time later the Statistique générale de France (1833) was set up, which was to remain in charge of the country's official statistics for more than a century.[13] This rapid growth meant mathematicians such as Poisson and Fourier had far more information at hand than their predecessors. At the beginning of the nineteenth century the technical prospects for social mathematics were more favourable than ever. Concorcet's proposals were nonetheless disputed and superseded by new interpretations of probability.[14]

Condorcet worked from the individualistic model of classical probability theory, which viewed each decision as the outcome of individual and rational considerations. Classical probability theory, as Laplace observed, was nothing but 'common sense reduced to arithmetic'. The model was descriptive and normative at the same time, descriptive because it formalized existing chances and considerations, and normative because one type of conduct was taken as the norm and all the other types were viewed as non-rational. Social questions were approached in the same fashion. The subject was a collective, government, state or society, but the model remained geared towards a reasonable subject that acted in a rational manner.

With the breakthrough of modern statistics, rival models came to the fore. It no longer concentrated on the choices and decisions of rational subjects, but on distributions and trends. Quetelet's work, as Lorraine Daston notes, presented a good example of this transition. His studies were a combination of statistical facts, individualistic assumptions and a deterministic scientistic ideal. Quetelet's *mécanique* or *physique sociale* was an imitation of Laplace's celestial mechanics. Quetelet followed this determinist programme by interpreting any variation as a deviation or error and consistently restoring them to averages. With the aid of these averages, he believed it would be possible to formulate laws as irrefutable as those of mechanics.[15] Social physics was the science of the average man, *l'homme moyen*, with statistics producing the material of which he was composed. Quetelet's reasoning was reminiscent of the individualistic assumptions of classical probability calculations and the mechanical conceptions of causality of Laplace's school. At the same time it was one of the most important contributions to modern statistics, from which these models were gradually to disappear. Statistics became an activity for officials and administrators focused on the periodical and numerical description of sectors, groups and regions. Mathematicians and physicists no longer played a role. It was not until the end of the nineteenth century that a new series of innovations was introduced. However, the new techniques of Galton and Pearson centred no longer on averages but on variance and distribution. They were interested in the extremes, the deviations from the average, and in particular in determining the distance between the 'genius' and the 'degenerate'.[16] This resulted in totally different statistical computations from Quetelet's averages.

Cabanis and the idéologues

> It is indeed from physical sensibility, or from the organization it
> determines and modifies, that ideas, feeling, passions, and virtue
> and vice are derived. . . . The movements of the soul have the same
> origin as health or bodily ailments: this true source of morals is in
> the human organization, on which both our faculty and our
> manner of feeling depend.
>
> Cabanis

The *idéologues*, a school that took shape during the Revolution, played a prominent role in the human sciences and philosophy until the start of the Empire.[17] The careers and work of the *idéologues* were linked to the revolutionary changes. Many of the problems they dealt with were rooted in the new relations, and the way they approached these problems was determined by the new prestige of the natural sciences. Unlike Condorcet, however, their orientation was not towards the mathematical but towards the life sciences. They had little or no interest in mathematical and statistical techniques, and generally viewed them as inappropriate methods for social sciences. Cabanis felt calculating probabilities was a 'spurious and dangerous approach'.[18] Medical and human sciences studied phenomena that were rarely quantifiable. The 'energy' and 'intensity' of human passions, or so Destutt de Tracy held, could not be expressed in numbers.[19]

Almost all the members of the group, born between 1750 and 1760, were a good ten years younger than Condorcet, and their publications date back to after 1789. Most of the *idéologues* were actively involved in the first stage of the Revolution. A number of them were delegates at the National Assembly (Destutt de Tracy, Volney), others turned to journalism (Garat) and virtually all of them were active in such clubs as the Société de 1789. After the Terror, when a number of them were imprisoned (Daunou, Destutt de Tracy, Volney), they played an instrumental role in the forging of a new school system. The *écoles centrales* were based upon plans drawn up by a few *idéologues* and carried out by people who sympathized with them. As of 1795, *idéologues* rose to key positions in the department of the Institut de France devoted to the 'moral and political sciences'. It was then that a real 'group' emerged and that the word *idéologistes* came into use. Years later it was Napoleon's bantering that led to the group's being called *idéologues*. At the time, however, their prominent role had already declined and under the Empire the group split up. Cabanis died in 1808, others retained their positions, but the younger members of the group sought new and different paths.

The *idéologues* had their first contact with each other at the salon of Madame Helvétius. After her husband's death she had settled in Auteuil just outside Paris, where until her death in 1800 she was the hub of a circle of scientists, *philosophes* and reformers.[20] The guests at her salon sometimes included such elder celebrities as d'Alembert, Condillac or Turgot, though it was frequented more regularly by the circle around Holbach, younger writers such as Chamfort, and future *idéologues* such as Cabanis and Volney. There was a great deal of sympathy in the group for the new independence of the United States and for Turgot's reform policies. During the Revolution there was even greater political interest, and such well-known politicians as Siéyès, Talleyrand and Mirabeau came to the *société d'Auteuil* as well.

The *idéologues* and other guests at Auteuil belonged to the republican intelligentsia. It consisted largely of professional intellectuals with moderate revolutionary leanings. First and foremost they wanted to put an end to the role of the church, particularly in education and health care. They were also critical of the *mondaine* culture, which was dominated by the aristocracy. The most important organ of these groups was the *Décade philosophique* (1794–1807), which published on scientific and cultural matters. Politically, it was a platform for movements defending the revolutionary achievements against Royalists and Jacobins alike. To this end they alluded to the legacy of the Enlightenment. After 1800 this occurred mainly in heated debates with Fontanes and Chateaubriand's *Mercure de France*.

The contents of the *Décade philosophique* accurately reflected the intellectual mood of the revolutionary period. A great deal of attention was devoted to the sciences, especially physiology and the various branches of medicine. In that sense, the *Décade* was diametrically opposed to the *Mercure de France*, where very little space was allotted to the sciences and virtually nothing was written about medicine or physiology.[21] Since so many medical practitioners refused to accept the existence of a 'soul', the branches of medicine were viewed by the circles around the *Mercure* as consisting of 'materialistic' doctrines.

The prominent position of the medical sciences was also evident in the curricula vitae of the *Décade's* editorial staff. Almost half of them had a background in the natural sciences, and the other half consisted of almost 30 per cent men of letters, with a small group of *érudits* and a small group of amateurs. There were very few writers who devoted all their time and attention to literature in the traditional sense. The large majority of the staff with a background in the natural sciences came from the various branches of medicine or pharmacy. There were relatively small numbers of mathematicians, chemists and engineers, and a somewhat larger number of naturalists.[22] The prominent place accorded to the medical sciences was also illustrated by the careers of the *Décade's* staff. Two professional groups dominated: teachers (and professors) and physicians.

In general, the *Décade philosophique* was the organ for the somewhat younger intellectual bourgeoisie. For this group the sciences were significantly more important than literature. Only a small role was reserved for the mathematical sciences, which had become inaccessible to laymen. However, the life sciences, not requiring such specialized knowledge, served as an important intellectual model. There was similarly a great deal of interest in the newer social sciences. The *philosophe* most widely acclaimed in the *Décade* was Condorcet. He was lauded as a mathematician, as a co-worker of Turgot, and as the man who further developed Turgot's idea of progress.[23] In a social sense, the circle around the *Décade* was more homogeneous than the group responsible for the *Encyclopédie*. Almost all of them were professional intellectuals, mainly teachers and physicians, whose positions were based largely upon their cultural capital. They had very few ties with the *monde* and looked down upon the *bohème*. Despite many similarities in their political attitudes, they had no contact, for example, with the more cosmopolitan and aristocratic group around Madame de Staël. There were no longer any *philosophes*, as Regaldo noted, among the *Décade* authors, just *médecins philosophes*, *magistrats philosophes* and *professeurs philosophes*.[24]

What was true of the *Décade* also held true of the *idéologues*. Most of them were from the intellectual bourgeoisie; they were strongly geared towards the sciences, particularly the branches of medicine, and were in their thirties when the Revolution broke out. Their backgrounds differed – Volney was a geographer, Garat a barrister and Cabanis a physician – but their common aim was to develop an integral science of man and society. The results of these branches of knowledge ought to be taught at various institutions, they felt, and the administration of the state should be based upon the insight they produced. The Moral and Political Science Department at the Institut de France provided an institutional setting for the development of the sciences.

The moral and political science class consisted of six sections (philosophy, moral theory, law, political economy, history and geography), each of which had six members. The *idéologues* were concentrated in the philosophy section. The members of the second class came in part from the intellectual sector and in part from political administration (high officials, ambassadors). Many of them had been involved in the Revolution. More conservative views were dominant only in the geography and history sections. The historians were almost all former members of the Académie des inscriptions and had rarely played any role in the Revolution.[25]

The close ties with the new state were evident from Destutt de Tracy's proposal to found a college for the 'moral and political sciences'. It was to serve the same function as the Ecole polytechnique for the mathematical sciences. Higher public offices would only be open to people with a thorough knowledge of the social sciences. Nothing ever came of this proposal. Shortly afterwards the reconciliation with the church was officially confirmed, symbolizing the final break between Napoleon and the *idéologues*.

The work of the *idéologues* was part of a broad offensive on the part of the intellectual bourgeoisie to reinforce its position. Their efforts were directed against the position of the First and Second Estates in the cultural sector. The call for scientific standards was of central significance in this campaign, as was the promise of application possibilities. The work of the *idéologues* fitted well into this framework. Their activities were focused upon developing a scientific foundation for the social sciences. This orientation gave rise to two questions. Firstly, which sciences and methods were best suited to serve as examples? Just as Condorcet had called for mathematical techniques, the *idéologues* propagated a science of society that was based upon physiology. In *Rapports du physique et du moral de l'homme* (1802) Cabanis reconnoitred the field. Physiology was viewed as a worthy replacement for unscientific notions regarding the 'soul' and for the unsystematic psychology of the *moralistes*.

If the human sciences could thus be provided with a stricter scientific foundation, the question arose as to whether there was any future for philosophy. The man who set out to solve this problem was Destutt de Tracy. In the tradition of Condillac, he felt philosophy had one and only one task: to analyse the human mind. Condillac called analyses of this kind 'metaphysics', though his successors spoke of an *analyse des sensations et des idées.* This term was also used for the philosophy section at the Institut de France. It was before this audience that Destutt de Tracy presented his first work from 1796 to 1798, sketching the contours of a new science that was to replace philosophy. Since ideas could also be analysed in a scientific fashion, he held that philosophy should be transformed into 'ideology', the science of ideas. Ideology would be an empirical science with the physiology of the senses and the mind as its foundation, and in this sense ideology was part of zoology. There was also a more philosophical branch, studying the expression of ideas (grammar) and their combination (logic).

With its subject matter consisting of ideas, ideology was an extra-ordinary science. As the study of the foundations and methods of scientific knowledge, it was the science of sciences. To Destutt de Tracy, ideology was the only conceivable scientific philosophy and the only feasible philosophical foundation for the sciences.[26] It was a science, but as the science of sciences it was simultaneously a means towards scientization.

From this perspective, Destutt de Tracy viewed the work of Kant, for example, as a reversion to old-style metaphysics. In France the first books about Kant were not published until 1801, twenty years after the *Kritik der reinen Vernunft*.[27] These publications were reviewed at the Institut de France. It was one of the tasks of the Institut to maintain relations with foreign institutions. Correspondents could be appointed for this purpose, but on account of the war situation not much had come of it. What is more, the political rulers were not in favour of international exchanges. France was at war with virtually all the other European powers, and the Minister of Home Affairs stated that enlightened ideas were certainly not to be expected from Germany. The philosophers at the Institut nonetheless felt that Kant's writings deserved some attention. This was, as Jules Simon observed, an unexpected honour.[28] However, there was not much interest in it. To Destutt de Tracy, Kant's philosophy proved that Germany was still overrun by sects. Kant himself headed one of those sects, where his theories were taught in the same dogmatic fashion as theology. In France all this was a thing of the past. Destutt de Tracy was unimpressed by the contents of Kant's teachings. It is true that he did not read Kant's work in the original, since he did not know German, but he perused a Latin translation and was familiar with a summary. In his opinion its author, the Dutchman Johannes Kinker, had clearly conveyed Kant's line of thinking. His criticism of the German philosopher was that his thinking was based on misuse of words and faulty abstractions. Pure reason did not exist, nor did pure knowledge, and a critique of pure reason was consequently totally superfluous. To Destutt de Tracy, transcendental analyses were no more than a new variation on the old metaphysics. Other *idéologues* were in agreement with him. Garat concluded that the Latin edition was teeming with odd phrases, apparently Germanisms, so that Kant's teachings could be assumed to be as 'barbarian' as his Latin.

References to Kant in the *Décade philosophique* were of the same nature. Here, again, the sarcastic tone masked an ignorance as vast as the lack of interest. The anti-metaphysical mood and feelings of national superiority obstructed a fair appraisal of Kant's ideas. It was not until Madame de Staël's *De l'Allemagne* was published in 1814 that interest in German literature and philosophy was really aroused. Her depiction of Germany as a nation of poets and thinkers was to dominate the French image of it for years to come. Exiled from France by Napoleon, Madame de Staël had settled in Coppet, Switzerland, where a small group of intellectuals gathered, including Benjamin Constant and Sismondi. Via August Wilhelm Schlegel they became acquainted with German literature and philosophy. Degérando was the only *idéologue* to be well informed on matters of German philosophy. But he was the youngest member of the group, opted for a career in civil service, and was overshadowed by Destutt de Tracy and Cabanis.

Alongside Destutt de Tracy, Pierre-Jean-Georges Cabanis was the other major *idéologue*. It was he who formulated the physiological foundations of the doctrine. Cabanis grew up in the Limousin, where relations were cordial between his father and Turgot, the *intendant* of the region. With a letter of recommendation from Turgot, Cabanis arrived in Paris in 1771. He was initially interested mainly in literature. He translated part of the *Iliad* for a contest at the Académie française, and at the salon of his tutor, the poet Antoine Roucher, he made the acquaintance of Chamfort and Garat. When Turgot was appointed Minister, Roucher came into office as well. As his literary activities were not yet sufficiently remunerative, this enabled him to earn a living. Cabanis had high hopes of a similar arrangement, but the fall of Turgot seemed to ruin his chances. Cabanis was forced to choose an occupation, and it was in part upon the urging of his father that he decided to study medicine. By way of his relations with Roucher and Turgot, shortly after the start of his studies he was introduced at Madame Helvétius' salon. Madame Helvétius treated Cabanis like her own son. He lived at her home, which she left to him in her will together with her other possessions. Soon after he met Madame Helvétius Cabanis joined a Freemason's lodge, where he came into contact with Lacépède, Dupont de Nemours, Benjamin Franklin and such future *idéologues* as Destutt de Tracy, Volney, Garat and Daunou.

He completed his first discourse, *Du degré de certitude de la médecine*, shortly before the Revolution. It was a well-reasoned defence of medicine written in the form of a refutation of the most common arguments against medical science. After the Revolution broke out Cabanis focused his attention on more pressing matters such as hospital reforms. He published *Observations sur les hôpitaux* (1790) and joined the Société de 1789. Through his friends Garat and Volney, both fully immersed in politics by this time, he came in touch with political leaders and for a while even wrote speeches for Mirabeau. However, Cabanis had a marked preference for more administrative functions and became involved in welfare work for the poor and hospital management in Paris. During the Revolution he came into more intensive contact with Condorcet as well. Revolutionary scientists moved in rather small circles, as is illustrated by the fact that Cabanis married Condorcet's sister-in-law. After the Terror Cabanis was invited to join the Institut de France and was appointed to the Ecole de santé in Paris. In acknowledgment for his active support of Napoleon's coup, he and several other *idéologues* also became members of the Senate.

From the angle of medical science, Cabanis' work was probably not that original. He did not make any discoveries, nor were his theoretical insights particularly innovative.[29] Yet the fact remains that Cabanis was one of the leading physicians of the revolutionary period and the most important spokesman of a science of man based on physiology. In this respect, his originality was comparable with Condorcet's. Both of them worked to expand existing insights and methods, Condorcet demonstrating the use of probability calculus to analyse social processes and Cabanis focusing on the physiology of mental phenomena. In Cabanis' view, there was a direct link between the expansion of medical research and the Revolution. His first discourse, *Du degré dé certitude de la médecine* (1788), was still confined to the traditional field of medicine. When it was published ten years later, Cabanis added a preface attributing to medicine a totally new function. Medical research, he stated, could also serve as a 'basis' for philosophy and moral science. The laws of the organic *sensibilité* were grounds not only for illness and health, but also for mental phenomena such as passions and ideas. Medical science could thus provide a sturdy foundation for a better understanding of how human beings act and think. Every effort to influence their conduct by way of education or politics should be based upon insight into the 'source' of mental processes. The moral human being was nothing but an aspect of the physical one.[30]

By the time this discourse was published in 1798, Cabanis had already been engaged for some time in elaborating upon this programme. Starting in 1796 he held lectures about it at the Institut de France, which were published in a more detailed version as *Rapports du physique et du moral de l'homme* (1802). According to Cabanis, the physician and the moralist should both be interested in the physical human being. The physician was interested in health and illness, and the moralist in thoughts and emotions, but this division was debatable. Even the most complex mental operations were linked to organs, and organs were subject to the same laws as other parts of the body. By studying the organic foundations of mental phenomena, the moral sciences would be able to acquire a sturdy basis. What Cabanis presented were still 'only' physiological studies, but they were focused on functions that were of crucial importance to a science of man and society. In this conception, 'physiology', the 'study of ideas' and 'morals' were three branches of the same science. Cabanis called it the science of man, *science de l'homme*. His use of this term put him in the tradition of Barthez. Germans, he observed, preferred the term 'anthropology'.[31]

The point of departure for this science of man was the organization of the *sensibilité physique*. People were 'sensory beings', open to impressions that were either internal or external. Processing external impressions led to ideas, and processing internal impressions led to instincts. Feelings were generally produced by a combination of the two. The processing of impressions was not a mechanical process, but was shaped by the 'organization' of the human body, in other words by how the organs interacted and worked together. In the first instance, physiology thus provided an invariant model of the organic foundations of mental processes. This model could subsequently be specified according to age, sex, temperament, illnesses, habits and climate. Cabanis wrote separate treatises on the 'influence' of all these variables. At the end of his lengthy study there was a separate section on how mental phenomena could affect physiological processes. Sudden anxiety, for example, could upset the digestion, and in general the brain exerted considerable influence on countless parts of the body.[32]

Firstly, Cabanis' psychophysiology could be distinguished from the spiritualistic model, according to which higher human capacities were localized in the incorporeal 'soul'. In that sense, his work clashed with ecclesiastical doctrines and other conceptions that drew a sharp distinction between the body and the mind. In principle, Cabanis did not see any difference between products of the mind and of other organs. Like the other organs, the brain 'processed impressions' and excreted a product: thoughts.[33] On the grounds of statements like these, Cabanis was frequently categorized as a materialist. He himself refuted this label and it might be preferable to speak of monism.[34] Cabanis did not claim that everything could be reduced to matter, he merely denied any essential distinction between physical and mental phenomena. Mental phenomena also had an organic 'basis' or 'origin', so that the human sciences ought to be based upon physiology.

Secondly, Cabanis' approach could be distinguished from the mechanical ones. In this sense, he adhered to the vitalist notions of the Montpellier school. Living bodies were not machines; their functioning was grounded in sensory stimuli. *Sensibilité* was the most important property of living beings, and the way it was organized was the subject matter of the life sciences. Far more than the Montpellier school, however, Cabanis focused on the relevance of physiology to problems of knowledge formation and human behaviour. Barthez had already headed in this direction in *Nouveaux éléments de la science de l'homme* (1778). Cabanis went even further, and his work was far more systematic than that of his predecessors.[35]

Medical circles exhibited avid interest in Cabanis' work. Numerous physicians were sympathetic to the idea of studying cognitive and moral phenomena from a physiological perspective. Some of them, such as Philippe Pinel, had frequented the salon in Auteuil before the Revolution and held similar ideas; others had been Cabanis' pupils and students at the new *écoles de santé*. The younger ones joined the active Société médicale d'émulation (1796), where followers of the *idéologues* played an important role.[36]

Arguments in favour of an integral science of man did not remain confined to eloquent declarations or incidental examples. Efforts were also made to conduct organized research, particularly at the Société des observateurs de l'homme (1799–1805), which was closely linked to the *idéologues*. Its aim was to 'observe the physical, intellectual and moral aspects of mankind'.[37] Criticism of speculative theories was accompanied by a strong emphasis on observation and comparison, a mentality supported by the physicians and naturalists who dominated the society.

The Société des observateurs de l'homme was founded immediately after Napoleon's coup. What the founders expected was undoubtedly that the human sciences would also benefit from Napoleon's aspirations. Scientists had viewed the Egyptian expedition as a promising example, which was one of the reasons why the *idéologues* had supported the coup.

As usual, the society organized lectures and contests. The contest instructions were, for example, to determine by way of 'observations' what the influence was of 'various occupations on the character of the people who engage in them', or to ascertain via 'daily observations' how the physical, intellectual and moral capacities of children developed. Instructions of this kind were in keeping with the efforts of the *idéologues* to develop a science of the human mind. Since experimentation was not excluded in advance, the notion was considered of asking the government for permission to observe a number of children for ten or fifteen years in a 'purely natural environment'. It would shed light upon the origins of language and other mental capacities.

A great deal of attention was devoted to variations in man's physical and moral constitution. Just as physicians had started with a medical topography of France, a plan was conceived to draw up an anthropological topography as well. For each region, material would be gathered about the physical and moral features of the inhabitants. A more exact assessment of the influence of the climate, for example, could then be made on the grounds of this information. This avid interest was in no way confined to the local population. When an expedition to Australia was scheduled in 1800, two members of the society wrote a list of instructions for the travellers. The expedition was financed by the government and accompanied by numerous scientists. Cuvier instructed them on the comparative anatomy of races and explained how worthwhile it would be to collect skulls and skeletons. He provided them with information on how to preserve these and made a few suggestions on how to get them, for example by going to cemeteries.

The *idéologue* Degérando wrote extensive guidelines for observing the customs of natives. He discussed the most common shortcomings of travel accounts, stressing the importance of detailed observations on a wide spectrum of subjects such as upbringing, marriage, family relations, the position of women and sensations such as 'shame' or 'love'. Degérando worked from the assumption that the only differences were in the developmental stage people were at. Primitive societies were not interesting as examples of fundamentally different races, but as examples of earlier developmental stages. By becoming acquainted with these cultures, one could gain insight into the past of humanity.

Say and Saint-Simon

[My] friends, we are organized bodies.

Saint-Simon

The nucleus of the Société des observateurs de l'homme consisted of physicians and naturalists. Cabanis, Pinel and Moreau de la Sarthe were members, as were Cuvier and Lamarck. Via their work, physiological models also began to serve as models outside the life sciences, as had the early examples of Destutt de Tracy, Degérando and other *idéologues*. What they were mainly interested in was developing a new science of man that would shed light on how physiological and mental processes were related. This insight was a prerequisite for the intended changes in upbringing, education and health care. The work of Jean-Baptiste Say and Claude-Henri de Saint-Simon were later examples of a science of man based on physiology. However, the discourses by Say and Saint-Simon, whose work was related to that of the *idéologues*, were also illustrations of a new tendency. Their central concept was no longer *sensibilité*, it was 'organization'. They based their writing far more upon social frameworks, and went on to interpret them by using this concept of organization. The emphasis was no longer on a new science of man that would make it possible to formulate well-founded policies, but on social processes that were relatively detached from political decision-making. This model was commonly used to emphasize that 'social order' was a spontaneous occurrence. It came to the fore after 1800, when the *idéologues* and like-minded colleagues were divested of their political power. The period of reform was over, and the political role of the *idéologues* was a thing of the past. Viewed in this light, the work of Say and Saint-Simon was an effort to preserve the theoretical orientation of the *idéologues* under different circumstances.

The child of a Protestant family of merchants, Jean-Baptiste Say was cut out for a future in the world of trade and industry. Active as a journalist in the Revolution, he was one of the founders of the *Décade philosophique* in 1794. As a member of the *Décade*'s editorial staff he wrote about a wide range of subjects, but gradually came to concentrate more on economic analyses. Together with several like-minded *idéologues* he was appointed by Napoleon to the Tribunate. It was the task of this institution to evaluate bills proposed by the Cabinet. Just as in the Senate, Napoleon initially appointed numerous intellectuals to the Tribunate. However, it was not long before disputes arose with the future emperor. Like the *idéologues* and the group around Madame de Staël, Say belonged to the liberal opposition. In 1802 and 1803 Napoleon dismissed many of these liberal intellectuals (Say, Benjamin Constant and such *idéologues* as Daunou, Ginguené and Laromiguière) from their functions at the Tribunate. Say withdrew to the provinces as a cotton and thread manufacturer and continued to devote his attention to political economy. For generations his *Traité d'économie politique* (1803) was to remain a standard work in France, and in the Restoration period Say was selected to occupy the first professorial chair in this field. He propagated a more empirical approach to economic phenomena than the physiocrats. Economic processes should be analysed regardless of political or judicial questions of rights and obligations. The physiocrats had viewed political economy as an application of natural law. Basing his work on that of Adam Smith and the physiology of Cabanis, Say advocated a more positive approach. The subject matter of political economy was a 'complex and living totality'. As a science of society, economics ought to study the various 'social organs', their needs and ways to satisfy these needs. Using this more physiological strategy, he repudiated Condorcet's social mathematics and accorded statistics a limited and purely descriptive function.[38]

Saint-Simon was a more marked example of this orientation. He too viewed the work of Cabanis and other physiologists as the most appropriate example for a social science. Unlike Say and the *idéologues*, however, he was an intellectual outsider. Saint-Simon was an ambitious self-taught man, an aristocrat from an impoverished Parisian family who did not intend to allow anyone to keep him from what he saw as his task. In keeping with tradition, he began his career in military service. Under La Fayette's command, he fought side by side with other French officers on the side of the American rebels against the English. By speculating, he amassed a small fortune during the Revolution, but soon after he discovered the sciences in 1797 he decided to abandon his commercial activities. He moved to premises across the street from the Ecole polytechnique and played host to young scientists who told him about the work of Laplace and Lagrange. In 1801 he moved to the vicinity of the Ecole de médecine and saw to it that he was similarly informed as regards the medical sciences and physiology.

All this information convinced Saint-Simon there was a great future in store for the modern sciences. He himself decided to devote his time and energy to their most general aspects, to *la science générale*.[39] Although it was not clear just exactly what this 'general science' entailed, Saint-Simon felt a need to return to 'general ideas'. Even the greatest scientists had too one-sided a view of reality. It was time for a new synthesis, a kind of super-science, which was to be the start of the 'great scientific revolution' he foresaw.

What this science had to offer was first and foremost a new form of spiritual power. Priests and theologians, he felt, should be replaced by scientists. This new spiritual power would usher in a 'positive' and 'organic' era to succeed the 'revolutionary' and 'critical' period. In this new order secular power would be in the hands of the producers. Saint-Simon devised multifarious plans to effect this transition. He proposed erecting monuments for scientists and appointing scientific councils and collected funds for a new encyclopedia, but his grand spirit of enterprise failed to lead to more than a few pamphlets.

To a certain extent, this held true of his 'scientific' work as well. Saint-Simon felt it was important not to stop at the work of Newton or Locke but to go a step further, and his *Introduction aux travaux scientifiques du 19e siècle* (1807–8) outlined this kind of step. Newton's work could be generalized to a universal law on the forces of attraction, a law that could then serve as the basis for structuring a new society and a new morality. In addition, Saint-Simon formulated a thought to which he attached great importance, that the universe consisted of solid and liquid parts, and that changes were the result of the 'battle' between the two. In an accompanying letter Saint-Simon stated once again just exactly what his contribution was: he had devised a better system than Newton, a better classification of the sciences than Bacon and a better method than Locke. The members of the Bureau de longitudes, whom he presented with his manuscript, were not impressed by these innovations, but it was not until later that Saint-Simon discovered the reason for their unenthusiastic reaction. In *Mémoire sur la science de l'homme* (1813) he noted two kinds of bodies, *corps bruts* and *corps organisés*. Mathematicians and physicists studied the former, and physiologists the latter. The members of the Bureau de longitudes were, however, unaware of the existence of *corps organisés*. They were astronomers and mathematicians who had taken no notice whatsoever of the most recent advances. In the nineteenth century, according to Saint-Simon, physiology was to be at the vanguard of progress. It was time to accept this and put an end to the domination of the *brutiers*.[40]

This was not the first time Saint-Simon highlighted the importance of physiology. In one of his earliest writings, *Lettres d'un habitant de Genève* (1802), he distinguished four sciences: astronomy, physics, chemistry and physiology. Since human beings were organized bodies, 'social relations' should be viewed as 'physiological phenomena'. With the intensity of a veritable prophet, he concluded that it was the task of physiologists to oust the 'philosophers and moralists', just as astronomers had ousted the astrologers and chemists the alchemists. Soon afterwards he wrote his *Essai sur l'organisation sociale* (1804), in which he referred to the need to turn the 'science of social organization' into a positive science. Initially, however, Saint-Simon was more interested in *science générale* than a social science. It was not until he was treated in such an ungentlemanly manner by the *brutiers* that he turned his attention to physiology and social science and emphasized the conflict between the sciences of 'dead' and 'living' nature. He signed letters with a *salut physiologique* and scoffed at Laplace and Lagrange. During the Restoration there was once again a change in his interest. It was no longer scientists, not even physiologists, on whom he pinned his hopes, but industrialists. *L'industrie* (1817) and *L'organisateur* (1819–20) promulgated the new message, which Saint-Simon codified in his last writings into a *Catéchisme des industriels* (1823–4) and *Le nouveau christianisme* (1825).

Compared with those of Say and the *idéologues*, the writings of Saint-Simon were vague and confused, although several themes did recur in a rather coherent fashion. The transition from the eighteenth to the nineteenth century, from a 'critical' to a 'positive' period, was the central theme. According to Saint-Simon, the social basis of the new society consisted of producers and scientists and the concept that characterized the new society was 'organization'. Saint-Simon had borrowed the term from physiology, and upheld the pretence of being the first to transform the 'science of social organization' into a coherent body of knowledge. Most of what he knew of physiology had been taught to him by Jean Burdin, a young physician who frequented Saint-Simon's salon. Saint-Simon felt the most important contributions to the new science had been made by Vicq-d'Azyr, Cabanis and Bichat by way of their physiological work, and by Condorcet by way of his philosophy of history. All the important questions, in Saint-Simon's opinion, had been addressed by these four men, but had not been summarized in one book, 'organized' into a whole. This then was the task he set for himself, and, with the help of the new science, 'disorganization' would cease and 'reorganization' commence. From this quasi-physiological perspective, Saint-Simon stressed the contrast between 'critical' and 'organic' stages. He viewed politics, legislation and moral codes as 'rules' with a 'hygienic' function. They differed in various eras, but ought to serve the health of society.[41]

In his study on Saint-Simon, Henri Gouhier emphasized that his originality lay more in his temperament than his ideas.[42] Saint-Simon, in Gouhier's view, was not capable of finishing any of the things he started. He was not even able to earn a living, and remained financially dependent on his associates and relatives, and later on donations from well-to-do industrialists. The only exception was in the revolutionary period, when he and Count Redern engaged in some extremely successful financial transactions. What Saint-Simon excelled in was speculation. He had a great talent for acting at the right moment, buying, convincing others and selling. It didn't matter what he bought, as long as it did not require any special know-how or demand much time. Saint-Simon had the energy and the drive to make a success of these quick business ventures. Just as he speculated with property, he later speculated with ideas. However, he was never able to match his earlier financial success. Successful transactions on the intellectual market turned out to require a kind of capital Saint-Simon did not have. The illusion upon which Saint-Simon's entire 'scientific' career was based was that he could obtain ideas in the same way as he could obtain money. But this was not the case, and in this sense his career illustrates *a contrario* the specific features of the accumulation of intellectual capital. Intellectual capital proved to be far more strongly linked to the individual who possessed it than economic capital, it required investments on a longer term than Saint-Simon was accustomed to, and his familiarity with the market in question clearly left much to be desired. Saint-Simon had neither the knowledge nor the intellectual proclivity to be a success as an intellectual broker or impresario. What is more, in the Empire conditions were far less conducive to ventures of this kind than during the Revolution.

Up until 1814, as Gouhier observed, Saint-Simon was a 'magnificent failure'.[43] Then something changed. *De la réorganisation de la société européenne* was published in 1814. Its style, construction and reasoning made it his first real book. Grand plans and prophecies made way for an analysis that could vie with any of the comparable writings. In part it was why his work began to attract attention. The reason for this sudden change was Augustin Thierry, a young historian who acted as his co-author and secretary. He was replaced in 1817 by Auguste Comte. If a somewhat coherent doctrine emerged, and after the death of Saint-Simon even a movement, it was largely thanks to the efforts of Saint-Simon's assistants and co-workers. They eliminated the most speculative elements in his thinking, primed his revelations and systematized his brainstorms. In their journals and organizations, a Saint-Simon arose whose fame was ultimately to endure. The would-be scientist who felt it was below his dignity to be compared with Newton soon faded into oblivion. What remained was the reformer, the prophet of industrial society.[44]

By the time Saint-Simon formulated his proposals for a new social science the tide had already turned. At the time of the Empire the intellectual climate was hardly conducive to projects of this kind, and Saint-Simon was headed down a path that had just come to an end. His explanations exhibited the perseverance of someone who is rowing against the current, but has failed to notice. As an outsider, Saint-Simon was not familiar with exactly how things were done, and his unwavering self-confidence exempted him from the questions by which newcomers were ordinarily tormented. Following the advent of the Empire, virtually all the younger *idéologues* headed in a direction opposite to Saint-Simon's. They began to doubt the possibilities for a strict scientization of the human sciences and took an interest in themes more in keeping with the spiritualist opposition.

After 1802 the *idéologues* soon suffered one defeat after another. Ever since the Concordat they had been on the side of the opposition. Some of them were dismissed from the Tribunate, and in the Senate Cabanis and Destutt de Tracy held their tongues. After the *écoles centrales* were closed down the Institut de France was reorganized. In 1803 the separate class for the 'moral and political sciences' was abrogated, and its members divided between the other classes. A few geographers were transferred to the natural science department, eleven former classmates joined the literary department, and twenty-two opted for the department of historical sciences, which offered opportunities to conduct research in the field of 'moral and political sciences'. However, this research could be conducted only under the condition that it pertained to the past and did not cause any 'disturbance' to 'internal harmony'. The abrogation of the second class had been directly motivated by Napoleon's aversion to the opposition, although recommendations to this effect had also been made by members of the Institut, particularly men of letters and historians.[45] From then on this field of study once again fell within their province. After the abrogation of the second class the Société des observateurs de l'homme also came to an end, and in 1807 the *Décade philosophique* was banned.

After these setbacks the *idéologues* split into two groups, one focused on medicine and the other on philosophy. The effect of this split was that joint endeavours towards an integral human and social science were replaced by growing rivalry between the physiological and the more psychological approach. Even during the Empire and the Restoration, in the fields of medicine and physiology a monistic or materialistic vision of human nature was long to remain prevalent.[46] Gall's phrenology and Broussais' physiology were continuations of the attempt to study links between organic and mental phenomena from a medical point of view. Magendie's work was another illustration of how widely accepted these notions were in medical circles. He was viewed as one of the founders of a strictly experimental and positive branch of physiology. He avoided premature generalization, but it was based upon the notions formulated by Cabanis that he arrived at his insights.[47]

The philosophers went in the opposite direction. Maine de Biran, Degérando and Laromiguière began to take an interest in the autonomy of the mind *vis-à-vis* the brain and the nervous system. In 1804 or 1805 Maine de Biran departed from the teachings of Destutt de Tracy. He had hitherto spoken of 'ideology', which then became 'subjective ideology', only to turn into 'psychology' in 1807.[48] Psychology was defined as the science of man's 'internal sense' or 'consciousness'. Introspection was an important source, and Maine de Biran's *Journal* became one of his most renowned works. Degérando shared this interest in the self and the internal, and combined it with his interest in the history of philosophy. Laromiguière dealt with these same themes in the lectures he gave starting in 1809 at the new Faculty of Letters in Paris. All of them had started as *idéologues* and, after the reorganizations of the Napoleonic era, increasingly focused their attention on what was independent from physiology. This 'other' and 'nobler' part of man was beyond the scope of physiologists, and in Degérando's view could only be observed by the 'inner eye' or by using other subjective methods.[49] After the fall of Napoleon, Victor Cousin elaborated upon this spiritualist variant. He gave a prominent position to spiritualist psychology in the philosophy curriculum. For several generations to come this rendition was to be taught as official French philosophy.

The scientization of social theory

The efforts towards the scientization of social theory were made in a period when the French natural sciences were witnessing an unprecedented heyday. Research opportunities were first expanded during Turgot's term in office as Minister, leading to several new professorial chairs, the foundation of the Société de médecine and the expansion and reorganization of the Académie des sciences. This was also the era of the first great successes (Lavoisier, Laplace, Lagrange's arrival in Paris). The expansion continued throughout the revolutionary period and was accompanied by far-reaching reorganization. It was during these years that the sciences attained unparalleled prestige. Innumerable new institutions, societies and journals were founded, and the Académie des sciences lost its monopoly position. The decades around 1800 were thus a period of differentiation and discipline formation. From then on scientists were able to publish in their own journals and discuss their work at more specialized societies. Within a relatively short period of time the practice of the natural sciences had become a disciplined and respected profession. The prestige of literature declined during the Revolution, so that some writers and philosophers also began to express themselves increasingly in the language of the sciences.

The scientization of social theory was one component of this vast restructuring of the intellectual regime. In the first instance, scientization was the result of the extension of natural science methods to other fields of research, which was implemented mainly by authors whose own origins had been in the natural sciences. The first stage transpired in the years from 1775 to 1789. The second stage coincided with the Revolution and the Empire. Mathematicians were the ones to take the initiative, but in the second stage the torch was more or less handed over to the life sciences.

The first manifestation of this scientization of social theory was Condorcet's mathematization. His project arose in response to the demand for scientific expertise upon which to base Turgot's reform policies. At the same time it was linked to Laplace's efforts to mathematize new fields of science. This point is often overlooked. Condorcet's project was the outcome of two independent tendencies. It was the result neither of purely 'external' developments (the new demand for scientific expertise) nor of purely 'internal' developments in mathematics (Laplace's new techniques and his endeavour to mathematize new fields of research). More than any other member of the Académie des sciences, Condorcet was in a position to take advantage of the opportunities. He had the required mathematical capacities and was deeply committed to Turgot's reform policies. He gave up his former mathematical work to devote his time to new applications of probability calculus. In the Revolution he generalized his insights into a programme for 'social mathematics', which he defined as a 'separate science'. Parts of it were further pursued by Laplace and a number of his pupils.

The second effort at the scientization of social theory was linked to the expansion of the medical sciences. In a sense, the rise of this orientation dates back to before the Revolution. Ever since the founding of the Société de médecine, various steps had been taken to introduce innovations in the field of medicine, and representatives of the Montpellier school (Barthez) had been in favour of a more comprehensive *science de l'homme*. The first to elaborate upon this line of thought systematically was Cabanis, who viewed physiology as the foundation for a new human science. This work came to occupy a central position in the writings of the *idéologues*, and for some time this was the direction in which Saint-Simon continued. These efforts were less technical than Condorcet's social mathematics, and held the interest of republican intellectuals for a while to come.

Attempts to found a social science on natural science procedures also inspired the emergence of anti-scientific social theories, whose major spokesmen were de Bonald and de Maistre. They contested the fact that, as de Bonald observed, the moral sciences were reduced to a 'branch of anatomy and physiology'.[50] These conservative and counter-revolutionary doctrines, first formulated by emigrants, were well received in literary circles after 1800. By the time de Bonald wrote that the moral sciences were still only a branch of medical research, the *idéologues* had already suffered their most severe defeats. The young and more philosophically oriented members of the group were increasingly responsive to the anti-scientific mood prevailing in the literary intelligentsia. This romantic and 'spiritualistic' reaction was the start of French Romanticism and the point of departure for the schools of philosophy that came to the fore during the Restoration.

Part III
Foundations of Sociology

Introduction

> Instead of blindly searching for a sterile scientific unity, as
> oppressive as it is illusory, in the vicious reduction of all
> phenomena to one single order of laws, the human mind
> will finally regard the different classes of events as having
> their specific laws.
>
> Auguste Comte

The fall of Napoleon heralded a period of renewed interest in the
social sciences. Napoleon had supported the natural sciences and used
the arts for his imperial aspirations, but there was no place for the
social sciences. The work of the *idéologues* had been obstructed,
censorship was intensified and the 'moral and political science' department at the Institut de France no longer existed. The Restoration
(1814–30) was marked by a new interest in political and social
questions. When the warfare ended contact was renewed with foreign
countries, publication opportunities expanded and the mounting
rivalry between 'conservatives' and 'liberals' stimulated interest in
social questions. Virtually all the debates were initially centred round
aspects of the Revolution. Conservative groups saw the Revolution as
a heinous transgression, and their goal was to restore the alliance between the throne and the pulpit. Chateaubriand and de Bonald were
among the conservative spokesmen. The path pursued by the liberals
was midway between those of the Revolution and the Restoration.
They defended certain revolutionary achievements, propagated parliamentary control and advocated a constitutional monarchy. Conservative intellectuals were the ones with the most ties to the landed
gentry and the church. Liberal intellectuals frequently came from the
urban bourgeoisie and often held positions in the school system. Many
university historians and philosophers were thus closely linked to the
liberal opposition. During the July Monarchy (1830–48) they took
the initiative of founding the Académie des sciences morales et politiques
(1832), which, for several generations to come, remained the centre
for the official forms of social science. At the meetings of this bastion
of bourgeois liberal thinking, historians (Guizot, Mignet) made the

acquaintance of philosophers (Cousin), economists, independent authors (Tocqueville) and socio-medical researchers (Villermé). Up to the end of the nineteenth century this academy remained the dominant social science institution.[1]

In addition to these conservative and liberal groups, contributions to the social sciences were also made by men from the natural sciences. Their work was less in the limelight and less closely linked to political movements of the day. Several mathematicians who continued the work of Condorcet and Laplace incorporated new statistical data, which seemed to grant them unprecedented possibilities. 'Eventually', Lacroix wrote, 'everything will be able to be counted and measured, and consequently extricated, at least for the most part, from the realm of the imagination.'[2] However, Lacroix's expectations were not fulfilled. Condorcet's social mathematics became increasingly controversial, even among mathematicians, and major innovations in this field were no longer French, but resulted from the efforts of the Belgian Adolphe Quetelet. His work marked the transition from probability calculus to statistics.

Contributions to the human sciences were also made by various branches of medicine. Cabanis' psychophysiology was still widely respected in medical circles. Broussais, for example, who had served as a medic in Napoleon's army, engaged in a heated polemic in the Restoration against the revival of spiritualistic philosophy. His work was popular among medical students, and represented a continuation of the revolutionary legacy in a political sense as well.[3]

The decades after 1814 exhibited a sharp upturn and a further differentiation of social theory. There was greater diversity in the writings and it is more difficult to detect a dominant trend than in the previous periods. The work of Auguste Comte is a good illustration. His writings were among the most original of the period, but were published outside the framework of established groups and institutions. Comte was neither a conservative nor a liberal intellectual. Nor was his work representative of the natural sciences. It is true that he was a mathematician, but he did not hesitate to reject the use of mathematics in more complex sciences such as biology or sociology. Although he had a positive attitude to the work of physicians and biologists, they were two more groups to which he did not belong.

Comte was one of the younger members of the generation that came to the fore after 1814. His career roughly coincided with the political history of the period. Since he had no established position, he was more dependent on changing circumstances than his peers with steady employment. Comte grew up in the Napoleonic era. In the

Restoration he was one of the victims of the reorganization of the Ecole polytechnique and was in contact with the liberal opposition. During the July Monarchy he was employed at the Ecole polytechnique and was able to elaborate upon his ideas in his *Cours de philosophie positive* (1830–42). Unlike most of the liberal intellectuals of his generation, however, Comte lost his position again. He gradually came to spurn strictly intellectual activities and began to formulate his ideas in more philosophical terms. His later writings were largely published after 1848 and dealt with philosophical and subjective facets.

Although Comte addressed the central problems of his day, his career was just as out of the ordinary as the theoretical direction for which he opted. In this respect, he occupies a different position from most of his predecessors. Comte's work is not typical of any particular stage in the development of the social sciences. Montesquieu, Rousseau, Condorcet, Cabanis – all were prominent and respected writers at the time. This was not the case with Comte. There are connections and similarities with other thinkers, but, contrary to what is generally assumed, his work was original in an uncustomary manner. His unsung originality is the first reason why Comte's work occupies a central position in this part of the book. The second reason is that his theory provided a new theoretical orientation for the social sciences. At the end of the nineteenth century this orientation was to serve as the foundation for the French sociological tradition.

Two overall interpretations have been given of Comte's writings. Firstly, as regards the political, social or religious connotations: against the background of the ideological crisis of post-revolutionary France, his work has been examined in relation to such schools as Saint-Simonism and conservatism or as an effort to find a secular substitute for Catholicism. This type of interpretation is based largely upon Comte's later work.

In the second type of interpretation, the emphasis has been different. Here Comte is viewed primarily as a theorist. His earlier work occupies a central position and his later activities are only sarcastically referred to in passing. In this case, Comte's originality has been linked to his 'positivism' and his 'sociology'. Positivism is taken to be the core of his theory of knowledge and sociology as a specific outcome or application of it. Up to now this has been the most prevalent and most neutral description. This is the Auguste Comte who is presented in the textbooks.

I do not agree with either of these interpretations. Since it overlooks everything Comte wrote about the sciences, the validity of the first interpretation is doubtful. If Comte did indeed primarily have political or ideological intentions, then it remains a mystery why he initially focused mainly on the development of the various sciences. It is also unclear why he directed his efforts to scientists and members of the Académie des sciences. These efforts were essentially an intellectual endeavour and ought to be viewed as such, as is done in the second interpretation. And yet this interpretation is misleading as well. Neither Comte's positivism nor his sociology was particularly original. Nor did either of them play an especially significant role in a historical perspective. This requires further elaboration.

The term positivism can mean two very different things. Firstly, it refers to the imitation of natural science methods in the social sciences. In terms of this definition, Hobbes would probably be the first positivist. Condorcet and Cabanis were positivists and perhaps Saint-Simon, but Comte criticized imitations of this kind and, contrary to what even specialists claim, he was certainly not a positivist in this sense.[4]

Positivism can also refer to anti-metaphysical conceptions of knowledge, according to which valid knowledge consists solely of what is positively given: validity is restricted to testable statements. Statements about 'first' or 'final' causes are not testable, nor are those about the 'meaning' or 'essence' of things, and questions such as these consequently have no place in science. Comte was undoubtedly a positivist in this sense. But the question is whether he made such a special contribution to the formulation of this conception. He gave it a name, but whether he did much more than that remains doubtful. Positivism in this sense emerged simultaneously with the classical natural sciences. Newton expressed a wish to abandon what he called 'hypothetical questions'. In the course of the eighteenth century this attitude became increasingly widespread at the Académie des sciences. Debates were confined to observable phenomena and the regularities or laws they exhibited.[5] This 'phenomenalism' represented a position that was articulated by various authors in the eighteenth century.[6] The repudiation of metaphysical questions was common practice among French scientists around 1800. 'Positive' studies were published on a myriad of subjects, 'positive sciences' were discussed, and the notion that one should confine oneself to 'positive statements' in whatever science one engaged was generally accepted throughout scientific circles.[7]

Comte never disputed that these positivist or proto-positivist ideas were widely accepted among French scientists. In fact, he was himself of the opinion that this positivism was nothing new. When he addressed the Académie des sciences in 1835, for example, he opened his lecture by stating that scientific hypotheses ought to be subjected to 'positive verification'. This was an 'indispensable prerequisite' for validity and 'generally acknowledged' as such.[8] Comte expressed this same standpoint in his *Cours de philosophie positive*. It was useless, he wrote, to devote any attention to 'the principle' that distinguished positive conceptualization from metaphysical knowledge. Anyone who had any advanced knowledge of the sciences was 'familiar' with this principle.[9] Comte made no claim to originality in this respect. He simply adopted ideas that were generally accepted in the sciences of his day. In his later writings the term positivism came to have a far broader meaning. Then 'positive' no longer meant mainly 'restricted to observable phenomena' or 'testable'; it also meant 'useful', precise' and 'certain'.[10] This expansion of the definition was part of positivism in a more philosophical sense. Although this form of positivism was undoubtedly original, it is an aspect of his work that will not be dealt with here.

The same can be said of Comte's sociology as of his positivism. He coined the term, but his concepts were not particularly new. For example, the law of the three stages, which Comte viewed as the core of his entire sociology, had already been formulated by Turgot. According to Turgot, the human mind developed in three stages. Before people had any idea of the 'real relations', they assumed that invisible beings, gods, performed all the acts for which people were not themselves responsible. Philosophers criticized these assumptions, but, since they had no insight into the true causes, they formulated explanations in terms of abstract entities. It was not until much later that the first scientific explanations were drawn up with the help of mathematics.[11] Either directly or via the work of Condorcet, Comte was probably familiar with this text.[12] It is similarly difficult to view other components of Comte's sociology (the distinction between what is 'static' and what is 'dynamic' or between 'secular' and 'spiritual' power) as important innovations.

Comte did undoubtedly contribute towards the formulation of positivist and sociological conceptions. Although it has never been studied in detail, his most important contribution was probably that he systematized existing ideas. There is, however, little reason to view this work as truly innovative. Moreover, in a historical perspective Comte's work failed to play a particularly important role in either of these senses. 'Sociology' became an academic discipline and 'logical positivism' developed within philosophy, but in both cases the connection to Comte's work remained little more than nominal.

The programme of the logical positivists was characterized by their pursuit of a demarcation criterion and was driven by a reductionist ideal of science, both of which Comte had rejected. To him, there were no general and purely logical principles of science. In his opinion the pursuit of criteria with which scientific statements could be distinguished once and for all from non-scientific statements was nothing but an intellectual illusion. In his *Cours* he called notions of this kind an 'absurd utopia'.[13] Comte also refuted the notion that all forms of scientific knowledge could or should be reducible to one prototype. In each of these senses, Comte's work belonged to a different tradition from logical positivism as it later developed.

Comte's views also differed in another sense from those of the logical positivists. He felt it was pointless to study methods without examining how they were actually put to use in scientific practice. Otherwise studies would only produce 'vague generalities' without any real significance for the progress of research. What he felt was a central issue in any method was good 'intellectual habits'. Insight into these habits could be gained only by conducting detailed studies of the use of certain methods *en action*.[14] Comte did not write a general *Discours de la méthode positive* and it is a mistake to interpret him as a methodologist, as Larry Laudan does.[15] In reality, Comte's view of the theory of knowledge is closer to a historicizing pragmatism than to logical positivism.

So it is no wonder that not a single representative of logical positivism can be named to whom Comte's writings were of any importance. For their orientation they looked mainly to new developments in logic and mathematics. In surveys on logical positivism usually only one mention is made of Comte, and that is when the term positivism is discussed. Sometimes he isn't mentioned at all, as in Bertrand Russell's *History of Western Philosophy*.

Much the same holds true of Comte's sociological insights. Emile Durkheim, the sociologist who owes the most to Comte, viewed the law of the three stages as a 'historical oddity'. Comte's other specifically sociological insights similarly failed to impress him.

The conclusion to be drawn from all this is that either Comte was not a particularly original and important thinker, or something has been overlooked. With very few exceptions,[16] the former possibility is accepted. But unjustly so, for every attempt to reduce Comte's intellectual contributions to his positivism and his sociology means a failure to appreciate his theory of science. Whatever the precise significance of his positivism and his sociology might have been, Comte's theory of science was more original and of far greater import. In short, Comte can be viewed as the very first to develop a *historical* and *differential theory of science*. He relinquished the idea that the validity of knowledge could be ascertained with the help of a non-historical and universally valid principle. He thus rejected virtually all the classical theories. Descartes had ascertained the validity of knowledge in a non-historical subject, Leibniz had called upon logic for this purpose, and all the classical theories had assumed the existence of a timeless and general principle of truth.[17] This principle, whether it involved the *cogito*, logic or reason, was thought to be valid for all the sciences. This assumption fulfilled an extremely important function in the early modern era, founding the unity of the sciences *vis-à-vis* theology. For authors around 1800, this assumption lost something of its significance, but Condorcet and the *idéologues* still reasoned largely along these lines.

Comte's departure from the premises of the classical theory of science was the result of two operations. Firstly, he approached the formation of knowledge as a historical phenomenon. In this respect he followed Turgot and Condorcet. Statements on scientific knowledge, he concluded, ought to be statements on historical developments and not on universals. In comparison with developments in other countries (German historicism, Hegel) this was not out of the ordinary. The second operation was a more original one. Comte differentiated the various sciences according to the specific properties of their objects. He refuted monistic or reductionist theories of science and replaced them by a differential theory. In line with this view, what is scientific depends not only on historical phases, but also on the particular field of science. It was impossible to reduce the various sciences to one and the same basic type. Sciences differ from one another and, depending on the features of their specific objects, different methods have to be used.

It was at first an observation that Comte drew attention to the cognitive heterogeneity of the sciences. With the expansion and accelerated differentiation of the natural sciences around 1800, conflicts arose between the mathematical or mechanical disciplines and the life sciences. Mechanists and vitalists alike felt that their orientation was the most general. Condorcet viewed mathematics as a legitimate method for every conceivable subject; Laplace viewed mechanics as a model that was also appropriate for chemical reactions. Representatives of the life sciences frequently held the opposite opinion. Cabanis, for example, viewed physics as a special case of physiology. Gravity was actually nothing but a specific form of 'affinity' or *sensibilité*. In this sense, affinity was the most universal property of matter, and physiology was consequently a more general science than mechanics.[18]

With the formation of disciplinary natural science, it was increasingly difficult to adhere to the assumptions of the classical theory of knowledge. From the seventeenth century until the Enlightenment, theories of science had been based upon the unity and immutability of reason. This changed around 1800 and the theory of science became a field for what might be called competing monisms. An intellectual regime had emerged that was characterized by more differentiated conceptions and modes of organization. In the new constellation, no single group could any longer make a claim to a monopoly on judgements. Like the differentiation of the 'two cultures', the differentiation of various fields of science had been made possible mainly by the disappearance of the rivalry with theology and the church. Unity with regard to ecclesiastical authorities no longer had to be maintained, and, with the expansion of secular institutions, in a relatively short period of time new lines of division emerged. Science and literature disbanded, and the rise of 'biology' and 'physics' in the modern sense was a sign of a fundamental differentiation within the world of the natural sciences.

Auguste Comte can be viewed as one of the first to have examined this new constellation with any detachment. He rejected the generalizations of the various parties and specified the conditions under which certain methods were more useful than others. The result was a differential theory of science based upon distinguishing various levels of complexity. Astronomy studied the workings of mechanical forces between heavenly bodies; they appeared to be simple processes for which there were mathematical descriptions, thus eventuating exact predictions. Physics was somewhat more complicated, but the phenomena were still simple and distinct enough for mathematical description. In chemistry, substances and reactions were studied that were subject not only to physical laws, but also to the principles of 'chemical affinities'. Biology studied living creatures: since their conduct could not be explained on the basis of physical forces or chemical reactions, they were more complex than inanimate objects. It is true that biological processes did depend on physical and chemical phenomena, but they were determined by the specific 'organization' of bodies, in other words by the anatomy and the physiology of the species. Since human beings have the capacity to learn and their actions are not purely instinctive, social phenomena were even more complex.

The sciences, Comte argued, form a series of increasing complexity and decreasing generality. The laws of mechanics are the least complex and apply to all bodies, small and large, animate and inanimate. These laws are simple, general and independent. The laws of biology are considerably more complicated. Moreover, they are less general because they apply solely to living creatures and depend on processes at lower levels of complexity. The laws of social phenomena are the most complicated of all and apply only to human societies. Social phenomena are the smallest subset, as it were, of all natural phenomena. Here the laws of physics, chemistry and biology hold true to no less an extent, but human behaviour is the result of a specific type of regularity, which is the object of a relatively autonomous science: sociology.

In Comte's view, this series of increasing complexity also explains the history of the sciences. The human mind first discovered the features of the simplest objects and then gradually proceeded to explore the more complex ones. Chemistry did not become a positive science until the eighteenth century, biology was in the making, and in sociology the first steps had barely been taken.

In his *Cours de philosophie positive*, Comte transformed this basic idea into a comprehensive theory of science, a theory that pertained to the various sciences and how they were interrelated. Of course Comte acknowledged that these sciences have certain features in common – mainly the developmental pattern of the three stages. The 'positive' stage is characterized by the formation of knowledge, whereby metaphysical and theological questions have made way for a controlled interchange between theory and research. Comte gave a rather elementary description of this positive stage.

The *Cours de philosophie positive* is generally viewed as a positivist treatise. This is a misconception. The subject of these six volumes was not the question 'what are the common features of the positive sciences as compared with metaphysics?' Comte's *Cours* was not about the 'demarcation' between science and metaphysics. What the author was addressing was the question of how developments in the various sciences could be interpreted in view of his theory of increasing complexity and decreasing generality. It is consequently erroneous to view the *Cours* as a positivist textbook. Strange as it might sound, positivism did not play a main role; what was presented as 'positivist theory' was not a theory about what was 'positive science' and what was not. Comte was a positivist, but in the minimal definition of the word, and basically in the same way as most of the French scientists of his day. In this sense positivism was an assumption rather than a result of his theory. What the *Cours de philosophie positive* has to offer is primarily a differential theory of science.

If this interpretation is correct, Auguste Comte can be viewed as one of the first modern theorists of science. Despite the laconic contempt with which he is usually treated, Comte's theory of science signified a major intellectual breakthrough. His differential approach implied a radical repudiation of claims to monopolies on knowledge and put an end to the illusion of universal methods. The anti-reductionist and historicizing epistemology was of great importance to French philosophy of science as well as to French sociology. What Durkheim derived from Comte was mainly this theory of science. What in short deserves further examination is neither Comte's positivism nor his sociology, but this very theory.

This examination requires two steps. First, the question should be posed as to how it was possible to formulate a theory such as this. The reply to this question was given in Part I and Part II. Not only did sciences other than the mathematical disciplines emerge; fundamental changes took place in the structure of the scientific world itself. The monopolistic organization around the Académie was replaced by a more differentiated culture of science where various fields and methods were recognized, including the social sciences. With the rise of journals, separate societies and specific syllabuses, the formation of disciplines became dominant. What was unclear in this new constellation, and a matter of permanent controversy, was the question of how these sciences were to be ranked. Representatives of the established disciplines developed ideologies to legitimate the supremacy of their own particular field. These conflicts occurred mainly between mathematicians and representatives of the emerging life sciences. The position of the social sciences was an extremely precarious one, as was evident from the abrogation of the 'second class' at the Institut de France in 1803 and in the debates that preceded it. Conservative groups opposed every claim to scientificity and numerous men of letters backed them on this point, whereas representatives of the natural sciences put their faith mainly in their own branch of science. These controversies and disputes were the background against which Comte's work was conducted. Without this truculent process of intellectual differentiation, a differential theory of science would have been inconceivable. That was the first condition for Comte's theory.

The second question to be posed is how this possibility was effectuated, in other words how and why Auguste Comte interpreted these developments as he did. This, then, will be elaborated upon in Part III.

11

The Interrupted Career of Auguste Comte

A provincial in Paris

Isidore-Auguste-Marie-François-Xavier Comte was born in 1798, towards the close of the Revolution, in Montpellier. His father, Louis Comte, worked for the province as treasurer and is described as a meticulous and straightforward man. His daily schedule was as strict as his principles: he would get up at five, have breakfast three hours later, leave for work at nine and stay there until five 'without ever leaving the work site for a quarter of an hour'.[1] Louis Comte led a frugal and worthy life devoted predominantly to his work. He did not join any clubs or parties or go to theatres or coffee shops. His only hobbies were cultivating flowers and breeding birds. He would have liked to go horseback riding, but his income did not allow for it. Though he was certainly not well-to-do, scholarships enabled him to send his elder son to the Ecole polytechnique and his younger to the medical faculty. Later, when various members of the family were stricken by lengthy illnesses, Louis Comte was unable to make ends meet and went into debt. One of the reasons this upset him so much was because he could no longer help support his son, who consequently lost faith in him. Isidore-Auguste's father was a model civil servant: precise, dutiful and upright – and unable ever to understand why his talented son refused to consider a career in the civil service.

Comte's mother, Rosalie Boyer, was twelve years older than her husband. She was a sensitive woman resolutely devoted to her family even though her health was as poor as that of her husband and children. It weighed heavy on her that she seldom heard from her elder son after his departure for Paris. Despite the strife between the young Comte and his parents, Isidore-Auguste was attached to his mother. In his 'second career' – his mother had died by then – he began to venerate her as one of his 'three angels'. Her affection and generosity counterbalanced his father's 'banality'. Besides Isidore-Auguste, who was the oldest, there were two other children, a girl called Alix and a boy by the name of Adolphe. Alix remained in Montpellier, where she led a pious life. Plagued by one illness after the other, she nonetheless cared for her sickly father. Adolphe, the younger son, hesitated between a financial career and medicine. In the end he decided to register at the medical faculty, but failed to complete his studies there. After a conflict with his father he left for the colonies, where he died less than a year later.

The Comtes were Catholics and royalists, but in a cautious manner. The virtues of the petty bourgeoisie dominated the family: order, regularity, frugality. In a spirit of patient faith and commitment, Louis Comte devoted his energy to his work just as Rosalie devoted hers to her family. Risks and adventure were best to be avoided. Improvements could be attained only by conscientiously performing the tasks that had to be done. In this sense, Auguste Comte's lifestyle did not differ much from that of his parents. He was no less strict than his father; he too left nothing to chance and made every effort to arrange all the aspects of his life down to the very last detail. This attitude was also evident in his work. First and foremost, Comte was systematic. He had very little interest in factual research: the passion for research and the urge to discover something new were virtually non-existent in his life. He was barely interested in separate problems and theories, but all the more in how they were interrelated and ordered. In later life this led him to design a wide range of positivist systems (calendar, library, catechism). Some passages, as Henri Gouhier notes, bring to mind the cash books so carefully kept by his father.[2]

However, neither Isidore-Auguste nor his brother Adolphe could accept a lifestyle like their father's. Both of them deprecated the banality of life as a civil servant in the provinces. Isidore-Auguste's resistance was first stimulated by his success at school, enabling him to choose another path and giving him the confidence and ambition that were to characterize his career. Comte's school career began at the age of nine at the local lycée. He was an excellent pupil, won various prizes and was soon known for his superb memory. Of all his teachers only Daniel Encontre, his mathematics master, made an impression on him. Encontre wrote a number of books and his teaching skills had earned him a fine reputation. He was said to teach mathematics and physics 'as if he himself had invented them'.[3] Daniel Encontre was Comte's first example. Under his supervision, by 1812 Comte was adequately prepared for the admission examinations at the Ecole polytechnique.

He was too young, however, and had to remain in Montpellier one more year, during which time he replaced Encontre for a short period. The fifteen-year-old pupil was viewed as a good substitute.

One thing with which Comte had trouble at the lycée was the military discipline Napoleon had imposed there. In a number of disputes with military 'trainers', his masters intervened to shield their headstrong pupil from overly rash punishments. Comte's resistance was driven by his intellectual abilities, which also inspired his habit of scoffing at figures of authority who he felt did not 'deserve' their positions. These meritocratic sentiments, reinforced by Comte's forthright and tenacious temperament, led to many of the conflicts in his life. He would go on where other people thought that enough was enough. Concessions and compromises were hard for him to make. All this not only meant there was a certain rigidity and tactlessness in his conduct, it also led to the rigour that characterized his work.

In 1814 Comte was admitted to the Ecole polytechnique. Seventy-five of the hundreds of candidates were selected to attend this prestigious school. Three boys from Paris did better in the examinations, and Comte's name was fourth on the list. In October of that year Comte left for Paris, where his teachers included some of the most renowned scientists of the day: the mathematicians Poinsot and Arago, the chemist Thénard and the physicists Petit and Poisson. His letters to his friends in Montpellier were extremely enthusiastic. The information about Comte's years at the Ecole polytechnique is in much the same tone as at the lycée. He was one of the best pupils in every subject except drawing, he made an impression on his fellow pupils and teachers, and his lecture notes indicate considerable scientific interest. He took part in the ritual recreational activities which were part of the life at a closed institution such as the Ecole polytechnique. And he became acquainted with Paris: he explored its neighbourhoods, attended its theatres and visited its less respectable districts. A few years later that was where he was to meet the woman he would marry.

In one sense, Comte did not meet with the requirements. Starting in the second trimester, his conduct was described as 'utterly reprehensible'.[4] There were no problems with his teachers, but he had numerous altercations with the school administration and supervisors. Most of the incidents were of negligible importance (he would whistle in the study hall or fail to do exercises that bored him), but this kind of conduct was not tolerated at a militarized institution. At the end of the first year Comte lost the rank of corporal and was demoted. After a similar conflict a year later he had to terminate his studies.

In the spring of 1816, after Napoleon's '100 days' and during the initial stage of the Restoration, a dispute broke out at the Ecole polytechnique between the pupils and one of the teachers. The man had a poor reputation. On behalf of the pupils, a number of delegates requested him to alter his method of posing questions, but the man refused to listen to their complaints. Instead the pupils' spokesmen were punished. Their fellow pupils then collectively declared their solidarity, so that the conflict was now between the school administration and the entire student body. In order to lend force to their demands, fifteen pupils addressed the teacher in writing. They politely requested him to leave the school premises. Comte was one of the pupils to sign the letter. In the hope of gaining the confidence of the conservative government, the school administration decided strict disciplinary action was called for. The Minister was asked to expel the fifteen pupils. Auguste Comte was one of them. In government circles, however, the entire Ecole polytechnique was viewed as a breeding ground of Jacobins and Bonapartists, and the Minister took advantage of the opportunity to close the school and dismiss the staff. The government paid the travelling expenses for the pupils to return home, and thus Comte found himself back at Montpellier.

Closing the Ecole polytechnique was a political decision pertaining to an institution founded during the Revolution and known as a republican hotbed. It was not an isolated incident, for in the same year, 1816, the Institut de France was 'purged' as well. Although Comte was more directly involved in the conflict than many others, he never viewed it as a personal affair. The cause lay in government policies and efforts to turn back the clock. This attitude was similar to that of Comte's fellow pupils and much of their generation.

Most of the pupils at the Ecole polytechnique were opposed to the Restoration. They feared their position would be weakened, and in circles of engineers and scientists Comte's republican sympathies were no exception. His attitude was also linked to the problems of his generation, members of which hoped to reap the benefits of their diplomas in the years after 1814, but were confronted with attempts to restore the power of the church. Numerous priests were once again being appointed in the school system, and, if there were no suitable candidates among their ranks, pious Catholics were selected instead. In this sense Comte found himself in a position similar to that of many of his peers. In order to assess the more specific aspects of his position I shall first discuss several more general ones.

The Restoration and the July Monarchy

With the 1814 defeat, the Empire had come to an end. In the years that followed, industrial developments advanced, interest in developments abroad increased and, although the Bourbons returned to the throne, it was under new conditions. The legislative basis for the regime was a constitution, the Charter, which in principle guaranteed civil freedom and equality before the law. One of the rights entailed was freedom of the press. With the end of the wars and the renewed contact with other countries, this was one of the most important prerequisites for the cultural and intellectual revival at the time of the Restoration (1814–30).

There were more ample opportunities to organize and publish, as was most clearly illustrated by the emergence of organized political persuasions such as 'conservatism' and 'liberalism' with their own newspapers and magazines. Their formation was closely linked to the new political structure. The constitution provided for two chambers. The Upper Chamber was appointed by the monarch and the Lower Chamber was elected. Only males above the age of thirty who paid more than three hundred francs in taxes were eligible to vote, and only people above the age of forty who paid a minimum of a thousand francs in taxes could be elected to office. These requirements excluded the middle classes from the political arena, and political differentiation remained confined to well-to-do 'worthies'.

This elite of dignitaries was divided into two factions. The aim of the traditional faction or 'legitimists' was to restore the old-style monarchy, whereas the more liberal faction was in favour of a constitutional monarchy. The legitimists were mainly large landowners, noblemen and representatives of the church. De Bonald and Chateaubriand belonged to the radical wing of this group, the 'ultras'. The liberals were predominantly progressive-minded noblemen and well-to-do citizens such as bankers, traders and manufacturers. They had fewer ties with the church, were more frequently employed in the modern sectors and in the cities, and had contact with Protestants and the intellectual bourgeoisie.[5]

There were shifts in the power relations between the two groups in the years from 1814 to 1848. Louis XVIII was initially supported by liberal as well as ultra-royalists. After the murder of the heir apparent in 1820, the ultras gained more power, and still more under Charles X (1824–30). Former emigrants received large sums of money in damages, the Jesuits returned and schools were put under church supervision. This shift to the right stimulated the formation of a better organized opposition, and by 1828 the opposition had a majority in Parliament. After several conflicts between the Cabinet and Parliament, the Cabinet instituted measures that altered the entire situation: the two chambers were disbanded, the suffrage system was changed and the press was censored. These measures led in turn to the July Revolution in 1830. On behalf of the opposition, Louis-Philippe, duc d'Orléans, now came to power.

The new government relied more on the well-to-do bourgeoisie and less on the nobility and the church. In the formulation and implementation of government policies, a number of intellectuals (Guizot, Thiers, Cousin) played instrumental roles. Many of them had university positions and had earned a reputation during the Restoration as spokesmen of the liberal opposition. Refounded in 1832, the Académie des sciences morales et politiques became the liberal intellectual centre, and from 1830 to 1848 this group played a political role comparable with that of the scientists from 1789 to 1814.

Sweeping changes affected the cultural sector after 1814, the revival being most striking in literature and the arts. Immediately after the defeat in 1814, various publications appeared on the new English and German literature. In 1810, upon the orders of Napoleon's police, the first edition of De l'Allemagne by Madame de Staël had been destroyed. In 1814 a new edition appeared, leading to one of the first major debates on Romanticism.[6] Ample attention was also devoted to English writers, for example, in Stendhal's controversial Racine et Shakespeare (1822), and shortly beforehand the first Romantic journals were published. Lamartine, Vigny and Victor Hugo innovated poetry, Delacroix painted his first pictures and audiences listened to music composed by Berlioz. Developments of this kind continued throughout the July Monarchy, but without the excitement and enthusiasm that had inspired the Romantics during the Restoration.

Advances in the natural sciences occurred somewhat outside the range of public interest. Firstly, the new rulers had been quick to divest the natural sciences of their prominence. Not only were the four classes at the Institut de France given back their old academic names in 1816; Louis XVIII also went so far as to grant special privileges to members of the Académie française. Members of other academies were excluded from these privileges, and this demonstrative restoration of the supremacy of literature was accompanied by a 'purge' at the academies. Napoleon had abrogated the second class at the Institut, but had not been willing or able to dismiss any of its members; they were simply transferred. Louis XVIII was less dependent on the support of intellectuals and less scrupulous. More than twenty members of the Institut were discharged from their positions (the painter David, such scientists as Monge and Carnot and the revolutionary politicians Sieyès and Grégoire).

Despite this political intervention, in the natural sciences there was still a certain continuity with the years around 1800. Scientists lost their political power and in part their public esteem, but a few of them, particularly Laplace and Cuvier, retained leading positions in the scientific world. There were thorough reorganizations at numerous institutions, but education and research remained concentrated in the ones set up during the Revolution and the Empire. Unlike the newer generation of poets, scientists were unlikely to foster much sympathy for the Restoration. Members of the Académie des sciences were of humbler social backgrounds than those at all the other academies, they held political positions less frequently, and a considerable number of them lacked the property that would entitle them to vote.[7] Many scientists were still sympathetic when it came to the revolutionary period.

Among intellectuals, it was mainly poets and writers who had ties with the 'legitimists'. A few prominent representatives were of aristocratic lineage themselves (Lamartine, Musset, Vigny). Their great example was Chateaubriand, a former emigrant and of noble descent himself. The ties university intellectuals had were mainly with the 'orleanists' or liberals. While contesting the republican and scientistic schools of thought that emerged around 1800, these groups defended the public education system from the claims of the church. Their work was inspired by the wish to find the golden mean between Restoration and Revolution. They all believed in a form of secular spiritualism. They rejected 'materialism' and 'determinism', which they associated with the natural sciences, and stressed the significance of 'higher values', but without relating them to religious faith. Madame de Staël and Benjamin Constant were early examples of this development. Laromiguière and Maine de Biran, the youngest *idéologues*, had proceeded in the same direction, and after 1815 Victor Cousin served as the leading spokesman of this spiritualist philosophy.

The ties scientists had with the elite of dignitaries were probably the weakest. Legitimist preferences were rare, liberal ones more prevalent, but unlike the professors at the liberal arts faculties, particularly historians and philosophers, even during the July Monarchy scientists had relatively few political ties. In the first half of the nineteenth century, 20 per cent of all the professors at the Sorbonne were members of the Upper or Lower Chamber. There was a sharp decline in this percentage in the second half of the century: universities became more autonomous, and by 1900 only 4 per cent of professors were represented in the Parliament or Senate.[8] No comparable figures are available on professors in the natural sciences, but their political involvement in this sense does seem to have been weaker. Many scientists exhibited a certain distrust as regards established politics, and in principle Comte's opinions did not differ from those of his fellow scientists. Revolutionary or Napoleonic sympathies probably survived longest in these circles.

Having lost his religious faith at school, Auguste Comte became a republican. During Napoleon's short-lived return he had confidence that the Emperor would mend his ways, but this illusion was soon abandoned. During the Restoration Comte's sympathies were with the liberal opposition, though without his having much contact with its spokesmen.

The generation of 1820

I see, although a bit late, that the simple manifestation of competence is not sufficient.

Comte to Eichtal, 1825

Comte belonged to the generation born between the early years of the Revolution and the start of the Empire. This post-revolutionary generation attended the Napoleonic lycée, studied at the Napoleonic university, the Ecole polytechnique or the Ecole normale supérieure and expected to hold leading positions in the great French Empire. Napoleon's fall came as a great shock to them. It was not just the military defeat; with it came an abrupt end to the promise to lead an Empire. Instead the Bourbons returned and emigrants and emissaries of the church demanded the positions from which they had previously been excluded.[9]

These young people, whose careers began after 1815, were divided as it were into two categories. On the one hand there were the Romantic poets and writers, who distanced themselves from the Classicist tradition. They were dependent on the literary audience, on the salons, and on the groups in the *monde* who traditionally served as patrons of the arts and literature. Chateaubriand was their leading example, and they welcomed the Restoration as the end of a regime hostile to literature. On the other hand there were the novices whose careers were to be based upon their school education and whose futures depended on official positions in education and research. In general they were opposed to the Restoration, belonged to the liberal opposition, and were particularly adamant in their disapproval of the new power of the church. This group's major spokesmen came from the Ecole normale supérieure and the Ecole polytechnique.

The new generation of poets and writers published their first works around 1820. Alphonse de Lamartine, born in 1790, was the oldest of this group. The publication of his *Méditations poétiques* (1820) caused quite a stir. It was soon followed by the debuts of Alfred de Vigny and Victor Hugo. These writers were organized around such new magazines as *Conservateur littéraire* (1819–21) and *La muse française* (1823–4), the periodical of Chateaubriand's young admirers. The Romantic poets initially set all their hopes on the new regime. Their ties with the new rulers were such that Lamartine and Hugo were commissioned to compose odes for the coronation of Charles X. Despite the extraordinary honour this implied, the latter years of the Restoration were tempered by reservations. Chateaubriand, who became Minister in 1822, was discharged from office in 1824. His dismissal was the first disillusionment. At the same time *Globe* (1824–32), an organ by and for young liberals, began to show interest in the new literature. This led to a rapprochement between Victor Hugo and the liberals. In 1827 Hugo described Romanticism as 'liberalism in literature' and it was not long before he abandoned his Catholic friends and defected to the other side. Despite this surprising manoeuvre, there were still very important differences between writers and other intellectuals.

The young people who attracted the most attention were the *normaliens*. The idol of this group of future teachers and professors was Victor Cousin, who began to lecture at the university in 1815, though he was not twenty-four. Cousin's philosophy was a spiritualist version of the Scottish common-sense philosophy. In *Du vrai, du beau et du bien*, he argued that there were universal standards for knowledge, art and morality. He worked from the assumption that God existed, and countered the determinism of the natural sciences by emphasizing free will and the autonomy of the 'soul'. Cousin's doctrine provided a philosophy that was 'secular but not atheist, liberal without being revolutionary'.[10] Although his ideas were not very original, his lectures were perceived as a 'veritable philosophical revolution'.[11] One important reason for this was that Cousin was an inimitable speaker. If he had not studied philosophy, Cournot wrote, he would have become France's greatest barrister.[12] Cousin's highly successful lectures were banned in 1820. Two years later, with Bishop Frayssinous presiding at the universities, the Ecole normale was closed, and Cousin was not able to continue teaching until 1828. The July Monarchy put Cousin and his associates in command: given a chair as professor and appointed director of the Ecole normale supérieure, he held numerous high official positions, including one as Minister. He was also selected to join the Senate, the Académie française and the Académie des sciences morales et politiques. The philosophy taught at the lycée and the university after 1830 was Cousin's creation. He compiled the curriculum and selected the teachers, and this 'regiment', as it was called, represented the official philosophy of France for decades to come.

In addition to the philosophers there was an important group of historians among the *normaliens*. They too were primed for teaching careers, opposed the renewed influence of the church, and were active in the liberal opposition. Their vocation made direct confrontation with the political disputes of their day more or less inevitable. The interpretation of their national history was a fixed component of the dispute between liberals and conservatives. History was the language in which numerous political conflicts were fought.[13] There were close ties between the liberal politicians and the young historians. François Guizot was to the historians what Cousin had been to the philosophers. And, even more intensely than Cousin, Guizot combined a political career with an academic one. For some time during the Restoration his lectures at the Sorbonne had been prohibited. In addition he acted as spokesman for the older liberals, the *doctrinaires*. For years after 1830 he combined a position as Minister with an academic career.

The ideas of the young historians and philosophers were best expressed in *Globe*, a magazine founded in 1824 by young liberals, most of whom had been educated at the Ecole normale. As journalists and politicians, they played an important role in the July Revolution of 1830.[14] Many of them were to have successful careers during the July Monarchy.

In addition to the poets around *La muse française* and the *normaliens* around *Globe*, the *polytechniciens* constituted a third network of young people in the opposition. A few of them, particularly Prosper Enfantin and Olinde Rodriques, played key roles in the Saint-Simonian movement. Supported by several industrialists and bankers, in 1825, shortly after Saint-Simon's death, they founded the *Producteur*. As at the magazines referred to above, the average age of the staff was young, and here only thirty.[15] The aim of the journal was to unite industrialists, scientists and artists. Their attention was focused less on cultural and political problems than on what they viewed as the requirements of technical and scientific civilization. The Saint-Simonians managed to recruit numerous *polytechniciens* and played an active role in industrial projects (railroad construction, the Suez Canal).

Despite their differences, these three groups of young people had a certain attitude in common. Alfred de Musset described this generation of lycée graduates as 'ardent, pale and nervous'. What was ailing them was the well-known 'maladie du siècle'. Tormented by feelings of 'malaise' and 'despair', they were apt to succumb to feverish impetuosity.[16] Musset described a group whose great expectations had all come to nought in the Restoration. Their disappointment was owing largely to the fact that, after 1814, far fewer positions than candidates were at hand. For young people, the revolutionary period and the Empire had been extremely favourable. Older people had to make way, and their positions were filled by young people; these were still in place at the start of the 1820s, thus blocking access for the new generation to higher official functions and the professions. With the fall of the Empire, moreover, there was a sharp reduction in the number of official functions, but, as a result of the return of emigrants and former Empire functionaries, an abundance of candidates to fill them.[17] Colonial expansion was proposed by some as a solution, but all the government had to offer to most of the young people was patience and piety.

Against this background there were 'incidents' at tens of schools and universities in the period from 1815 to 1824.[18] For years, uprisings and outbursts had been the rule rather than the exception; the events at the Ecole polytechnique in 1816 were neither the first nor the last. Protests were frequently followed by drastic measures, which in turn led to new resistance. The bone of contention was often the dismissal of insurgent teachers or the reintroduction of church duties. After the Ecole polytechnique, in 1819 the law faculty in Toulouse and the medical faculty in Montpellier were closed as well. In 1822 the same fate awaited the medical faculty in Paris and the Ecole normale. In the years from 1820 to 1822, resistance led to the formation of secret societies such as the Carbonari. By means of clandestinely organized groups, the aim of the Carbonari was to instigate the downfall of the government. A total of thirty thousand people were actively involved in the plots. Students, young intellectuals and army officers disappointed by Napoleon's fall were the most active.[19] In the end the whole conspiracy was a fiasco, and opposition in the following years was continued by peaceful means. Former Carbonari (Thierry, Jouffroy) played a role in founding such magazines as *Globe*. Others (Bazard, Buchez) joined the Saint-Simonian movement or applied themselves to their studies.

It was the discrepancy between the anticipated and the actual chances that constituted the social basis for the intellectual and cultural revival during the Restoration. The revival was bolstered by a generation faced with fundamentally altered occupational chances. They had had a good education but, since the demand for teachers, physicians and barristers remained far below the supply, many of them had no choice but to select other routes. Greater freedom of the press made a career in journalism one of the options. In 1825 more than two thousand newspapers and magazines were published in France, fourteen times as many as in the last years of the Empire.[20] Since the new periodicals regularly opposed the policies of the government, freedom of the press was a recurrent political theme. Legislation in this field was altered on various occasions, and proposals to censor the press thoroughly were what led to the Revolution of 1830, in which journalists, many of whom belonged to the generation of 1820, played an important role.[21]

12

Politics, Science and Philosophy

Comte belonged to the generation of 1820. A victim of the fact that the Ecole polytechnique was closed down, he was in a position comparable with that of other young men for whom there was no place. He had ties with the opposition, and in the first instance the end of the Restoration meant an improvement for him as well. In 1832 he was appointed as tutor at the Ecole polytechnique. A few years later he was also appointed as examiner. He never succeeded, however, in finding a permanent position, and in the end he even lost his modest functions at the Ecole polytechnique.

The Ecole polytechnique

I am enchanted with the excellent spirit that reigns at the school
and with this intimate friendship existing among all the pupils,
making them happy on the inside and formidable on the outside.

Comte to Pouzin, 1814

Of the three young oppositional networks, Comte was furthest removed from the poets and writers. He did not frequent the salons, had very little interest in literature, and what he called 'positive' was quite the opposite of 'poetic'. It was not until his 'second career', when he rediscovered the power of emotion, that literature and music began to play a meaningful role in his life.[1]

As regards the second group, consisting of liberal intellectuals, Comte's attitude was ambivalent. He had nothing but contempt for Cousin's philosophical teachings. Spiritualist psychology used subjective methods such as introspection, which Comte held to be unscientific. On this point, he endorsed the criticism of physicians and physiologists (Broussais, Gall). Comte held that psychological phenomena could be reduced to either physiology or sociology. There was no room for a psychology such as Cousin's. According to Comte, Cousin owed his success mainly to his skills at 'mime', and his audience consisted largely of youngsters with no scientific schooling.[2] Comte was far more 'positive' when it came to the historians. As early as 1818 he had advised his friend Valat to read more history. Comte held the Scottish historians (Hume, Robertson) in high regard, he found the German 'historical school' far more important than Kant and Hegel, and he respected French historians as well. Moreover, before 1830 he had made the acquaintance of Guizot. Guizot praised one of Comte's earlier works and in a letter Comte once commented that Guizot was the only living French thinker who could be compared with him.[3] When Guizot became Minister in 1830, Comte appealed to his benevolence and entreated him to establish a chair in the history of science. Guizot failed to meet his request.

Despite a certain degree of sympathy for the liberal opposition, in the Restoration Comte had more contact with the *polytechniciens*. His first articles were published mainly in Saint-Simonian magazines, where Ecole polytechnique alumni were particularly active. Even after his break with Saint-Simon, Comte continued to publish in these periodicals. In 1826, for example, two more general essays by Comte appeared in *Le producteur*. In addition, Comte published in liberal magazines such as *Journal de Paris* and *Censeur européen*.

Comte's relations in Paris were dominated largely by his contacts with *polytechniciens*. Via these contacts he found the pupils to whom he gave mathematics lessons, met Saint-Simon and published his first work. These associations were based upon the *camaraderie* and *esprit de corps* alumni were apt to share, which facilitated social relations – another reason Comte was so attached to his status as former pupil at the Ecole polytechnique. He also kept in contact with the friends of his youth, but his social network was limited. In his letters he made allusions to his obstinate temperament and his inability to socialize in Parisian circles.

In the first instance, Comte's ideas developed in a critical dialogue with the notions prevalent among *polytechniciens*. He held engineers and scientists in extremely high esteem, and for a long time they served as his primary frame of reference. After the Ecole polytechnique was closed down and Comte returned to Montpellier, he served as secretary of the regional association of dismissed pupils, but Paris proved irresistible. Less than two months later he returned to the capital. He began to earn a living by giving mathematics lessons, and for sixteen years tutoring was to remain his main source of income.

Although Comte remained dependent on his earnings as a private tutor, this did not keep him from making plans. The most obvious solution to his financial problems was to register at a *concours* for an official position, an opportunity with which the government presented the dismissed pupils. Comte, however, had no such ambition. The 'sad vocation of clerk' did not appeal to him, nor did that of engineer. As 'impeccable conduct' was a requirement for success, he felt his chances were slim. Rather than take part in a *concours*, he hoped to depart for America. He had been offered a position as mathematics teacher at the American version of the Ecole polytechnique, which was being founded at the time. Comte was recommended for the position by General Campredon, a man from Montpellier, who had taken him under his wing before at the Ecole polytechnique. Comte learned English, read Monge's work, studied all the conceivable applications of descriptive geometry and was brimming with enthusiasm about the 'promised land'. He spent what little time that remained on philosophy. In his letters he mentioned having become a 'philosopher'. He despised the new regime, advised Valat to seek refuge in philosophy and reminded him of the miserable youth of his new idol, Benjamin Franklin. In 'philosophical isolation' he read, contemplated and led a studious life.

In 1817 the American dream went up in smoke when Congress postponed founding the polytechnical school. Comte decided to stay in Paris. Through a former teacher at the Ecole polytechnique, he was commissioned to translate an English geometry book. Complete with several footnotes by the translator, it was published in 1818. Shortly afterwards Comte informed Valat with delight that he was happy and had abandoned his stoic life. Against all expectations he was having an affair with an older Parisian lady. Although Comte had no doubts as to his intellectual capacities, he was extremely insecure in social situations, particularly with women. He was short, somewhat cross-eyed and had never believed, or so he wrote to Valat, that any woman could ever fall in love with him. The affair was short-lived, but gave Comte moments of unanticipated joy.

In the summer of 1817 Comte entered the employ of Saint-Simon, upon whose request he turned his attention to political economy, studying Smith and Say and editing a number of essays. Comte was fascinated by the energetic aristocrat. Saint-Simon taught him 'a myriad of things I would have sought in vain in books'.[4] To the young Comte, Saint-Simon was primarily a *professeur d'énergie*,[5] an example of someone with ambition, with plans and projects, and with unwavering confidence in himself and his capacities. Comte felt attracted to the dynamic Saint-Simon and liked the role of *publicist*. Although he was paid as Saint-Simon's secretary for only three months, they stayed in contact for six years. In the first two years Comte viewed himself as Saint-Simon's apprentice. But in 1819 he had the feeling there was nothing more he could learn from him; while their contact continued, Comte was now aware of his own originality.

Starting in 1818, in his letters Comte repeated again and again that he wanted to try to get a permanent position at the Ecole polytechnique, the Ecole normale or the Académie des sciences. This was the only ambition he had, though he did make some attempts in other directions. He considered emigrating to England or applying for some other position, but he was increasingly convinced of the significance of his insights. Moreover, his first lengthy publication was well received and he had the support of several former teachers. His perseverance was based upon actual possibilities, although it was 1832 before he was appointed as tutor at the Ecole polytechnique.

The fact that Comte persevered for sixteen years also undoubtedly had to do with Caroline Massin, the woman he married in 1825. He had met her several years earlier and their relationship lasted until 1842, when she left him after he completed his *Cours*. When Comte first met Caroline she was a young penniless prostitute with no relatives (Comte revealed the 'secret' of her past in a passage in his will). She was then being kept by a young barrister, but they met again a year later. Upon her request Comte gave her mathematics lessons, and soon he became quite fond of her. He doubted whether he would ever meet any other woman who would like him as much. He had no objections to the fact that she was destitute, and in fact he viewed her having no relatives as a great advantage. Tormented by feelings of inferiority, he felt that perhaps even her ignoble past might work in his own favour. By marrying her he felt that, if only out of gratitude, he would be assured of her affection and loyalty.[6]

Politics and mathematics

Comte's first publications date back to the period when he was employed by Saint-Simon. Four years after his first book was published in 1822, he began working on *Cours de philosophie positive*. Comte's theory was thus conceived and formulated during the period from 1816 to 1826, between the moment the Ecole polytechnique was closed and the moment he started his *Cours*. By consulting his letters and unpublished notes it is possible to reconstruct how his ideas took shape. This

reconstruction illustrates how illusory it is to analyse ideas as the outcome of rational choices. Comte's theory was produced by complex
social dynamics. Motives played a role that methodologists view as
improper, as did circumstances to which historians of ideas usually
avoid referring.

In his first years as *professeur ambulant* Comte grappled with two
problems. Both were related to the closing of the Ecole polytechnique
and the insecurity of his job situation.

The first problem was of a political nature. *Mes réflexions* (1816),
the earliest of Comte's writings known to us, castigated the 'horrific
alliance of kings and priests'.[7] The Restoration, Comte wrote, was no
less reprehensible than the despotism of Napoleon and the Reign of
Terror. If the *Ancien Régime*, the Terror and despotism were so widely
denounced, why wasn't the Restoration? Although his political sympathies did not alter much in the course of time, Comte was soon
confronted with the issue of a more scientific approach to politics. In
his early texts a great deal had been taken directly from Saint-Simon,
but the tone and style differed from the prophetism of his mentor.
Comte's ideas were close to those of the liberal opposition, but here
too there were major differences, the most important of which was
that his analyses went further than political commentaries. In politics
Comte was an outsider. He was less interested in parliamentary debates than in the concept of a new political science. He wrote, for
example, a text on tax reforms that was in fact an analysis of the
function of taxes in industrial society. He also wrote a critical piece on
liberal politicians, in which he held that it is not possible to engage in
and analyse politics simultaneously. The more one is involved in the
political game, the less one is able to develop an objective conception
of it. The reason so many authors were unable to see this was that
there was no positive political science. Even in these early political
pieces Comte expressed a scientific ambition fairly uncommon among
liberals. In 1818, long before he actually broke with Saint-Simon, Comte
specified what was lacking in his mentor's views. Saint-Simon expected
too much from the wrong groups and elaborated upon his ideas in the
wrong fashion. The problem was that 'positive ideas' had yet to be
formulated. The only 'reasonable politics' was political economy, but
it was not yet a science in the true sense of the word. There would be
a future for Saint-Simon's projects only if he had access to a true social
science.[8]

The second problem facing Comte had to do with mathematics,
which was the most important subject at the Ecole polytechnique
and the one at which he was best. He did not doubt its importance,

but was increasingly critical as to how it was used. He began to be especially disparaging of the boundless claims some mathematicians were apt to make. What was called for, he felt, was a theory of mathematics that would take into account the limitations of mathematical models. A theory of this kind would be useful for scientists and mathematics teachers alike. Comte felt he had arrived at a less biased perception of the mathematical spirit than prevailed at the Ecole polytechnique. However, the book he planned to write about mathematics was never published. The outline was completed in 1818, two fragments were written in 1819 and another two in 1821, but in the end he abandoned the project. He was convinced a new theory of mathematics ought to be based upon its role in science, and, more than a theory of mathematics, this required a theory of science.

It is clear from his early notes and writings that, by 1819, Comte was thoroughly convinced he had found something new. He succeeded in formulating a number of problems in a new manner and felt he was on the track of an interesting solution. His 'apprenticeship' was over, he wrote to a friend, and to solemnize the transition he changed his first name from Isidore to Auguste.

In a long letter Comte stated that many mathematicians were only 'calculators.'[9] Completely engrossed in one tiny problem, they could not even understand why the methods they used were so effective. It was essential to have a general theory of mathematics, which would clarify the limitations as well as the possibilities of mathematical models. The question was thus how this theory should be constructed. General reflections on the human mind were pointless. Cognition a priori led only to 'illusions'; 'logic, metaphysics, ideology' were all 'fantasies'. Comte was certain scientists were in agreement on this point, even though they might not all be aware of it. A positive theory of knowledge had to be based upon observable facts. These facts, in Comte's opinion, were the various sciences at their various stages of development. The 'only reasonable logic' was consequently a 'general philosophy of the sciences'. Its results would be of importance to all the sciences. Rigid specialization could be avoided and mathematicians could be liberated from their blind faith in mathematical procedures. Once they became acquainted with other sciences and other methods they would comprehend their own work better and no longer profess there was a mathematical solution to every scientific problem.

What Comte meant by these 'other sciences' were mainly the biomedical disciplines. The use of quantitative and mathematical methods was widely disputed in these fields. The most important tradition in this respect was the Montpellier School. Comte had only the greatest admiration for Barthez' methodical mind and called Bichat the 'true founder' of biology. On the positivist calendar, it was Bichat and not Galileo or Newton who was featured as the patron saint of the modern sciences.

The vitalistic ideas of the Montpellier School gave Comte an important clue to the theory of science for which he was looking.[10] As regards his rejection of mathematical models, Comte had been convinced mainly by Bichat's arguments. According to Bichat, it was in their irregularity that organic phenomena differed from inorganic ones. In a certain sense, even pathological phenomena were normal for living creatures. This was why it was impossible to look for the same regularities in biology as in astronomy or physics. Mathematical models were unsuitable and biology should be an independent science based upon the study of 'life forces' or 'life principles'. Comte was not an unconditional admirer of this conception. He reformulated certain aspects of it, although in principle he concurred with it. The recognition of biology as an essentially different science from physics gave Comte a fruitful analogy for a redefinition of social science. Social science would be to biology what biology was to chemistry. This line of reasoning first appeared in a piece written in 1819 entitled *Considérations sur les tentatives qui ont été faites pour fonder la science sociale sur la physiologie et sur quelques autres sciences*. Comte specifically criticized Cabanis' attempt to found the science of man on physiology. What he did was use the arguments of biologists to refute certain of the claims made by these same biologists. Comte used the very arguments biologists had employed against the mathematicians, but this time against the subordination of social science to biology.

If social science could indeed be viewed as analogous to biology, the question remained as to what were the specific features of social phenomena as compared with biological phenomena. The reply to this question can be found in an unfinished essay on Condorcet, also written in 1819. All things considered, Comte wrote, 'the gradual development of civilization' or 'the progress of the human mind' were specific features of the human species. This was the 'regulating' principle, the 'general force' that dominated all other forces, and Condorcet was the man who had discovered it.[11]

Although the elements for it were at hand, the 1819 writings did not contain any finished theory. Theorists of biology (Barthez, Bichat) had provided Comte with a clue to a non-reductionistic and differential theory of science based upon what was later to be referred to as 'relative autonomy'. This theory of science was the answer to the two problems with which he was grappling: mathematics and politics. In the hierarchy of the sciences, they were the two extremes.

First steps towards a theory

In the years around 1820 Auguste Comte wrote three types of articles and essays. The first type dealt with the philosophy of mathematics. If one was to formulate it, one had to study the role of mathematics in the various sciences. In Comte's first effort towards a book about it he devoted a special section to 'erroneous applications of mathematics'. In conclusion he wrote an entire chapter on the place of mathematics *vis-à-vis* other forms of knowledge. The book was meant for mathematicians, mathematics teachers and scientists in other disciplines. In the following years Comte devoted most of his time and energy to the study of other sciences[12] and the focus of his attention shifted to a general theory of science.

The second type of writing addressed social science. Before Saint-Simon, Comte was interested in political economy and efforts to formulate 'positive politics'. Like his mentor, he was convinced of the necessity for a positive political science and wrote various essays on the subject. He criticized earlier attempts in this connection and emphasized the historical nature of social science. It was in this vein that he wrote *Sommaire appréciation de l'ensemble du passé moderne* (1820). One of the problems was that, although social science was to be historical science, historical research was still at an unscientific stage.

The third type of writing focused on current events. Comte wrote articles such as the two dated 1819 about the freedom of the press, as well as book reviews and political commentaries. In the articles he similarly stressed the necessity of 'positive politics' and the importance of a scientific approach to political issues. In this sense, current events reinforced his interest in questions about the science of man.

These various interests came together for the first time in *Prospectus des travaux scientifiques nécessaires pour réorganiser la société* (1822), published in a series edited by Saint-Simon. Comte began his treatise with an elaboration that did not deviate in any way from the ideas of his mentor. But, the further he went, the clearer the differences became. In the opening lines he repeated that the important thing was to put an end to the prevailing 'anarchy'. The feudal-cum-theological point of view was just as reprehensible as the 'critical doctrine'. A new 'organic' system was called for, in which industrialists were entitled to secular power and scientists to spiritual power. If this new system were to be put into effect, Comte concluded, there were two tasks to be fulfilled. Firstly, a new system of ideas had to be worked out. Since they were the only ones with the capacities for it, and since they alone had sufficient intellectual authority, this was a task for scientists. Secondly, there was a practical task for industrialists as regards the organization of society. This second task was subordinate to the first.

The most urgent need was for a system of positive ideas. The first step in this direction was the creation of a political science. This science was to constitute the basis for the establishment of a new society, and consequently had high priority. It would be erroneous to start with 'practical activities', and Comte specified what he meant by the new science. It was in this framework that he first formulated his law of the three stages and his differential theory of science. The two were closely related. However, Comte presented this relatedness in a very peculiar manner. After the publication of his treatise he began to speak of the three stages as his 'grand law' formulated for the first time in this *opuscule fondamental*. This was also how he presented his ideas in *Cours de philosophie positive*. The law of the three stages was explained in the first lesson, and in the second lesson the 'hierarchy of the sciences' was discussed. This was the 'complement' of his discovery. In this mode of presentation the differential theory of science became a specification of the law of the three stages. His adherents followed this interpretation and his opponents never objected to it. Thus an image emerged of Comte's theory of science in which the law of the three stages was the central notion. The differential nature of his epistemology was of secondary importance, and its historical nature was reduced to the three stages. This depiction obfuscated the genesis as well as the meaning of Comte's work.

In so far as one can explore how Comte arrived at his ideas, his conception of the three stages and his differential theory of science emerged at more or less the same time. The two were closely linked, and there is little reason to assume the priority of either the one or the other in a historical or systematic sense. Historically, Comte's theory was the outcome of two types of reasoning, both of which were evident in his work.

In the first type of reasoning the notion of the three stages was a consequence of the necessity for a differential theory of science. Since sciences differed in their subjects and methods (the result of his work on the philosophy of mathematics), social science also ought to be based upon the specific features of its object. This gave rise to the question of how the human world differed from the plant and animal kingdom. The answer was that people had the ability to learn, particularly from previous generations. This was the property that made history feasible. If social science was to be a true science, it ought to be based upon a historical law. Comte found a first step in this direction in the work of Condorcet, whose insight he reformulated into his law of the three stages.

The second type of reasoning was quite different. Here the point of departure was not a differential conception of science, but the necessity for a political science. This was something on which Comte had focused his attention ever since the closing of the Ecole polytechnique. His interest was reinforced when he made the acquaintance of Saint-Simon and led him to the following line of reasoning. If political science was to become a real science, the question was how this process had taken place in other sciences. The development of human knowledge had gone through various stages. Like Turgot, Cuvier, for example, had also distinguished three stages: the fantastic, the contemplative and the descriptive stage.[13] Comte made a comparable classification: the theological or fictive stage, the metaphysical or abstract stage and the positive or scientific stage. This developmental pattern assumed the nature of an invariable law. The human mind could develop only in this manner. This was not the end of it, however, for the various sciences did not exhibit the same order of development. The sequence was not indiscriminate, it was determined by the complexity of the scientific object in question. Since the phenomena on which it focused were simple, astronomy had been the first to reach the positive stage. The more complex the phenomena were, the longer it took to reach the positive stage. According to this line of reasoning, the law of the three stages was the point of departure and the differential theory of science was a further specification of it.

In the years around 1820 Comte followed these two lines of reasoning simultaneously, but, as soon as he wanted to systematize his insights, a problem arose. If he followed the first line of reasoning, the emphasis would be on his differential theory and the law of the three stages would serve primarily as the foundation for one of these sciences. In this case the differences between the sciences would be stressed and the law of the three stages would serve mainly to underline the specifically historical nature of social science. In the other case the emphasis was on the similarities between the sciences: all of them developed according to the same pattern; only the sequence differed. Comte chose the latter option. He granted priority to the law of the three stages and presented it as the most general and prominent result of his thinking.

This choice on his part was undoubtedly of decisive importance for the manner in which Comte's work was perceived. Since then Comte has been viewed mainly as the apostle of the 'positive stage' that all the sciences will reach and that should be the foundation for the reorganization of modern society.

In keeping with this choice, Comte presented political science as an illustration of his three stages. The features of politics had also developed in three stages. The doctrine of *droit divin* represented the theological stage, the ideas on popular sovereignty the metaphysical stage. Positive politics would have to abandon absolute principles of this kind. Positive politics was based upon the acceptance of the primacy of observation over imagination. The subject of these observations was neither the state nor civil society, but the whole – in other words human civilization in the process of its development. Political problems could be comprehended only by realizing that societies were characterized by a certain civilizing stage. This stage was determined in turn by the development of the human mind. An exhaustive study of the development of civilization would thus have to be at the foundation of a true political science.

After this outline of a positive approach to politics, Comte concluded his *Prospectus* with a critical discussion of earlier efforts in this direction. He reviewed the work of Montesquieu, Condorcet and Cabanis. According to Comte, Montesquieu had no idea of the true interconnections between the phenomena. He lacked insight into the 'natural development of civilization'. Condorcet was the first truly to exhibit this kind of insight. Condorcet's classification of the eras, however, was quite confused, and he laboured under the illusion that mathematical procedures retained their validity in social science. Cabanis had come closer to the truth. He was familiar with a fundamental distinction between animate and inanimate nature, but failed to see that social science could not be reduced to physiology.

In his first lengthy publication Comte sketched the contours of a large-scale project. Its main feature was the priority accorded to intellectual reform. Not until this reform had been implemented would it be possible for political activities to commence. This attitude illustrated the difference between Comte on the one hand and Saint-Simon and many of the representatives of the liberal opposition on the other. However, it was not quite clear exactly what the intellectual tasks entailed. On the grounds of his first writings, three possibilities can be distinguished. The first and most general was that Comte would focus on the formulation of a philosophy based on his theory of knowledge. This meant he would have to draw up a theory on the positive stage.

The second possibility was that he would confine himself to the elaboration of his differential theory of science. It meant he would have to conduct further research into the development of the various fields of science. The third possibility was that he would concentrate on a new political science. This meant he would have to conduct research into the history of civilization. This is not a distinction Comte drew. In his opinion, the three possibilities were probably inseparable. Yet he was soon to make a clear choice.

13

The Shift to the Theory of Science

Prospectus des travaux scientifiques nécessaires pour réorganiser la société was Comte's first book. The 1822 edition, however, was a provisional one, and only a hundred copies were printed. Two years later two new editions were published. One of them, entitled *Système de politique positive*, was an expanded version of the *Prospectus* and contained a short explanatory note by Comte. Against his will, another version was published as well. It was entitled *Catéchisme des industriels* and contained a foreword by Saint-Simon, in which two 'imperfections' were cited: his 'pupil' found 'scientific capacity' more important than 'industrial capacity' and concentrated on the scientific part, unjustly overlooking the religious aspects of the doctrine. This second publication and its foreword led to the break between Saint-Simon and his 'pupil'. Comte had had his fill of being treated like an inferior. It was a long time since he had learnt anything from Saint-Simon, and it was time for him to head in his own direction.[1]

'My little intellectual revolution'

The text of the second edition differed from that of the first in two senses.[2] Firstly, Comte qualified his political stance. He had initially mentioned two parties – monarchists and advocates of popular sovereignty. The doctrines of both, based as they were upon absolute principles, were reprehensible. In the new edition he tempered this point of view and acknowledged that, for the time being, the constitutional monarchy advocated by the liberals was the most desirable regime. Although they set too much store on political reforms, in anticipation of a truly positive polity the liberals deserved to be supported. Comte wanted to examine the foundations of a truly 'positive polity' in a separate study. This is why he changed the title of his treatise and presented the text of *Prospectus* as Part I of a *Système de politique positive*. Part II, which was never published, was to contain an analysis of the development of human civilization.

Comte's second alteration pertained to epistemological questions. At the close of his text he added ten pages that were mainly about the methodology of the life sciences. In Comte's view, the sciences of inanimate nature had developed differently from those of animate nature. In the former case, insight into specific properties preceded insight into the interdependence of phenomena. In the life sciences the developmental sequence had been the reverse. The general features of organisms and species were frequently known earlier than the specific ones. Thus the whole was accessible earlier than the parts. From this 'important difference' Comte concluded that, like biology, social science ought to start at the most general level. This addition was in keeping with his intention to study the development of human civilization.

The two changes Comte made were related to the audience he wanted to reach. He sent out all the copies he had, and we know to whom.[3] In addition to friends and relatives, the *Système de politique positive* went to two groups of readers: liberal politicians and scientists. The change in his political stance was an opening to the liberals, and the additions about the scientific method were for the scientists. The liberals who received copies of the book included such leading figures as Benjamin Constant and Guizot, a number of economists (Say, Sismondi, Dunoyer, Charles Comte) and several bankers and industrialists. As to the scientists, Comte circulated virtually all the leading physicists and chemists of his day (Ampère, Arago, Gay-Lussac, Fourier, Laplace, Poinsot, Poisson). Strikingly enough, physicians and naturalists (Blainville, Burdin, Cuvier, Flourens) were less well represented. In the course of time this ratio was to alter in favour of life scientists. There was only an incidental mathematician or physicist among his later pupils, whereas relatively large numbers of physicians and biologists became interested in Comte's work.

Comte immediately sent off all the copies of his book, which indicates how important it was to him what other people thought of it. Until then his only public appearances had been as Saint-Simon's pupil. Now he wanted to make a name for himself. We do not know much about the public's reaction to this debut, but its author was extremely satisfied. For several weeks Comte enjoyed 'the most flattering comments' coming his way from all sides.[4] The success reinforced his intuition that an important task lay ahead of him. The question was just what exactly this task was to be.

Simultaneously with the publication of *Système de politique positive* and his break with Saint-Simon, Comte and Caroline Massin moved in together. A year later, early in 1825, they got married. From that moment on the irregularity of Comte's earnings was a serious problem. In 1825 he wrote several articles for *Le producteur*. At the time it was his only source of income. He no longer had any pupils and did not expect the situation to improve soon. Since it cost him too much time and distracted him too much from his real interest, Comte did not view journalism as a viable alternative. It was under these uncertain circumstances that he came up with the idea for a series of lectures. If he could manage to drum up a reasonable number of people to register to attend them, it would solve his financial problems and at the same time enable him to concentrate on his own work. At the beginning of 1826 he officially announced he was going to give a *cours*. For a year he was to present a survey of the positive sciences and the philosophy based upon them. He sent invitations to his friends and acquaintances and a number of prominent scientists. With very few exceptions (Guizot), this time liberal politicians and publicists were not invited.

The design of his *cours* and the selection of who was to be invited were indicative of a further and more precise elaboration of his project. In February 1826 Comte informed Blainville, a biologist who was a friend of his, that he had had a nervous breakdown and was not yet completely recovered. With short breaks he worked for almost eighty hours on end, and in this 'high strung state' suddenly realized what his task was in life. He decided not to write the second part of *Système de politique positive*, but to devote his time instead to systematizing his theory of science. In a letter to Blainville he spoke of 'a little intellectual revolution'.[5]

Ten years after the Ecole polytechnique was closed, Comte had outlined the framework for his theory of science. The most important elements were already evident in his early notes, his letters and his first book, but the plan for *Cours de philosophie positive* was not drawn up until 1826. He first formulated his ideas in his 1819 notes, but it was to be another seven years before he decided to expand them into a systematic theory of science.

The Crisis of 1826

Although Comte was still bothered by nervous symptoms in March 1826, and spoke to Blainville of *violents dérangements*, he began his *cours* a few weeks later. It was attended by Blainville, Alexander von Humboldt, the economist Dunoyer and several acquaintances, some of whom were *polytechniciens*. The meetings were to be held every Wednesday and Sunday. When the men arrived for the fourth session, they found the apartment closed. Due to illness, the meeting could not take place.

The crisis of 1826 was the worst Comte ever experienced. When he began his lectures he was overworked and in a state of great uncertainty. His financial situation was precarious and had led to conflicts with his wife. It had infuriated Comte when Caroline proposed returning to her old occupation. Comte had just started on his *cours* in April when she suggested renewing her contact with a former friend and patron. Comte refused to allow her to do so, Caroline left home and Comte fled in despair to the outskirts of the city. There his wife found him a few days later in a state of utmost confusion. Caroline appealed to Blainville for help, and it was through his mediation that Comte was admitted to Esquirol's clinic. He spent eight months there. The treatment of his 'mania', as his ailment was diagnosed, consisted of cold showers and bleeding. He was discharged from the clinic in December 1826; there was no money left to pay the bills. His depression continued for more than a year. In the spring of 1827 he tried to commit suicide, but in the following months there was a clear improvement.[6]

In 1828, two years after his crisis, Comte had recovered to the extent that he resumed his work. Once again he tried to find a position for himself in whatever way he could, including as an *ingénieur de commerce*. He wrote book reviews and articles about practical commercial problems and earned the recommendations of liberal politicians (Guizot) and scientists (Arago, Fourier, Poinsot). His chances were good, but at the last moment the funds for the new function appeared to be lacking.

In the summer of that year he published on a totally different subject, Broussais' *Traité de l'irritation et de la folie*. The review contained Comte's first extensive discourse on physiology. He observed that the great revolution in the life sciences was a recent and widely underestimated phenomenon. The major innovations dated back to the end of the eighteenth century. However, one could only speak of a positive science once mental phenomena also began to be studied from a physiological point of view. That was what Cabanis achieved. Broussais worked in this tradition and summoned the courage to oppose the fashionable psychology of Cousin and the spiritualists. Comte agreed with Broussais that psychology could not be separated from physiology.

It was only on minor points that Comte begged to differ with Broussais' convictions, the most important one being the proper treatment of mental illness. Broussais emphasized that 'moral and emotional care' were indispensable to therapy, but failed to note that, in this respect, there was 'extreme negligence'. Without studying the problem himself, according to Comte, Broussais would have been convinced that many patients simply became worse after being admitted. Comte spoke from experience: he had not begun to improve until after he left Esquirol's clinic. The 'loving care' of his wife had done far more for him than any official therapy.[7]

The review of Broussais' *Traité* enabled Comte to take a somewhat more objective view of his own crisis and at the same time to return to his true work. He wanted to resume his *cours* as soon as possible, and was indeed able to do so in January 1829. The new cycle consisted of seventy-two lessons over a period of eight months. The opening was attended by such prominent scientists as Fourier, the most important French physicist at the time, Navier and Poinsot, both former teachers of Comte's, and the biologists Blainville, Broussais and Esquirol. Their presence was indicative of their interest in Comte's ideas. Esquirol might have come to see how his patient was faring, and Broussais perhaps to meet a young admirer, but the rest of the scientists otherwise had little reason to come and be addressed by an unemployed mathematician. Fourier, Navier, Poinsot and Blainville were all members of the Académie des sciences, and Fourier was even its secretary. As a *polytechnicien*, of course Comte was not a nobody, but it could not have been enough to attract 'the great Fourier' to Comte's apartment for a course in 'positive philosophy'. These scientists must all have had some intellectual interest in what Comte had to say.

The seventy-two lessons of the *cours* met with such great acclaim that a private institution, the Athénée, invited Comte to come and repeat the lectures for a larger audience. He began to do so late in 1829. The first lessons of the new cycle were published as brochures and then as books. Volume 1 appeared in 1830. With some delay, the other five volumes were published by Bachelier, a publishing house specializing in mathematical works. Volume 2 on astronomy and physics was published in 1833, Volume 3 on chemistry and biology in 1838, and the last three volumes, all on sociology, in 1839, 1841 and 1842.

Cours de philosophie positive

In keeping with the plan drawn up in 1826, the *Cours* pertained mainly to epistemological research. Analysing the various fields of science, it was written primarily for scientists and appeared through a scientific publishing house of great repute. The philosophical and political aspects were secondary to the theory of science. Comte spoke of 'positive philosophy', but made it clear that he was not interested in philosophy in the traditional sense. He 'regretted' having to use the word philosophy. *Philosophie des sciences* would have been more accurate, but did not include social science. For lack of a better term, and in the hope that the word 'positive' would make it clear that something new was involved, he decided to use the term 'positive philosophy'.[8]

The *Cours* began with two survey lessons. In the first Comte explained the law of the three stages. In the positive or scientific stage, the process of conceptualization was confined to problems that provided testable answers. Statements that were not testable made way for questions pertaining to the 'relations of similarity and succession of phenomena'. These relations exhibited regularities, and the study of these regularities was the aim of every positive science. In order to arrive at a scientific statement it was not necessary to query the 'origin', the 'essence', or even the 'cause' of a phenomenon. It was enough to know its laws. Comte cited two examples of this type of positive knowledge: the law of gravity and Fourier's analytical theory of heat. Although the 'origin', 'essence' and 'cause' of gravity were unknown, Newton's law of gravity did provide an adequate explanation. Precisely the same held true for Fourier's theory of heat.

What Comte described as positive science was a compact summary of what many scientists before him propagated in mathematics and physics (from Newton to Fourier) as well as in the life sciences (Barthez). Comte himself viewed the rise of positive philosophy as a process that had been going on for two centuries, and historians of science have not discovered much that was original in his elaborations. Positivist conceptions had been widespread among French scientists well before Comte.[9] And Comte himself did not present his *Cours de philosophie positive* as a discourse on the positive method. The aim of his work was twofold. He wanted to contribute towards founding social science as a positive science. Once this 'gap' was filled, the system of positive sciences would be complete and it would be possible to formulate a theory of this system as a whole. This was the second goal. According to Comte, a theory of science of this kind was important for four reasons.

Firstly, it could counterbalance the negative repercussions of the division of scientific labour. This division of labour was the foundation of the modern sciences, and the pursuit of a general method, universal logic or all-encompassing science was an illusion. The need remained, however, for a theoretical perspective that would be more general than the separate sciences. Comte's theory of science was designed to fulfil this need. In addition to persons who practised the separate sciences, there was room for 'specialists in generalities'. This new specialism was all the more indispensable since the division into fields of science was not in any way a natural one. It was merely an *artifice* constructed to comprehend reality.

Secondly, the new epistemology had a didactic function. It was an important instrument in reforming the school system. The metaphysical and literary syllabus could be replaced by a positive curriculum based upon Comte's theory of science.

Thirdly, it could be useful for the development of the separate sciences. Advanced specialization largely overlooked the fact that scientific problems often need more points of view or a more general point of view. Thus analytical geometry had emerged from a combination of two formerly separate disciplines, algebra and geometry. As illustration of the same phenomenon, Comte cited the problems on the interface of chemistry and biology. They could be solved only by uniting the two points of view.

Fourthly, this epistemology could serve as a guideline for social reforms. In Comte's opinion, the prevailing intellectual anarchy was owing mainly to the simultaneous use of theological, metaphysical and positive ideas. By demonstrating that they were irreconcilable, Comte wanted to make it clear that the positive philosophy was a fruitful point of departure for social innovation.

Working from the law of the three stages, the first lesson dealt with what the positive sciences had in common. The second addressed what the differences were and how they should be interpreted. According to Comte, it was generally acknowledged that the existing divisions into sciences did not suffice. Any effort at division was even apt to be viewed with distrust. For many 'good minds' the differences between the sciences had become too great to put them into one scheme. Comte spoke of a 'general discredit'. These comments indicate that, around 1830, the processes of discipline formation had become so dominant that transdisciplinary conceptions had largely lost their significance. The situation was quite different from the one around 1800, when Laplace as well as his opponents were still formulating approaches that were more general than their specific field of research.

In the eighteenth century scientific specialization occurred to an extremely limited extent. There was only one institution, the Académie, where researchers would meet and compare notes, and it was not until 1775 that the first journals were founded. The establishment of a new educational system in the revolutionary period made it possible for them to work as teachers, and they soon had a variety of independent journals and began to unite in specialized societies. The process of disciplinary specialization began to play an increasingly dominant role. Researchers no longer solely conducted research, they also held professorial chairs, had students, wrote textbooks and now communicated mainly with the other members of their profession. This development led to the formation of 'disciplines' in the modern sense. From then on, scientific work was conducted within the framework of the discipline, in other words in organizational forms that served as units for research, teaching and professional association. They were essentially different from the predisciplinary and predominantly 'academic' organizational forms of the seventeenth and eighteenth centuries.

This process of the formation of disciplines was one of the most important problems in Comte's epistemology. He wanted to formulate a general theory of science, but without being reductionist. Without wanting to give up a more general ambition, he recognized the significance of scientific differentiation. According to Comte, an epistemology of this kind could be formulated only in one way, by approaching the sciences scientifically, in other words by working empirically. The naturalists had set the example: the sciences could be classified in much the same way as they had classified plants and animals. A study of this kind revealed that there was a distinction between fundamental or abstract sciences and applied sciences or specializations. In Comte's view there were six fundamental sciences which, logically considered, could be arranged in hundreds of different ways. Since the main point was to determine their relations with one another, the relations between their objects were of decisive importance. These objects could be classified according to the degree of complexity. The results would be commensurate with the phenomena's degree of dependence and were inversely proportional to the degree of generality. The more complex the object was, the more dependent it was and the more its degree of generality decreased. This classification led to the following sequence: mathematics, astronomy, physics, chemistry, biology or physiology, and social physics or sociology.

This epistemological model was Comte's most original contribution, and the *Cours de philosophie positive* was really nothing but a detailed elaboration of it. Comte refrained from revealing much about the sources of this model, but it is clear that he had consulted primarily the writings of physicians and naturalists. They had drawn the fundamental distinction between inanimate and animate nature. This distinction led the young Comte to realize where mathematics lost its validity. What is more, a number of these biologists *avant la lettre* had developed a conception that was more differentiated than the dichotomy between organic and inorganic. As far as I know, two authors were of special significance in this respect, Barthez and Cabanis. In contrast to mechanists such as Laplace and vitalists such as Bichat, Barthez and Cabanis both suggested a classification that was less 'absolute', and in Comte's terms consequently more positive. In *Nouveaux éléments de la science de l'homme* (1778), Barthez advocated a reorientation of the medical sciences. But before this could be achieved, a farewell to metaphysics was required. 'First causes' could not be known; in science only the 'laws' of the 'succession of phenomena' were studied. This formulation came quite close to what Comte called 'positive'. Barthez then distinguished various 'components' of nature. They each had their 'own activity' based upon a specific 'principle'. The first and simplest principle was the 'impulse'. The second was gravity, the third a combination of the two, and the fourth the 'force of life'. This scale was gradual and was characterized by increasing 'compositeness'.[10] Barthez held that physiology was the study of the order of phenomena that was dominated by 'life forces'. Cabanis went a bit further in elaborating upon this theme. He too distinguished four 'gradations of existence', be it in a somewhat different manner than Barthez. What he added was the principle that Comte called 'decreasing generality'. Cabanis stated that the laws of the 'first gradation of existence' also applied to the other three. The simplest properties were the ones the phenomena have in common.[11] Cabanis' formulations were unsystematic and rather imprecise, but they did mean a step towards Comte's idea that the degree of complexity and the degree of generality were inversely proportionate.

Compared with Barthez and Cabanis, the originality of Comte was unmistakable. In the first place, Comte's model was more comprehensive and more general. He granted mathematics and astronomy a place, and his arguments for social science paralleled those of the biologists for biology. In the second place, Comte's model was much more systematic. Works by Barthez and Cabanis did not contain much more than a descriptive and rather cursory sketch. Moreover, since he distinguished various 'gradations of existence', though adhering to a monistic point of departure, Cabanis was not consistent in his conception. In the third place, Comte expanded his insights into an empirically founded theory. In this sense there was also an important difference between the ten pages written by Cabanis and Barthez and the six volumes of Comte's *Cours*. Comte realized that the schemes drawn up by Barthez and Cabanis could be elaborated into a general and systematic theory of science. This was something his predecessors had failed to realize.

Comte's explications in the *Cours* bore witness to his didactic qualities and extremely thorough knowledge of the sciences and their history. His work contained no original natural science research. On only one occasion did he make any contribution to the scientific discussion of his day. That was in 1835, when he read a *mémoire* for the Académie des sciences on mathematical aspects of Laplace's cosmogony. The members of the Academy were not impressed by Comte's contribution, and in later years Comte concurred with their evaluation. The text of his lecture has only recently been published for the first time.[12] Consequently, Comte's work does not derive its significance from its scientific contribution, but from its didactic qualities and epistemological innovations. The *Cours* contained mainly epistemological research, and *Traité élémentaire de géométrie analytique* (1843) and *Traité philosophique d'astronomie populaire* (1844) were of a didactic nature.

Although they were not original contributions to the scientific discussion, Comte's analyses were not neutral surveys either. He presented his own interpretations in all the fields of science and did not refrain from adding clear recommendations for research. The best way to read the *Cours* is by bearing in mind the relation between Comte's interpretations and the developments in the particular field of science. This has unfortunately very rarely been done. Sociologists confine themselves to Comte's sociology, philosophers to his positivism, and only a few historians of science have focused on his interpretations of the natural sciences. However, this usually occurs in an extremely judgemental manner. Comte is said, for example, to have overlooked the significance of the mathematician Cauchy and underestimated the work of Fresnel, and Michel Serres does full justice to the anachronism by using twentieth-century developments to expose Comte's digressions.[13] Others have expressed far more positive opinions of Comte's insights, but the most striking point is still how little has been written on what was actually said in the *Cours*. A great deal has been written on Comte and positivism, but a few essays by Bachelard, Brunschvicg and Canguilhem are virtually all that can clarify anything of the relation between Comte's analyses and the developments in the natural sciences of his day.

Mathematics and astronomy

The first science Comte dealt with in the *Cours* was mathematics. Although it is the oldest and most perfected science, the ideas about it were 'vague and uncertain'. Ever since Lagrange, according to Comte, mathematics constituted a real unity. In *Mécanique analytique* (1787) Lagrange converted mechanics into a coherent analytical system, and in such later work as *Théorie des fonctions analytiques* (1797) he focused on the systematization of analytical techniques.[14] It was important to Comte, who had nothing but the greatest admiration for Lagrange, to determine what the relation was between these two works. The most significant distinction Comte made in his interpretation of mathematics was between 'abstract' and 'concrete' mathematics. His growing criticism of mathematicians was based upon this distinction. To Comte, abstract mathematics was essentially arithmetic, *calcul*. This component was of a purely logical or rational nature. Its significance, however, was completely instrumental, depending in other words on applications and consequently on concrete mathematics. The aim of concrete mathematics was to formulate equations regarding a certain class of phenomena. This task involved two disciplines, geometry and mechanics. A decisive contribution to modern geometry was made by Descartes as the founder of analytical geometry. Comte called it 'general geometry'. The most important contribution to the systematization of mechanics was made by Lagrange. Volume 1 of the *Cours* is organized round these distinctions. After a general introduction, first abstract mathematics is dealt with, in lessons 4 to 10, then geometry in lessons 10 to 15 and mechanics in lessons 15 to 19.

Comte's interpretation of mathematics, as Brunschvicg observed,[15] was a pragmatic one. Abstract mathematics was born of concrete mathematics, and in Comte's view served solely an auxiliary function. With this attitude, Comte turned against the emergence of pure mathematics that had begun in the early nineteenth century. Representatives of this new school spent their time studying mathematical foundations. Comte felt, however, that research of this type was too frequently purely speculative. Abstract mathematics ought to be subordinate to concrete mathematics, and according to Comte this concrete mathematics had no mathematical foundation. The construction of an analytical foundation for geometry or mechanics was based upon a misconception. Comte referred to the 'misuse' of analysis and of 'metaphysics'.[16] Geometry and mechanics were both based upon postulates that, in the end, could be traced back to observations. Geometry provided a description of bodies from a static point of view.

Mechanics, a bit more complicated and dependent on geometry, provided a description of bodies from a dynamic point of view. So, essentially, these disciplines were both natural sciences. They had developed into mathematical disciplines, however, and were used more as mathematical 'methods' than as natural science 'doctrines'.

Comte's criticism of mathematicians intensified in his later work. Although he continued to view mathematics as the most fundamental science, of all scientists mathematicians bore the brunt of his most severe censure. He referred to abstract mathematics as a 'sterile' endeavour. He was no less critical of the role of mathematicians in astronomy and physics. As long as they could apply their own techniques, they furthered the formulation of the most speculative hypotheses. In Comte's view probability calculus, for example, was thus little more than a mathematical alibi for dominating social science. Comte increasingly viewed mathematics as the last 'serious refuge for the absolute mind'.[17] Since mathematics was the only science that was not dominated by another science, mathematicians were not accountable to anyone for their limitations. Comte formulated this standpoint, already expressed in his early work, increasingly in moral and political terms as well.

The contrast between abstract and concrete mathematics probably had a political dimension from the very start. It was only as an outcome of Lagrange's later work that the 'pure mathematics' problem emerged. Its most important representative was Augustin Cauchy. Besides being a brilliant mathematician, Cauchy was also a devout Catholic and an ultra-conservative. When Monge and Carnot were ostracized from the Académie in 1816, the king appointed two royalists to replace them, one of whom was Cauchy. Cauchy accepted the appointment, and his colleagues were not quick to stop resenting him for it. In 1816, just as Cauchy was becoming an academician, Comte and his fellow students were turning against a tutor known for his royalist sympathies. The Ecole polytechnique was closed down and reorganized and one of the victims of the reorganization was Louis Poinsot, who was replaced by Cauchy. Poinsot was a liberal and a student of Monge, and together with Louis Navier he was to be Comte's most important patron. Poinsot was a geometrician; Navier had concentrated on mechanics and hired Comte as his assistant at the Ecole polytechnique in 1832.[18] These associations were evident in Comte's interpretation of mathematics. In response to the *algébristes*, Comte held that geometry and mechanics were the true foundations of mathematics, in other words that Cauchy ought to be subordinate to Poinsot and Navier.

The conflicts among various groups of mathematicians were also related to didactic considerations. Cauchy's pure mathematics was poorly suited to the syllabus at the Ecole polytechnique, designed as it was for engineers. What is more, Cauchy was a poor teacher. In his campaigns for a teaching position, Comte highlighted his own didactic qualities. For access to the Académie specialized publications counted, but for a teaching position at the Ecole polytechnique Comte felt didactic skills should be decisive. The lectures at the Ecole were excessively dominated by an erroneous use of 'algebraic customs'. As a result, 'form' had become more important than 'content' and 'analytical instruments' were more in the spotlight than 'the phenomena studied'.[19] By taking this stand, Comte gave his candidacy an aura of educational reform that was designed to put the *algébristes* 'in their place'. Comte's position and argumentation were in keeping with the interpretation of mathematics he presented in the *Cours*.

The only science directly linked to mathematics was astronomy. As it was also the only one to be fully liberated from theological and metaphysical influences it was a kind of model science. Questions regarding the 'origins' of the planets or the 'cause' of their movements had made way for the formulation of laws. In no other science did the concept of laws play such a clear role. Comte described astronomy as the study of celestial bodies as geometric and mechanical phenomena. As such, astronomy was directly dependent on concrete mathematics but differed from it in the importance it attached to observations. Since according to Comte it was impossible to study physical or chemical aspects of celestial bodies, astronomy did not depend on either physics or chemistry. Only the most simple properties of celestial bodies could be studied. The means astronomers had at hand were similarly limited. No methods other than observation were available. Experiments were not feasible, and, since knowledge was restricted to the solar system, the comparative method was inapplicable as well. Virtually no information was available on other galaxies, and Comte did not expect this situation to change soon.

Physics and chemistry

Physics was a newer and more complex science than astronomy. It was not until after Galileo's discoveries that a positive science began to emerge. Compared with astronomy, physics was less systematic and less precise. It differed from chemistry in ways that were less clear. Physics, Comte felt, was more general than chemistry. Physicists

242 FOUNDATIONS OF SOCIOLOGY

studied the general properties of bodies in so far as no changes occurred in their molecular structure.[20] These properties were linked largely to the mass of these bodies. Chemists, on the other hand, studied more specific phenomena.

Observation and experimentation were the methods used in physics. Mathematical procedures were significant but had fewer direct applications here than in astronomy. Physical phenomena such as heat, light, sound or electricity were more complicated than celestial mechanics and less suited to mathematical deductions. This was why physicists themselves were the ones who could best determine the role mathematics was to play. It would be wrong to leave this to the mathematicians. In general, it held true that the more complex the object was, the less chance there was for exact predictions. What mattered in all the positive sciences were the 'laws of phenomena', but in Comte's scheme the nature of these laws was not uniform. Referring to 'laws' gave the impression that every science studied the same type of regularity. However, this was not Comte's opinion. With changes in the level of complexity, the nature of regularities altered as well. Complexity meant compositeness and dependence. The more complex or composite a phenomenon was, the more it depended on other phenomena and the more difficult it was to make exact predictions.

Since physics was more an experimental than a mathematical science, it was important to devote attention to the research process itself. It was within this framework that Comte formulated his views on hypotheses. He was rather non-committal when it came to how hypotheses should be tested. Inductive and deductive procedures both played a role and Comte rejected the idea that either one had priority. In this sense as well, his views could best be described as realistic or pragmatic. The most important feature of scientific hypotheses is that they have to be testable. According to Comte, this meant all the assumptions having to do with 'ethers' had to be abandoned. After all, it was impossible to demonstrate even the existence of these substances, which were assumed to be invisible and imponderable. According to Comte, phenomena such as light, electricity and heat should be studied independently of assumptions as to their 'causes'. Comte did not present this view as a methodological prohibition, but as a historical generalization. In astronomy and various branches of physics, developments had gone in this direction. There was less and less of a tendency to look for the 'entities' that were the 'causes' of physical phenomena. By way of the 'historical comparative method',[21] greater insight could be gained into scientific problems.

Comte's attitude with respect to hypotheses was based predominantly upon the work of Joseph Fourier.[22] Not much information is available about the personal contact between Fourier and Comte. It was of the utmost importance to Comte that Fourier attend the opening of his *cours*. Fourier was not there in 1826, but he was at the reopening three years later. Shortly beforehand, Fourier also wrote a short letter of recommendation for Comte. So there was certainly some degree of personal contact. Comte's great admiration for Fourier was also evident from the fact that he dedicated the *Cours* to 'my illustrious friends' Fourier and Blainville. Fourier was a representative of the latest trends in mathematics and physics; Blainville represented the life sciences. In the introduction to his pioneering *Théorie analytique de la chaleur* (1822) Fourier expounded that 'first causes' could not be known and that he confined his study to a mathematical description of the conduction of heat through solids. In addition to the 'causes', Fourier also refrained from discussing the 'nature' of the phenomenon. He viewed heat as a general property of matter, and his work pertained only to its conduction. Fourier's work was to be long disputed by Laplace's school, but after 1815 it became one of the major contributions to the new physics. Fourier became a member of the Académie des sciences and was elected secretary in 1822.

To Comte, Fourier's work was important in two senses. Firstly, Fourier provided a more radical formulation of positivism. In so far as Comte defended a specific variant of positivism, it could be considered a generalization of Fourier's methodology. Secondly, Comte considered Fourier's theory of heat of paradigmatic importance. Fourier dealt with the phenomena of heat conduction as a separate area of research, independent of the mechanics viewed by Laplace and his followers as the general model for physics. To Comte, physics was no longer a unified science modelled after the example of celestial mechanics. As far as that was concerned, Fourier's mathematical theory of heat conduction could serve as an example for theories of sound, electricity, light and magnetism. All of them were 'phenomena sui generis' that could no longer be reduced to mechanics. The 'irrational pursuit of a scientific uniformity' had to be abandoned.[23] Comte compared Fourier's contribution with Lagrange's. Much as Lagrange provided a mathematical theory of mechanics without calling upon geometry, Fourier drew up a mathematical theory of heat conduction without calling upon a single principle from the field of mechanics.[24] Physics was thus a more varied science than astronomy. Comte's classification of physics was based upon his series of increasing complexity and dependence. The simplest branch of physics was 'barology'.

It was followed by the studies of heat, sound, optics and electricity. Comte devoted a chapter to each branch (lessons 29 to 35).

Comte's analysis of physics was directed against two schools of thought in the physics of his day. The first, postulating the existence of ethers, was in evidence mainly in England; it was defended in France by Cauchy and in some cases by Ampère.[25] The second, propagated by Laplace and his followers (Biot, Poisson), held that all physical phenomena could be reduced to forces between particles. Comte viewed this approach as reductionist. It had been dominant in France, but was supplanted in the decade from 1815 to 1825 by a number of physics studies no longer modelled after mechanics. Fresnel formulated his wave theory of light, Fourier his theory of heat, and Ampère his theory of electromagnetism.[26] Comte praised all these new developments and gave each of them a place in his classification of physics. There was nonetheless a clear preference on his part for Fourier's style. He wondered, for example, why Fresnel had assumed that light consisted of waves rather than particles. If he had used Fourier's method, he would not have had to make any assumption about the 'nature' of the phenomenon.[27]

Compared with his approach to physics, Comte's attitude to chemistry was highly critical. Most of the studies conducted in the field of chemistry barely deserved the term scientific.[28] Very few laws of chemistry had been formulated, and their predictive value was negligible. The complexity of the phenomena was the most important reason for this. Chemistry occupied a position somewhere between physics and biology. Its object consisted of changes in the composition of substances due to molecular alterations. In chemistry, the principles were studied that governed matters of 'composition and decomposition'. These principles were less general than those of physics. After all, there were any number of physical processes that had no chemical effects to speak of, whereas every chemical process had physical effects. Chemical processes were therefore always more comprehensive than physical ones.

On the grounds of this demarcation, Comte defended the position that chemistry was a fundamental science. It was no longer enough to accrue knowledge on individual elements; general phenomena and laws had to be sought as well. This was why Comte had the highest esteem for chemists such as Berthollet and Berzelius, who developed more systematic approaches.[29] In addition to the fundamental and abstract nature of chemistry, Comte emphasized the need for autonomy. It was of the utmost importance to develop specifically chemical theories and methods. Mathematics was virtually useless for chemical research. Physical concepts could serve a purpose, but were by no means sufficient.

In drawing up chemical theories, various methods could be used. The more complex the object of a science was, the more methods there were that could be used to study it. Opportunities for observation were thus more varied in chemistry than in the simpler sciences. In astronomy, only the sense of sight could be used for observations, and in physics the sense of hearing and of touch; but in chemistry the sense of taste and of smell could be utilized as well. As in physics, the experiment played a leading role. The comparative method had been developed mainly in the field of biology, but according to Comte it was also important in chemistry. One procedure that was specifically developed in chemistry was that of nomenclature. Chemical elements were relatively simple and uniform, so a naming system could be set up that was unambiguous and comprehensive.

Comte drew a dividing line between chemistry and biology that was just as clear as the one between physics and chemistry. To Comte, organic chemistry was a reprehensible compromise. In his view, anything that was organic did not belong in the field of chemistry, and anything that was chemical did not belong in the field of biology. Under the guise of organic chemistry chemists had appropriated topics that could be adequately studied only by biologists. The chemical composition of blood and saliva could be completely comprehended only from a physiological point of view. Of course physiologists should use chemical insights and methods in approaching matters of this kind, but the problem belonged in the field of biology. The way he dealt with organic chemistry is a good example of Comte's anti-reductionist intentions. Wherever questions of this type came up in the *Cours*, his response was increasingly vehement and polemic. Time after time Comte defended the newer, more complex sciences against the claims of the established ones. His theory of science was one vast defence against reductionism. He went in recurrent pursuit of borders and limitations in his efforts to defend the new disciplines' right to exist, and he knew that in every science there is the tendency to annex the following science in the name of an 'older and more established positivity'.[30] He countered these tendencies towards 'usurpation' by way of a well-reasoned defence of the principle of relative autonomy. Although this notion played a central role in Comte's theory of science, the term 'relative autonomy' was not coined until much later. Comte often used double negatives (not independent but not reducible either). The same held true of his followers and admirers. In sociology, Norbert Elias was probably the first to use the term systematically, but at approximately the same time it was also employed by Louis Althusser. Oddly enough, these two authors have been the only ones to note recently the importance of Comte.[31]

Biology and sociology

The lessons on biology occupy a special place in the *Cours* – firstly, because biological insights played an important role in Comte's own development. More than any other group, it was the theorists of the life sciences who inspired Comte as regards his differential theory of science. But it was not only that biologists were important to Comte; he in turn was important to them. In the first half of the nineteenth century biology was neither an institutionally nor a theoretically unified field of study. According to Comte it was the only positive science that had no autonomous organization. Biology was not a separate field of science at the Académie des sciences or the universities, and there was no learned society for biologists. Thus what Comte wrote about biology was less an interpretation of existing arrangements than an attempt on his part to achieve some measure of systematization. As a matter of fact, the first lesson on biology (lesson 40) is one of the longest of the entire *Cours*. For quite some time it was also the most authoritative. Despite a few exceptions,[32] there are no indications that Comte's analyses of mathematics, physics and chemistry made much of an impression on mathematicians, physicists or chemists. As to his writings on biology, however, the situation was totally different. Comte was one of the leading nineteenth-century theorists of biology in France.

It is indicative of this role that Comte was instrumental in spreading the very word 'biology'. The term dates from the years 1800 to 1802, but had long remained obscure. Comte had a marked preference for it, and frequently used it to refer to a general and fundamental science of life. According to historians of biology it is largely thanks to Comte and his students that the term came into such general use.[33]

This was not simply a question of a word. Just exactly how original Comte's analyses were is not quite clear. There is no doubt, however, that for various generations of French biologists they played a role of great significance. The Société de biologie (1848) was a clear illustration. Among the founders of this society were two physicians who explicitly viewed themselves as Comte's students. One of them, Charles Robin, edited the articles of association and a statement on the theoretical orientation of the group, basing his views upon Comte's theory of science and his classification of biology. Robin later held the first professorial chair in France for histology and wrote his most renowned work, *Dictionnaire de médecine*, together with another of Comte's students, Emile Littré. Claude Bernard, the most famous member of the Société de biologie, is also known to have been familiar with Comte's work. He seems to have read it 'with his pen in his hand'.[34]

From 1848 to 1880, according to Georges Canguilhem, there was not a single French biologist or physician who was not directly or indirectly affected by the Comtean interpretation of biology.[35] Biologists were the first and for quite some time the only academic group to know and appreciate Comte's work. This recognition was linked to the function Comte's epistemology served for a discipline like biology that had yet to become established. Comte countered the claims of certain chemists and physicists with arguments in favour of a more autonomous science of biology. Confronted with the clinical orientation of Parisian physicians, he emphasized that biology was a fundamental science. And in response to the institutional and cognitive heterogeneity of the new field, he provided a fruitful taxonomy. The programme Robin designed for the Société de biologie was based upon these three features.

Comte founded his survey largely upon information he garnered from Blainville's publications and lectures. (The *Cours* was dedicated not only to Fourier but also to Blainville.) They first met around 1824. Blainville was a pupil of Cuvier, who taught zoology and comparative anatomy. Comte's first book had made an impression on him. Despite growing differences of opinion, they maintained a lengthy friendship.

The most important property of Comte's analyses is that he described biology in such a way as to surmount the contrast between vitalistic and mechanical models. He put the spirits of Stahl and Boerhaave both in their proper perspective.[36] Comte felt that, essentially, it was Bichat who formulated the first positive definition, be it still an inadequate one, of life: 'life is the sum total of functions that resist death'. Bichat's reasoning was still overly affected by the assumption of an antagonism between life and death. Quite the opposite was the case. Biological processes could not be reduced to chemical and physical ones, but were characterized by dependence on the 'environment'. Thus the relations of organisms to the environment they lived in were part of the object of biology.[37] In response to the mechanists Comte emphasized the unity and specificity of living creatures, and in response to the vitalists he stressed the dependence on the environment. This provided an escape route from the old contradictions, which was one of the main reasons for the interest in Comte's work on the part of biologists.

Commensurate with the greater complexity of the object, in biology more methods could be used than in physics or chemistry. As in chemistry, each of the five senses could play its own observational role. And even more than in chemistry, instruments could be used to heighten the sense of sight (the microscope) or hearing (the stethoscope).

Biology also provided opportunities for experimentation, be it that, in general, the greater the complexity and dependence of the phenomena, the more limited these opportunities were. As physical phenomena were relatively independent, the experiment was especially suited to the field of physics. This was less true of chemistry, and in biology the interdependence of the phenomena was so great that experimental methods were only practicable to a limited extent. Biology did have an equivalent to the experimental method, namely pathology. Pathological phenomena could be viewed as 'spontaneous experiments' that provided insight into the normal state of organisms. The comparative method, however, was the most useful in biology. What could be compared went from parts of organisms, generations and developmental stages to variants of the same species and different species. In biology, conceptualization was based mainly upon these comparisons.

After biology, Comte devoted the last three volumes of his *Cours* to sociology. He introduced the term in Volume 4, and its use thereafter became more and more frequent. Much of the contents of the last three volumes of the *Cours* is quite familiar by now. Comte began by defending the necessity of a social science. In the following lessons earlier efforts were described and the relations to the other sciences were discussed. Volume 4 closed with an overview of the two branches of sociology, statics and dynamics. Statics pertained to a theory about the order and coherence of human societies, and dynamics viewed them from a historical point of view. Volume 5 and the beginning of Volume 6 continued to expand upon dynamics and contained a detailed historical elaboration of the law of the three stages.

Comte's sociology illustrated once again how important biology was to him: it was based for a large part upon biological notions, and a few of the key concepts, such as crisis, organization, consensus and organic system, came from the field of biology. His notion of diagnosis and remedy emulated a medical model.[38] And Comte even interpreted progress, the specific feature of the human species, from a biological perspective. He defined progress as the 'development of order', which was in fact why dynamics was subordinate to statics. This thought originated in pre-Darwinist biology, where development was still viewed as materialization rather than mutation. Developments were processes whereby already existing creatures simply unfolded their pre-existing properties. Seed and embryo were the appropriate metaphors.[39]

Despite the fact that Comte was the first to state the necessity for a relatively autonomous social science, he did not succeed in truly moving beyond a biological mode of thinking. His division of sociology into statics and dynamics and many of his key concepts were taken from biology. For other reasons as well, the volumes on sociology were less cogent than the first three. They seemed to lack the concentration of Comte's earlier works, and now and then the conviction was gone as well. Initially only one volume was to be devoted to sociology but in the end there were no fewer than three. These latter volumes contained a total of only fifteen lessons, which were considerably longer than the forty-five lessons of the first three volumes. Parallel observations can be made on the composition and style, as these last three volumes were filled with repetitions, the argumentation was roundabout and verbose, and the tone had changed. The statement with which Volume 4 opened was characteristic of this altered tone. In the very first sentence Comte vented his spleen on 'the intellectual ravings' of his day. In the sixth and final volume his discontent took an even more personal turn. He began with a 'personal foreword', drawing attention to his own misfortune and the injustice that had been done to him.

The difference between the first and the last three volumes of the *Cours* had to do with a rather sudden change in his expectations. In 1838, shortly before he began on the sociological part, there was a second crisis in Comte's life.[40] He was overworked and tense, and sombre prospects for the future put him off balance. He viewed his chances of gaining recognition for his sociology as even slimmer than for his earlier writings. For the first time he stated that 'any hope of support from scientists (. . .) had to be abandoned'.[41] Scientists 'distrusted' questions that crossed the borders of their own specialism and were only interested in their careers. If they engaged in politics at all, it was only to take the side of the established powers. Further on Comte noted their 'blind opposition' to his philosophy and commented that, 'exactly like priests', scientists exhibited a tendency towards mental 'oppression'.[42] It was when Comte lost all hope of support from the scientific world that his tone and style changed. He felt isolated, his self-discipline weakened, and, as he disliked going half way, in 1838 he suddenly stopped reading anyone else's work. This famous 'cerebral hygiene' symbolized his new attitude towards the intellectual world and was the start of his 'second career'. Comte wanted nothing more to do with the group he had hitherto addressed. A few years later, in 1844, his dismissal as examiner at the Ecole polytechnique was followed by a third crisis, and now his life conclusively took a different route. He met Clotilde de Vaux, and after an *année sans pareille* he devoted his remaining years to matters totally different than the theory of science on which his *Cours* had focused.

14

Response and Resistance

Social dynamics of an intellectual breakthrough

Auguste Comte's theory of science was the outcome of a dilemma. It was the work of a mathematician with an intense interest in science who was more or less excluded from the scientific world and the career opportunities his education had promised. This position marked his mode of thinking by a critical distance from his teachers and colleagues. His intention was to write a kind of *critique of mathematical reason*. Characteristic of Comte's ambition, this critique was to be constructive: based upon scientific insights, it was intended primarily for the very persons who were the object of his criticism. The only reference group he acknowledged for this scientifically founded critique of science consisted of the mathematicians and physicists at the Ecole polytechnique and the Académie des sciences. He made no effort to secure a chair anywhere else, and insisted that biologists and sociologists ought to study mathematics and physics before embarking upon the study of more complex matters.

What Comte reproached his former colleagues for was unjustly claiming a monopoly on knowledge. There were other positive sciences where mathematicians could learn procedures different from the ones to which they were accustomed. They could learn the experimental method from physicists, the comparative method from biologists and the historical method from sociologists. The notion that the same mathematical procedures were applicable to all these sciences bore witness to a belief in what he initially referred to as 'unfeasible perfection'.

In his criticism of mathematicians Comte used arguments from the field of biology, but he could not concur without reservations with the claims made by biologists. Biology studied a specific order of phenomena, but it was not an 'independent' order. On the contrary, a central feature of more complex phenomena was their dependence on less complex ones. Biological theories gave him insight into the limitations of mathematical models. At the same time his links with the Ecole polytechnique stimulated him to approach them in a critical fashion, so that the result was not a rejection but a reassessment of the significance of mathematics. Comte's departure from what he called 'intellectual absolutism'[1] was motivated by the fact that he had a different attitude towards the established sciences than did its practitioners. His differential theory of science was based upon a differential relation to the sciences. As a critical mathematician he became interested in biology; as an admirer of biological theorizing he once again focused his attention on mathematics, designed a theory of science that was more general, and then presented this theory to those same mathematicians. The result of this dynamic was a more comprehensive and differential theory of scientific knowledge.

There is no way of knowing how and when Comte first came into contact with the writings of biologists, but in view of his position it was bound to happen. Biologists were the only group who had expressed scientifically founded criticism of the claims made by mathematicians. There were numerous other forms of criticism, but Comte never felt attracted to the anti-scientific romanticism of Chateaubriand or the theological criticism of science voiced by de Maistre and de Bonald. What Saint-Simon wrote about scientific problems must have struck him as a kind of 'science fiction', and he felt only contempt for the spiritualist philosophy of Cousin. Comte stuck to a strict notion of positive science and his proposals were addressed to the scientific establishment. Perhaps this attitude can be explained largely by the fact that he had no other resources apart from his scientific abilities. His self-esteem and ambition were directly connected to his education and to the scientific capital he had thus accumulated.[2] He had been one of the best students at the Ecole polytechnique, but on account of his humble social background he was lacking in economic resources. Two-thirds of the students were from the well-to-do bourgeoisie, but Comte belonged to the 15 to 20 per cent who were of petty bourgeois descent.[3] Comte was also lacking in social capital. He came from Montpellier, knew very few people in Paris and accepted his inability to move in fashionable circles as his fate in life. In the world of receptions and parties he was condemned to 'philosophical observation', as he once noted in a letter.[4] He did not dance and abhorred the *gens comme il faut*. Comte's work was made possible by his scientific capacities, by the unique position in which he unwittingly found himself *vis-à-vis* the established sciences, and by his talent for systematization. His strategy was focused upon accumulating this specific intellectual capital. The tenacity with which he did so, and persisted to do so for years on end without any true recognition, grew from the dearth of other options. Comte persisted and persevered; his intellectual abilities enabled him to carry on, just as his inabilities kept him from turning in other directions.

Significance and restriction

Auguste Comte's theory of science resulted from the tension between a scientist and the scientific establishment from which he was excluded. His distance from it enabled him to see what insiders did not and outsiders could not perceive with sufficient precision. By elaborating upon the insights acquired in this fashion he hoped to win back what he had been deprived of. By constructing a differential model he limited the claims of the established sciences to what he felt was their proper perspective. It was in this model that his originality and intellectual significance lay. But this was not all. Comte's theory had an important shortcoming: restricted to the objects of scientific knowledge, it failed to take into account that the knowledge of these objects presumes active subjects. Conflicts of interpretation and social interests play a role in scientific pursuits as well, and this was not an issue to which Comte devoted systematic thought. Though his writings include noteworthy passages in a sociology of science vein, to Comte it was a matter of 'concomitant influences'[5] and not a fundamental problem. Comte viewed science as a dominion of 'the human mind' and felt its development was more a natural than a social process. Thus he could only explain the historical development of scientific theories in terms of his levels of complexity. It was a matter of necessity that the human mind first discovered the laws of the simplest phenomena and only then gradually proceeded to more complex ones. This model was inadequate to cover the factual history of the sciences. The main flaw in Comte's theory of science was its objectivism. By depicting science as a process without concrete subjects he eliminated all questions of interpretation and sociability. Recent studies have demonstrated that these hermeneutic and sociological dimensions, both of which are related to the persons who actually practise science, are indispensable for an adequate theory of science. Contemporary theorists tend, however, to make quite the opposite mistake. Some of them propagate a purely subjectivist theory in which the features of the object studied are no longer accounted for. There are only sly subjects that construct 'realities' independently of any ontological condition. These scientists without objects are the exact opposite of Comte's objects without scientists.

If recent epistemological research has revealed anything, it is indeed that no adequate theory of science can exist without doing justice to the practitioners' activities, interpretations, conflicts and interests. In the competition in which they engage, however, ontological conditions serve a function as well. And in questions of this kind distinctions between various levels of complexity are still one of the central problems. There is consequently no reason why contemporary contributions to the theory of science should be incompatible with Comte's differential approach.[6]

Positivist schools in France

The objectivism of Comte's theory of science was to play an unexpected role in his own development. His 'second career' was dominated by the rediscovery of the subject. Having abandoned the perspective of his first career, now it was not the objective properties of various integration levels that were of central importance, but the way they should be perceived as serving human needs. In Comte's later writings the primacy of the subject is always assumed.

The first signs of this reorientation were evident after his second crisis in 1838. Turning away from the 'pedantocrats', he took a sudden interest in music and literature. This was the start of a sequence of events in which the demands of the 'head' began to make way for the needs of the 'heart'.[7] On a number of occasions Comte had unsuccessfully applied for a chair at the Ecole polytechnique. Disappointment about his failures led him to pursue other possibilities and pleasures. Up to then he had championed the 'objective' method and ignored the 'subjective' one. This distinction, which he first drew in 1836, was decisive in his later work: emotional and moral problems now came into the spotlight and purely intellectual questions were increasingly relegated to the background. With this shift, the group he was addressing altered as well. Instead of the best educated groups, he expected more and more of the least educated ones, workers and women. In 1838 Comte claimed to have lost faith in scientists, though for some time he continued to hold that a good education called for a scientific syllabus. For several years he pinned all his hopes on foreign scientists. He later came to view an education in the sciences as a moral and emotional shortcoming. That had been the problem with his 'first career', marked as it was by 'inadequate emotional development'.[8] In *Système de politique positive* (1851–4) Comte introduced morality as the seventh science. His last project was a vast *Synthèse subjective*. The first volume appeared in 1856, but the remaining three were never published. Comte died in 1857.

Comte would not have had a second career had it not been for the failure of the first. The publication of his first book and the initial interest in his ideas stimulated him to continue working towards a new and comprehensive theory of science. In 1832 his perseverance was rewarded with his appointment as tutor at the Ecole polytechnique, followed several years later by the one as examiner. Efforts to rise to a professorial chair, however, were all in vain, and the response to the *Cours* was extremely disappointing. The first review was not printed in France until fourteen years after the publication of the first volume and two years after the completion of the entire work. For Comte, that was too late. In that same year, 1844, he lost his position as examiner at the Ecole polytechnique and fell in love with Clotilde de Vaux. Her affection promised to provide 'sacred compensation'[9] for all his misfortune.

The response to Comte's work illustrates once again what an unusual position he had occupied. In the early nineteenth century barely anyone else had comparable knowledge of the various fields of science. His classification of these fields was new, and, by taking complexity rather than 'certainty' or 'exactness' as a criterion, he helped create a space for such new sciences as biology and sociology. But no matter how significant his theory of science actually was, it appeared to be too critical for the scientific establishment and too scientific for men of letters and philosophers. This is the main reason why recognition failed to ensue. Comte's work did not become part of the intellectual canon. It lived on only among his followers, for whom positivism mainly fulfilled other needs. They developed his ideas in a political and ideological sense but conducted barely any original research.

Comte's followers were divided into two groups, an orthodox one round the Société positiviste and a heterodox one round Emile Littré. The Société positiviste was founded by Comte himself in 1848 with the aim of establishing a new 'spiritual power' that would put an end to the crisis in which the West had been since 1789. Comte openly voiced his approval of the Second Republic, but emphasized the importance of spiritual and moral reforms. In the first year there were eighteen registered members, and by Comte's death in 1857 forty-three persons had joined the Société.[10] They were predominantly young people, most of whom (33 of the 43) had been born in the provinces. Professionally they belonged to the intellectual middle class (16) or were skilled workers (15). There were quite a few physicians (10) among the intellectual members, but none of them held a high position in health care or at a university. In fact the only member who held a university position at all was a foreigner, the English chemist Williamson. There were very few traditional craftsmen among the skilled workers, but quite a few persons engaged in the new technical occupations.

After Comte's death Pierre Laffitte gradually took over the leadership of the Société. Twenty-five years old in 1848, he was a mathematics teacher who first met Comte in his capacity as examiner. Comte felt Laffitte was unfit to be a *polytechnicien*, but later came to appreciate him as a faithful positivist. By way of lectures and brochures Laffitte and the others went about spreading the word, and found an audience with a somewhat more willing ear after the Third Republic was founded in 1870. The *Revue occidentale* (1878–1914) became the organ of the movement. In 1892 Laffitte was appointed to the new chair for the history of science at the Collège de France.[11] It was less in recognition of his own merits than as a late tribute to his mentor.

Despite Laffitte's position at the Collège de France, Comte's followers failed to play a role at the university. This was evident from their surprised reactions to the rise of a university-oriented sociology. All the *Revue occidentale* published about sociology was a single summary of Comte's later views.[12] When the first doctoral dissertation in sociology appeared in 1877, the journal noted that, for the very first time, a university philosopher had paid 'satisfactory' tribute to Comte. There was less enthusiasm about the fact that the author had been influenced mainly by Spencer.[13] Shortly afterwards the publication of the *Année sociologique* was received with a mixture of awe and scepticism. Emile Durkheim's 'highly learned discussions' did arouse some admiration, but the fact that no mention was made of Comte's views on religion gave rise to wariness.[14]

The orthodox positivists were a tiny group without connections in the political and academic elites. They were 'neither esteemed nor monied', as one of them put it.[15] This held true to a much smaller extent of the apostates round Littré. Emile Littré, who was only a few years younger than Comte, had studied medicine and was reputed as an *érudit* and journalist. For his translation of the collected works of Hippocrates, in 1839 he was elected to the Académie des inscriptions. In 1844 his articles on the *Cours* in *National*, a republican periodical, were the first to appear on Comte's work in French. According to

Littré, the *Cours* was neither a point of departure for the 'religion of humanity' nor a purely epistemological work. In Littré's view Comte had provided the groundwork for a positive philosophy. All his life, Littré defended this philosophy against deviations, including Comte's later ideas. Their rift took place in 1851. Littré refused to accept the 'subjective method' and disagreed with Comte's political opinions. At the time of the Second Empire (1851–70) Littré became one of the leading intellectuals. Together with Taine, Renan and others, he combated the spiritualist philosophy that still had a monopoly at the universities and *lycées*. His *Dictionnaire de médecine* (1855) earned him membership of the Académie de médecine, and his *Dictionnaire de la langue française* (1863–78) a seat at the Académie française.[16]

His erudition made Littré a highly respected man and his political standpoints earned him the sympathy of anti-clerical circles, but his admiration for Comte merely made him a target of mockery. Littré helped popularize Comte's ideas but could not do much to earn them academic respectability. His journalistic and political writings were important in the history of republican thinking,[17] but his journal *La philosophie positive* (1867–83) never played any role at the universities.

In contrast to the more ideological and educational positivism propagated by the orthodox positivists, Littré's positivism was mainly political, as is clearly illustrated by the story of the Société de sociologie, with Littré as its chairman. Founded in 1872 for 'the scientific study of social and political problems', it was the world's first sociological society. For approximately a year it stood firm, though it never progressed much beyond the point at which the 'immortal founder of sociology' had stopped. Littré acknowledged this fact and gave an interesting explanation for it. In the course of the society's discussions it had become evident that the members tended to use 'biological language' to formulate sociological problems. But in sociology, Littré felt, biological terms could be used only as 'analogies or metaphors'. In sociology organs and functions were thus not the same as they were in biology. It was necessary to eliminate this source of misunderstandings. By creating their own sociological vocabulary sociologists would be able to accustom themselves to thinking sociologically. For this purpose Littré introduced a whole list of neologisms, for example, 'sociodynamics' and *sociomerie* to replace dynamics and statics. However, his lexicographic ingenuity surpassed his sociological insight, and the idea produced no greater fruits than a few pages in his journal.[18]

Littré was well aware that Comte's sociology was not quite consistent. Comte emphasized that sociology was relatively autonomous, but at the same time he borrowed a great deal from biological theories. Without explicitly criticizing Comte, Littré advocated a more autonomous conceptualization.[19] And yet the sociology of Littré and his associates amounted to little more than paraphrases of Comte's work. The main reason for this failing was that political commitment prevailed above scientific interest. The members of the Société de sociologie were markedly better educated than the orthodox positivists.[20] A majority of them (seventeen out of twenty-five) had attended a university, and several of them (Littré, the biologist Charles Robin) held academic positions. However, a university career was very much an exception. The large majority of them were in one way or another engaged in a political or administrative career. A total of sixteen of the twenty-five members had political functions: three were political writers, five were government officials, five were Members of Parliament and another three were Ministers. At the time of the Second Empire Littré and his associates had belonged to the republican opposition. Their average age (forty-eight) was quite advanced in 1872, and the founding of the Third Republic gave them an opportunity to pursue political ambitions. It can be concluded from the sizeable numbers of Members of Parliament, Senators and Ministers, amounting to 30 per cent of the total membership, that they accounted for a significant group within the new republican elites. Their political involvement was also evident from their educational backgrounds. As was the case with the orthodox positivists, more than half the members with a university diploma had studied medicine. This was the major similarity between the two groups. But in that a relatively large number of them were jurists, they differed from the orthodox positivists.

In view of the development of sociology, the most striking fact was perhaps the absence of university philosophers. In neither of the positivist networks was there anyone with a position at the Faculty of Letters. In addition to a large group of physicians and a small group of jurists, there were a few writers or journalists, but not only was there not a single person employed at the Faculty of Letters, there was virtually no one who had even studied there. In the decades after 1870 most sociologists were graduates of the Ecole normale supérieure who sought careers in the Faculty of Letters. They were the ones who turned sociology into a university subject. Comte's followers did not play any role in this process.

Reactions in England, the Netherlands and Germany

The *Cours* was reviewed earlier, more frequently and more favourably in England than in France. The earliest evidence of this interest, which was concentrated outside the established centres at Oxford and Cambridge,[21] was a review written by a Scottish physicist, David Brewster. Lengthy and highly complimentary, it was printed in the *Edinburgh Review* in 1838. First and foremost the author used Comte's work to denounce the views of his rival William Whewell, who lectured at Cambridge and was one of the central figures in the English university establishment. Brewster could not help but express a word of caution as regards the Frenchman's atheism. He thanked his lucky stars the British situation did not allow for that kind of thing.[22] Comte's strict distinction between theology, metaphysics and science did not cause much of a furore in France, but it was precisely what drew attention in England. Against the background of the Anglican mixture of religion and science, Comte was read in England as a positivist. What was involved here was positivism in all its capacities, as theory of knowledge, as world view, and as religion of humanity.

Comte owed his English fame mainly to the circle around John Stuart Mill. In 1837 Mill read the first two volumes of the *Cours* followed by Volume 3 several years later, and in 1841 he expressed his admiration in a letter to the author. An extensive correspondence ensued, and in 1844 Mill organized financial support for the former examiner. Though this enthusiasm was soon to flag, for years to come Comte's English reputation remained based upon what Mill wrote about him in his *System of Logic* (1843). In this widely read and extremely successful work, Comte was lauded as the most important modern-day philosopher. Here English admirers and followers made their first acquaintance with the hitherto unknown Frenchman. In later editions Mill put a bit of a damper on his praise, but as soon as Mill broke off contact with Comte his intermediary role was taken over by George Henry Lewes. Lewes not only published a book on *Comte's Philosophy of the Sciences* (1853), he had already demonstrated his high esteem of the author in his *Biographical History of Philosophy* (1845–6). In fact the third edition of this popular book was renamed *History of Philosophy from Thales to Comte* (1867). When a somewhat abridged English translation of the *Cours* was added to the publications by Mill and Lewes in 1853, Comte's presence on the English stage was secured.

In the 1850s and 1860s positivism was the topic of innumerable discussions in England. Criticism was initially mainly of a religious and theological nature. At regular intervals Mill and Lewes both advised Comte to be a bit more cautious in his statements on the *canaille théologique*. Slowly but surely, criticism other than the religious variant began to emerge. Mill, Lewes and Harriet Martineau, who had translated the *Cours*, raised objections to Comte's later work, which was propagated in England by a group round Richard Congreve and Frederic Harrison. For decades they were the nucleus of the more orthodox positivists. Critical comments expressed by scientists such as Herschel, Huxley and Spencer were even more important than the theological criticism and Mill's reservations. The aim of their arguments was to demonstrate that Comte's ideas had no foundation in science.

Thirty years after he first came across the *Cours*, Mill felt it was time to take stock. In *Auguste Comte and Positivism* (1866) he had barely anything good to say about Comte's personality, his political and social views or his later writings. His wording was more favourable when it came to sociology: the term was a 'convenient barbarism',[23] and Comte's historical schemes had been useful, though this had certainly not been the case with Comte's aversion to psychology ('a big mistake') and his opinions on political economy ('extraordinarily superficial'). In an epistemological sense Comte's writings were admirable, but, more than in earlier statements, Mill now emphasized a difference of opinion on methodological questions. According to Mill philosophy of science consisted of two parts, one pertaining to research methods and the other to modes of argumentation and proof. Comte's theory of science pertained to the first part, and was unsurpassed in this respect. As regards the second part, however, Comte had nothing to offer but disheartening words.[24] Mill was right. Comte refused to conduct research into the 'general criteria' for validity in which Mill was so interested. To Comte, methods were 'intellectual customs' that derived their meaning from the research practice in a given field of science. Questions on logical criteria for argumentation had thus lost their central significance. What Mill was putting into words anticipated the problematic of logical positivism (particularly Reichenbach's distinction between the 'context of discovery' and the 'context of justification'). This criticism serves to remind us that it was only in a trivial sense that Comte belonged to the genealogy of logical positivism.

After England, for some time the Netherlands was a centre of positivist activities. This was at any rate the opinion of Comte himself, who spoke with the highest esteem of *notre foyer hollandais* as early as 1848.[25] Later Comte appointed three Dutchmen to the group of thirteen that was to supervise the execution of his last will and testament. On the grounds of this fact, historians including Lucien Lévy-Bruhl were convinced that positivism was of comparable importance in the Netherlands and England. This was not the case. Neither a movement nor a journal was ever launched in the Netherlands, and for a long time academic circles failed to devote any attention at all to Comte. At a relatively early stage, however, a small group of men came together with a shared interest in Comte's work. Members of this group, which consisted of military officers concentrated in The Hague,[26] translated the first two lessons of the Cours and published them in 1846. It was presumably via their relations with the Ecole polytechnique that these young men had come into contact with positivism. Their receptiveness had to do with their scientific training at the Artillery and Engineering Corps. Strikingly enough, the three officers who played the most prominent roles were all members of the aristocracy: Count van Limburg Stirum, Squire van Capellen, and Baron Constant Rebecque. All three were among those who supervised the execution of Comte's last will and testament. Perhaps their aristocratic descent brought them into closer contact with France than was customary in bourgeois circles. Their efforts were focused upon disseminating positivism as a secular and scientifically founded doctrine. As a means to this end, they translated a number of Comte's dissertations, raised funds to finance his work and wrote summaries and commentaries. In Comte's work they found an 'all-inclusive doctrine of laws' that could put an end to 'the revolutionary state in which civilized Europe has long found itself'.[27] The group did not remain in existence for long; it disbanded after the death of Constant in 1862. Unlike the circle round Mill, however, the Dutchmen had no ties with the ruling liberal intellectuals. It was characteristic of this lack of contact that De Gids refused to publish an essay by one of them about positivism because its 'tone' vis-à-vis the theological mode of thinking was so 'uncompromising and rash'.[28]

The response in Germany was in stark contrast to the widespread interest in England and the relatively early but isolated interest in the Netherlands. No positivist society or journal was ever founded there, and whatever interest there was in Comte's work was limited and late. The first publication did not appear until 1859, twenty years after Brewster's review and more than ten years after the first Dutch ones. Comte's reputation in England played an important role in the German reception. Comte was bracketed together with Mill, and the differences between the two were referred to very rarely. German authors saw it largely as their task to construct an alternative to these 'positivist' or 'empiricist' modes of thinking. Their sources of inspiration, German idealism (Kant, Fichte, Schelling) and neo-humanist philology, had emerged in the period from 1780 to 1820, with German universities in the midst of a crisis and French natural sciences rising to international repute.[29] After the Napoleonic era both of these schools of thought played prominent roles in the expansion of the modernized universities and acted as a methodological counterbalance to the English and French schools, which were oriented primarily towards the natural sciences. Thus it could happen that, even before Comte had achieved any fame to speak of, in Germany positivism was already of ill-repute. Goethe commented in 1826 that the French were *gute Köpfe*, but that in their view everything had to be 'positive', and if it was not 'positive' they would make it 'positive'.[30] This anti-positivist tendency, further advanced in the second half of the nineteenth century, was to dominate the German humanities.

In the first instance, Comte was reviewed by academic outsiders in Germany as well. The most prominent of them, Karl Twesten, one of the theorists of the Progress Party in Prussia, published a lengthy article on the 'life and work of Auguste Comte' in *Preussische Jahrbücher* in 1859. It was one of the very first German-language publications on Comte.[31] In his review Twesten included references to Mill and the English historian Buckle. Comte, Mill and Buckle were cited as examples of a new science of history which was thought to cover more than just political history, and to pursue 'laws' rather than simply give descriptions of 'individual persons' or special 'events'. The fact that Twesten's references pertained solely to foreign authors characterized his viewpoint. Around 1860 there was virtually no one in Germany who shared this attitude.

In circles of university historians, Droysen was the one to respond to Twesten's scientific challenge: he reviewed Buckle's *History of Civilisation in England* (1857–61) in the official journal for historians. The German historian opposed the notion that only the pursuit of 'laws' was truly scientific. The historical sciences or 'humanities' did not have the same foundation as the natural sciences. According to Droysen the 'essence' of the historical method was *forschend zu verstehen*. This position marked the 'hermeneutic turn' in the German human sciences.[32] The hermeneutic and the historical sciences were united, and this synthesis served as the foundation for the methodology of the humanities to be further developed by Dilthey and others. From that moment on, German developments were dominated by the dualism of explanation and interpretation, the natural sciences and the humanities.

Although references were made to 'positivism' in the German debates, Comte's work did not make much of an impression. Unlike Mill and Buckle, Comte was virtually unknown to historians.[33] He was slightly more important to Dilthey, but solely as the spokesman of a positivist doctrine. Dilthey addressed Comte as a 'naturalist' and a 'reductionist'. He rejected introspection and other subjective methods and viewed science as equivalent to the pursuit of 'laws'. For Dilthey, this was sufficient reason to conclude that Comte was one of the most dogmatic spokesmen of a 'nomothetic' mentality – as it was called shortly afterwards by Windelband. In the German debates no note was taken of the fact that Comte had also emphasized that the pursuit of laws occurred via a wide variety of methods and that these laws were of a different nature in the various sciences.[34]

Despite the difference in how he was evaluated, Comte was read in much the same way in Germany as in England. Here again, it all revolved around positivism. Though there was widespread appreciation of this school of thought in England, the German human sciences developed mainly as an alternative to it. Neither in England nor in Germany or the Netherlands was Comte's work viewed primarily as a theory of science.

The Comtean legacy

With the exception of the life sciences, it was only at a late stage that Comte began to play a role in academic discussions in his own country. There were numerous practising physicians among the orthodox positivists, and the heterodox positivists even included one with an academic position (Robin). Comte was also quite well known among other medical specialists outside the group of adherents. In the circles round the medical faculty and the Société de biologie he was seen as an important theorist, and there was a great deal of sympathy throughout the medical world for the philosophical aspects of positivism. Science on behalf of human progress was a popular ideal in these circles.[35]

Besides the physicians, before 1870 there was not a single other group of French intellectuals to whom Comte was important. Interest in the sciences did increase after 1860, as did opposition to the spiritualist philosophy, but Comte played no role in these developments. Neither Taine nor Renan attached the slightest importance to Comte's work. In Renan's opinion, Comte had not understood anything of philology and the historical sciences, and for the rest his work 'repeated in poor French what scientists had been saying ever since Descartes'.[36] In *Les philosophes classiques du XIXe siècle* (1857) Taine drew a distinction between two philosophies, spiritualism and positivism. One was 'rhetorical' and purely for 'literary use', the other was to be used solely among scientists.[37] Taine's whole book was an assault on spiritualism, but it did not devote any attention to positivism. In 1864 he wrote a review of the second edition of the *Cours*, but it was dominated by his criticism of Comte's style and his 'incompetence' in metaphysics, history, literature and psychology.[38]

The advent of the Third Republic was accompanied by quite a few changes. Comte was slowly but surely accepted as deserving of academic attention. Renan noted in 1882 that Comte was becoming an important author. Although it was an 'error', he expected Comte to occupy 'an important place in future accounts of the history of philosophy'.[39] This shift was related to the university reforms after 1870 and the new international situation. A new educational system was instituted in the first decades of the Third Republic. There was a growing demand for teachers, and the humanities and natural science faculties mushroomed. This university expansion favoured more autonomous disciplines. New journals were established, and there was room for points of view other than spiritualism.[40] The new approaches were focused more upon original research than didactic surveys and elegant essays. In the new philosophical journal *Revue philosophique* (1876), in addition to Kant there was a great deal of interest in Spencer and such new disciplines as psychology and sociology. The rise of this more scholarly and science-oriented approach was linked to efforts to find a viable response to the supremacy of German science. After the defeat in the war with Prussia in 1870, this objective was viewed by republican politicians and intellectuals as a matter of the greatest urgency.[41] New journals kept their readers informed about German science, and more attention was devoted to French achievements that might stand a chance of rivalling German scientific achievements. It was under these circumstances that Comte made his entrance. One of the very first university philosophers to whom Comte's work became important was Emile Boutroux. In his doctoral dissertation *De la contingence des lois de la nature* (1874) he used Comte's theory of science and combined it with neo-Kantian points of view. Boutroux argued that the rapid development of the sciences did not necessarily mean human freedom was an outdated tenet. The existence of laws and regularities did not justify a deterministic outlook. In Comte's footsteps, he conceived reality as consisting of various levels that could not be reduced to one another. Since there were no necessary relations between physical and biological phenomena, or between biological and psychological ones, Boutroux concluded that the higher, more complex levels were contingent with respect to the lower ones. The more complex they were, the greater the contingency was. In other words, necessity existed only in logic; the burgeoning of the empirical sciences had only emphasized human freedom.[42]

French neo-Kantians such as Boutroux were the first to read Comte as a theorist of science. The positivist doctrine of knowledge that had drawn all the attention in England and Germany alike was now in the background. Thanks to the efforts of Boutroux and a few other neo-Kantians such as Renouvier, Comte slowly gained repute as an important philosopher and his theory of science became an object worthy of academic consideration. Dissertations were written that dealt with Comte, and his work was included in the syllabus for philosophy students. This recognition meant a decisive step in the formation of two intellectual traditions, *historical epistemology* and *Durkheimian sociology*. Both were based upon Comte's theory of science, both were developed by university philosophers, and both marked a specifically French development.

Historical epistemology grew into an original school of thought in the theory of science. In this approach, the pursuit of a logical foundation for scientific knowledge was replaced by a problematic in which scientific conceptualization was considered historically and regionally bound. Its consistent linking of the history and theory of science with an anti-reductionist stance distinguished this tradition from the logical positivism that became dominant in the Anglo-American world. The same can be said of the sociology of the Durkheim School. It too was based upon Comte's differential model of science and developed into an original and specifically French tradition.

Historical epistemology included such figures as Paul Tannery, Abel Rey and Léon Brunschvicg. Tannery and Rey were more historically oriented. Like Boutroux, Brunschvicg was more interested in philosophy, but all of them wrote commentaries on Comte's theory of science.[43] The most important representatives of this school of thought, however, were Gaston Bachelard and Georges Canguilhem. Abel Rey and Brunschvicg conferred a PhD degree on Bachelard in 1927, after which he published widely on the development of modern physics. In 1940 he succeeded Abel Rey at the Sorbonne.[44] The title of his chair, 'philosophy and history of the sciences', emphasized the link between the theory and history of science, whereas the plural form 'sciences' alluded to the differential approach. Bachelard was succeeded in 1955 by Canguilhem, who applied himself to the history of the life sciences.

Although this tradition is not well known outside France, Bachelard and Canguilhem were among the most important examples for the generation of intellectuals that came to the fore after Sartre (Althusser, Foucault, Bourdieu). It is not common practice to link names such as these to a tradition that goes back to Auguste Comte. And, as far as I know, there is only one author who ever suggested such a link. Strikingly enough it was Louis Althusser, who referred in *Pour Marx* to the 'pitiful history' of French philosophy since 1789. The 'only' philosopher he felt was worth studying was Comte.[45] Althusser repeated this position once more and, besides Comte, made a reference to Durkheim as well.[46] The mention of Emile Durkheim touched upon the second tradition to which Comte's name is linked. Durkheim was a student of Boutroux and dedicated his doctoral dissertation to him. Unlike his mentor, however, Durkheim was not interested in the classical problem of freedom and necessity. He viewed it as a 'metaphysical question' that bore no relation to science.[47] But, as he said himself, it was indeed Boutroux's doing that even at the Ecole normale supérieure, his mind had already been 'permeated' with the idea that every science had to develop its own principles for research and conceptualization. He then 'applied' this idea to sociology, 'reinforced' in the process by reading Comte.[48]

One of the problems with which Durkheim grappled as a young man was that the epistemological orientation of Comte and Boutroux did not have much more to offer than a general guideline. Comte's sociology had not come much further than the law of the three stages. The organicist social theories that later developed might have been based upon erroneous assumptions, but they did have extensive systematics. In order to do more than simply repeat his mentors, in the first instance Durkheim began to use the schemes he came across in the work of Spencer and Schäffle. Since it was the only way to make a start on true research, he adapted and varied them. At his opening lecture in 1887 he defended this method and stated that the analogy could be 'an extremely valuable instrument'. Societies were not biological phenomena, but they did fulfil comparable functions as organisms. Further research in this field was called for, and Spencer's work could be useful in this connection.

This attitude was born of a certain research pragmatism, but also implied fundamental criticism of one of Comte's ideas. Comte had emphasized that social phenomena were related to one another and constituted a class of their own. It was upon this idea that the unity and specificity of sociology were based, and in this sense Durkheim was a Comtean from the very start. But Comte had in fact gone a bit further. He stressed the interdependence of social phenomena, adding that it was impossible to study them separately. The study of the whole had absolute priority. Comte rejected specialization and exhibited only the greatest indifference when it came to factual research. Social science ought to start at the most general level, which was the development of humanity.

Durkheim's reconsideration of Comte began at this point. Durkheim agreed that social phenomena constituted a class of its own, but disagreed in that he felt they were not congeneric. Not every social formation necessarily went through the same development, and not every social phenomenon was part of one and the same process. It had been Comte's illusion that there was one law governing the development of all of humanity, and that different societies were no more than particularizations of this general pattern. Instead of analysing, comparing and translating his theory into research, Comte had just kept on repeating his great law of human evolution. By doing so, Durkheim wrote, he immediately cut off the pathway that had just opened up.[49]

From this critical assimilation of Comte, the project emerged to which Durkheim's name was to be linked. The 'age of generalities' could be closed, and from then on sociology was to develop on the basis of detailed research. For the first few years his lectures were about such topics as the family, crime and law, suicide and education. Comte's sociology was no longer of much importance for this work, nor for all the articles that were to appear in *Année sociologique* (1898–1912). To Durkheim, the law of the three stages was no more than a 'historical curiosity'.[50] The idea, however, that 'social facts' had to be accounted for on the basis of other 'social facts' continued to be Durkheim's point of departure. It was his rendering of Comte's idea of relative autonomy. Durkheim thus distinguished his sociology from organicist and individualistic sociologies. This was also the difference between the *Année sociologique* and an eclectic enterprise such as René Worms' *Revue internationale de sociologie*.[51]

Emile Durkheim was the first to transform Comte's idea of social science as a relatively autonomous field into a workable research programme. Durkheim succeeded in effectuating what Comte had made feasible, and he did it in a way that earned him academic recognition. Sociology in France had become conceivable with Auguste Comte, but it was not until Durkheim that it became practicable as well.

Conclusion

The historical understanding of modern social science has substantially improved over the past two decades. Research has become a more scholarly endeavour, specialized journals and research groups have been established and new questions have transformed the conventional accounts. What has not changed, however, is that most research is conducted from a disciplinary perspective. Research questions are still very much shaped by disciplinary demands and divisions. The history of sociology is written by sociologists for sociologists; the same holds for the other social sciences. Most of this work, therefore, focuses on matters related to the contemporary identity of the disciplines, while the diffuse period of their 'early history' is widely neglected.

But disciplinary social science is a fairly recent phenomenon, dating from no earlier than the last decades of the nineteenth century, and most disciplines have become fully institutionalized only since World War II. Since the disciplinary division of labour is more of a problem than a solution, disciplinary histories can be of only limited use. For a more accurate account of the genesis of the social sciences, a broader and a more long-term perspective is needed. It is simply not possible to understand fully the categories of economic thought or the concepts of sociological theory without critically examining the trajectories that have preceded the establishment of these disciplinary communities.

The usual opposition between a 'history' still considered relevant and an 'early history' one is allowed to forget is therefore best replaced by a distinction between two stages: a *predisciplinary* and a *disciplinary stage*. One of the main arguments of this study has been that modern social science is the outcome of a process which is much longer than is generally assumed. For an analysis of this process a theoretical perspective and a research programme need to be formulated, a few elements of which may be recalled in conclusion.

Central to the predisciplinary stage, from about 1600 to the first half of the nineteenth century, was the elaboration of modern notions of 'state', 'economy' and 'society'. These concepts often became the core of more or less distinctive *intellectual genres*, each with a specific vocabulary and a related set of questions. Political theory became centred around the modern notion of the state, originating in the work of Machiavelli, Bodin and their successors. Political economy was a genre directly linked to state matters, but from the end of the seventeenth century onwards it developed in a somewhat more independent way. Moral philosophy and moralistics were also relevant genres of their own, although they are almost entirely ignored by contemporary social scientists. Social theory, finally, became something of a recognizable intellectual genre in the course of the eighteenth century.

These genres were not part of a unified corpus of knowledge (as Aristotelian practical philosophy had been). Although they represented more or less distinctive discourses, they were not separate 'disciplines'. All were part of a secular or secularizing intellectual culture which emerged with the expansion of intellectual networks independent of the church and most universities. The institutional centre of these networks was academies and learned societies. Those involved in them communicated with one another on the basis of a common epistemic code, structured by three key terms: 'nature', 'reason' and 'philosophy'. Work carried out on this basis entailed the search for natural principles and natural laws. These could be approached through rational and reasonable enquiry, and such enquiries were considered branches of philosophy, whether 'natural philosophy' or 'moral philosophy'. The different intellectual genres of the early modern period were thus generally conceived of as being part of a universal discourse, founded on a common set of assumptions and procedures and practised in similar types of institutions.

This intellectual movement emerged in the late Renaissance, became well established in the seventeenth century and functioned for most of the eighteenth century. Its general principle, both intellectually and socially, was to provide an alternative model to theology and university scholasticism. This so-called natural system of knowledge was in part a response to the new demands of worldly elites in cities and around courts.

One of the difficulties of understanding the genesis of social theory is that, initially, it was part of these early modern arrangements, but it was fairly soon affected by another transformation. From approximately 1770 to 1830 a fundamental transformation of the intellectual regime occurred. The early modern intellectual genres tended to give way to more specialized and more strictly organized 'disciplines'. As a result the exchanges *between* intellectual endeavours weakened, whereas the ties *within* the disciplines strengthened considerably. Disciplines were not only more specialized, but, as the word indicates, also more constraining arrangements.

The transition from rather flexible intellectual genres to more organized disciplines was directly linked to the institutional shift from academies and learned societies to re-formed universities and new professional schools. Disciplines in the modern sense thus became the central unit of the modern intellectual regime. What was previously ranked under the common heading of 'natural philosophy' now became disciplined and led to a division in mathematics, physics, chemistry and biology. A similar transition occurred somewhat later from 'natural law' and 'moral philosophy' to the different social sciences. The best single indicator of this process is that philosophy also became a discipline which was now conceived of as being independent not only of theology, but also of the different sciences. In different ways both Kant and Comte redefined philosophy in this sense.

That disciplines were more specialized areas of research was reinforced by the fact that transdisciplinary codes ('reason', 'nature') lost their appeal and supradisciplinary forms of control weakened. The two were linked to the demise of the academies. Academies had been both general platforms for exchange and arbiters in intellectual debate. In the new intellectual regime they lost these functions and tended to become honorific institutions. Their previous role was taken over by university departments and disciplinary journals and associations.

Contrary to the intellectual genres of the early modern period, disciplines were units, not only for research, but also for teaching and professional organization. Disciplines fulfilled more functions, including teaching activities (standard courses, exams, textbooks) and professional strategies.

In order to understand the predisciplinary social sciences, it thus seems inevitable to take into account the entire intellectual constellation and its transformation during the decades around 1800. One of the central arguments of the analysis was, indeed, that it is not possible to account for the rise of social theory independently of a much wider range of intellectual enterprises. It is quite typical, for example, that the early social theorists came from very different intellectual backgrounds: Montesquieu was trained in law, Condorcet in mathematics and Cabanis in medicine, whereas Saint-Simon was an energetic autodidact. All of them contributed to the definition of social theory by importing categories and habits of thought they had acquired earlier on. All of their projects, furthermore, depended on the power relations between different intellectual groups. Social theory was thus an integral part of the intellectual field, in Pierre Bourdieu's sense, and can therefore be understood only by reconstructing the structure of this field and its successive transformations.

The analysis of social theory thus led me to questions concerning law, medicine and mathematics, about the literary world as well as about the societal conditions under which all of this intellectual work took place. Following Wolf Lepenies, one may think of social theory as a core genre of the 'third culture', oscillating between literary practice on the one hand and more scientific models on the other. Understanding social theory then requires an investigation of the connections with these other intellectual cultures. But in doing so, social theory appears to be an interesting indicator for the changing relations between the two cultures. Examining social theory may thus be a way to analyse the intellectual field as a whole.

In all parts of the book I have tried to realize this type of analysis on two levels simultaneously. Avoiding the usual separation of text and context, product and producer, intellectual history was systematically combined with social history. The main reason for this dual approach is that it is otherwise impossible to find explanations for the patterns observed. Historians of ideas may very well detect theoretical affinities and patterns of intellectual development, but they can only explain their findings by explicitly taking into account the social dynamics of intellectual production. Textual and historical interpretation thus need to be combined with a sociological perspective.

This broad approach was also adopted to grasp the distinctiveness of social theory. Since intellectual identities can be established only in a relational manner, other intellectual genres and their theoretical models need to be examined. As it emerged in the eighteenth century, social theory did represent something of a new intellectual genre because it effectively transcended the existing division in political theory, political economy and moral philosophy. Perhaps it was above all a synthesis of moral philosophy and political theory. The synthetic ambition was realized chiefly by integrating considerations of state forms and political regimes with insights about morals and manners. The result of these efforts was most evident in the modern notion of 'society', which was thought of as a differentiated, or decentred, yet interconnected whole. Social theory thus became a discourse on the social world, centred on the structures of interdependence of human groups in time and space.

In the decades around 1800 social theory developed in a more scientific direction. Older theoretical models, drawn mainly from natural law, gave way to scientific approaches, derived either from mathematics (Condorcet) or from the life sciences (Cabanis). The Comtean project of 'sociology' subsequently provided social theory with a new theoretical model. By insisting that both natural law and natural science were inadequate frameworks, Comte's differential theory of science laid the foundation for sociology as a relatively autonomous science.

All contributors to this new intellectual tradition adhered to a specific vocabulary, a language centred around the notion of society and social relations. The new idiom allowed a redefinition of what was previously conceived in political, moral or economic terms. It is rather misleading, however, to identify social theory with a specific political outlook, with liberalism, conservatism or any form of progressive ideology. The origins of sociology have most often been associated with conservatism (Zeitlin, Nisbet). But a closer look at the whole development reveals that the political orientation of social theorists has varied greatly, including moderate reform (Montesquieu) and revolutionary engagement (Condorcet) as well as political conservatism (de Bonald, de Maistre).

Throughout this analysis, France was taken to be the main centre of predisciplinary social theory. There were, no doubt, major contributions from other countries, and for a while France and Scotland were competing centres. For the period from 1730 to 1850 as a whole, however, there is little doubt that Paris was its intellectual capital. Nowhere else was there such a consistent pattern of intellectual innovation over such a long period of time. In no other country were there six or seven successive generations of leading social theorists. From the generation of Montesquieu and Voltaire up to that of Auguste Comte, French social theorists shared a sense of continuity, of critique and counter-critique, of moving ahead or of deliberately reactivating older notions.

Whereas the first half of the nineteenth century witnessed an unprecedented variety of social theories and social movement, the revolution of 1848 marked the end of an era. The years of the Second Empire (1851–70) saw nothing in any way comparable with the previous intellectual ferment. Despite Cournot's work and Tocqueville's incisive plea for a 'new political science', intellectual innovation in French social science practically came to an end. Independent work

was obstructed by censorship and political repression. Only conservative Catholics such as Le Play found support, and even the Académie
des sciences morales et politiques ran into trouble with the political
authorities.

The leading social theorists now came from the German-speaking
countries and from England. Marx in Germany and Spencer in England were only the best-known representatives. In France it was not
until after the establishment of the Third Republic (1870) that significant contributions were made once again. The references for these
renewals generally came from abroad and were motivated by a widely
felt need to catch up with the Germans and the English. Supported by
the republicans who had come to power, new initiatives created the
institutional infrastructure for years to come. The Ecole libre des sciences politiques (1871), a training school for civil servants, became a
centre for political studies. Economics entered the Faculty of Law,
which formed the institutional basis for a new generation of economists and their journal, the *Revue d'économie politique* (1887). In the
same period the Faculty of Letters provided the institutional context
for psychology and sociology. The philosopher Ribot introduced the
new psychology, and Espinas and then Durkheim dedicated themselves to sociology.

The intellectual challenge represented by Spencer and a variety of
German authors was explicitly acknowledged by the young Emile
Durkheim. After he had studied in Germany his early reviews were
chiefly concerned with the recent scholarship abroad (Schäffle, Tönnies,
Wagner, Schmoller, Spencer) and with older French writers
(Montesquieu, Saint-Simon, Comte). The tension between the advances
in Germany and England, and the decline of French contributions was
one of Durkheim's major concerns. His own work represented a way
to overcome this tension. By adopting a Comtean scheme, according
to which social facts had to be explained by other social facts, Durkheim
managed to revive a French tradition, but one that was now based
largely on the most recent work of foreign scholars. In the extraordinary sociological workshop that was the *Année sociologique*, this tendency was all too clear. The vast majority of the books were published
in foreign languages, but their work soon gained prominence as the
French school of sociology.

But Durkheimian sociology, along with Ribot's psychology and the
economics of the *Revue d'économie politique*, had already ushered in
a new era. Since the 1880s social science was becoming a field of disciplines, dominated by professors and organized around university chairs
and disciplinary journals. The university professors redistributed the

subject matter of the social sciences, fixed their boundaries, specified its concepts and methods and rewrote its history accordingly. The various disciplines were not only carefully delineated from one another, but also from their predisciplinary past. Predisciplinary social science now appeared merely as prehistory.

Twentieth-century social science, then, turned into a self-conscious disciplinary endeavour, often with distinct national profiles and subdivided into a variety of different specialties. For many decades this seemed the natural order of things. It was fundamentally questioned only in the more recent past. Breaking the routines of disciplinary research, innovative scholars from different quarters have paved the way for truly interdisciplinary work, and, thereby, for a critical reflection upon disciplinary biases. Woken from our disciplinary slumbers, we may now also reinvestigate the predisciplinary stage of modern social science. Such a project will not be merely of historical concern. It should also contribute to the collective self-understanding of social scientists, and may indeed be of use for the formulation of new questions and the discovery of forgotten problems. Rethinking contemporary social science along these lines is no doubt the best way to do justice to past achievements.

Notes

Introduction

1   Cf. the contributions in W. Lepenies (ed.), *Geschichte der Soziologie*, Frankfurt am Main, Suhrkamp, 1981 (4 vols).
2   Of the more recent literature, see especially G. Hawthorn, *Enlightenment and Despair: A History of Social Theory*, Cambridge, Cambridge University Press, 1976; J. Szacki, *History of Sociological Thought*, London, Aldwych Press, 1979; S. Seidman, *Liberalism and the Origins of European Social Theory*, Oxford, Blackwell, 1983.
3   On disciplinary history, see L. Graham, W. Lepenies and P. Weingart (eds), *Functions and Uses of Disciplinary Histories*, Dordrecht, Reidel, 1983.
4   Cf. R. Stichweh, *Zur Entstehung des modernen Systems wissenschaftlicher Disziplinen: Physik in Deutschland 1740–1890*, Frankfurt am Main, Suhrkamp, 1984.
5   Q. Skinner, *Foundations of Modern Political Thought*, Cambridge, Cambridge University Press, 1978; Q. Skinner, 'The state', in T. Ball, J. Farr and R. L. Hanson (eds), *Political Innovation and Conceptual Change*, Cambridge, Cambridge University Press, 1989, pp. 90–131.
6   Cf. J.-C. Perrot, 'Economie politique', in *Handbuch politisch-sozialer Grundbegriffe in Frankreich. 1680–1810*, Munich, Oldenbourg, 1988, No. 8, pp. 51–104. On classical conceptions of 'economy', see O. Brunner, 'Das "ganze Haus" und die alteuropäische ökonomik', in *Neue Wege der Sozialgeschichte*, Göttingen, Vandenhoeck and Ruprecht, 1956, pp. 33–61.
7   Cf. J.-C. Perrot, 'Nouveautés: l'économie politique et ses livres', in H.-J. Martin and R. Chartier (eds), *Histoire de l'édition française*, Paris, Promodis, 1984, vol. 2, pp. 240–57.
8   Cf. N. Elias, 'On the sociogenesis of sociology', *Amsterdams Sociologisch Tijdschrift*, 11, 1984, pp. 14–52; E. Fox-Genovese, *The Origins of Physiocracy: Economic Revolution and Social Order in Eighteenth-*

Century France, Ithaca, Cornell University Press, 1976.

9 J. Goudsblom, *Sociology in the Balance*, Oxford, Blackwell, 1977, pp. 15–18.

10 On the role of jurists in the process of state formation, see P. Bourdieu, *La noblesse d'Etat: grandes écoles et esprit de corps*, Paris, Minuit, 1989, pp. 533–59. On the formation of the French state, see N. Elias, *The Civilizing Process*, Oxford, Blackwell, 1978, 1982 (2 vols).

11 Cf. W. F. Church, *Richelieu and Reason of State*, Princeton, Princeton University Press, 1972.

12 For an earlier formulation of this pattern, see J. Heilbron, 'Ueber die Genese der Soziologie in Frankreich', in *Wissenschaftskolleg Jahrbuch*, Berlin, Siedler, 1987, pp. 267–79.

13 See N. Luhmann, *Gesellschaftsstruktur und Semantik: Studien zur Wissensoziologie der modernen Gesellschaft*, Frankfurt am Main, Suhrkamp, 1980, 1981 (2 vols).

14 For surveys viewed from a variety of national traditions, cf. D. R. Kelley, 'Horizons of intellectual history: retrospect, circumspect, prospect', *Journal of the History of Ideas*, 48, 1987, pp. 143–69; R. Chartier, 'Intellectual history or sociocultural history? The French trajectories', in D. LaCapra and S. L. Kaplan (eds), *Modern European Intellectual History: Reappraisals and New Perspectives*, Ithaca, Cornell University Press, 1982, pp. 13–46; R. Koselleck (ed.), *Historische Semantik und Begriffsgeschichte*, Stuttgart, Klett-Cotta, 1979.

15 The publication of *The Structure of Scientific Revolutions* (1962) by Thomas Kuhn is frequently viewed as the start of a succession of innovations in thinking about science. One reason why Kuhn's book made so much of an impression was that it was the first study in a long time to be simultaneously theoretically interesting, historically reliable and sociologically relevant. Its success illustrates the extent to which the theory, history and sociology of science had parted ways. The formulation of theories was the province of philosophers, historical research the realm of historians, and debates on the 'norms' of the academic community a matter for sociologists. It is striking that Kuhn's book drew far less attention in the country where this division of labour was far less marked, namely in France. French historical epistemology in the tradition of Gaston Bachelard and Georges Canguilhem is still largely unknown outside France. For an overview of more recent research in the history and sociology of science, but confined to the English-speaking world, see S. Shapin, 'History of science and its sociological reconstructions', *History of Science*, 20, 1982, pp. 157–211.

16 For Bourdieu's theory of cultural production fields, see especially his recent *Les règles de l'art: genèse et structure du champ littéraire*, Paris, Seuil, 1992.

17 Auguste Comte used the term 'intellectual regime'. In fact he described his three well-known stages as different 'intellectual regimes'. I use the term as analogous to 'medical regime', 'religious regime' and 'ecological

regime', see, respectively, A. de Swaan, *The Management of Normality*,
London, Routledge, 1990; M. Bax, *Religieuze regimes in ontwikkeling*,
Hilversum, Gooi en Sticht, 1988; J. Goudsblom, *Fire and Civilization*,
London, Allen Lane, 1992; J. Goudsblom, E. L. Jones and S. Mennell,
Human History and Social Process, Exeter, University of Exeter Press,
1989.

18   W. Lepenies, *Between Literature and Science: The Rise of Sociology*, trans.
R. J. Hollingdale, Cambridge, Cambridge University Press, 1988.

Part I Introduction

1   On several of these themes, see N. Elias, 'On the sociogenesis of
sociology', *Amsterdams Sociologisch Tijdschrift*, 11, 1984, pp. 14–52;
A. Swingewood, 'Origins of sociology: the case of the Scottish
Enlightenment', *British Journal of Sociology*, 21, 1970, pp. 164–180.

2   For a brief overview, cf. J. G. A. Pocock, *Virtue, Commerce and History:
Essays on Political Thought and History, Chiefly in the Eighteenth
Century*, Cambridge, Cambridge University Press, 1985, pp. 1–34. His-
torians of political theory have also made important contributions to
methodological questions. In addition to that of Pocock and John Dunn,
Skinner's work has been of particular significance. His most important
essays have been compiled in J. Tully (ed.), *Meaning and Context: Quentin
Skinner and his Critics*, Cambridge, Polity Press, 1988.

3   Cf. P. Favre, 'Les sciences de l'Etat entre déterminisme et libéralisme:
Emile Boutmy (1835–1906) et la création de l'Ecole libre des sciences
politiques', *Revue française de sociologie*, 22, 1981, pp. 429–65;
D. Damamme, 'Genèse sociale d'une institution scolaire: l'Ecole libre
des sciences politiques', *Actes de la recherche en sciences sociales*, 70,
1987, pp. 31–46.

4   F. Braudel, *Ecrits sur l'histoire*, Paris, Flammarion, 1969, p. 7.

5   On this division, see J. Heilbron, 'The tripartite division of French social
science: a long-term perspective', in P. Wagner and B. Wittrock (eds),
Discourses on Society: The Shaping of the Social Science Disciplines
(Sociology of the Sciences Yearbook, vol. 15), Dordrecht, Kluwer
Academic, 1991, pp. 73–92.

6   P. Gay, *The Enlightenment*, London, Weidenfeld & Nicolson, 1967,
vol. 1, pp. 140–1.

7   R. Hubert, *Les sciences sociales dans l'Encyclopédie*, Paris, Alcan, 1923,
p. 366.

8   The fact that systematic comparisons have come to be more or less
automatically abandoned is evident, for example, from R. Porter and
M. Teich (eds), *The Enlightenment in National Context*, Cambridge,
Cambridge University Press, 1981. In this anthology, one of the few of
its sort, the articles about different countries are presented side by side,

without any attempt at comparison having been made. For a comparative view of the Enlightenment see R. Wuthnow, *Communities of Discourse: Ideology and Social Structure in the Reformation, the Enlightenment, and European Socialism*, Cambridge (MA), Harvard University Press, 1989.

Chapter 1   Intellectuals between Academy and Salon

1   A. Viala, *Naissance de l'écrivain: sociologie de la littérature à l'âge classique*, Paris, Minuit, 1985, p. 29.
2   See, in this connection, N. Heinich, 'La perspective académique; peinture et tradition lettrée: la référence aux mathématiques dans les théories de l'art au 17e siècle', *Actes de la recherche en sciences sociales*, 49, 1983, pp. 47–70; and "Arts et sciences à l'âge classique', *Actes de la recherche en sciences sociales*, 66–7, 1987, pp. 47–78.
3   Cf. P. O. Kristeller, *Renaissance Thought II*, New York, Harper & Row, 1965, pp. 163–227.
4   E. Zilsel, *Die sozialen Ursprünge der neuzeitlichen Wissenschaft*, Frankfurt am Main, Suhrkamp, 1976, especially pp. 49–65.
5   J.-B. Biot, *Essai sur l'histoire générale des sciences pendant la Révolution française*, Paris, Duprat, 1803, p. 38. Recent research has demonstrated that Biot's witticism was not exaggerated, cf. L. W. B. Brockliss, 'Aristotle, Descartes and the new science: natural philosophy at the University of Paris, 1600–1740', *Annals of Science*, 38, 1981, pp. 33–69.
6   F. Yates, *The French Academies of the Sixteenth Century* (1947), Nendeln, Klaus Reprint, 1968, pp. 275–316.
7   K. Mannheim, 'Die Bedeutung der Konkurrenz im Gebiete des Geistigen' (1929), in K. Mannheim, *Wissensoziologie*, ed. Kurt H. Wolff, Berlin, Luchterhand, 1964, pp. 566–613.
8   Cf. R. Hahn, *The Anatomy of a Scientific Institution: the Paris Academy of Sciences, 1666–1803*, Berkeley, University of California Press, 1971. On the relation of the Académie des sciences to other academic institutions, see C. C. Gillespie, *Science and Polity in France at the End of the Old Regime*, Princeton, Princeton University Press, 1980, pp. 74–184.
9   M. Crosland, 'The French Academy of Sciences in the nineteenth century', *Minerva*, 16, 1978, pp. 73–102.
10 These terms have been taken from W. Oosterbaan Martinius, *Schoonheid, welzijn, kwaliteit: kunstbeleid en verantwoording na 1945*, The Hague, Gary Schwartz/SDU, 1990.
11 With respect to this entire development, see N. Elias, *The Court Society*, trans. E. Jephcott, Oxford, Blackwell, 1983, and *The Civilizing Process*, trans. by E. Jephcott, Oxford, Blackwell, 2 vols, 1978–82.
12 N. Elias, *The Civilizing Process*, vol. 2, pp. 191–2.

13 Wolf Lepenies referred to this double function of the salons in *Melancholie und Gesellschaft*, Frankfurt am Main, Suhrkamp, 1969.

14 A. Viala, *Naissance de l'écrivain*, Paris, Minuit, 1985, p. 133.

15 C. C. Lougee, *Le paradis des femmes: Women, Salons and Social Stratification in Seventeenth-Century France*, Princeton, Princeton University Press, 1976.

16 P. van Tieghem, *Les influences étrangères sur la littérature française (1550–1880)*, Paris, Presses Universitaires de France, 1967, pp. 113–19 and 194–8.

17 Cf. R. Zuber, *Les 'belles infidèles' et la formation du goût classique*, Paris, Armand Colin, 1968.

18 A. Viala, *Naissance de l'écrivain*, Paris, Minuit, 1985, p. 135.

19 Quoted in R. Picard, *Les salons littéraires et la société française. 1610–1789*, New York, Brentano's, 1943, p. 150.

20 Quoted in R. Picard, ibid., p. 90.

21 E. Renan, *Questions contemporaines* (1868), in *Oeuvres complètes*, Paris, Calmann-Lévy, 1947, vol. 1, p. 206.

22 E. Durkheim, *L'évolution pédagogique en France*, Paris, Presses Universitaires de France, 1969, pp. 270–331. On the relation between educational systems and national intellectual styles, see also P. Bourdieu, 'Systèmes d'enseignement et systèmes de pensée', *Revue internationale des sciences sociales*, 19, 1967, pp. 367–88.

23 Montesquieu, *De l'esprit des lois* (1748), in *Oeuvres complètes*, Paris, Gallimard, 1951, vol. 2, p. 262.

24 See P. Bourdieu, *Distinction*, Cambridge (MA), Harvard University Press, 1984.

25 T. W. Adorno, 'Der Essay als Form', in *Gesammelte Schriften*, Frankfurt am Main, Suhrkamp, 1974, vol. 11, pp. 9–33.

26 Although the universities in the Protestant countries played a role of greater importance than in France, philosophy as an academic occupation is said to have begun with Kant. Kant was the first to have developed the concept of philosophy as a discipline that was not only independent of theology, but of the various sciences as well. Cf. R. Rorty, *Philosophy and the Mirror of Nature*, Princeton, Princeton University Press, 1979, especially pp. 133–9.

27 R. Darnton, *The Business of Enlightenment: A Publishing History of the Encyclopédie, 1775–1800*, Cambridge, Belknap Press, 1979.

28 R. Bray, *La formation de la doctrine classique en France* (1926), Paris, Nizet, 1966.

29 U. Ricken, *'Gelehrter' und 'Wissenschaft' im Französischen: Beiträge zu ihrer Bezeichnungsgeschichte vom 12.–17. Jahrhundert*, Berlin, Akademie, 1961, p. 37.

30 Madame de Staël, *De l'Allemagne* (1810), Paris, Garnier Frères, n.d., vol. 2, p. 101.

31 Cf. V. L. Tapié, *Baroque et classicisme*, Paris, Librairie générale française, 1980.

32 A. Viala, *Naissance de l'écrivain*, Paris, Minuit, 1985, p. 291.
33 H. Peyre, *Qu'est ce que le classicisme?*, Paris, E. Droz, 1933, p. 32.
34 Cf. W. Kühlmann, *Gelehrtenrepublik und Fürstenstaat: Entwicklung und Kritik des deutschen Späthumanismus in der Literatur des Barockzeitalters*, Tübingen, M. Niemeyer, 1982, pp. 306–18.
35 Montaigne, 'Du pédantisme', in *Essais* (1580), Paris, Garnier Frères, 1962, vol. 1, pp. 141–54.
36 Quoted in F. Brunot, *Histoire de la langue française des origines à 1900*, Paris, A. Colin, 1913, vol. 4, p. 412.
37 F. Brunot, ibid., p. 413.
38 A. Viala, *Naissance de l'écrivain*, Paris, Minuit, 1985, p. 283. On the decline of the humanist tradition, see also H. Gillot, *La querelle des anciens en des modernes en France* (1914), Geneva, Slatkine Reprints, 1968, pp. 323–53.
39 Cf. R. Pintard, *Le libertinage érudit dans la première moitié du XVIIe siècle* (1943), Geneva, Slatkine Reprints, 1983.
40 M. Fumaroli, *L'âge de l'éloquence: rhétorique et 'res literaria' de la Renaissance au seuil de l'époque classique*, Geneva, Droz, 1980, pp. 585–646.
41 N. Elias, *The Civilizing Process*, Oxford, Blackwell, 1978, vol. l.
42 Madame de Staël, *De l'Allemagne* (1810), Paris, Garnier Frères, n.d., vol. 1, p. 49.
43 I. Kant, *Beobachtungen über das Gefühl des Schönen und Erhabenen*, quoted in F. Schalk, *Studien zur französischen Aufklärung*, Frankfurt am Main, Vittorio Klostermann, 1977, p. 46.
44 This attitude continued to exist at French colleges and universities; cf. P. Bourdieu, J.-C. Passeron, *Les héritiers*, Paris, Minuit, 1964, pp. 106–15.

Chapter 2   Conflict over Reason

1 A. Viala, *Naissance de l'écrivain*, Paris, Minuit, 1985, pp. 51–7.
2 Cf. P. van Tieghem, *Les influences étrangères sur la littérature française. 1550–1880*, Paris, Presses Universitaires de France, 1967, pp. 61ff.
3 Voltaire, 'Lettres philosophiques' (1734), in *Mélanges*, Paris, Gallimard, 1961, pp. 97–100.
4 R. Pomeau, *La religion de Voltaire*, Paris, Nizet, 1969, p. 192.
5 Voltaire, 'Le siècle de Louis XIV' (1751), in *Oeuvres historiques*, Paris, Gallimard, 1957, p. 1018.
6 H. U. Gumbrecht and R. Reichardt, 'Philosophe, philosophie', in *Handbuch politisch-sozialer Grundbegriffe in Frankreich, 1680–1820*, Munich, R. Oldenbourg, 1985, vol. 3.
7 Cf. the introduction by A. Calame in Fontenelle, *Entretiens sur la pluralité des mondes* (1686), Paris, Marcel Didier, 1966.
8 Cf. L. Brunel, *Les philosophes et l'Académie française au dix-huitième*

siècle (1884) , Geneva, Slatkine Reprints, 1967.

9 On these questions of intellectual tactics, see J. N. Pappas, *Voltaire and d'Alembert*, Bloomington, Indiana University Press, 1962.

10 Cf. R. Darnton, *The Great Cat Massacre and Other Episodes in French Cultural History*, New York, Basic Books, 1984, pp. 191–214.

11 d'Alembert, 'Discours préliminaire' in *Encyclopédie ou dictionnaire raisonné des sciences, des arts, et des métiers* (articles choisis), Paris, Flammarion, 1986, vol. 1, p. 152.

12 Cf. B. Toscanne, *L'idée de nature en France dans la seconde moitié du XVIIe siècle*, Paris, Klincksieck, 1978; R. Mercier, *La réhabilitation de la nature humaine, 1700–1750*, Villemomble, La Balance, 1960; J. Ehrard, *L'idée de nature en France dans la première moitié du XVIIIe siècle*, Paris, Sevpen, 1963.

13 R. Hahn, 'Scientific research as an occupation in eighteenth-century Paris', *Minerva*, 13, 1975, pp. 501–13.

14 C. Salomon-Bayet, *L'institution de la science et l'expérience du vivant*, Paris, Flammarion, 1978, p. 273.

15 Entry on 'Gens de lettres', *Encyclopédie ou dictionnaire raisonné des sciences, des arts et des métiers*, Paris, 1757, vol. 7.

16 Entry on 'Philosophe', *Encyclopédie ou dictionnaire raisonné des sciences, des arts et des métiers*, Neuchâtel, 1765, vol. 12.

17 E. Cassirer, *The Philosophy of the Enlightenment* (1932), Princeton, Princeton University Press, 1968, esp. chaps 1 and 2.

18 R. Chartier, 'Les livres de voyage', in H.-J. Martin and R. Chartier (eds), *Histoire de l'édition française*, Paris, Promodis, 1984, vol. 2, pp. 216–17.

19 Cf. S. Auroux and B. Kaltz, 'Analyse, expérience', in *Handbuch politisch-sozialer Grundbegriffe in Frankreich 1680–1820*, Munich, Oldenbourg, 1986, vol. 6, pp. 7–40.

20 I. F. Knight, *The Abbé de Condillac and the French Enlightenment*, New Haven, Yale University Press, 1968.

21 T. L. Hankins, *Jean d'Alembert, Science and the Enlightenment*, Oxford, Clarendon Press, 1970.

22 Cf. T. L. Hankins, *Science and the Enlightenment*, Cambridge, Cambridge University Press, 1985; G. Buchdahl, *The Image of Newton and Locke in the Age of Reason*, London, Sheed & Ward, 1961.

23 Buffon, *Histoire naturelle générale et particulière*, The Hague, 1750, vol. 1, p. 10, quoted in F. Schalk, *Studien zur französischen Aufklärung*, Frankfurt am Main, Vittorio Klostermann, 1970, p. 45.

24 R. Darnton, *Mesmerism and the End of the Enlightenment in France*, Cambridge (MA), Harvard University Press, 1968; M. Dumont, 'Le succès d'une fausse science: la physiognomie de Johann Kaspar Lavater', *Actes de la recherche en sciences sociales*, 54, 1984, pp. 2–30.

25 On the cognitive and psychological aspects of this salon science, see G. Bachelard, *La formation de l'esprit scientifique*, Paris, Vrin, 1938. Bachelard held that an autonomous culture of science, which he referred

to as a 'scientific spirit', did not emerge until the end of the eighteenth century. Historians of science ignored his analysis, since they were writing the history of discoveries and theories, and were not traditionally concerned with the context within which science was practised. Viewed from this perspective, the 'scientific revolution' of the seventeenth century occupied a central position. And a depiction such as Bachelard's of the eighteenth century as a 'pre-scientific stage' is apt to strike orthodox historians of science as extremely odd.

26 J. d'Alembert, 'Essai sur la société des gens de lettres et des grands' (1753), in *Mélanges de littérature, d'histoire, et de philosophie*, Amsterdam, Zacharie Chatelain, 1759, vol. 1.

27 R. Grimsley, *Jean d'Alembert (1717–83)*, Oxford, Clarendon Press, 1963, pp. 79, pp. 125–31.

28 D. Roche, *Le siècle des lumières en province: académies et académiciens provinciaux, 1680–1789*, Paris, Mouton, 1978, vol. 1, pp. 286–90.

29 F. Furet, 'La librairie du royaume de France au 18e siècle', in G. Bollème et al., *Livre et société dans la France du XVIIe siècle*, Paris, Mouton, 1965, pp. 3–32.

30 R. Chartier, *Lectures et lecteurs dans la France d'Ancien Régime*, Paris, Seuil, 1987, pp. 166–80.

31 J. E. McClellan III, 'The Académie des sciences, 1699–1793: a statistical portrait', *Isis*, 72, 1981, pp. 541–67. On the natural science syllabus at military training schools, see the contributions by Roger Hahn and Réné Taton in R. Taton (ed.), *Enseignement et diffusion des sciences en France au XVIIIe siècle*, Paris, Hermann, 1964, pp. 511–615.

32 E. Walter, 'Les auteurs et le champ littéraire', in H.-J. Martin and R. Chartier (eds), *Histoire de l'édition française*, Paris, Promodis, 1984, vol. 2, pp. 383–99; R. Darnton, 'The facts of literary life in eighteenth-century France', in K. M. Baker (ed.), *The Political Culture of the Old Regime*, Oxford, Pergamon Press, 1987, pp. 261–91.

33 E. Walter, ibid., p. 391.

34 This and other information to come has been taken from R. Darnton, ibid., p. 266.

35 Cf. J. R. Jacob and M. C. Jacob, 'The Anglican origins of modern science', *Isis*, 71, 1980, pp. 251–67; J. Morrell and A. Thachray, *Gentlemen of Science: Early Years of the British Association for the Advancement of Science*, Oxford, Clarendon Press, 1981, pp. 25, 224–9.

36 Cf. J. Ben-David, *The Scientist's Role in Society: A Comparative Study*, Englewood Cliffs (NJ), Prentice-Hall, 1971, p. 84.

Chapter 3   French Moralists and the Social Order

1 H. Maier, *Die ältere deutsche Staats- und Verwaltungslehre*, Munich, Deutscher Taschenbuch Verlag, 1980, pp. 281–8.

2   H. Denzer, *Moralphilosophie und Naturrecht bei Samuel Pufendorf*, Munich, C. H. Beck, 1972, esp. pp. 296–300.

3   This has been extensively documented by Manfred Riedel. See especially M. Riedel, *Studien zu Hegels Rechtsphilosophie*, Frankfurt am Main, Suhrkamp, 1969, pp. 135–66; 'Gesellschaft, bürgerliche', in O. Brunner, W. Conze and R. Koselleck (eds), *Geschichtliche Grundbegriffe*, Stuttgart, 1972, vol. 1, pp. 672–725. Riedel's work is far less convincing when he refers to literature in English or French. However, no comparable studies are available for these linguistic areas.

4   L. W. B. Brockliss, *French Higher Education in the Seventeenth and Eighteenth Centuries*, Oxford, Clarendon Press, 1987, pp. 331–3.

5   I do not know in what context the term 'moral and political sciences' was first used. At any rate, in 1767 the physiocrat Nicolas Baudeau published his *Principes de la science morale et politique sur le luxe et les lois somptuaires*.

6   W. Dilthey, 'Das natürliche System der Geisteswissenschaften im 17. Jahrhundert', in *Gesammelte Schriften*, Stuttgart, B. G. Teubner, 1960, vol. 2, pp. 90–245.

7   On historicization and 'Verzeitlichung', cf. G. H. Nadel, 'Philosophy of history before historicism', *History and Theory*, 3, 1964, pp. 291–315; R. Koselleck, *Vergangene Zukunft*, Frankfurt am Main, Suhrkamp, 1979; P. H. Reill, *The German Enlightenment and the Rise of Historicism*, Berkeley, University of California Press, 1975.

8   Cf. D. R. Kelley, *Foundations of Modern Historical Scholarship: Language, Law and History in the French Renaissance*, New York, Columbia University Press, 1970.

9   W. F. Church, 'The decline of the French jurists as political theorists, 1660–1789', *French Historical Studies*, 5, 1967, pp. 1–40.

10   Cf. R. Mousnier, *Les institutions de la France sous la monarchie absolue, 1598–1789*, Paris, Presses Universitaires de France, 1980, vol. 2, p. 651.

11   Quoted in W. F. Church, 'The decline of the French jurists as political theorists, 1660-1789', *French Historical Studies*, 5, 1967, pp. 1–40.

12   D. Roche, *Le siècle des lumières en province: Académies et académiciens provinciaux, 1680–1789*, Paris, Mouton, 1978, vol. 1, p. 102.

13   P. Janet, *Histoire de la science politique dans ses rapports avec la morale* (1858), Paris, Alcan, 1913, vol. 2, p. 307; J. Klaits, 'Men of letters and political reform in France at the end of the reign of Louis XIV: the founding of the Académie politique', *Journal of Modern History*, 43, 1971, pp. 577–97.

14   Entry on 'académicien', in J. B. R. Robinet, *Dictionnaire universel des sciences morale, économique, politique et diplomatique*, London, 1777–83 (30 vols).

15   J. Portemer, 'Recherches sur l'enseignement du droit public au XVIIIe siècle', *Revue historique de droit français et étranger*, 37, 1959, pp. 341–97.

16   See, e.g., the important study by N. O. Keohane, *Philosophy and the*

State in France: From the Renaissance to the Enlightenment, Princeton, Princeton University Press, 1980.

17   Cf. P. O. Kristeller, *Renaissance Thought II*, New York, Harper & Row, 1965, pp. 20–68.

18   H.-J. Martin, *Livre, pouvoirs et société à Paris au XVIIe siècle (1598– 1701)*, Geneva, Droz, 1969, pp. 826–830, 1074.

19   Cf. D. Steland, *Moralistik und Erzählkunst von La Rochefoucauld und Mme de Lafayette bis Marivaux*, Munich, Wilhelm Fink, 1984.

20   See N. Elias, *The Court Society*, trans. E. Jephcott, Oxford, Blackwell, 1983, pp. 106–10; *The Civilizing Process*, vol. 2, Oxford, Blackwell, 1982, pp. 272–6.

21   Madame de Staël, *De l'Allemagne* (1810), Paris, Garnier Frères, n.d., vol. 1, p. 74.

22   F. Nietzsche, 'Jenseits von Gut und Böse' (section 254), in *Werke*, ed. K. Schlechta, Frankfurt am Main, Ullstein, 1979, vol. 2, pp. 721–23. See also the comments in 'Menschliches, Allzumenschliches' (sections 35 and 214), ibid., vol. 1.

23   Cf. H. Friedrich, *Montaigne*, Berne, A. Francke, 1949, p. 226.

24   Quoted in H. Friedrich, ibid., p. 220.

25   Cf. L. van Delft, *Le moraliste classique*, Geneva, Droz, 1982, pp. 235– 89. See Also A. Levi, *French Moralists: The Theory of the Passions, 1585 to 1649*, Oxford, Clarendon Press, 1964.

26   On 'parliamentarization', see N. Elias and E. Dunning, *Quest for Excitement: Sport and Leisure in the Civilizing Process*, Oxford, Blackwell, 1986, esp. pp. 19–62, 150–74.

27   Madame de Staël, *De la littérature considérée dans ses rapports avec les institutions sociales* (1800), Geneva, Droz, 1959, p. 213.

28   A. O. Hirschman, *The Passions and the Interests*, Princeton, Princeton University Press, 1977. See also A. J. Krailsheimer, *Studies in Self-Interest: From Descartes to La Bruyère*, Oxford, Clarendon Press, 1962.

29   See H.-J. Fuchs, 'Interesse', in *Historisches Wörterbuch der Philosophie*, Darmstadt, Wissenschaftliche Buchgesellschaft, 1976, vol. 4, pp. 479– 85.

30   H.-J. Fuchs, *Entfremdung und Narzissmus: semantische Untersuchungen zur Geschichte der 'Selbstbezogenheit' als Vorgeschichte von französisch 'amour-propre'*, Stuttgart, J. B. Metzler, 1977.

31   P. Bourdieu, 'Le capital social: notes provisoires', *Actes de la recherche en sciences sociales*, 31, 1980, pp. 2–3. On the relation to other forms of capital, see P. Bourdieu, 'The forms of capital', in J. G. Richardson (ed.), *Handbook of Theory and Research for the Sociology of Education*, London, Greenwood Press, 1986, pp. 241–58.

32   Voltaire, *Oeuvres historiques*, Paris, Gallimard, 1957, p. 1017.

33   d'Alembert, *Eloges lus dans les séances publiques de l'Académie française*, Paris, Panckoucke, 1779, p. XIII.

34   C. Buffier, *Traité de la société civile, et du moyen de se rendre heureux en contribuant au bonheur des personnes avec qui l'on vit*, Paris, Briasson,

1726, p. 15.
35 R. Mauzi, *L'idée du bonheur dans la littérature et la pensée françaises au XVIIIe siècle*, Paris, A. Colin, 1960.
36 Abbé Pluquet, *De la sociabilité*, Yverdon, 1770, vol. 1, p. 2; see also vol. 2, p. 217. On Pluquet, see R. Mauzi, *L'idée du bonheur dans la littérature et la pensée françaises au XVIIIe siècle*, Paris, A. Colin, 1960, pp. 255–258.
37 Condorcet, *Mathématique et société* (choice of texts and comments by R. Rashed), Paris, Hermann, 1974, p. 96.
38 On Mandeville, see especially T. A. Horne, *The Social Thought of Bernard de Mandeville: Virtue and Commerce in Early Eighteenth-Century England*, London, Macmillan, 1978.
39 Cf. N. O. Keohane, *Philosophy and the State in France. The Renaissance to the Enlightenment*, Princeton, Princeton University Press, 1980.

Chapter 4   The Construction of Social Theory

1   Voltaire, "Essai sur les moeurs" (1756), in *Oeuvres complètes*, Paris, Hachette et cie., 1876, vol. 10, p. 43.
2   The word *civilisation* was used for the first time in a publication dated 1756, and then spread quite rapidly. The terms *civilité* and *civiliser* are much older and have their origins in the field of law (*civil*). For a recent overview of the history of these words, see J. Starobinski, *Le remède dans le mal: critique et légitimation de l'artifice à l'âge des Lumières*, Paris, Gallimard, 1989, pp. 11–59.
3   See, in this connection, R. Koselleck, *Kritik und krise: eine Studie zur Pathogenese der bürgerlichen Welt*, FrankfurtamMain, Suhrkamp, 1973.
4   P.-H. T. d'Holbach, *Système de la nature, ou des lois du monde physique et du monde moral* (1770), Hildesheim, Georg Olms, 1966, p. XXIX.
5   Cf. E. C. Ladd, 'Helvétius and d'Holbach: "la moralisation de la politique"', *Journal of the History of Ideas*, 23, 1962, pp. 221–38. See also D. Mornet, *Les origines de la Révolution française, 1715–1787*, Paris, A. Colin, 1933, pp. 100–4; A. C. Kors, *d'Holbach's Coterie: an Enlightenment in Paris*, Princeton, Princeton University Press, 1976.
6   See especially the comments made by Montesquieu in 'De l'esprit des lois' (1748), *Oeuvres complètes*, Paris, Gallimard, 1951, vol. 2, pp. 518, 1137.
7   R. Shackleton, *Montesquieu: A Critical Biography*, London, Oxford University Press, 1961, p. 27.
8   G. Lanson, *Histoire de la littérature française* (1894), Paris, Hachette, 1982, p. 711.
9   R. Shackleton, ibid., p. 72.
10 R. Shackleton, ibid., p. 74.

11   Studies are available on many of the facets of Montesquieu's work. The greatest attention has been focused on his significance in the field of political theory, but a great deal has also been written about the sociological and judicial aspects of his work. In particular, *Lettres persanes* has been subject to frequent analysis by historians of literature. For a concise overview of secondary sources, cf. C. P. Clostermeyer, *Zwei Gesichter der Aufklärung: Spannungslagen in Montesquieu's 'Esprit des lois'*, Berlin, Duncker & Humblot, 1983. The significance of moral philosophy and moral science for Montesquieu has been largely overlooked. As far as I know, there is only one more extensive study in this field: C. Rosso, *Montesquieu moraliste: des lois au bonheur*, Bordeaux, Ducros, 1971. Rosso disputes the claim that *De l'esprit des lois* contains a coherent theory. He feels the systematics is 'illusory' (p. 66), and fails to detect anything more in Montesquieu's major work than a collection of maxims.   But how Montesquieu came into contact with the whole field of moral science, what it was about it that caught his interest, and how he went on to use moral themes . . . these are all questions that Rosso did not address.

12   Montesquieu, *Oeuvres complètes*, Paris, Gallimard, 1949, vol. 1, p. 114.

13   R. Shackleton, *Montesquieu: A Critical Biography*, London, Oxford University Press, 1961, p. 314.

14   Montesquieu, *Oeuvres complètes*, Paris, Gallimard, 1951, vol. 2, esp. p. 58.

15   J. Goudsblom, *Sociology in the Balance*, Oxford, Blackwell, 1977, pp. 15–18. See also S. S. Wolin, *Politics and Vision: Continuity and Innovation in Western Political Thought*, London, Allen & Unwin, 1960, pp. 290–3.

16   The term society is not referred to in Pierre Bayle's *Dictionnaire historique et critique* (1695–7). In the *Dictionnaire universel* (1690), compiled by Furetière, and Richelet's *Nouveau dictionnaire françois* (1719 edition) its definition as a judicially recognized form of association predominates. Furetière defined a society as an association of various people to serve their mutual needs. Richelet defined it as 'an agreement made in good faith by which something is shared in order to benefit from it in a fair manner'.

17   Montesquieu, *Oeuvres complètes*, Paris, Gallimard, 1949, vol. 1, p. 62.

18   R. Chartier, *Lectures et lecteurs dans la France d'ancien régime*, Paris, Seuil, pp. 45–86.

19   Cf. M. Duchet, *Anthropologie et histoire au siècle des lumières*, Paris, Flammarion, 1977, p. 191.

20   F. Brunot, *Histoire de la langue française des origines à nos jours*, Paris, A. Colin, 1966, vol. 6 (first part), pp. 101–5.

21   B. Groethuysen, *J.-J. Rousseau*, Paris, Gallimard, 1949, p. 390.

22   J.-J. Rousseau, 'Emile, ou de l'éducation', in *Oeuvres complètes*, Paris, Gallimard, 1969, vol. 4, p. 524.

23 E. Cassirer, *Le problème Jean-Jacques Rousseau* (1932), Paris, Hachette, 1987.

24 J.-J. Rousseau, 'Du contrat social (le version)', in *Oeuvres complètes*, Paris, Gallimard, 1964, vol. 3, p. 284.

25 See in this connection J. Starobinski, *Jean-Jacques Rousseau, la transparence et l'obstacle*, Paris, Plon, 1957.

26 See R. Derathé, *Jean-Jacques Rousseau et la science politique de son temps*, Paris, Presses Universitaires de France, 1950.

27 On the history of contract theories, cf. J. W. Gough, *The Social Contract: A Critical Study of its Development*, Oxford, Clarendon Press, 1936.

28 Cf. the letter to C. de Beaumont in J.-J. Rousseau, *Oeuvres complètes*, Paris, Gallimard, 1969, vol. 4, pp. 966–7.

29 J.-J. Rousseau, 'Emile', in *Oeuvres complètes*, Paris, Gallimard, 1969, vol. 4, p. 524.

30 The dictionaries held that the word 'social' was a neologism. Comte de Mirabeau even commented in 1775 that it was a dangerous term on account of its vague connotations (see F. Gohin, *Les transformations de la langue française pendant la deuxième moitié du 18e siècle (1740–1789)*, Geneva, Slatkin Reprints, 1970, p. 318). The section on it in the *Encyclopédie* stated only that 'social' was a new word that referred to the qualities that made man a useful member of society. *The Dictionnaire de Trévoux* (1771) compiled by the Jesuits was a bit more extensive. There was no reference to 'usefulness' and 'social virtues' were defined as civilized conduct. These virtues were best served by the doctrine of *charitas*. This definition, referring as it did to the aristocracy and the church, was typical of the Jesuit mentality. The word social was probably most widely used by the physiocrats. In their circle it was common after 1770, to speak of the desirability of an *art social*. Holbach's *Système social* (1773) would seem to have been directly inspired by Rousseau, but is far less coherent.

31 Cf. E. Angermann, 'Das Auseinandertreten von "Staat" und "Gesellschaft" im Denken des 18. Jahrhunderts', in E.-W. Böckenförde (ed.), *Staat und Gesellschaft*, Darmstadt, Wissenschaftliche Buchgesellschaft, 1976, pp. 108–30.

32 G. T. Raynal, *Histoire philosophique et politique des établissements et du commerce des européens dans les deux Indes*, Geneva, Jean-Leonard Pellet, 1781, vol. 9, p. 156.

33 E. Burke, *Reflections on the Revolution in France* (1790), Harmondsworth, Penguin Books, 1968, esp. p. 182. This was also the point of view of L. G. Crocker, *Nature and Culture: Ethical Thought in the French Enlightenment*, Baltimore, Johns Hopkins Press, 1963. Crocker described the French Enlightenment philosophy as the 'pseudo-scientific expression of egotistical and hedonistic doctrines'.

Chapter 5 Theoretical Models Compared: France and Scotland

1 On this argument, cf. C. Lévi-Strauss, 'Jean-Jacques Rousseau, founder of the sciences of man', in *Structural Anthropology*, London, Allen Lane, 1977, vol. 2, pp. 33–43.
2 M. H. Waddicor, *Montesquieu and the Philosophy of Natural Law*, The Hague, Martinus Nijhoff, 1970, p. 24.
3 R. Derathé, *Jean-Jacques Rousseau et la science politique de son temps*, Paris, Vrin, 1970.
4 Cf. R. Derathé, ibid., pp. 32–3.
5 On natural law, cf. O. Gierke, *Natural Law and the Theory of Society, 1500 to 1800*, Boston, Beacon Press, 1957; H. Welzel, *Naturrecht und materiale Gerechtigkeit*, Göttingen, Vandenhoeck & Ruprecht, 1962; G. Gurvitch, *L'idée du droit social*, Paris, Recueil Sirey, 1932; R. Tuck, *Natural Rights Theories: Their Origins and Developments*, Cambridge, Cambridge University Press, 1980.
6 M. H. Waddicor, *Montesquieu and the Philosophy of Natural Law*, The Hague, Martinus Nijhoff, 1970.
7 Cf. D. R. Kelley, 'The prehistory of sociology: Montesquieu, Vico, and the legal tradition', *Journal of the History of the Behavioural Sciences*, 16, 1980, pp. 133–44.
8 J. M. M. de Valk, *De evolutie van het wetsbegrip in de sociologie*, Assen, Van Gorcum, 1960.
9 J. d'Alembert, 'Réflexions sur l'usage et sur l'abus de la philosophie dans les matières de goût' (1757), in *Mélanges de littérature, d'histoire, et de philosophie*, Amsterdam, Zacharie Chatelain, 1759, vol. 4, pp. 301–20.
10 R. Darnton, *The Literary Underground of the Old Regime*, Cambridge (MA), Harvard University Press, 1982.
11 See H.-U. Thamer, *Revolution und Reaktion in der französischen Sozialkritik des 18. Jahrhunderts*, Frankfurt am Main, Akademische Verlagsgesellschaft, 1973.
12 J. Ehrard, *L'idée de nature en France dans la première moitié du XVIIIe siècle*, Paris, Sevpen, 1963, p. 786.
13 On the Scottish Enlightenment, see especially N. T. Phillipson, 'Culture and society in the 18th-century province: the case of Edinburgh and the Scottish Enlightenment', in L. Stone (ed.), *The University in Society*, Princeton, Princeton University Press, 1974, vol. 2, pp. 407–48; A. C. Chitnis, *The Scottish Enlightenment: A Social History*, London, Croom Helm, 1976.
14 See especially the third volume of D. Hume, *A Treatise of Human Nature* (1739–40), Harmondsworth, Penguin, 1969, pp. 507–670.
15 Quoted in E. C. Mossner, *The Life of David Hume*, Oxford, Clarendon Press, 1980, p. 301.
16 D. Forbes, *Hume's Philosophical Politics*, Cambridge, Cambridge University Press, 1975.

17 David Hume, 'My own life', in E. C. Mossner, *David Hume*, p. 612.
18 Cf. R. L. Emerson, 'The social composition of enlightened Scotland: the Select Society of Edinburgh, 1754–1764', in *Studies on Voltaire and the Eighteenth Century*, 114, 1973, pp. 291–329.
19 See A. S. Skinner, *A System of Social Science: Papers Relating to Adam Smith*, Oxford, Clarendon Press, 1979, p. 9; H. Medick, *Naturzustand und Naturgeschichte der bürgerliche Gesellschaft*, Göttingen, Vandenhoeck & Ruprecht, 1973, p. 191.
20 For good overviews on recent research, see I. Hont and M. Ignatief (eds), *Wealth and Virtue: The Shaping of Political Economy in the Scottish Enlightenment*, Cambridge, Cambridge University Press, 1983; A. S. Skinner and R. H. Campbell (eds), *The Origins and Nature of the Scottish Enlightenment*, Edinburgh, John Donald, 1982. In recent studies, however, not much attention is devoted to the social and intellectual significance of the natural sciences; cf. R. L. Emerson, 'Science and the origins of the Scottish Enlightenment', *History of Science*, 26, 1988, pp. 333–66.
21 A. Smith, 'Letter to the Edinburgh Review' (1756), in *Essays on Philosophical Subjects*, Oxford, Clarendon Press, 1980, pp. 242–54.
22 J.-J. Rousseau, 'Discours sur l'origine et les fondements de l'inégalité' (1755) , in *Oeuvres complètes*, Paris, Gallimard, 1964, vol. 3, p. 193.
23 J.-J. Rousseau, ibid., p. 132.
24 See R. L. Meek, *Social Science and the Ignoble Savage*, Cambridge, Cambridge University Press, 1976; P. Stein, *Legal Evolution: The Story of an Idea*, Cambridge, Cambridge University Press, 1980. On the development and function of genetic models, see J. Goudsblom, 'Over de bijdrage van de geschiedenis aan de sociologie', *Tijdschrift voor Geschiedenis*, 101, 1988, pp. 589–99.

PART II Introduction

1 B. W. Head, 'The origins of "la science sociale" in France, 1770–1800', *Australian Journal of French Studies*, 19, 1982, pp. 115–32; K. M. Baker, *Condorcet: From Natural Philosophy to Social Mathematics*, Chicago, University of Chicago Press, 1975, pp. 391–5. Head's and Baker's studies were not mentioned in F. R. Shapiro, 'A note on the origin of the term social science', *Journal of the History of the Behavioral Sciences*, 20, 1984, pp. 20–2. Shapiro cited 1825 as the earliest date for the term 'social science' in English.
2 Condorcet, *Mathématique et société*, texts chosen by R. Rashed, Paris, Hermann, 1974, p. 197.
3 Cf. J. Godechot, *La pensée révolutionnaire en France et en Europe, 1780–1789*, Paris, Armand Colin, 1964.
4 J. Belin, *La logique d'une idée-force: l'idée d'utilité sociale pendant la*

Révolution française (1789–1793), Paris, Hermann, 1939, p. 34.
5 On 'nation' and 'fatherland', see the contributions by M. Cranston and
   N. Hampson in C. Lucas (ed.), *The Political Culture of the French Revolution*, Oxford, Pergamon Press, 1988, pp. 97–104, 125–37.
6 H. Kohn, 'France between Britain and Germany', *Journal of the History
   of Ideas*, 17, 1956, pp. 283–99.
7 B. Bensaude-Vincent, 'Une mythologie révolutionnaire dans la chimie
   française', *Annals of Science*, 40, 1983, pp. 189–96.
8 C.-H. de Saint-Simon, 'Introduction aux travaux scientifiques du 19e
   siècle' (1808), in *Oeuvres*, Paris, Anthropos, 1966, vol. 6, p. 13.
9 Destutt de Tracy, *Eléments d'idéologie* (1803), Paris, Vrin, 1970, vol. 2,
   p. 10.

Chapter 6   Reform, Revolution and the Napoleonic Era

1 On the first stage of the Revolution, cf. M. Vovelle, *La chute de la
   monarchie, 1787–1792*, Paris, Seuil, 1972. An overview of the period
   covering the Revolution and the Empire can be found in D. M. G.
   Sutherland, *France 1789–1815: Revolution and Counterrevolution*,
   London, Fontana Press, 1985. In the recent interpretations of the Revolution there is a great deal of emphasis on political processes and ideas,
   cf. F. Furet and M. Ozouf (eds), *Dictionnaire critique de la Révolution
   française*, Paris, Flammarion, 1988; K. M. Baker (ed.), *The Political
   Culture of the Old Regime*, Oxford, Pergamon Press, 1987; C. Lucas
   (ed.), *The Political Culture of the French Revolution*, Oxford, Pergamon
   Press, 1988.
2 Cf. M. Bouloiseau, *La République jacobine*, Paris, Seuil, 1972; R.
   Darnton, 'What was revolutionary about the French Revolution?', *New
   York Review of Books*, 19 January 1989.
3 Cf. L. Bergeron, *L'épisode napoléonien: aspects intérieurs*, Paris, Seuil,
   1972; J. Lovie and A. Palluel, *L'épisode napoléonien: aspects extérieurs*,
   Paris, Seuil, 1972; J. Tulard (ed.), *Dictionnaire Napoléon*, Paris, Fayard,
   1987.
4 These figures have been taken from a study conducted by J. Tulard, quoted
   in L. Bergeron, *L'épisode napoléonien: aspects intérieur*, Paris, Seuil,
   1972, p. 84.
5 Cf. D. M. G. Sutherland, *France 1789–1815: Revolution and Counterrevolution*, London, Fontana Press, 1985, p. 386.

Chapter 7   Intellectual Transformations around 1800

1 On this shift from a long-term perspective, see B. Kempers, *Painting, Power and Patronage: The Rise of the Professional Artist in Renaissance Italy*, London, Penguin/Allen Lane, 1992.

2 U. van de Sandt, 'La peinture: situation et enjeux', in J.-C. Bonnet (ed.), *La carmagnole des muses: l'homme de lettres et l'artiste dans la Révolution*, Paris, Armand Colin, 1988, pp. 333–57; D. L. Dowd, 'The French Revolution and the painters', *French Historical Studies*, 1, 1959, pp. 127–48.

3 P. Frantz, 'Pas d'entracte pour la Révolution', in J.-C. Bonnet (ed.), Ibid., pp. 381–98.

4 B. Foucart, 'L'artiste dans la société de l'Empire: sa participation aux honneurs et dignités', *Revue d'histoire moderne et contemporaine*, 17, 1970, pp. 709–19.

5 M. Dorigny, 'Le Cercle social ou les écrivains au cirque', in J.-C. Bonnet (ed.), Ibid., pp. 49–66; G. Kates, *The Cercle social, the Girondins and the French Revolution*, Princeton, Princeton University Press, 1985.

6 R. Darnton, *The Literary Underground of the Old Regime*, Cambridge (MA), Harvard University Press, 1982.

7 Cf. C. C. Gillispie, *Science and Polity in France at the End of the Old Regime*, Princeton, Princeton University Press, 1980, pp. 290–330.

8 M. Weber, *Wirtschaft und Gesellschaft*, Tübingen, J. C. B. Mohr, 1976, pp. 308, 313–14.

9 D. Outram, 'The ordeal of vocation: the Paris Academy of Sciences and the Terror, 1793–95', *History of Science*, 21, 1983, pp. 251–73; F. Waquet, 'La Bastille académique', in J.-C. Bonnet (ed.), Ibid., pp. 19–36.

10 R. Hahn, *The Paris Academy of Sciences, 1666–1803*, Berkeley, University of California Press, 1971, p. 118.

11 Cf. J. Fayet, *La Révolution française et la science, 1789–1795*, Paris, Marcel Rivière, 1960, pp. 236–57.

12 J. B. Biot, *Essai sur l'histoire générale des sciences pendant la Révolution française*, Paris, Duprat, 1803.

13 Madame de Staël, *De la littérature considérée dans ses rapports avec les institutions sociales* (1800), Geneva, Droz, 1959, p. 325.

14 L. de Bonald, *Mélanges littéraires, politiques et philosophiques*, Paris, D'Adrien Le Clere, 1852, esp. pp. 47, 66–87, 169–206. The comment that literature is the 'expression of the society' comes up in an article Bonald wrote in 1805 and was elaborated upon shortly afterwards in articles about the theatre (1805) and about 'style and literature' (1806).

15 R. Mortier, 'Les héritiers des philosophes devant l'expérience révolutionnaire', *Dix-huitième siècle*, 6, 1974, pp. 45-57; E. Joyau, *La philosophie en France pendant la Révolution (1789–1795)*, Paris, Arthur Rousseau, 1893.

16 R. Fargher, 'The retreat from Voltairianism, 1800–15', in W. Moore et

al. (ed.), *The French Mind: Studies in Honour of Gustave Rudler*, Oxford, Clarendon Press, 1952, pp. 220–37; S. Moravia, *Il tramonto dell' illuminismo: filosofia e politica nella società Francese (1770–1810)*, Bari, Laterza, 1968; R. Mortier, *Le 'Tableau littéraire de la France au XVIIIe siècle': un épisode de la 'guerre philosophique' à l'Academie française sous l'Empire (1804–1810)*, Brussels, Palais des Académies, 1972.

17 The texts of the various proposals and the political debates about them were published in C. Hippeau, *L'instruction publique en France pendant la Révolution*, Paris, Didier, 1881, 1883 (2 vols).

18 J. Fayet, *La Révolution française et la science, 1789–1795*, Paris, Marcel Rivière, 1960, pp. 420–33.

19 L. P. Williams, 'Science, Education and the French Revolution', *Isis*, 44, 1953, pp. 311–30; see also the theme issue of *Annales historiques de la Révolution française*, 53, no. 243, 1981.

20 M. Crosland, *The Society of Arcueil: A View of French Science at the Time of Napoleon I*, London, Heinemann, 1967, pp. 4–55; J. Fischer, *Napoleon und die Wissenschaften*, Stuttgart, Franz Steiner, 1988.

21 N. and J. Dhombres, *Naissance d'un nouveau pouvoir: sciences et savants en France (1793–1824)*, Paris, Payot, 1989, pp. 104, 815–16.

22 N. and J. Dhombres, ibid., p. 732.

23 Cf. J.-L. Halperin, 'Sénat', in J. Tulard (ed.), *Dictionnaire Napoléon*, Paris, Fayard, 1987.

24 L. P. Williams, 'Science, education and Napoleon I', *Isis*, 47, 1956, pp. 369–82.

25 See the account by the Danish astronomer Bugge, who spent six months in Paris in 1798, in M. Crosland (ed.), *Science in France in the Revolutionary Era*, Cambridge (MA), MIT Press, 1969.

26 C. Maxwell, *The English Traveller in France. 1698–1815*, London, Routledge, 1932, esp. pp. 44, 223, 231.

27 J. Dhombres, 'Books: reshaping science'. in R. Darnton and D. Roche (eds), *Revolution in Print: The Press in France, 1775–1800*, Berkeley, University of California Press, 1989, pp. 177–202.

28 Earlier references were made to this split between science and literature, but always more or less in passing, and as far as I know it was never analysed in greater detail; cf. A. W. Brown, 'Some political and scientific attitudes to literature and the arts following the French Revolution', *Forum for Modern Language Studies*, 2, 1966, pp. 230–52; M. Crosland, 'The development of a professional career in science in France', *Minerva*, 13, 1975, pp. 38–57.

29 K. Mannheim. 'Die Bedeutung der Konkurrenz im Gebiete des Geistigen' (1929), in K. Mannheim. *Wissenssoziologie*, selected texts ed. Kurt H. Wolff, Berlin, Luchterhand, 1964, pp. 566–613.

Chapter 8   Natural Science and Revolution

1   D. Roche, *Les républicains des lettres: gens de culture et lumières au XVIIIe siècle*, Paris, Fayard, 1988, p. 170.
2   On this entire period, see C. C. Gillispie, *Science and Polity in France at the End of the Old Regime*, Princeton, Princeton University Press, 1980.
3   B. Willink, *Burgerlijk sciëntisme en wetenschappelijk toponderzoek: sociale grondslagen van nationale bloeiperioden in de negentiende eeuwse bètawetenschappen*, PhD dissertation, Amsterdam, 1988.
4   This generation classification was based on N. and J. Dhombres, *Naissance d'un nouveau pouvoir: sciences et savants en France (1793–1824)*, Paris, Payot, 1989, pp. 153–71.
5   H. Guerlac, 'Chemistry as a branch of physics: Laplace's collaboration with Lavoisier', *Historical Studies in the Physical Sciences*, 7, 1976, pp. 193–276.
6   Cf. N. N. Stuloff, 'Über den Wissenschaftsbegriff der Mathematik in der ersten Hälfte des 19. Jahrhunderts', in A. Diemer (ed.), *Beiträge zur Entwicklung der Wissenschaftstheorie im 19. Jahrhundert*, Meisenheim am Glan, A. Hain, 1968, pp. 71–89. On the French mathematicians in this period, see J. Dhombres, 'Mathématisation et communauté scientifique française (1775–1825)', *Archives internationales d'histoire des sciences*, 36, 1986, pp. 249–93.
7   Cf. W. Scharlau, 'The origins of pure mathematics', in H. N. Jahnke and M. Otte (eds), *Epistemological and Social Problems of the Sciences in the Early Nineteenth Century*, Dordrecht, D. Reidel, 1981.
8   On these last two schools of thought, see I. Grattan-Guinness, 'Mathematical physics in France, 1800–1840: knowledge, activity and historiography', in J. W. Dauben (ed.), *Mathematical Perspectives: Essays on Mathematics and its Historical Development*, New York, Academic Press, 1981, pp. 95–135; E. Glas, 'De samenhang tussen sociale en cognitieve factoren in de Franse mathematische revolutie (1794–1814)', *Kennis en methode*, 10, 1986, pp. 169–90.
9   R. Fox, 'The rise and fall of Laplacian Physics', *Historical Studies in the Physical Sciences*, 4, 1974, pp. 89–136.
10   M. Crosland, *The Society of Arcueil: A View of French Science at the Time of Napoleon I*, London, Heinemann, 1967.
11   N. and J. Dhombres, *Naissance d'un nouveau pouvoir: sciences et savants en France (1793–1824)*, Paris, Payot, p. 182.
12   Cf. R. H. Silliman, 'Fresnel and the emergence of physics as a discipline', *Historical Studies in the Physical Sciences*, 4, 1974, pp. 137–162; T. S. Kuhn, 'Mathematical vs. experimental traditions in the development of physical science', *Journal of Interdisciplinary History*, 7, 1976, pp. 1–31; E. Frankel, 'J. B. Biot and the Mathematization of experimental physics in Napoleonic France', *Historical Studies in the Physical Sciences*, 8, 1977, pp. 33–72.

13 The history of the mathematization of the *sciences physiques* still remains largely to be written. The cooperation between Laplace and Lavoisier which in a certain sense constitutes the first chapter, is an interesting episode because Laplace initially exhibited very little enthusiasm for an enterprise of this kind. His reluctance was indicative of the social and cognitive hierarchy within the *Académie des sciences*; cf. D. I. Duveen and R. Hahn, 'Deux lettres de Laplace à Lavoisier', *Revue d'histoire des sciences*, 11, 1958, pp. 337–42.

14 I. Grattan-Guinness 'Mathematical physics in France, 1800–1835', in H. N. Jahnke and M. Otte (eds), *Epistemological and Social Problems of the Sciences in the Early Nineteenth Century*, Dordrecht, D. Reidel, 1981, pp. 349–70. On the ramifications of the new French natural sciences, see M. Crosland and C. Smith, 'The transmission of physics from France to Britain: 1800–1840', *Historical Studies in the Physical Sciences*, 9, 1979, pp. 1–61.

15 M. Bradley, 'Scientific education versus military training: the influence of Napoleon Bonaparte on the Ecole polytechnique', *Annals of Science*, 32, 1975, pp. 415–49; T. Shinn, *Savoir scientifique et pouvoir social: l' Ecole polytechnique 1794–1914*, Paris, Presses de la Fondation nationale des Sciences Politiques, 1980.

16 Cf. M. Foucault, *Les mots et les choses*, Paris, Gallimard, 1966 (esp. chap. 5).

17 C. Limoges, 'The development of the Musée d'histoire naturelle of Paris, 1800–1914', in R. Fox and G. Weisz, *The Organization of Science and Technology in France, 1808–1914*, Cambridge, Cambridge University Press; Maison des Sciences de l'Homme, 1980, pp. 211–240.

18 D. Outram, *Georges Cuvier: Vocation, Science and Authority in Post-Revolutionary France*, Manchester, Manchester University Press, 1984.

19 M. Foucault, *Les mots et les choses*, Paris, Gallimard, 1966; 'La situation de Cuvier dans l'histoire de la biologie II', *Revue d'histoire des sciences*, 23, 1970, pp. 63–9, followed by a discussion, pp. 70–92.

20 O. Temkin, *The Double Face of Janus*, Baltimore, Johns Hopkins University Press, 1977, p. 363.

21 P. Corsi, *The Age of Lamarck: Evolutionary Theories in France, 1790–1830*, Berkeley, University of California Press, 1988.

22 See W. Lepenies, *Das Ende der Naturgeschichte: Wandel kultureller Selbstverständlichkeiten in den Wissenschaften des 18. und 19. Jahrhunderts*, Frankfurt am Main, Suhrkamp, 1978.

23 N. D. Jewson, 'Medical knowledge and the patronage system in 18th-century England', *Sociology*, 8, 1974, pp. 369–85; 'The disappearance of the sick man from medical cosmology, 1770–1870', *Sociology*, 10, 1976, pp. 225–44.

24 See T. Gelfand, *Professionalizing Modern Medicine: Paris Surgeons and Medical Science and Institutions in the 18th Century*, Westport (CT), Greenwood Press, 1980.

25 Cf. J. Roger, 'The living world', in G. S. Rousseau and R. Porter (eds),

The Ferment of Knowledge, Cambridge, Cambridge University Press, 1980, pp. 255–83.

26 C. Hannaway, 'The Société royale de médecine and epidemics in the Ancien Régime', *Bulletin of the History of Medicine*, 46, 1972, pp. 257–73; A. F. La Berge, 'The early nineteenth-century French public health movement: the disciplinary development and institutionalization of *hygiène publique*', *Bulletin of the History of Medicine*, 58, 1984, pp. 363–79.

27 Cf. T. D. Murphy, 'The French medical profession's perception of its social function between 1776 and 1830', *Medical History*, 23, 1979, pp. 259–78.

28 M. Foucault, *Naissance de la clinique* (1963), Paris, Presses Universitaires de France, 1972; E. H. Ackerknecht, *Medicine at the Paris Hospital, 1794–1848*, Baltimore, Johns Hopkins Press, 1967; I. Waddington, 'The role of the hospital in the development of modern medicine', *Sociology*, 7, 1973, pp. 211–24; D. M. Vess, *Medical Revolution in France, 1789–1796*, Gainesville, University Presses of Florida, 1975.

29 O. Temkin, 'The role of surgery in the rise of modern medical thought', in *The Double Face of Janus*, Baltimore, Johns Hopkins Press, 1977, pp. 487–96; T. Gelfand, *Professionalizing Modern Medicine: Paris Surgeons and Medical Science and Institutions in the 18th Century*, Westport (CT), Greenwood Press, 1980.

30 J. E. Lesch, *Science and Medicine in France: The Emergence of Experimental Physiology. 1790–1855*, Cambridge (MA), Harvard University Press, 1984; W. R. Albury, 'Experiment and explanation in the physiology of Bichat and Magendie', *Studies in the History of Biology*, 1, 1977, pp. 47–131.

31 Cf. W. R. Albury, 'Heart of Darkness: J. N. Corvisart and the medicalization of life', in J.-P Goubert (ed.), La médicalisation de la société française 1770–1830, *Historical Reflections/Réflexions historiques*, 9, 1982, pp. 17–31.

32 J. Dhombres, 'Books: reshaping science', in R. Darnton and D. Roche (eds), *Revolution in Print: The Press in France, 1775–1800*, Berkeley, University of California Press, 1989, pp. 177–202.

33 Cf. J.-P. Goubert (ed.), La médicalisation de la société française, 1770–1830, *Historical Reflections/Réflexions historiques*, 9, 1982.

34 M. Crosland, 'The development of a professional career in science in France', *Minerva*, 13, 1975, pp. 38–57; J. Ben-David, *The Scientist's Role in Society: A Comparative Study*, Englewood Cliffs (NJ), Prentice-Hall, 1971, pp. 98–9.

35 C. C. Gillispie, *The Edge of Objectivity: An Essay in the History of Scientific Ideas*, Princeton, Princeton University Press, 1960, p. 177.

36 J. E. McClellan III, 'The scientific press in transition: Rozier's journal and the scientific societies in the 1770s', *Annals of Science*, 36, 1979, pp. 425–49.

37 Cf. R. Stichweh, *Zur Entstehung des modernen Systems wissenschaftlicher*

Disziplinen: Physik in Deutschland, 1740–1890, Frankfurt am Main, Suhrkamp, 1984, p. 52.

38   B. Hoppe, 'Le concept de biologie chez G. R. Treviranus', in J. Schiller (ed.), *Colloque international Lamarck*, Paris, A. Blanchard, 1971, pp. 199–237; T. Lenoir, *The Strategy of Life: Teleology and Mechanics in Nineteenth-Century German Biology*, Dordrecht, D. Reidel, 1982; J. Schiller, *La notion d'organisation dans l'histoire de la biologie*, Paris, Maloine, 1978.

39   A. O. Lovejoy, *The Great Chain of Being*, Cambridge (MA), Harvard University Press, 1936.

40   R. Darnton, *The Business of Enlightenment: A Publishing History of the Encyclopédie, 1775–1800*, Cambridge, Belknap Press, 1979, pp. 430–54.

Chapter 9   The Literary Opposition

1   C. A. Sainte-Beuve, 'Espoir et voeu du mouvement littéraire et poétique' (1864), in *Oeuvres*, Paris, Gallimard, 1949, vol. 1, pp. 369–77.

2   G. Lanson, *Histoire de la littérature française*, Paris, Hachette, 1951, pp. 853–906.

3   M. Albert, *La littérature française sous la Révolution. l'Empire et la Restauration (1789–1830)*, Paris, Société française d' Imprimerie et de Librairie, 1898, p. 77.

4   Quoted in J. Charpentier, *Napoléon et les hommes de lettres de son temps*, Paris, Mercure de France, 1935, p. 30.

5   On this intellectual reorientation, see F. Baldensperger, *Le mouvement des idées dans l'émigration française (1789–1815)*, Paris, Plon, 1924. The size and social composition of this group of *émigrés* are dealt with in D. Greer, *The Incidence of the Emigration During the French Revolution*, Cambridge (MA), Harvard University Press, 1951. It is clear from this study that only very few professional writers and scientists emigrated. There were 23 writers and 34 scientists and professors, but almost 600 physicians and surgeons and more than 1,700 jurists. However, many writers were not professional, and information is available only on the professions of half of the emigrants of aristocratic descent, the group to which Chateaubriand belonged.

6   On several facets of these debates, see S. Moravia, *Il tramonto dell'illuminismo: filosofia e politica nella società francese* (1770–1810), Bari, Laterza, 1968, pp. 462–509, and especially P. Bénichou, *Le sacre de l'écrivain, 1750–1830*, Paris, José Corti, 1973, pp. 111–263.

7   L. de Fontanes, 'De la littérature, considérée dans ses rapports avec les institutions sociales, par madame de Staël-Holstein', *Mercure de France*, no. I, 1er Messidor an 8 (20 June 1800), pp. 13–37. The second

part of the review was in no. III, 1er Thermidor an 8 (20 July 1800), pp. 171–96.

8 Chateaubriand, 'Lettre au C. Fontanes, sur la seconde édition de l'ouvrage de Mme. de Staël', *Mercure de France*, no. XIII, 1er Nivose an 9 (22 December 1800), pp. 14–38.

9 Chateaubriand, *Essai sur les Révolutions; Génie du christianisme* (1802), Paris, Gallimard, 1978, p. 817.

10 Chateaubriand, *Mémoires d'outre-tombe* (1848), Paris, Gallimard, 1946, vol. 1, p. 467.

11 A. de Lamartine, *Oeuvres poétiques complètes*, Paris, Gallimard, 1963, p. 5. On the same theme, cf. Reflexion, dated 1830 (ibid., p. 500):

L'esprit humain fendant la mer d'obscurité, Trompé par chaque écueil, crie en vain: Vérité! Sur ces bords ignorés plane une nuit divine; Ce monde est une énigme: heureux gui la devine! . . .

12 Quoted in N. and J. Dhombres, *Naissance d'un nouveau pouvoir: sciences et savants en France (1793–1824)*, Paris, Payot, 1989, p. 326.

13 Madame de Staël, *De l'Allemagne* (1813), Paris, Garnier Frères, n.d., vol. 2, pp. 203–68.

14 A. de Lamartine, 'Des destinées de la poésie' (1834), in Lamartine, *Oeuvres choisies*, ed. by M. Levaillant, Paris, A. Hatier, 1930, pp. 553–4.

15 G. Flaubert, Letter to E. Chevalier, 24 June 1837, in *Correspondance*, Paris, Gallimard, 1973, vol. 1, pp. 23–5.

16 D. Outram, *Georges Cuvier: Vocation, Science and Authority in Post-Revolutionary France*, Manchester, Manchester University Press, 1984, pp. 76–8.

17 J.-B. Biot, 'De l'influence des idées exactes dans les ouvrages littéraires' (1809), in *Mélanges scientifiques et littéraires*, Paris, Michel Lévy Fréres, 1858, vol. 2, pp. 1–19.

18 M. Regaldo, *Un milieu intellectuel: la Décade philosophique (1794–1807)*, Paris, Champion, 1976, vol. 3, p. 1137.

19 Cf. M. Regaldo, ibid., vol. 2, p. 1022.

20 According to Isaiah Berlin, Vico was the first to state in so many words that the natural sciences and the humanities were characterized by essentially different forms of knowledge; see I. Berlin, *Against the Current*, London, Hogarth Press, 1979, pp. 80–110. Until about 1800, however, it was no more than an individual opinion.

21 Cf. I. Jenkens, 'Art for art's sake', in P. Wiener (ed.), *Dictionary of the History of Ideas*, New York, Charles Scribner's Sons, 1968–73; A. Cassagne, *La théorie de l'art pour l'art en France chez les derniers romantiques et les premiers réalistes*, Paris, Hachette, 1906.

22 Cf. A. Cunningham and N. Jardine (eds), *Romanticism and the Sciences*, Cambridge, Cambridge University Press, 1990.

23 L. de Bonald, 'Des sciences, des lettres et des arts' (1807), in *Mélanges littéraires, politiques et philosophiques* (1819), Paris, D'Adrien le Clerc,

1852, pp. 294–320.

24 L. de Bonald, *Mélanges littéraires, politiques et philosophiques*, Paris, D'Adrien le Clerc, 1852, p. 114.

25 L. de Bonald, 'Sur la guerre des sciences et des lettres', in *Mélanges littéraires politiques et philosophiques*, Paris, D'Adrien le Clerc, 1852, pp. 387–9.

26 See P. H. Beik, 'The French Revolution seen from the right: social theories in motion, 1789–1799', *Transactions of the American Philosophical Society*, 46, 1956, pp. 3–122; J. Godechot, *La contre-révolution: doctrine et action, 1789–1804*, Paris, Presses Universitaires de France, 1961.

27 J. de Maistre, *Les soirées de Saint-Pétersbourg*, Paris, Garnier Fréres, n.d., vol. 2, p. 103. On de Maistre's criticism of science, cf. R. Lebrun, 'Joseph de Maistre, Cassandra of science', *French Historical Studies*, 6, 1969, pp. 214–31.

28 L. de Bonald, *Mélanges littéraires, politiques et philosophiques*, Paris, D'Adrien Le Clerc, 1852, p. 39. On de Bonald, cf. A. Koyré, 'Louis de Bonald', *Journal of the History of Ideas*, 7, 1946, pp. 56–73.

29 A. Comte, 'Premier aperçu d'un travail sur le gouvernement parlementaire considéré comme régime transitoire' (1817), in *Ecrits de jeunesse*, Paris, Mouton, 1970, p. 71. On the general significance that Comte attached to this statement, see his 'Lettre à Valat, le 15 mai 1818', in *Correspondance générale et confessions*, Paris, Mouton, 1973, vol. 1, p. 37.

30 P. Bénichou, *Le temps des prophètes: doctrines de l'âge romantique*, Paris, Gallimard, 1977, pp. 200–5 and 423– 5.

Chapter 10   Models for a Social Science

1 Quoted in K. M. Baker, *Condorcet: From Natural Philosophy to Social Mathematics*, Chicago, University of Chicago Press, 1975, p. 10.

2 Ibid., p. 23.

3 Condorcet, 'Discours de réception' (1782), in *Oeuvres de Condorcet*, Paris, A. Condorcet O'Connor, M. F. Arago, Firmin Didot Fréres, 1847–9, vol. 1, p. 392.

4 K. M. Baker, ibid., p. 85.

5 G. T. Guilbaud, 'Les théories de l'intérêt général et le problème logique de l'agrégation', *Economie appliquée*, 5, 1952, pp. 501–84; G.-G. Granger, *La mathématique sociale du marquis de Condorcet*, Paris, Presses Universitaires de France, 1956; D. Black, *The Theory of Committees and Elections*, Cambridge, Cambridge University Press, 1958, esp. pp. 156–80.

6 It was this paradox that made Condorcet famous. If sixty voters choose from the mutually non-exclusive alternatives A, B and C, it might result in the following:

23 choose the sequence A, B, C
19 choose the sequence B, C, A
16 choose the sequence C, B, A
2 choose the sequence C, A, B

A is the first choice of the largest group (23 voters). But, at the same time, B and C are both preferred by a majority (19 and 16) of the voters above A. Cf. C. C. Gillispie, 'Probability and politics: Laplace, Condorcet, and Turgot', *Proceedings of the American Philosophical Society*, 116, 1972, pp. 1–20. For Condorcet's work in the political and academic context, see especially E. Brian, *La mesure de l'Etat: géomètres et réforme administrative à la veille de la Révolution*, Paris, Albin Michel, 1994.

7   C. C. Gillispie, *Science and Polity in France at the End of the Old Regime*, Princeton, Princeton University Press, 1980, pp. 36–50.

8   C. C. Gillispie, 'Probability and politics: Laplace, Condorcet and Turgot', *Proceedings of the American Philosophical Society*, 116, 1972, pp. 1–20.

9   K. M. Baker, 'Politics and social science in eighteenth-century France: the *Société de 1789*', in J. F. Bosher (ed.), *French Government and Society, 1500–1800*, Bristol, Athlone Press, 1973, pp. 208–30.

10   Condorcet, 'Tableau général de la science qui a pour objet l'application du calcul aux sciences politiques et morales' (1793), in *Mathématique et société*, ed. R. Rashed, Paris, Hermann, 1974, pp. 196–216.

11   For comments on Condorcet's working method, see G.-G. Granger, *La mathématique sociale du marquis de Condorcet*, Paris, Presses Universitaires de France, 1956, pp. 151–63.

12   L. J. Daston, 'Mathematics and the moral sciences: the rise and fall of the probability of judgments, 1785–1840', in H. N. Hahnke and M. Otte (eds.), *Epistemological and Social Problems of the Sciences in the Early Nineteenth Century*, Dordrecht, D. Reidel, 1981, pp. 287–309.

13   Cf. B. Gille, *Les sources statistiques de l'histoire de la France: des enquêtes du XVIIe siècle à 1870*, Geneva, Droz, 1964; J.-C. Perrot and S. J. Woolf, *State and Statistics in France, 1789–1815*, Chur, Harwood Academic Publishers, 1984.

14   L. J. Daston, 'Rational individuals versus the laws of society: from probability to statistics', in L. Krüger, L. J. Daston and M. Heidelberger (eds), *The Probabilistic Revolution*, Cambridge (MA), MIT Press, 1987, vol. 1, pp. 295–304.

15   Cf. T. M. Porter, *The Rise of Statistical Thinking, 1820–1900*, Princeton, Princeton University Press, 1986, pp. 100–9.

16   See D. MacKenzie, *Statistics in Britain, 1865–1930: The Social Construction of Scientific Knowledge*, Edinburgh, Edinburgh University Press, 1981; A. Desrosières, 'Histoires de formes: Statistiques et sciences sociales avant 1940', *Revue française de sociologie*, 26, 1985, pp. 277–310.

17   See especially S. Moravia, *Il pensiero degli idéologues: scienza e filosofia in Francia (1780–1815)*, Firenze, Nuova Italia, 1974; G. Gusdorf, *La*

conscience révolutionnaire: les idéologues, Paris, Payot, 1978; Cabanis, *Oeuvres philosophiques*, Paris, Presses Universitaires de France, 1956, vol. 1, p. 103.

18 Cabanis, ibid.

19 Quoted in S. Moravia, *Il pensiero degli idéologues: scienza e filosofia in Francia (1780-1815)*, Firenze, Nuova Italia, 1974, p. 740.

20 A. Guillois, *Le salon de Madame Helvétius. Cabanis et les idéologues*, Paris, C. Lévy, 1894.

21 M. Regaldo, *Un milieu intellectuel: la Décade philosophique (1794-1807)*, Paris, Champion, 1976, vol. 1, p. 16

22 Ibid., vol. 1, p. 181.

23 Ibid., vol. 2, p. 583.

24 Ibid., vol. 3, pp. 1626-7.

25 M. Staum, 'The class of moral and political sciences, 1795-1803', *French Historical Studies*, 11, 1980, pp. 371-97. See also J. Simon, *Une Académie sous le Directoire*, Paris, Calmann Lévy, 1885.

26 Cf. M. Foucault, *Les mots et les choses*, Paris, Gallimard, 1966, pp. 253-4. For a more extensive analysis, see B. W. Head, *Ideology and Social Science: Destutt de Tracy and French Liberalism*, Dordrecht, Martinus Nijhoff, 1985.

27 J. Ferrari, 'L'oeuvre de Kant en France dans les dernières années du XVIIIe siècle', *Les études philosophiques*, 1981, pp. 399-411.

28 J. Simon, *Une Académie sous le Directoire*, Paris, Calmann Lévy, 1885, pp. 213-15. See also E. Kennedy, *A Philosophe in the Age of Revolution: Destutt de Tracy and the Origins of 'Ideology'*, Philadelphia, American Philosophical Society, 1978, pp. 117-20.

29 Cf. G. Canguilhem, 'Cabanis', in *Dictionary of Scientific Biography*, New York, Charles Scribner's Sons, 1971, vol. 3, pp. 1-3.

30 Cabanis, *Oeuvres philosophiques*, Paris, Presses Universitaires de France, 1956, vol. 1, pp. 35-7.

31 Ibid., p. 126.

32 Ibid., pp. 600-17.

33 Ibid., p. 196.

34 See M. S. Staum, *Cabanis: Enlightenment and Medical Philosophy in the French Revolution*, Princeton, Princeton University Press, 1980.

35 On the medical context of Cabanis' work see S. Moravia, *Il pensiero degli idéologues*, Firenze, Nuovo Italia, 1974, pp. 13-288; S. Moravia, 'Philosophie et médecine en France à la fin du XVIIIe siècle', *Studies on Voltaire and the Eighteenth Century*, 89, 1972, pp. 1089-151.

36 M. S. Staum, *Cabanis: Enlightenment and Medical Philosophy in the French Revolution*, Princeton, Princeton University Press, 1980, pp. 172-3 and 245-55.

37 Various of this society's texts have been compiled and commented upon in J. Copans and J. Jamin (eds), *Aux origines de l'anthropologie française*, Paris, Le Sycomore, 1978. See also G. W. Stocking, 'French anthropology in 1800', *Isis*, 55, 1964, pp. 134-50.

38 C. Ménard, 'Three forms of resistance to statistics: Say, Cournot, Walras', *History of Political Economy*, 12, 1980, pp. 524–41; T. E. Kaiser, 'Politics and political economy in the thought of the ideologues', *History of Political Economy*, 12, 1980, pp. 141–60; M. S. Staum, 'The institute economists: from physiocracy to entrepreneurial capitalism', *History of Political Economy*, 19, 1987, pp. 525–50; G. Faccarello and P. Steiner (eds), *La pensée économique pendant la Révolution française*, Grenoble, Presses Universitaires de Grenoble, 1990.

39 Cf. C.-H. de Saint-Simon, 'Histoire de ma vie', in *Oeuvres*, Paris, Anthropos, 1966, vol. 1, p. 109. On Saint-Simon, see especially H. Gouhier, *La jeunesse d'Auguste Comte et la formation du positivisme*, Paris, J. Vrin, 1936, vol. 2.

40 C.-H. de Saint-Simon, 'Mémoire sur la science de l'homme' (1813), in *Oeuvres*, Paris, Anthropos, 1966, vol. 5, pp. 28–37.

41 Cf. also 'De la physiologie sociale' (1825), in C.-H. de Saint-Simon, *Oeuvres*, Paris, Anthropos, 1966, vol. 5.

42 H. Gouhier, *La jeunesse d'Auguste Comte et la formation du positivisme*, Paris, J. Vrin, 1936, vol. 2, esp. pp. 152–3.

43 Ibid., p. 348.

44 Cf. S. Charléty, *Histoire du Saint-Simonisme (1825–1864)*, Paris, Paul Hartmann, 1931.

45 See M. S. Staum, 'The class of moral and political sciences, 1795–1803', *French Historical Studies*, 11, 1980, pp. 371–97.

46 L. S. Jacyna, 'Medical science and moral science: the cultural relations of physiology in Restoration France', *History of Science*, 25, 1987, pp. 111–46.

47 O. Temkin, 'The philosophical background of Magendie's physiology', in *The Double Face of Janus*, Baltimore, Johns Hopkins University Press, 1977, pp. 317–39.

48 F. Azouvi, 'Psychologie et physiologie en France, 1800–1830', *History and Philosophy of the Life Sciences*, 6, 1984, pp. 151–70.

49 Cf. Degérando's overview that was presented to Napoleon in 1808 in M. Dacier, *Rapport historique sur les progrès de l'histoire et de la littérature ancienne depuis 1789, et sur leur état actuel*, Paris, L'Imprimerie Impériale, 1810, p. 255.

50 L. de Bonald, *Mélanges littéraires, politiques et philosophiques*, Paris, D'Adrien le Clerc, 1852, p. 123.

PART III Introduction

1 No systematic studies are available on this academy. For information, see E. Seillière, *Une académie à l'époque romantique*, Paris, Ernest Leroux, 1926; Y. Knibiehler, *Naissance des sciences humaines: Mignet et l'histoire*

philosophique au XIXe siècle, Paris, Flammarion, 1963; E. Feller and J.-C. Goeury, 'Les archives de l'Académie des sciences morales et politiques', *Annales historiques de la Révolution française*, no. 222, 1975, pp. 567–83.

2 S. F. Lacroix, *Traité élémentaire du calcul des probabilités* (1816), Paris, Bachelier, 1833, p. 301.

3 Cf. J.-F. Braunstein, *Broussais et le matérialisme: Médecine et philosophie au XIXe siècle*, Paris, Méridiens Klincksieck, 1986.

4 See, for example, the Introduction by Gertrud Lenzer in *Auguste Comte and Positivism: The Essential Writings*, ed. Gertrud Lenzer, Chicago, University of Chicago Press, 1975, esp. p. xxi.

5 R. Hahn, *The Paris Academy of Sciences, 1666–1803*, Berkeley, University of California Press, 1971, p. 34.

6 Cf. G. Misch, *Zur Entstehung des französischen Positivismus*, Darmstadt, Wissenschaftliche Buchgesellschaft, 1969.

7 H. Gouhier, *La jeunesse d'Auguste Comte et la formation du positivisme*, Paris, Vrin, 1936, vol. 2, pp. 5–62; N. and J. Dhombres, *Naissance d'un nouveau pouvoir: sciences et savants en France (1793–1824)*, Paris, Payot, 1989, p. 450.

8 A. Comte, 'Premier mémoire sur la cosmogonie positive' (1835), in *Ecrits de jeunesse, 1816–1828*, Paris, Mouton, 1970, p. 585.

9 A. Comte, *Cours de philosophie positive*, Paris, J. B. Baillière, 1864, vol. 1 (lesson 1), p. 16.

10 Cf. A. Comte, *Discours sur l'esprit positif* (1844), Paris, Vrin, 1983, pp. 64–5.

11 Turgot, 'On universal history' (1750), in *On Progress, Sociology and Economics*, Cambridge, Cambridge University Press, 1973, pp. 102–3.

12 Cf. H. Gouhier, *La jeunesse d'Auguste Comte et la formation du positivisme*, Paris, Vrin, 1941, vol. 3, pp. 395–403.

13 A. Comte, *Cours de philosophie positive*, Paris, J. B. Baillière, 1864, vol. 6 (lesson 58), p. 601.

14 Ibid., vol. 1 (lesson 1), p. 34. See also vol. 4 (lesson 48), p. 209.

15 L. Laudan, *Science and Hypothesis: Historical Essays on Scientific Methodology*, Dordrecht, D. Reidel, 1981, pp. 141–62.

16 See especially N. Elias, *What is Sociology?*, London, Hutchinson, 1978, pp. 33–49; J. Goudsblom, 'Sociale wetenschappen: kenmerken en criteria', *Grafiet*, 1983, pp. 14–37.

17 Cf. R. McRae, *The Problem of the Unity of the Sciences: Bacon to Kant*, Toronto, Toronto University Press, 1961; E. Kennedy, 'Destutt de Tracy and the unity of the Sciences', *Studies on Voltaire and the Eighteenth Century*, 171, 1977, pp. 223–39.

18 Cf. M. S. Staum, *Cabanis: Enlightenment and Medical Philosophy in the French Revolution*, Princeton, Princeton University Press, 1980, pp. 179–82.

Chapter 11   The Interrupted Career of Auguste Comte

1   H. Gouhier, *La jeunesse d'Auguste Comte et la formation du positivisme*, Paris, Vrin, 1933, vol. 1, p. 32. See also H. Gouhier, *La vie d'Auguste Comte*, Paris, Gallimard, 1931. The biographical information has been taken largely from Gouhier's work.

2   Ibid., p. 33.

3   N. and J. Dhombres, *Naissance d'un pouvoir: sciences et savants en France (1793–1824)*, Paris, Payot, 1989, p. 207.

4   H. Gouhier, ibid., p. 103.

5   A.-J. Tudesq, *Les grands notables en France (1840–1849): étude historique d'une psychologie sociale*, Paris, Presses Universitaires de France, 1964.

6   Cf. E. Eggli, P. Martino, *Le débat romantique en France 1813–1830*, Paris, Belles Lettres, 1933.

7   Cf. A.-J. Tudesq, ibid., pp. 457–63.

8   C. Charle, *Dictionnaire biographique des universitaires aux XIXe et XXe siècles*, Paris, Institut National de Recherche Pédagogique/Editions de CNRS, 1985, p. 11.

9   A. B. Spitzer, *The French Generation of 1820*, Princeton, Princeton University Press, 1987.

10 D. S. Goldstein, 'Official philosophies in modern France: the example of Victor Cousin', *Journal of Social History*, 1, 1967, pp. 259–79.

11 Sainte-Beuve, 'M. Victor Cousin', in *Oeuvres*, Paris, Gallimard, 1951, vol. 2, p. 921.

12 A. Cournot, *Souvenirs (1760–1860)*, Paris, Hachette, 1913, p. 172.

13 S. Mellon, *The Political Uses of History: A Study of Historians in the French Restoration*, Stanford, Stanford University Press, 1958; P. den Boer, *Geschiedenis als beroep: de professionalisering van de geschiedbeoefening in Frankrijk (1818–1914)*, Nijmegen, SUN, 1987.

14 D. H. Pinkney, *The French Revolution of 1830*, Princeton, Princeton University Press, 1972.

15 A. B. Spitzer, *The French Generation of 1820*, Princeton, Princeton University Press, 1987, p. 153. See also S. Charléty, *Histoire du Saint-Simonisme*, Paris, Gonthier, 1931.

16 A. de Musset, *La confession d'un enfant du siècle* (1836), Paris, Gallimard 1973 (esp. chap. 2).

17 G. de Bertier de Sauvigny, *La Restauration*, Paris, Flammarion, 1955, pp. 101–3, 320–3. See also L. O'Boyle, 'The problem of an excess of educated men in Western Europe, 1800–1850', *Journal of Modern History*, 42, 1970, pp. 471–95.

18 A. B. Spitzer, ibid., pp. 35–43.

19 A. B. Spitzer, *Old Hatreds and Young Hopes: The French Carbonari Against the Bourbon Restoration*, Cambridge (MA), Harvard University Press, 1971.

20   G. de Bertier de Sauvigny, *La Restauration*, Paris, Flammarion, 1955, p. 447.
21   Cf. A. Jardin, A.-J. Tudesq, *La France des notables: l'évolution générale 1815–1848*, Paris, Seuil, 1973, pp. 225–30.

Chapter 12   Politics, Science and Philosophy

1   W. Lepenies, *Between Literature and Science: The Rise of Sociology*, trans. R. J. Hollingdale, Cambridge, Cambridge University Press, 1988.
2   A. Comte, *Correspondance générale et confessions*, Paris, Mouton, 1973, vol. 1, p. 132. See also p. 231, where Cousin is described as a 'sophist'.
3   A. Comte, *Correspondance générale*, vol. 1, p. 132.
4   Ibid., p. 28.
5   H. Gouhier, *La jeunesse d'Auguste Comte et la formation du positivisme*, Paris, Vrin, 1941, vol. 3, p. 2.
6   Cf. A. Comte, *Correspondance générale*, Paris, Mouton, vol. 1, 1973, pp. 115–16.
7   A. Comte, *Ecrits de jeunesse, 1816–1828*, Paris, Mouton, 1970, pp. 417–31.
8   A. Comte, 'Deux lettres à M. Saint-Simon' (1818), in *Ecrits de jeunesse*, pp. 439–49.
9   'Letter to Valat, 24-9-1819', in *Correspondance générale*, vol. 1, pp. 51–62.
10   Cf. G. Canguilhem, *Etudes d'histoire et de philosophie des sciences*, Paris, Vrin, pp. 61–80.
11   A. Comte, 'Sur les travaux politiques de Condorcet' (1819), in *Ecrits de jeunesse*, pp. 483–9.
12   Cf. H. Gouhier, *La jeunesse d'Auguste Comte et la formation du positivisme*, Paris, Vrin, 1941, vol. 3, pp. 234–40.
13   Cf. E. H. Ackerknecht, 'Cuvier and medicine', *Gesnerus*, 45, 1988, pp. 313–15.

Chapter 13   The Shift to the Theory of Science

1   Cf. A. Comte, *Correspondance*, vol. 1, pp. 76–7.
2   Cf. H. Gouhier, *La philosophie d'Auguste Comte*, Paris, Vrin, 1987, pp. 65–77.
3   P. Laffitte, 'De la circulation des ouvrages d'Auguste Comte', *Revue occidentale*, 1893, vol. 2, pp. 315–24.
4   A. Comte, *Correspondance*, vol. 1, pp. 89, 92, 101.
5   Ibid., pp. 185–90.

6   On this crisis, see especially H. Gouhier, *La vie d'Auguste Comte*, Paris, Gallimard, 1931.

7   Cf. the comments in the 'personal foreword' that opens the last volume of *Cours*.

8   A. Comte, *Cours de philosophie positive*, vol. 1, p. 5.

9   For one of the few detailed studies, see K. J. S. Boughey, *Studies in the Role of Positivism in Nineteenth-Century French Chemistry*, PhD dissertation, University of Leeds, 1972 (unpubd).

10 P.-J. Barthez, *Nouveaux éléments de la science de l'homme*, Montpellier, Jean Martel, 1778, pp. 1–5.

11 Cabanis, 'Coup d'oeil sur les révolutions et sur la réforme de la médecine' (1804), in *Oeuvres philosophiques*, Paris, Presses Universitaires de France, 1956, vol. 2, pp. 175–8.

12 A. Comte, 'Premier mémoire sur la cosmogonie positive' (1835), in *Ecrits de jeunesse*, pp. 585–608.

13 Cf. his comments in A. Comte, *Philosophie première. Cours de philosophie positive, leçons 1 à 45*, ed. M. Serres, F. Dagognet and A. Sinacoeur, Paris, Hermann, 1975. This edition, which was presented as the 'first scientific edition', contains useful notes but the index is missing, as is oddly enough the four-page *avertissement* in which Comte elaborated, for example, upon the term 'positive philosophy'.

14 On Lagrange cf. J. V. Grabiner, 'Changing attitudes towards mathematical rigor: Lagrange and analysis in the eighteenth and nineteenth centuries', in H. N. Jahnke and M. Otte (eds), *Epistemological and Social Problems in the Sciences in the Early Nineteenth Century*, Dordrecht, D. Reidel, 1981, pp. 311–30.

15 L. Brunschvicg, *Les étapes de la philosophie mathématique*, Paris, A. Blanchard, 1972, p. 292.

16 A. Comte, *Cours de philosophie positive*, vol. 1 (lessons 11 and 15), pp. 294, 393.

17 A. Comte, *Système de politique positive*, Paris, L. Mathias, 1851, vol. 1, p. 462. On this theme, see M. Boudot, 'De l'usurpation géométrique', *Revue philosophique*, 110, 1985, pp. 387–402.

18 Cf. B. Belhoste, *Cauchy: un mathématicien légitimiste au XIXe siècle*, Paris, Belin, 1985. On Poinsot and Navier, cf. *Dictionary of Scientific Biography*, New York, Charles Scribner's Sons, 1970–80, vols 10 and 11.

19 A. Comte, *Correspondance*, vol. 1, pp. 262–5.

20 Cf. A. Comte, *Cours de philosophie positive*, vol. 2 (lesson 28), p. 275.

21 Ibid., p. 313.

22 On Fourier, see J. Herivel, *Joseph Fourier: The Man and the Physicist*, Oxford, Clarendon Press, 1975. On the relation between Fourier and Comte's work, see G. Bachelard, *Etude sur l'évolution d'un problème de physique: la propagation thermique dans les solides*, Paris, Vrin, 1928, pp. 33–72.

23   A. Comte, *Cours de philosophie positive*, vol. 2 (lesson 33), p. 446.

24   Cf. L. Brunschvicg, *L'expérience humaine et la causalité physique*, Paris, Presses Universitaires de France, 1949, pp. 324–30.

25   K. L. Caneva, 'Ampère, the etherians and the Oersted connexion', *British Journal for the History of Science*, 13, 1980, pp. 121–38.

26   R. Fox, 'The rise and fall of Laplacian physics', *Historical Studies in the Physical Sciences*, 4, 1974, pp. 89–136; E. Frankel, 'Corpuscular optics and the wave theory of light: the science and politics of a revolution in physics', *Social Studies of Science*, 6, 1976, pp. 141–84.

27   Cf. A. Comte, *Cours de philosophie positive*, vol. 2 (lesson 33), p. 463.

28   Ibid., vol. 3 (lesson 35), p. 7.

29   Comte was influenced mainly by Berthollet; cf. M. Crosland, 'Comte and Berthollet: a philosopher's view of chemistry', *Actes du XIIe congrès international d'histoire des sciences* (1968), Paris, A. Blanchard, 1971, vol. 6, pp. 23–7.

30   A. Comte, *Système de politique positive*, Paris, L. Mathias, 1851, vol. 1, pp. 50–1.

31   N. Elias, *What is Sociology?*, London, Hutchinson, 1978; L. Althusser, *Lire le Capital*, Paris, Maspero, 1975, vol. 1, pp. 71, 121, 124–5.

32   Cf. R. Fox, *The Caloric Theory of Gases: From Lavoisier to Regnault*, Oxford, Clarendon Press, 1971, pp. 262–70.

33   W. Coleman, *Biology in the Nineteenth Century: Problems of Form, Function and Transformation*, New York, John Wiley & Sons, 1971, p. l.

34   G. Canguilhem, *Etudes d'histoire et de philosophie des sciences*, Paris, Vrin, 1983, pp. 61–74; E. Gley, *Essais de philosophie et d'histoire de la biologie*, Paris, Masson, pp. 168–312; V. Genty, *Un grand biologiste: Charles Robin (1821–1885)*, Lyon, A. Rey, 1931. For critical though unconvincing comments on Gley and Canguilhem, see H. W. Paul, *From Knowledge to Power: The Rise of the Science Empire in France, 1860–1939*, Cambridge, Cambridge University Press, 1985, pp. 60–92.

35   G. Canguilhem, ibid., p. 71.

36   A. Comte, *Cours de philosophie positive*, vol. 3 (lesson 40),

37   On the concept of environment in the history of biology, see G. Canguilhem, *La connaissance de la vie*, Paris, Vrin, 1985, pp. 129–54.

38   G. Canguilhem, 'Histoire de l'homme et nature des choses selon Auguste Comte', *Etudes philosophiques*, 1974, pp. 293–7.

39   G. Canguilhem, G. Lapassade, J. Piquemal and J. Ulmann, *Du développement à l'évolution au XIXe siècle*, Paris, Presses Universitaires de France, 1985, pp. 22–5.

40   Cf. G. Dumas, *Psychologie des deux messies positivistes: Saint-Simon et Auguste Comte*, Paris, Alcan, 1905, pp. 153–75.

41   A. Comte, *Cours de philosophie positive*, vol. 4 (lesson 46), p. 162.

42   Ibid., vol. 6 (lesson 57), pp. 434, 478.

306 NOTES

Chapter 14 Response and Resistance

1 A. Comte, *Cours de philosophie positive*, vol. 4 (lesson 48), p. 217.
2 For an elucidating analogy with Nietzsche, see J. Goudsblom, *Nihilism and Culture*, Oxford, Blackwell, 1980.
3 Cf. A. Daumard, 'Les élèves de l'Ecole polytechnique de 1815 à 1848', *Revue d'histoire moderne et contemporaine*, 5, 1958, pp. 226–34.
4 A. Comte, *Correspondance générale*, vol. 1, p. 23.
5 A. Comte, *Cours de philosophie positive*, vol. 3 (lesson 40), p. 194.
6 Cf. J. Heilbron, 'Theory of knowledge and theory of science in the work of Auguste Comte', *Revue de Synthèse*, 1991 (1), pp. 75–89.
7 Cf. A. Comte, *Correspondance générale*, vol. 3, pp. 78–83.
8 A. Comte, *Système de politique positive*, Paris, L. Mathias, 1851, vol. 1, p. 8.
9 A. Comte, *Correspondance générale*, vol. 4, p. 23.
10 For the composition of the *Société positiviste*, see 'Liste chronologique des membres de la Société positiviste', in A. Comte, *Correspondance générale*, vol. 4, pp. 306–8.
11 Cf. H. W. Paul, 'Scholarship and ideology: the chair of the general history of science at the Collège de France, 1892–1913', *Isis*, 67, 1976, pp. 376–9.
12 For a typical exception see P. Laffitte, 'De l'institution subjective de la sociologie par la prépondérance de la morale', *Revue occidentale*, 6, 1883, pp. 1–13.
13 Review of Espinas' PhD dissertation by Dr Bazalgette in *Revue occidentale*, 2, 1879, 260–76.
14 O. d'Araujo, 'Emile Durkheim, l'Année sociologique', *Revue occidentale*, 19, 1899, pp. 305–10.
15 Dr Robinet, 'Le positivisme et M Littré', *Revue occidentale*, 4, 1881, pp. 80–104.
16 On Littré, see S. Aquarone, *The Life and Works of Emile Littré, 1801–1881*, Leyden, A. W. Sythoff, 1958, and the issue about him of *Revue de synthèse* (no. 106–8), 1982.
17 Cf. C. Nicolet, *L'idée républicaine en France (1789–1924): essai d'histoire critique*, Paris, Gallimard, 1982, pp. 187–277; L. Legrand, *L'influence du positivisme dans l'oeuvre scolaire de Jules Ferry*, Paris, Marcel Rivière, 1961.
18 E. Littré, 'Plan d'un Traité de sociologie', *La philosophie positive*, 1872, pp. 153–60.
19 E. Littré, 'De la condition essentielle qui sépare la sociologie de la biologie' (1868), in *La science au point de vue philosophique*, Paris, Didier, 1873, pp. 348–75. For sociological studies by people who shared Littré's views, see E. de Roberty, *La sociologie: essai de philosophie sociologique*, Paris,

G. Baillière, 1881; C. Mismer, *Principes sociologiques*, Paris, G. Fischbacher, 1882.

20 The composition of the Société de sociologie was published in *La philosophie positive*. Biographical information on the twenty-five members has been taken from biographical reference books and other material at the Documentation Department of the Bibliothèque administrative in Paris.

21 For overviews, see W. M. Simon, *European Positivism in the Nineteenth Century*, Ithaca, Cornell University Press, 1963; M. J. Murphy, *Positivism in England: The Reception of Comte's Doctrines, 1840–1870*, PhD dissertation, Columbia University, 1968 (unpubd); T. R. Wright, *The Religion of Humanity: The Impact of Comtean Positivism on Victorian Britain*, Cambridge, Cambridge University Press, 1986.

22 Cf. R. Olson, *Scottish Philosophy and British Physics, 1750–1880*, Princeton, Princeton University Press, 1975, pp. 178–85.

23 J. S. Mill, *The Logic of the Moral Sciences* (1843), London, Duckworth, 1987, p. 83.

24 J. S. Mill, *Auguste Comte and Positivism* (1866), Ann Arbor, University of Michigan Press, 1961, pp. 54–7.

25 A. Comte, *Correspondance générale*, vol. 4, p. 181.

26 H. van 't Veer, 'Het oudste positivisme in Nederland: het positivisme van W. Baron de Constant Rebecque (1807–1862)', *Tijdschrift voor Filosofie*, 24, 1962, pp. 279–302.

27 Cf. the foreword in A. Comte, *Algemeene grondslagen der stellige wijsbegeerte*, The Hague, Gebroeders Belinfante, 1846. The translation and foreword were anonymous. It was noted merely that the publication was edited by 'several advocates of positive philosophy'.

28 Quoted in H. van 't Veer, ibid.

29 R. Collins, 'A Micro-macro theory of intellectual creativity: the case of German idealist philosophy', *Sociological Theory*, 5, 1987, pp. 47–69.

30 J. P. Eckermann, *Gespräche mit Goethe in den letzten Jahren seines Lebens*, Munich, Deutscher Taschenbuch, 1976, p. 190.

31 Cf. W. M. Simon, *European Positivism in the Nineteenth Century*, Ithaca, Cornell University Press, 1963, pp. 238–263.

32 M. Riedel, *Verstehen oder Erklären? Zur Theorie und Geschichte der hermeneutischen Wissenschaften*, Stuttgart, Klett-Cotta, 1978, pp. 114–33; H. Schnädelbach, *Philosophie in Deutschland, 1831–1933*, Frankfurt am Main, Suhrkamp, 1983, pp. 71–4, 148–53.

33 M. Maclean, 'History in a two-cultures world: the case of the German historians', *Journal of the History of Ideas*, 48, 1988, pp. 473–95.

34 On Dilthey's criticism of Comte and Mill, cf. S. Mesure, *Dilthey et la fondation des sciences historiques*, Paris, Presses Universitaires de France, 1990.

35 Cf. J. Léonard, *La France medicale au XIXe siècle*, Paris, Gallimard, 1978, pp. 236–42.

36 E. Renan, *L'avenir de la science: pensées de 1848*, Paris, Calmann-Lévy, n.d., pp. 148–51; *Souvenirs d'enfance et de jeunesse*, Paris, A. Colin, 1959, p. 144.

37 H. Taine, *Les philosophes classiques du XIXe siècle en France* (1857), Paris, Ressources, 1979, p. vi.

38 D. G. Charlton, *Positivist Thought in France during the Second Empire, 1852–1870*, Oxford, Clarendon Press, 1959, p. 135.

39 E. Renan, 'Réponse au discours de réception de M Pasteur' (1882), in *Oeuvres complètes*, Paris, Calmann-Lévy, 1947, vol. 1, p. 767.

40 Cf. J.-L. Fabiani, *Les philosophes de la République*, Paris, Minuit, 1987.

41 Cf. C. Digeon, *La crise allemande de la pensée française (1870–1914)*, Paris, Presses Universitaires de France, 1959.

42 A good summary can be found in E. Boutroux, *De l'idée de loi naturelle dans la science et la philosophie contemporaines*, Paris, Vrin, 1925.

43 Cf. P. Tannery, 'Auguste Comte et l'histoire des sciences', *Revue des sciences*, 16, 1905, pp. 410–17. Brunschvicg has been quoted above (see Chapter 13, notes 15 and 24). On Abel Rey, see W. M. Simon, *European Positivism in the Nineteenth Century*, Ithaca, Cornell University Press, 1963, pp. 120–2.

44 J. Heilbron, 'Gaston Bachelard', in C. P. Bertels and E. J. Petersma (eds), *Filosofen van de 20e eeuw* (7th ed), Assen, Van Gorcum, 1981 pp. 207–20.

45 L. Althusser, *Pour Marx*, Paris, Maspéro, 1965, p. 16.

46 L. Althusser, *Lénine et la philosophie*, Paris, Maspéro, 1972, p. 11.

47 E. Durkheim, 'Cours de science sociale' (1887), in *La science sociale et l'action*, Paris, Presses Universitaires de France, 1970, p. 83.

48 E. Durkheim, 'Réponse à Simon Deploige' (1907), in *Textes*, Paris, Minuit, 1975, vol. 1, pp. 402–5.

49 E. Durkheim, 'La science sociale selon de Greef' (1886), in *Textes*, Paris, Minuit, 1975, vol. 1, p. 39.

50 E. Durkheim, 'La sociologie' (1915), in *Textes*, Paris, Minuit, 1975, vol. 1, pp. 109–18.

51 On Durkheim and Comte see J. Heilbron, 'Ce que Durkheim doit à Comte', in P. Besnard, M. Borlandi and P. Vogt (eds), *Division du travail et lien social: la thèse de Durkheim un siècle après*, Paris, PUF, 1993, pp. 59–66. On the Durkheim school, see the contributions by Karady, Besnard et al. in P. Besnard (ed.), *The Sociological Domain*, Cambridge, Cambridge University Press, 1983; see also J. Heilbron, 'Les métamorphoses du durkheimisme, 1920–1940', *Revue française de sociologie*, 26, 1985, pp. 203–37.

Index